ISBN 978-1-330-71195-8
PIBN 10095641

This book is a reproduction of an important historical work. Forgotten Books uses
state-of-the-art technology to digitally reconstruct the work, preserving the original format
whilst repairing imperfections present in the aged copy. In rare cases, an imperfection in
the original, such as a blemish or missing page, may be replicated in our edition. We do,
however, repair the vast majority of imperfections successfully; any imperfections that
remain are intentionally left to preserve the state of such historical works.

1 MONTH OF
FREE
READING

at
www.ForgottenBooks.com

By purchasing this book you are eligible for one month membership to ForgottenBooks.com, giving you unlimited access to our entire collection of over 1,000,000 titles via our web site and mobile apps.

To claim your free month visit:
www.forgottenbooks.com/free95641

Publications of the Bureau of Social Hygiene

Prostitution in Europe

BY

ABRAHAM FLEXNER

INTRODUCTION BY

JOHN D. ROCKEFELLER, Jr.
Chairman of the Bureau of Social Hygiene

NEW YORK
THE CENTURY CO.
1914

CONTENTS

INTRODUCTION

In presenting to the public the second volume of the series to be issued by the Bureau of Social Hygiene, it is appropriate to state briefly the origin and plans of the Bureau and to indicate the place assigned to the present study in the scheme which the Bureau has undertaken to develop.

The Bureau of Social Hygiene was created as a result of the work of the Special Grand Jury which investigated the white slave traffic in New York City in 1910. It was organized only after a thorough inquiry had been made, involving conferences with over a hundred leading men and women in the city as to the relative value of a public commission as compared with a private organization. The opinion prevailed that a permanent, unofficial organization, whose efforts would be continuous, would probably be more lasting and effective; the Bureau of Social Hygiene was therefore established in the winter of 1911. Its present members are Miss Katharine Bement Davis, Superintendent of the New York State Reformatory for Women, at Bedford Hills, New York; Paul M. Warburg, of the firm of Kuhn, Loeb & Company; Starr J. Murphy, of the New York Bar; and John D. Rockefeller, Jr.

As was stated in the introduction to the previous volume, spasmodic efforts to deal with the problem of prostitution have been made from time to time throughout

Introduction

the course of history. They have failed for several reasons: First, because, as a rule, there has been too little accurate information as to the facts of the situation to be dealt with; again, because they have taken too little account of the teachings of experience elsewhere; finally, because they have been too explosive, too discontinuous, to be effective, even if soundly conceived.

The first book of the present series, entitled, "Commercialized Prostitution in New York City," was written by Mr. George J. Kneeland, upon the completion of a careful study of conditions of vice in Manhattan, carried on under his direction by a corps of trained investigators. Its aim was simply descriptive; it presented a faithful picture of contemporaneous conditions in New York.

The present book carries the work a step further. Without raising any question as to how far European experience is significant for America, the author describes prostitution in Europe and discusses the various methods of handling it now employed in the large cities of Great Britain and the Continent. The subject is a highly controversial one. For this reason, its investigation was assigned to one who had, on the one hand, previously given it no critical thought or attention, but whose studies of education in this country and abroad had demonstrated his competency to deal with a complicated topic of this nature. Mr. Flexner was absolutely without prejudice or preconception, just as he was absolutely unfettered by instructions. He had no previous opinion to sustain; he was given no thesis to prove or disprove. He was asked to make a thorough and impartial examination of the

Introduction

subject and to report his observations and conclusions. He enjoyed the fullest possible facilities for his inquiries and to them and the writing of this book devoted almost two years.

It is difficult to summarize the contents of the volume. It touches many different aspects of the problem,—the nature of modern prostitution, the factors determining demand, the sources of supply, the various methods used in its regulation or control, their operation and value, the effect of abolishing regulation, and the general outcome of European experience. Though Mr. Flexner has in no way taken America into consideration, without question the facts he has assembled will be highly pertinent to any discussion in this country as to the merits of proposed legislation; for his account makes it clear that widespread misapprehension prevails as to the policies pursued by European cities, and their results.

Two volumes are still to appear: an account of European police systems, by Mr. Raymond B. Fosdick, a member of the staff of the Bureau, and formerly Commissioner of Accounts of New York City; and a final volume dealing with prostitution in the United States in which it is hoped that a program soundly based may be suggested.

JOHN D. ROCKEFELLER, JR.

New York, Nov. 1, 1913.

PROSTITUTION IN EUROPE

PROSTITUTION IN EUROPE

CHAPTER I

PROSTITUTION: DEFINITION AND EXTENT

Scope of investigation.— General uniformity of phenomena.— Prostitution an urban problem.— Medieval and modern prostitution differ.— Prostitution defined.— Need of broad conception.— Immorality distinguished from prostitution.— Prevalence and significance of immorality.— Prostitution not necessarily a permanent status,— Mortality of prostitutes.— Number of prostitutes.— Forms taken by prostitution.— Influence of alcohol.—Homosexuality.— The pimp.— The Paris prostitute.— The cost of prostitution.

PROSTITUTION will be studied in these pages from the standpoint of the practical experience of European countries. An effort will be made to ascertain its forms and extent, the sources from which it is recruited, the conditions that either cause or conduce to it, the procedure of different communities in dealing with it and with the conditions responsible for it, the measures which have been employed by way of combat or control, and the results which have been thus obtained. Material will be drawn from extended personal inquiry and observation in the larger cities of England, Scotland, France, Italy, Belgium, Switzerland, Holland, Denmark, Norway, Sweden, Germany, Austria-Hungary,[1] — from the coun-

[1] The following cities were visited: London, Liverpool, Birmingham, Manchester, Glasgow, Edinburgh, Paris, Lyons, Rome, Brussels, Berlin, Hamburg, Dresden, Frankfort-on-Main, Cologne,

Prostitution in Europe

tries, in a word, that may be grouped as Western Europe, because they are characterized by a considerable degree of similarity in all that pertains to social life, national ideals, and political institutions.

In the countries just specified, neither law nor opinion is strictly homogeneous: in consequence, the phenomena under consideration respond to differences of viewpoint or pressure by somewhat altering their external manifestations. The resulting divergencies are at times only superficial, at times important enough to affect, perhaps, the volume of vice itself. None the less at bottom the situation is sufficiently similar to support the generalized method of treatment which has been adopted in this book. Distinctions will not be ignored; but on the whole it will appear that they serve rather to emphasize fundamental agreement. Recent investigation, indeed, tends to show that such agreement is of far wider scope than is here assumed; for in prostitution, if nowhere else, the old adage holds — "There is nothing new under the sun." The source-books of both ancient and medieval worlds disclose an amazing identity with modern times in this melancholy respect.[2]

Such differences as still persist — in regard to viewpoint, form, or public policy,— are, at least in the area here dealt with, in a fair way to disappear. The progress of democratic thought and government, increas-

Hamm, Stuttgart, Munich, The Hague, Amsterdam, Rotterdam, Copenhagen, Stockholm, Christiania, Geneva, Zurich, Vienna, Budapest.

[2] This has been conclusively established by the researches of Dr. Iwan Bloch in his great work *"Die Prostitution,"* (Berlin, 1912), one volume of which has already appeared. Dr. Bloch has courteously placed the proof sheets of the second volume at my disposal.

4

Prostitution: Definition and Extent

ingly easy and unobstructed trading, the advance of industrialism with the revision of the ethical code following in the wake of practical sex equality, finally, even deliberate imitation are rapidly developing decided homogeneity of attitude and effort in reference to many fundamental human concerns. The student of the particular subject with which we are occupied is, therefore, nowadays, more and more likely to be struck by the uniformity of phenomena rather than by local or national peculiarities, in the course of an inquiry that begins in Glasgow and concludes in Budapest.

At the outset it is important to observe that throughout Western Europe prostitution has in the last few centuries undergone essentially the same evolution. Prostitution is an urban problem, its precise character largely dependent on the size of the town. Now the medieval town in Western Europe was small. The really great cities of the middle ages were all Islamic: Constantinople, Bagdad, and Cairo numbered more than a million souls apiece, Seville and Cordova were each half as large. Beside these the main cities of Western Europe were in point of size insignificant: Paris had a dubious 200,000; Vienna, 50,000; London, 35,000; Cologne, 30,000; Hamburg, 18,000; Dresden, 5,000. Towns without water communication rarely reached 25,000; many important places did not exceed 5,000.[3] Size largely determined the character of urban life and therewith the nature of medieval European prostitution. The inhabitants of these hardly more than villages were well known to one

[3] The evidence and authorities are exhaustively given by Bloch, *loc. cit.*, Vol. I, pp. 685, etc. Constantinople became Islamic in 1453.

5

Prostitution in Europe

another; the family was still an intact organization; the floating population — aside from organized movements like the crusades, pilgrimages, or armies,— was not voluminous; at any rate the stranger was known as such. Medieval prostitution was, in the main, of two varieties, resident or itinerant: the former more or less commonly living in regular houses of prostitution — the so-called bordells; the latter, either vagrant or informally attached like the camp-follower to the temporal or spiritual armies that swept to and fro across the continent, now waging war, now fulfilling religious vows. But whether resident or itinerant, the prostitute was a marked woman in the small medieval community. Even if her vocation was plied secretly, her true character inevitably and quickly became notorious; still more so, of course, if carried on professionally, for then she was visibly to be discriminated by garb, appearance, abode, and outward manner of living. The distinction between the vicious and the virtuous woman was thus in the middle ages uncommonly broad and clear.

Modern conditions contrast strongly with those that I have just sketched. The cities, themselves huge, are for practical purposes still further enlarged by the subsidiary communities that hang about their fringes. Berlin, for example, so late as 1816 a town of 197,000 inhabitants, contained in 1910, 2,071,257; Charlottenburg, to mention only one of the suburbs practically indistinguishable from it, adds 305,978. London numbers 7,-252,963; Liverpool, 760,357; Glasgow, 784,496; Paris, 2,888,110; Lyons, 523,796; Vienna, 2,031,498; Budapest, 881,600; Munich, 596,467; Hamburg, 931,035;

6

Prostitution: Definition and Extent

Dresden, 548,308; Amsterdam, 580,960; Stockholm, 346,599; Copenhagen, 476,806; Brussels itself, strictly speaking, a town of only 175,000, is increased to 659,-000 by nine contiguous self-governing suburbs which, for all practical purposes, merge into it. The mere quantitative difference between the medieval town and the modern city qualitatively transforms the problem of prostitution. In these latter-day Babylons, the family is frequently shattered; thousands of detached, more or less friendless, more or less irresponsible, girls and boys pour into them to earn a livelihood under conditions that, so far from forming, actually disintegrate character and ambition. The situation is still further complicated by the continuous presence of a huge floating population, in Paris, Berlin, and London reaching into hundreds of thousands, restlessly surging in and out, in search of trade, excitement, or amusement. Within the more or less tightly closed circle, characteristic of a simple community, the members of which are known to one another, mutual demands in the matter of conduct uphold the accepted ideal and tradition; family and clan morality thus sustain the weaker members. Moreover, whatever individuals may be, they are known to one another as such. But in the modern Babylons of which I am speaking, one no longer knows one's nearest neighbors. Temptation and inducement wax strongest, precisely where protection and restraint have become feeblest; the conditions favor not only irresponsibility but concealment. The mere numerical increase and the absolute impossibility of classifying women and men as virtuous or vicious on account of sheer ignorance of their life and character thus profoundly differentiate medieval from modern prostitution. The former was at once limited and definite; the latter is not only huge but vague.

From a practical point of view, these are facts of unmistakable importance. While thirty lewd women in a town of 3,000 inhabitants and 5,000 in a town of half a million represent precisely the same proportion — one percent in both cases — nevertheless the quantitative increase makes an enormous difference in the feasibility of measures designed to deal with one aspect or another of the situation. A device that might conceivably be effective on the smaller scale would probably break down completely if applied on the larger. Economically, administratively, hygienically, the problem thus changes its character, the moment the numbers involved pass beyond a certain point.

An additional difficulty is due to mere size; the prostitute can not be strictly discriminated in the huge modern city. Wherever professional prostitution has flourished, so-called clandestine prostitution has existed. But in the middle ages clandestine prostitutes were individually so notorious that, even when they avoided the bordell, they frequently lived in the bordell quarter. In any event, there was no doubt as to their business and character. In precisely the same way, there exists to-day in Europe the avowed professional prostitute and the equally notorious and unmistakable so-called clandestine prostitute,— both perfectly obvious to the police as well as to the casual observer. But a highly important distinction must be noted: of modern prostitution this known contingent, partly outright professional, partly so-called clandestine,[4] is the smaller and, from many points of view, the less significant fraction. Neither by garb, appearance, abode, or apparent manner of living are the majority of women subsisting wholly or partly on the proceeds of sexual irregularity any longer to be recognized. The frankly avowed prostitute is only one, and perhaps not the most important, of the types with which this account must deal; and this complication originates in the size of the modern city and in the industrial and other conditions to which city growth is due.

In the endeavor to arrive at an accurate definition of prostitution no little effort has been expended. Different conceptions are possible from different points of view. The continental police define prostitution from the standpoint of registration or inscription: as a rule they register or, where the system has been discontinued, used to register, only professional prostitutes,— women, that is, who have no other means of support than prostitution. From the police point of view the prostitute is therefore an inscribed woman, or a woman who, somehow eluding inscription, ought to be inscribed, or one who is at any rate liable to inscription, on the ground that she earns her livelihood through sexual promis-

[4] It looks like a contradiction in terms to speak of known clandestine prostitution. Current usage on the Continent construes "professional prostitute" to mean a woman who has been registered by the police; any prostitute who is not registered is therefore called clandestine. Many of these so-called clandestines are just as notorious as the registered professionals. The clandestine class therefore nowadays contains known, but unregistered women, as well as unknown or not reliably known prostitutes. It is this last named contingent that was insignificant in medieval, and has become so numerous in modern towns.

cuity. Vast numbers, however, escape through the wide
meshes of this net. Many prostitutes are actually engaged
in some sort of remunerative work. The barmaids of
the German "Animierkneipe,"[5] the singers and dancers of low grade Varietés are prostitutes who obtain their
customers by means of their occupations; yet they are
usually exempt from inscription as professional prostitutes because gainfully employed, and being exempt from
inscription they fall outside the police definition of professional prostitution. The mere fact that partial or even
pretended employment is a protection against police interference leads many prostitutes to keep up a more or less
nominal connection with work. Of 1,177 venereally diseased women, undoubtedly prostitutes, treated in the
municipal hospital of Zurich, only 7.9% owned to being
prostitutes; 6.7% more confessed to no employment, but
all the others — 85.4% — claimed a vocation of some
sort.[6] It is therefore obvious that the police definition
fails to square with the facts. Parent-Duchatelet, following an official declaration, uses the term prostitution,
where " several mercenary acts of immorality have been
legally established, when the woman involved is publicly
notorious, when she has been caught in the act by other
witnesses than her accuser or the police agent."[7] From
this definition, however, all really clandestine prostitution
is quite omitted; it suffices only for the most obvious and

[5] The Animierkneipe is a low-grade drinking-resort in which the
barmaid drinks with her customer, often in a screened nook or
corner, if he can be induced to occupy one.
[6] Müller: *Zur Kenntnis der Prostitution in Zürich.* (Zurich,
1911), pp. 11 and 44. Abundant additional illustrations will appear in subsequent chapters, e. g. Chap. III, V, VII, etc.
[7] A.-J.-B. Parent-Duchatelet: *De la Prostitution dans la Ville
de Paris.* (2 volumes, Paris, 1857) Vol. I, p. 25.

Prostitution: Definition and Extent

necessary police purposes. By way of contrast with the narrow conceptions above given, I shall, for reasons that will shortly appear, consider prostitution to be characterized by three elements variously combined: barter, promiscuity, emotional indifference. The barter need not involve the passing of money, though money is its usual medium; gifts or pleasures may be the equivalent inducement. Nor need promiscuity be utterly choiceless; a woman is not the less a prostitute because she is more or less selective in her associations. Emotional indifference may be fairly inferred from barter and promiscuity. In this sense, any person is a prostitute who habitually or intermittently has sexual relations more or less promiscuously for money or other mercenary consideration. Neither notoriety, arrest, nor lack of other occupation is an essential criterion. A woman may be a prostitute, even though not notorious, even though never arrested, even though simultaneously otherwise employed in a paid occupation.

The scope of the term is thus greatly, and, as I hope to show, justifiably, nay necessarily, extended. Barter, emotional indifference, and more or less promiscuity do not in modern cities characterize the sex relations of the avowed or professional prostitute alone. They are equally characteristic marks of the clandestine prostitute, using the term in its literal meaning to designate the numerous class of professional prostitutes whose real character is known only to their own clientele and their close female companions; of the occasional prostitute, — women who alternately emerge from and relapse into an irregular life; of the incidental prostitute,— those

Prostitution in Europe

who carry on more or less prostitution without interrupting some honorable employment; of women who practise prostitution under cloak of other occupations; of women, who ceasing to be kept as mistresses practise prostitution as a stop-gap until a firmer footing is once more found; of women who reserve themselves by express arrangement for a small group, none of whom can alone afford their support; of women, who faithul to one individual at a time are still taken up by a succession of men paying for favors; finally of married women, by no means always of the lowest classes, who, perhaps irreproachable in the eyes of the world, are not above earning through ignominy the price of luxuries.[8] Here are eight different categories, falling outside the narrow conception of prostitution, but nevertheless belonging to prostitution, if prostitution is conceived to be characterized by barter, emotional indifference, and promiscuity.

For this broad construction there exist the most substantial of grounds. Why do we object to prostitution at all? Obviously, it is repugnant for one or more of several reasons: in the first place, because of the personal demoralization it entails; in the second, because of economic waste; again, because it is by far the main factor in the spread of venereal disease; finally, because of its intimate association with disorder or crime. Unques-

[8] Adrien Mithouard in *Rapports au nom de la 2e Commission sur la Prostitution*, etc. (Conseil Municipal de Paris, 1904) p. 110. A. Moll: *Handbuch der Sexualwissenschaften* (Leipzig, 1912) p. 354, describes the same type as known in Germany: "To clandestine prostitution are to be reckoned also girls and women of better families who sell themselves in the salons of the pander." So also S. Leonhard: "Girls and women who live in comparative luxury, who have a calling and a good social position are often prostitutes." *Die Prostitution* (Munich, 1912) p. 23; also p. 20.

Prostitution: Definition and Extent

tionably the full-time notorious prostitutes who are the especial objects of police care exemplify all the counts in this indictment; they are themselves demoralized and they spread demoralization; they cause enormous waste; they inevitably and invariably spread disease; as a rule they have criminal or quasi-criminal connections. But there could be no greater mistake than to suppose that the other categories above specified are free from objection on these scores. Part-time prostitution, occasional prostitution, pretentious prostitution,— all the various kinds and grades above enumerated naturally and inevitably conduce to similar results. They may be less conspicuous or less offensive, but they are equally dangerous. If then prostitution is objectionable because of demoralization, waste, disease, or crime, then it is necessary so to define it as to include all the varieties to which one or more of the unfortunate results in questions is attributable. The lowest forms are most closely connected with crime and disorder, and as the police are mainly concerned with crime and disorder, they content themselves with a working conception of prostitution that goes no further. But the general concern of society must regard as hardly less serious menaces to its highest welfare the personal demoralization, the economic loss, the spread of disease equally associated with the less gross forms of the evil. For these are attended by personal degradation, even though some individuals, on the whole a considerable number, ultimately react vigorously enough to recover their self-respect; and they involve enormous economic waste, increasing rather than diminishing with the degree of dignity with which the

Prostitution in Europe

business is surrounded, so that what externally least resembles commercial prostitution is perhaps from the economic standpoint most severely to be reprobated as such.

It is, however, in respect to disease that the wide definition can be most readily and fully justified. Venereal disease is the certain harvest of any degree of promiscuity in the sex relation. The diminution of venereal disease is one of the most pressing objects of hygienic effort; it can be accomplished only by some sort of interference with prostitution. It would therefore be absurd to define prostitution so narrowly that many of the regular foci of infection remain outside the definition and hence beyond the reach of any policy contrived for the purpose of dealing with them. How numerous the foci are which a narrow conception would thus ignore will be more fully shown in subsequent chapters;[9] but enough must be said in this connection to warrant the extension of the definition beyond the usual police lines. A statistical study of venereal disease at Mannheim covering nine years (1892–1901) showed that 63% of the infections were traceable to professional prostitutes in the narrow police sense of the term, no less than 37%, however, to the occasional, incidental, and other prostitutes here explicitly included in the term; among whom girls in active service as waitresses, servants, and shop-hands are the most important.[10] A subsequent investigation of 594 cases disclosed 278 professionals and 316 — over

[9] Particularly Chapter VII. It is obvious that there is wide room for error in tracing the source of an infection, but allowance may be made for this without affecting the argument here made.

[10] H. Loeb: *Statistiches über Geschlechtskrankheiten in Mannheim. Zeitschrift für Bekämpfung der Geschlechtskrankheiten* (Leipzig). Band II, pp. 93 etc. Loeb admits a few persons whom

Prostitution: Definition and Extent

50% — girls serving in one capacity or another (waitress, seamstress, laundress, actress, etc.) as the sources of infection.[11] A similar statistic from Hanover proves in the same way that it is from the standpoint of sanitation absurd to limit prostitution to the absolutely indiscriminate, professional and notorious activity: of 330 women, to whom infections were traced, 42% (139) were outright professionals, though only partly inscribed, the remaining 58% being mainly girls who were simultaneously engaged in paid employments in shops, taverns, domestic service, theaters, etc.[12] Such conditions prevail generally on the Continent. The Munich police have lately made a most careful study of the callings in which 2,574 clandestine prostitutes well known to them are simultaneously engaged: 721 are servants, 608 are waitresses, 250 factory workers, 246 seamstresses, 60 are connected with the stage, 52 are laundresses, 40 dressmakers, 28 models, etc. Similar results can be cited from other sources. Of 100 venereal patients at Rouen, only 31 of the infections could be traced to inscribed prostitutes; 69 cases were attributed to clandestines, partials, etc.[13] Of 297 traceable infections in Stockholm, 146 — practically one-half — were attributed to girls also engaged in work.[14] The police of Hamburg are

my definition would exclude,— viz., mistresses, etc., who ought to be excluded so long as they are attached to one individual. This valuable publication will be referred to henceforth as *Zeitschrift*.

[11] Lion & Loeb, *Zeitschrift* VII, p. 295.

[12] F. Bloch: *Die nicht-gewerbsmässige Prostitution. Zeitschrift*, Band X, p. 70. Bloch's patients come from all social classes. In *Zeitschrift* XII, pp. 314 etc., Oppenheim and Neugebauer deal with the infection of laborers alone.

[13] Georges Hébart: *Où se prennent les malades vénériennes?* Thèse de Paris, 1906, pp. 31–34.

[14] *Zeitschrift*, V., p. 286.

Prostitution in Europe

at any rate logical, for there girls employed in bars and
fish-shops may be registered as prostitutes; in certain
smaller North German cities prostitution is so commonly
associated with employment as barmaid that the latter
is practically merged with the former. Under conditions in which barmaids, shop girls, servants, chorus-
girls, etc.,[15] are either permanently or intermittently engaged in prostitution, and when so engaged bring about
precisely the same sort of damage that is wrought by
prostitutes who are nothing else, it is manifestly illogical
to use the term so as to designate the latter class only.
The fact that complication with disorder attaches only to
the lower types is assuredly no reason for restricting the
designation of prostitution to them, once we realize that,
on the score of personal demoralization, economic waste,
and the danger of disease, the more sophisticated or
subtle forms of commercialized immorality are equally
dangerous and destructive. Prostitution will therefore
in these pages be construed to mean more or less promiscuity — even transient promiscuity,— of sex relationship
for pay, or its equivalent.

The definition just given is intended to exclude both
immorality and unconventionality in the sex relation,
though, for reasons that will appear, they require incidental discussion in an account of prostitution. Of
these unconventional or irregular sex relationships there
are in Western Europe many varieties, more or less widespread. Most substantial is the informal union which
serves as a substitute for marriage. In these combinations mutual fidelity is expected, as well as complete

[15] See, for example, Müller, *loc. cit.*, pp. 11-13.

Prostitution: Definition and Extent

responsibility for such children as may be born. A combination of this sort is occasionally permanent; occasionally it is converted into marriage; oftener, perhaps, it binds only during mutual congeniality, being dissolved when congeniality ceases, or more frequently when one or the other member has already entered on the stages preliminary to another combination. In the city such informal mating of industrial workers of opposite sexes is common;[16] the shop girl contracts an alliance of this kind with a clerk of her own class, or not infrequently with a student or professional man, more or less above her in rank. Of the non-legalized cohabitation of the artisans of London, Booth remarks that at times " they behave best if not married to the women with whom they live ";[17] occasionally two parties to previous but unsuccessful matrimony pair off again without the intervention of the divorce court, and " as a rule, are faithful to each other."[18] Somewhat similar is an informal relationship continued as such until a child is born — or shortly after — whereupon the neglected rites may be duly performed. The high percentage of illegitimacy is thus partly accounted for: In Berlin 20% of the births are outside of wedlock; in all Germany, almost 10%.[19] The incident is so common among the lower classes, especially in the rural districts, as hardly to carry any stigma at all. " Frequent illegitimacy," writes

[16] Paul Kampffmeyer: *Die Prostitution als soziale Klassenerscheinung.* (Berlin, 1905) p. 26.
[17] Charles Booth: *Life and Labor in London* (final volume, London, 1903) p. 41.
[18] Ibid p. 42.
[19] *Statistisches Jahrbuch für das Deutsche Reich* — quoted by J. Marcuse: *Die Beschränkung der Geburtenzahl* (Munich, 1913) p. 22.

Prostitution in Europe

Adele Schreiber, "may be the expression of wholesome monogamous conditions, as indeed is often the case in mountainous countries. Premarital relations are there common, are characterized by mutual fidelity and, with exceptions of course, look forward to marriage when a child is born and the parents are able to establish a home." [20] These relations must be distinguished from the episodic connection that is a mere incident in the course of casual companionship. Mainly in this latter sense, "immoral relations before marriage among the lower classes are not unusual and are indulgently regarded," [21] writes Charles Booth of London. Devon, describing Glasgow conditions, observes to the same effect that "girls do not seem to suffer in self-respect nor greatly in the esteem of others, if they yield themselves to the lad who is their sweetheart for the time. If decency is observed, morals are taken for granted." [22] On the Continent these conditions also exist. "Extra-marital, especially pre-marital intercourse is everywhere in the country very frequent," [23] declares Moll. Of certain communities in Saxony it has been deliberately asserted that "no girl over sixteen is still a virgin"; the German peasant is declared to have no conception of the meaning of chastity.[24] Welander dealing with 452

[20] Adele Schreiber: *Mutterschaft* (Munich, 1912) p. 260.
[21] *Loc. cit.,* p. 44.
[22] James Devon: *The Criminal and the Community* (London and New York, 1912) p. 158.
[23] Moll: *loc. cit.,* p. 371. Also: Kampffmeyer: *loc. cit.,* p. 20.
[24] Wohlrabe: *Schäden und Gefahren der sexuellen Unsittlichkeit* (Leipzig, 1908) pp. 8–10. Fuller accounts have been published by Wittenberg and Hückstädt: *Die geschlechtlich-sittlichen Verhältnisse der evangelischen Landbewohner ım Deutschen Reich* (Leipzig, 1895). These authors are all clergymen and may take too unfavorable a view.

prostitutes who could give a clear account of their first lapse, found that 299 had erred while still living at home or before leaving the country to take a position in Stockholm.[25]

Episodic laxity unquestionably exposes the girl to dangers that readily result in prostitution, just as it develops in her comrade the appetite that leads him to consort with prostitutes. But in itself mere laxity is not to be confused with prostitution. The instances above given show indeed how widely immorality varies in ethical quality. An irregular sex relation may indicate only carelessness of the convention that restricts sexual congress to the married relation; it may, at the other extreme, indicate total indifference to the ethical standard that forbids sexual commerce unaccompanied by high emotional sanction, mutual respect, complete responsibility for the natural result. The former is a marriage in all but form; the latter is simple depravity; but neither involves prostitution. A lapse — one or several — does not imply prostitution; nor is the paid mistress a prostitute so long as her relations, emotionally indifferent and mercenary though they be, are free from promiscuity. It must be remembered, therefore, that irregular sex connection may not only lack barter or promiscuity, but on the woman's side at least may possess high emotional coloring, whether she be mistress, unwedded wife, or compliant sweetheart.

In the designation of prostitute there is nothing final or irretrievable. It is indeed one of the peculiar earmarks of modern prostitution that thousands who floun-

[25] *Zeitschrift*, Vol. XI, p. 410. An opinion differing somewhat from that in the text is held by J. Kyrle, *Zeitschrift* VIII, p. 352.

Prostitution in Europe

der for a while eventually escape from the bog. The
tendency is undoubtedly towards complete disintegration;
women who drift into it may drift more and more
deeply into the morass. But the numerically more powerful drift is nevertheless outwards; while some are overwhelmed, thousands emerge. Having apparently started
on the descent, they somehow arrest their downward
progress and clamber out,— sometimes from the very
bottom, more frequently and more hopefully, before the
lower depths have been reached.[26] Modern prostitution
is therefore unprecedentedly fluctuating in character.
Johansson's admirable studies of the data contained
in the Inspection-bureau of Stockholm "show that the
same woman who one month is in domestic service or
at other work will the next month register with the
police and thus enter the ranks of professional prostitution; the third month she will have her position again
and be freed from the requirement to undergo inspection; thus the thing shifts for years and years."[27] During the first three years of registration a considerable
number of the women leave Stockholm, give up prostitution and become domestic servants or factory
hands.[28] This has been the case since modern urban

[26] This will appear clearly in the statistics given in Chap. V.
[27] I Reglementeringsfragen; (Upsala, 1911) p. 63.
[28] Ibid, p. 49. Carefully compiled tables covering the years,
1870–1904, are given in Prof. Johansson's report prepared for the
Swedish Commission appointed to study the regulation of prostitution. This report is published in four volumes in the Swedish
language (Stockholm, 1910). I shall refer to it as Report Swedish
Commission. Prof. Johansson's researches are contained in Vol.
III. For the tables here referred to, see pp. 19–20. In 1900–4,
31.7% of the registered prostitutes were dropped from the police
rolls and of these 73.4% engaged in some decent occupation. As
this volume goes to press, a new book by Prof. Johansson appears:

20

Prostitution: Definition and Extent

conditions began: "Let us recollect," wrote Parent-Duchatelet, "that for the majority of public women prostitution is a transitory estate; they quit for the most part after a year; very few indeed remain until death." [29] The Munich barmaid who is sexually more or less indiscriminate inflicts upon society for the time being the same sort of damage as the notorious prostitute; she herself deteriorates, she exposes herself to disease, in the spread of which she is subsequently a factor; she is therefore a prostitute. But once she rehabilitates herself, her status changes. She is barmaid now, prostitute no longer. The prostitution of European cities to-day is characterized by the abundance of cases that oscillate in this way to and fro across the dividing line. Our definition must be capable of including these at one moment, even if they have to be omitted at another.

We are thus enabled to understand what has long figured as a mystery. What becomes of the ordinary prostitute? For the common notion that her expectation of life is some five or six years, there is no basis in fact whatsoever.[30] It is demonstrably untrue even of

Reglementeringen I Stockholm (Stockholm, 1913). Table 6, p. 62, shows that of all women enrolled between 1859 and 1884, 36.6% left the life (sent home, obtained decent employment, married, etc.). If this is so often the case with the lowest type, whose emergence has been made difficult, it must be far oftener true of the clandestine not branded by the law. "Everything points to the likelihood that, if in their prostitution period they have succeeded in escaping enrolment, their return to a normal mode of life is much facilitated." *Ibid.*, p. 43.

[29] *Loc cit.*, Vol. I, p. 584.

[30] Parent-Duchatelet reports (*loc. cit.*, p. 582) two contrary opinions as current in his day: Some physicians hold that the prostitute has a constitution of iron ("santé de fer"), others that she dies before thirty. Neither view is sound. Parent-Duchatelet himself is able to trace the subsequent career of 1,680 women out of 5,081 who were stricken from the Paris list during a period of

Prostitution in Europe

the avowed professional or registered continental harlot. Though her resistance is weakened, an early death
need not and as a rule does not ensue. Of 3,517 women
inscribed at Paris, Parent-Duchatelet[31] notes that 980
—close to 28% — have been on the Paris list longer
than seven years; and the Paris list is neither the beginning nor the end of the careers of most of the women
inscribed. This is obvious from the further fact that
of the 3,517 women in question, 1,269 admitted the practice of professional prostitution during more than five
years.[32] Again, the average annual registration of professionals with the Paris police between 1888 and 1903
was 5,549; the average annual death rate among them
was 19.[33] Johansson has made an elaborate comparison
between the mortality of inscribed prostitutes and that
of the corresponding age groups of the female population of Stockholm; the inscribed women show the higher
rate, but by no means so large as is popularly supposed:[34]

	1870-4	75-79	1880-4	85-9	90-4	95-99	1900-3
Percentage of mortality among inscribed prostitutes	17.1	13.6	14.7	10.9	8.4	9.0	7.8
Among corresponding age groups of Stockholm's female population	12.0	9.1	7.6	6.4	5.7	4.8	4.7

The mortality among the registered prostitutes of
Vienna in the years 1879–1882, inclusive, averaged less

10 years. They returned to various occupations; probably many of
those whom heycould not follow up did likewise (*Ibid.,* pp. 584–5).
[31] Quoted by C. K. Schneider: *Die Prostituierte und die Gesellschaft* (Leipzig, 1908) p. 187.
[32] *Loc. cit.,* Vol I, p. 95.
[33] *Rapports, Conseil municipal, loc. cit.,* p. 31.
[34] *Report, Swedish Commission,* Vol III, pp.105–6.

than ½ of 1%; at Berlin for approximately the same period 1¼%;[35] for the years 1904–6, it was only ⅘ of 1%.[36] The mortality among the more cautious women, less exposed to wind and weather and alcohol, is probably lower still. The loss to the Paris registered list through death is negligible: of 3,582 inscribed women in 1880, 46 died in the course of the year; of 4,770 a decade later, 5 died; of 6,222 in 1900, 26 died. The total loss by death in twenty years was 485.[37] English statistics, though bearing less directly on the point, establish a similar presumption. Through the London Venereal Hospital[38] for women, some 400 patients annually pass; the average number of deaths during each of the last twenty years has been less than three. If there were 10,000 prostitutes in London — a low estimate,— there would be an annual death rate of 2,000, provided we assume a five year lease of life: yet out of 790,000 women between 18 and 35 resident in London, only 3,059 died in 1909. Finally, of the 11,823 women committed to Holloway Jail in 1908, many of them prostitutes of over five years' standing, only six died in the course of the year.[39] The explanation is to be sought in the fluctuating constitution of the prostitute army already pointed out. Prostitutes disappear rather

[35] J. Schrank, *Die Prostitution in Wien,* two volumes (Wien, 1886), Vol. II, pp. 220–2.
[36] Schneider, *loc. cit.,* p. 39.
[37] Fiaux, *La Police des Mœurs* (3 vols. Paris, 1907, 1910) Vol. III, p. 658. M. Fiaux is the most voluminous and indefatigable of European writers on the subject and his works are inexhaustible mines of information and argument.
[38] The Lock Hospital; the term "Lock" has no connection with "lock-up." Its meaning is obscure.
[39] Maurice Gregory, *The European Movement for Abolition.* (Tokyo, Japan, 1912), pp. 44–47.

than die,— a fact of great practical significance as we shall discover; only a part — it is uncertain of what size — remain prostitutes: a small fraction marry, a much larger fraction return to work; those who stick to the business wind up as the servants of younger prostitutes, occasionally as brothel-keepers; a few of them are found as aged hags, offering themselves for a copper coin below the bridges of Berlin or in the dark corners of Whitechapel.

The considerations just dwelt on make anything approaching an accurate estimate of the number of prostitutes in a given city entirely impossible. In the first place, because of the general flux above described; in the second, because particular causes — the conditions of trade, the season of the year, the presence or absence of local festivities, such as the Wakes and Bank Holiday in Great Britain, the October Fest at Munich, the Carnival at Cologne,[40] finally, the varying pressure of local authorities, all operate to disturb for better or worse the general movement above indicated. Only the roughest approximations can therefore be made by way of obtaining an imperfect picture; and for the most part, the guesses are not to be trusted too far, even for that purpose. At Paris, Maxime du Camp assessed the number at 120,000, — an estimate that has by common consent been rejected as manifestly absurd; M. Lépine, the able and accomplished ex-Prefect of Police, inclines to a figure varying from one-half to two-thirds as large, say 60,000 to 80,000 — itself generally viewed as much too high, even on

[40] At the proper time subsequently, these occasions are always followed by a perceptible rise in the illegitimacy curve.

Prostitution: Definition and Extent

a liberal interpretation of the terms; MM. Yves Guyot and Augagneur, distinguished publicists, estimate 30,-000;[41] Turot, still more conservatively, 20,000;[42] Carlier, formerly chief of the municipal police, cuts even this moderate estimate down: he concedes only from 14,000 to 17,000. His logic is worth noting, for I shall recur to a similar method of calculation. He assumes that for every clandestine prostitute actually arrested for solicitation, intoxication, etc., "there are at least five or six more who ought to be." Between 1872 and 1888, the non-registered prostitutes arrested averaged 2,797 annually; according as one employs as multiple five or six, the total would be 13,985 or 16,782. But the method is not reliable: in the first place, because in any case the multiple is probably too small; in the second because the fluctuation in arrests shows clearly that arrests do not increase "pari passu" with the increase in population, while clandestine prostitutes increase still faster.[43] There were, for instance, 1,932 arrests in 1888 — the last of the years considered by Carlier — as against 3,769 in 1872, the first. Moreover, from 1888 to 1903, the average annual arrests numbered 2,762, a slightly smaller figure than in the former period. Were the method sound, one must conclude that clandestine prostitution had not increased between 1872[44] and 1903,

[41] Louis Fiaux: *La Police des Mœurs* Vol. I, p. 160.

[42] These estimates deal with clandestine prostitution alone, meaning thereby, as I have already pointed out, unofficial prostitution, some of it notorious, some concealed. Official or registered prostitution is too small to be a factor in calculations of this kind.

[43] F. Schiller in *Zeitschrift* II, p. 312.

[44] Disturbed local conditions might be assigned as the explanation of this figure; but it is practically repeated in 1880, when the arrests reached 3,544.

despite the fact that population rose from 1,851,792 to 2,660,559.

An estimate of 80,000 was once current for London, — an unquestionable exaggeration. The Home Office reported in 1837 that the total number of prostitutes known to the police as living in houses of ill-fame, walking the streets and infesting low neighborhoods was 9,-409; [45] twenty years later a similar return made by Sir Richard Mayne, Commissioner of the Metropolitan Police, based on detailed reports from the several districts yielded a total somewhat smaller, 8,600; a decade later the number similarly reached had fallen to 6,515.[46] An unofficial count recently made disclosed 8,000. If the figures for 1837 and 1857 are fairly representative, the later ones are certainly much too low. The probabilities are, however, that all these estimates include only notorious and unmistakable prostitutes, excluding the numerous clandestines and partials who figure in the continental calculations.

Equally uncertain calculations have from time to time been put forth respecting other great cities. Dufour estimated the clandestine prostitutes of Berlin at 50,-000 in 1896, at a time when just above four thousand were enrolled, assuming, that is, 12 clandestine for every registered woman.[47] In three successive years, 1889, 1890, 1891, the morals police arrested for solicitation and similar offences 3,220, 3,537, and 4,019 women respec-

[45] Gregory, *loc. cit.*, p. 46.
[46] William Acton, *Prostitution* (London, 1870) p. 4. Acton quotes also (p. 3) a police estimate of 6,371, for 1839.
[47] P. Pollitz: *Die Psychologie des Verbrechers*. (Leipzig, 1909) p. 85.

tively; of these, 640, 735, and 792 respectively were registered by the police on the ground that they were incorrigible;[48] the rest were warned and released, despite the fact that with probably few exceptions they were at the moment practising professional prostitution.[49]   It would appear, therefore, that, as the police register only 1-5 of those they arrest, clandestine prostitution is at least five times as extensive as professional; on this basis we must assume 20,000 clandestine prostitutes for the German capital — probably an underestimate, since, large numbers of clandestines never being arrested at all, five is too small a multiple to employ.

It is perhaps needless to quote similar estimates for other places, except by way of driving home the enormous extent of the evil, even if it can not be definitely appraised.   The prostitutes of Vienna have been rated at 30,000, of Glasgow at 17,000,[50] of Cologne at 7,000, of Munich at 8,000.   The police records of Rome show 5,000 women who have been in their hands latterly for some offence connected with prostitution;[51] a Dutch register in process of compilation at police headquarters, Amsterdam, already contains upwards of 7,-000 names; in that city the police have the names and addresses of 968 women well known for this avocation;[52]

[48] The figures are official; they may be found in various sources, e. g., A. Grotjahn, *Soziale Pathologie* (Berlin, 1912) p. 153.
[49] Studies of this point have been made in Paris by O. Commenge: *La Prostitution clandestine à Paris* (Paris, 1904) Chap. II.
[50] *Memorandum on a Social Evil in Glasgow*, published by authority of the Parish Council, October, 1911, p. 43.   The Chief Constable in a report to the Magistrates Committee, November 20, 1911, holds this estimate to be a gross exaggeration.
[51] Personally communicated by Police Brigadier.
[52] Personally communicated by officials.

Prostitution in Europe

in Rotterdam 1,206.[53] For the German Empire as a whole, a not unreasonable calculation of 330,000 has been ventured, side by side with a serious, though mistaken guess of one and one half million.[54] But the only safe data refer to the number of registered women and the number of arrests; and though the former are confessedly only a small fraction, their sum total is itself not to be passed over lightly from whatever standpoint the matter is regarded: Paris with its 6,418 (1903), Berlin with 3,559, Hamburg with 935, Vienna with 1,689, Budapest with 2,000. If the evil is, on the average, only five times as extensive as these figures indicate, there is enough to be alarmed at, without a panic-stricken incursion into the realms of baseless fancy.

Left to itself or to unhampered exploitation prostitution seeks everywhere the same sort of outlets; the free professional, the clandestine, the occasional, the partial, hunt their prey, openly or furtively, according to circumstances, in the crowded thoroughfares of retail trade, or loiter in cafés and theater promenades. Having found their victim, they repair to their own rooms, to hotels, assignation houses, etc. A large number avoid publicity and obtain their clientele in the guise of friends through introduction or recommendation or through the keepers of *rendezvous*-houses, who arrange appointments by means of photographs and fill orders for patrons desiring a person of particular type. A small and steadily

[53] Th. M. Roest Van Limburgh: *In den Strijd tegen de Ontucht*. (Rotterdam, 1910) p. 17.
[54] The last named figures are quoted by Moll, *loc. cit.*, p. 371. For a discussion as to the probable number of prostitutes in Hamburg, see *Zeitschrift* IV, p. 183.

Prostitution: Definition and Extent

decreasing number of prostitutes suffer themselves to be immured in bordells, i. e., houses of prostitution licensed or authorized by the police in certain towns, e. g., in Germany, France, Austria-Hungary, Italy, and in Geneva, and conducted by a proprietor or mistress who collects the entire income, paying the inmates a stipulated percentage. In places where bordells are forbidden as well as in places where they exist, a non-licensed and more or less similar establishment has sprung up,— the brothel, which commonly represents itself as a boarding-place, where a certain number of prostitutes have their own rooms, pay the keeper a fixed sum for their keep and retain whatever else they earn. Into such establishments the police of Hamburg, Bremen, Dresden, Cologne, having the right to designate the registered prostitute's dwelling-place, yet being forbidden to license bordells, force as many of the women as they can lay hold of,— a violation of the statute in spirit, as we shall shortly perceive. In London and Berlin, the brothel takes a looser form, and amounts usually to nothing more than the casual combination of a few women who utilize their joint premises for carrying on their business. It is worth noting, as we pass, though we shall return to the point, that, whether the police favor the licensed bordell or, by stretching their authority, force women into barracks or brothels, a segregated district, into which the prostitutes of a city are confined, exists nowhere in Europe, and is nowhere supposed to be either desirable or feasible. A few streets — in Hamburg for example, are tenanted either only or almost entirely by prostitutes under police pressure; but they do not form a district, for

29

they are widely separated, and they contain in any event
only a fraction of the total number of local prostitutes,
— not even all the registered women of the city. A
single street in Bremen is inhabited altogether by prostitutes; but it is absurd to speak of segregation in reference to seventy-five women in a town containing hundreds of others living at large. Elsewhere, at Paris,
Rome, Geneva, Vienna, Budapest, where the bordells are
officially recognized and even favored,— they are scattered throughout the respective cities, no single street
usually containing more than one or two.

Prostitution tends, further, to associate itself with the
sale of alcohol; in consequence of which loose women
congregate in low-grade drinking and amusement-places,
and are utilized wherever law and custom do not interfere, to assist in the sale of drink. I have already called
attention to the low morality of the barmaid in certain
portions of the Continent. In the German cities, outright prostitutes are employed to push the sale of drink,
by drinking with and otherwise entertaining their already
more or less intoxicated patrons; screened corners and a
quick succession of new faces characterize the so-called
Animierkneipe and American-bars,[55] which are bitterly denounced as perhaps the most demoralizing form
that prostitution has as yet assumed. Hardly more than

[55] These bars often advertise "new service weekly." A statistical
return on the waitresses of Berlin shows that 57.2% remained in
one place three months or less. Of 1,108 cases examined, 732 had
more than six places in one year, 200 more than ten, and 63
more than 20! Henning, *Denkschrift über das Kellnerinnen-Wesen*
(Berlin, no date) pp. 13, 14. See also: A. Meher, *Die geheime
und öffentliche Prostitution in Stuttgart*, etc. (Paderborn, 1912)
p. 133, etc. See also: *Das Animierkneipenwesen in Frankfurt a. M.
Zeitschrift* VIII, p. 59; also, same volume, pp. 70 and 75.

Prostitution: Definition and Extent

a variation of Animierkneipe is the dance-hall, varieté, or cabaret, where the "artiste" is a prostitute mingling freely with the audience at the conclusion of her turn and relying largely on alcohol to make her way quickly with her casual acquaintances. Finally, pretended employments,— cigar shops, massage-establishments, and employment agencies illustrate in one place or another at once the timidity and the stubbornness of the phenomenon; for though prostitution easily takes fright and abandons any one shape under the frown of unfavorable opinion or the pressure of the law, it tends to reappear in another guise. We shall subsequently consider these efforts to control or suppress particular aspects of the evil, and their consequences.[56]

One more word is required here by way of mere description. Prostitution in Europe as an organized business is by no means limited to the intercourse of persons of opposite sexes. A homosexual prostitution,— prostitution, that is, in which the parties belong to the same sex,— has developed on a considerable scale. Notorious resorts for those addicted to homosexuality are to be found not only in Paris but in smaller towns, like Hamburg. Berlin is, however, probably the main mart. In prominent thoroughfares, bars exist to which only women resort as well as bars to which no woman gets access; and at intervals, large homosexual balls are given, attended only by persons of a single sex. I witnessed one such affair, at which some 150 couples, all men, appeared. It is estimated that between 1,000 and 2,000 male prostitutes live in Berlin; forty homosexual resorts are toler-

[56] See Chapter XI — *The Outcome of European Experience.*

Prostitution in Europe

ated by the Berlin police; and it is reported that some 30,000 persons of marked homosexual inclination reside in the German capital.

The prostitute is everywhere attended by a complementary phenomenon — the pimp, who lives upon her earnings, in return for which she is as a rule treated with brutality.[57] The police estimate that something like 50% to 90% of the prostitutes of the large European cities support men in this fashion — not only the street-walkers and scattered prostitutes, but, not infrequently, bordell inmates, as well.[58] The tie is easy to describe, difficult to understand. No practical advantage accrues to the woman, for in Europe the pimp affords her absolutely no protection against the police; indeed, the reverse is apt to be the case, for the police, tolerant of an inoffensive prostitute though they be, are unrelenting in their hostility to the pimp whom they rightly regard as a criminal, either actual or in the making. The woman may be compromised by the association; she certainly can not be protected. One is thrown back for an adequate explanation on the fundamental fact of sex relation. The woman has no attachment whatsoever with her stream of casual customers; but the pimp belongs to her. A vestige of affection, a sense of property lies at the bottom of the connection; her blunted sense does not revolt from the price she pays for it. This view is strongly favored by the fact that the woman's loyalty

[57] The pimp is called "bully" in England, "souteneur," "Louis" or "Alphonse" in France; "Zuhälter" in Germany.

[58] The pimp is said to be less common in Scandinavia than elsewhere: See Hjalmar von Sydow, *Om Soutenörväsendet* in *Report, Swedish Commission*, Vol. IV, p. 12.

Prostitution: Definition and Extent

will endure every strain that her mate may put upon it, — abuse, deprivation, or what not,— every strain, except competition. The difficulties of obtaining a conviction are practically insuperable unless jealousy loosens the woman's tongue.[59]

Despite the general similarity to which I have repeatedly adverted, there is a notion current that prostitution in Paris is subtly different from that in other great cities, that the women are less mercenary, the practice less odious or repulsive. Parisian prostitution enjoys indeed the glamour of a Bohemian background and a more picturesque tradition; but beyond this I saw no reason to think the notion well grounded. In my observation, prostitution is even more uniform internally than externally: it is everywhere purely mercenary, everywhere rapacious, everywhere perverse, diseased, sordid, vulgar, and almost always filthy. In her bloom, the Parisian cocotte possesses a bit of Gallic grace and verbal cleverness that is perhaps denied to English, German, or Scandinavian women of the same class. But it is soon brushed away by excess, drink and perversion. The refined courtesan of the books is practically as rare in Paris as in London and Berlin. Pretentious prostitution is indeed nowadays international; there is no distinction in type, origin, or bearing between the women of Monte Carlo, Ostende, the Ambassadeurs, or the Palais de Dance. At different times the same individuals may be found in all these resorts. At the lower level, all is equally sordid everywhere. The grisette of the Bal Tabarin is, like her English or German sister, a pathetic figure, whose

[59] See pp. 96-7.

33

Prostitution in Europe

livelier speech and simulated gaiety does not hide poverty, loneliness, vulgarity, or the ravages of overwork, irregular hours, disease, and absinthe. A day at St. Lazare or police headquarters — and thither those who remain prostitutes eventually come — quickly dispels any illusion one may entertain on this score: Holloway Jail and the Inspection bureaus of Hamburg, Vienna, and Stockholm have nothing more degraded or repulsive to show.

The cost of prostitution, near and remote, direct and indirect, outruns any calculation that one would dare to formulate. Payment for service varies from a few copper coins to several hundred marks or francs; incidental expense for accommodations, amusements, liquor, gratuities, gifts, may double the immediate outlay. The Berlin street girl of fair grade demands five or ten marks;[60] with her customer she takes a cab or taxi, for which he pays; they resort to a hotel or room of which she has the use and for which he pays perhaps six marks more; she demands pin-money for herself, the maid or concierge. Money is the sole object of her effort, the whole burden of her talk. "The Berlin street-walker," writes Schneider, "immediately asks the stranger whom she accosts: 'what will you give me?' Once at home with her, the bargaining begins anew, for, now that she has him, she can raise her demands."[61] Impossible as it is to be definite, one fact stands out: the prostitute living at large is swindled by every one who has dealings with her: her landlord, by way of recompense for the legal

[60] $1.25 to $2.50.
[61] Schneider: *loc. cit.*, p. 32.

risk he may run,[62] the dressmaker, milliner, grocer, butcher, etc. The London street-walker pays three guineas in rental where an honest family pays one. Nor is her outlay limited to her own necessities, for she must earn enough to satisfy the rapacity of her pimp, besides. Her business interest and bad taste lead her to indulge in shoddy and relatively expensive luxuries, soon worn out or discarded. The price of all this, mere livelihood, extravagance, and rascality, her patrons pay; from them every sou is obtained.

A clearer picture can be obtained in the case of the bordell, where business methods prevail.[63] The more elaborate of these establishments represent large investments. The latest bordell of Budapest required an initial outlay of 500,000 crowns ($100,000), on which a very liberal return is expected. Fiaux cites a second-class establishment in Paris that yields an annual profit of 70,000 fr. and notes that the same proprietors often run a chain of houses.[64] In these places, a minimum price for service is usually fixed; entrance fee, tips, and alcohol are of course " extra." In Paris, the entrance fee at pretentious establishments is 20 francs; from that it ranges downward as low as five. The inevitable bottle of wine at the former also costs 20 francs; at the latter, whatever can be wheedled or coaxed.[65] Rendezvous establishments, incurring greater risk, charge

[62] For a shabby room in Berlin, the author of the *" Diary of a Lost One "* (Berlin, 1905) p. 137, paid 180 marks a month.

[63] The subject is more fully discussed in Chapter VI.

[64] *Loc. cit.*, p. 220. A well-known Berlin resort is capitalized at 1,000,000 marks and has recently declared a dividend of 20%. (*Berliner Tageblatt,* May 2, 1912.)

[65] Fiaux, *loc. cit.,* I, pp. 215-6, 220-221.

Prostitution in Europe

correspondingly; 40 francs, if modish; five, if utterly wretched. Those with a carefully guarded clientele sometimes exact as much as 100 francs! At Stockholm, the charge varies from a few pennies to twenty-five crowns (about $7.50).

In the long run, whatever the women earn, they rarely have anything to show for it. The bordell-keeper plies them hard and then manages to keep them in her debt. Despite the fact that they may entertain anywhere from five to fifty guests in twenty-four hours, they do not own the clothes on their back, when they make up their mind to leave! Schneider calculates the minimum payment of a girl for bare living in the better bordells of Hamburg, Leipzig, and Vienna at 300 to 600 [66] marks a month — an underestimate, as he himself subsequently avers. Seventy-five wretched creatures are ‚harbored in the barracks of Helenenstrasse, Bremen, independently of each other; several of them figured out for me the amount they must earn merely to live; from which it appeared that 10,000 marks a year each barely sufficed: the first charge for their support was therefore 750,000 marks! In the Roman brothels, the girls must average 10 to 12 men a night, in order to earn the high charges made for their keep; in the lowest resort of Altona, the wretched inmate pays 75 marks a week for her mere board and lodging; at Dresden, the bordell women are charged up with 100 marks a week for the same bare necessaries. Among the common prostitutes of Stockholm are found women who claim to earn — and to spend — sums ranging from 3,000 to 12,000 crowns annually.

[66] $75 to $150.

36

Prostitution: Definition and Extent

A careful study was made by Dr. Lindblad of 712 cases;[67] the number of customers ran from less than one on the average daily to as high as 20 when business was brisk; assuming 225 working days per year,[68] the women must have averaged incomes of $1,080 each annually. Of 569 from whom information could be obtained, 513 save absolutely nothing, and only seven claimed to have saved a tidy sum.[69]

I have spoken thus far only of the money immediately involved,— the sums paid to the prostitute for her service, the sums paid out by her for her keep. But the account is not so simple. We may not overlook the loss involved in the unproductiveness of this army of women; expenditure on alcohol, gifts and demoralizing amusements; the long score chargeable to venereal disease, including the loss in earnings, the outlay for treatment, both of the immediate victims and those still more unfortunate on whom, though innocent, some part of the curse and its cost not infrequently devolves. Upwards of 10,000 individuals are now annually treated for venereal complaints in the public hospitals of Berlin alone. These are essential items in the cost of prostitution. Of the total loss only the roughest guesses can be made; but it is worth noting that any estimate that endeavors to include all the factors, direct and indirect, soon reaches into the millions. Losch, for example, has reckoned the annual cost of prostitution to the German Empire at some-

[67] *Report, Swedish Commission,* Vol. III, p. 50.
[68] Prof. Johansson calculated that a woman averages one-fourth of a year in hospital, prison, etc.
[69] *Ibid,* p. 54.

thing between 300 and 500 million marks.[70]   This outlay may be contrasted with that spent by the Prussian Government on its entire educational system: its universities, secondary schools, elementary school system, technical and professional institutions of all kinds involving a budget in 1909 of a little less than 200,000,000 marks.[71] Assuredly the economic burden imposed on society by prostitution is comparable with that due to standing armies, war, or pestilence.

[70] Quoted by Kampffmeyer, *loc. cit.,* p. 34.
[71] *Statistiches Jahrbuch* (Berlin, 1910) pp. 242-3.

CHAPTER II

THE DEMAND

Prostitution involves two parties.— Extent of demand in Europe. — Theory of its necessity.— Is physiological impulse irresistible? — Analysis into various factors.— Demand emanating from woman.— Effect of improvement in social status.— Changed attitude of medical profession.—Reduction of demand through education.— Sex education in Europe.— Influence of demoralizing literature.— Recent improvement.

PROSTITUTION is usually described and discussed from the standpoint of the women involved alone; but the problem cannot be understood so long as it is approached solely from that angle. In every act of prostitution at least two parties, usually, but not always, of opposite sex, are concerned. Now one, now the other, is either initially or more highly responsible. Not infrequently, however, these two individuals are so far from constituting the entire situation that they may be mere puppets in the hands of others: the man, the victim of shrewdly devised suggestion or excitement; the woman, the bait cunningly dangled by pimp, brothel-keeper, or publican. Under such circumstances it is plainly absurd to speak of prostitution as if it were only or even mainly the act of the woman; as if women took to prostitution simply because they were marked out for a vicious life by innate depravity or even forced into it by economic pressure. Inclination on the one hand, need on the other, are among the factors that will assist us to understand the

39

problem; but a fundamental and antecedent condition is the existence of a market, clamoring for wares of a particular kind and furnishing an opportunity for the forced sale of such wares as do not themselves immediately find buyers. Instead, therefore, of explaining prostitution as if it were caused by certain conditions affecting solely or primarily the constitution or environment of women, I shall view it from the standpoint of demand and supply. In utilizing these terms I do not mean to imply that a certain volume of demand exists, to begin with, and that this is satisfied and has to be satisfied through the production somehow of a corresponding supply. We shall find that both demand and supply are variable factors. The demand can within limits be stimulated or checked; the supply can be increased or decreased; and the increase of supply can be so manipulated as to increase demand. Moreover, a given supply can be made to satisfy a smaller or a larger demand, so that the volume of prostitution is a matter not only of the number of those engaged, but of the intensity of their activity. The two partners — the man and the woman — thus not only interact on each other, but are both played upon by agencies lying outside themselves. This method will have the advantage of demonstrating the interlocking relations of the man, the woman, and the exploiter.

That this procedure is both fair and sound a moment's consideration will show. If the prostitution of women had specific causes, in the sense in which the term cause is used in science, then, wherever such causes are present, prostitution should result. There are, however, no conditions of which this can be affirmed. Of the number

The Demand

of women of whom any particular fact or set of facts is characteristic, only a small portion ever become prostitutes. For example: prostitutes have often been, as we shall see, domestic servants. Yet service, even under unfavorable conditions, cannot be said to cause prostitution, for more servants escape than succumb. The conditions of service at most indicate whence part of the supply will be drawn. Moreover, once engaged in prostitution, the woman does not passively wait to be sought out by ungratified spontaneous demand; in order to earn her own livelihood or to satisfy the cupidity of a third party, she proceeds to create or develop the demand for what she has to sell. At every moment there exists a circle of habituated consumers, as well as numerous agencies,— the women and their exploiters, for example, — actively engaged in increasing the number of consumers and the urgency of their demands. Demand and supply thus interact upon each other in much the same fashion as characterizes the interplay of the market in reference to any other commodity. The application of this conception to the discussion of prostitution has therefore two obvious advantages: it brings out the dual nature of the phenomenon and it suggests the commercial side involved in the production and maintenance of prostitution on the grand scale.

At the present time, the demand on the part of the continental male European is practically universal;[1] so true is this, that until quite recently questioned, it has

[1] From this statement England is purposely excluded for two reasons: (1) accurate data covering different social classes are not obtainable; (2) family and religious life are so differently organized that there is a very strong presumption that correct living

41

Prostitution in Europe

been taken to be an ultimate and inevitable physiological fact. Male continence has not been required by either tradition or opinion. A low regard for women has practically left the matter one to be regulated by men on such standards as they themselves approve. Indulgence begins early: Meirowsky's investigations indicate that at least 20% of the boys in the highest gymnasium classes are already habituated;[2] of 106 venereally infected University students, 61% admitted intercourse before reaching the University.[3] In a Vienna statistic covering 10,-057 cases of venereal infection, over one-half were minors, and 67% under 25 years of age. Prof. Finger, Chief of the great Vienna clinic, concludes that these figures are actually representative,— that perhaps one-half of all venereal disease belongs to the youth of both sexes.[4] Welander found that of 582 Swedish men, 464 admitted intercourse before the end of the 18th year.[5] "In the country and in the urban proletariat, no one dreams of continence beyond adolescence," says Blaschko.[6] "Among the working classes, city or country, abstinence is excessively rare, and in the higher classes, practically insignificant."[7] Of 90 physicians interrogated by Prof. Neisser respecting their sexual history, only one denied all intercourse prior to marriage

is in certain strata of society distinctly more probable than on the Continent. Organizations like the White Cross Societies and The Alliance of Honor testify to the existence of sound sentiment and promote sound practice. But as to the extent to which continence prevails I have been unable to form a conception.

[2] *Zeitschrift* XI, p. 47.
[3] *Zeitschrift* XI, p. 5.
[4] *Zeitschrift* IX, pp. 66–68. See also pp. 37–65.
[5] *Zeitschrift* IX, p. 411.
[6] *Zeitschrift* XIII, p. 154.
[7] Blaschko, in *Zeitschrift* XIII, p. 104.

The Demand

and he attributed his exemption to an early engagement alone; twenty-eight, i. e., 32.9%, had indulged themselves while still in the secondary school.[8] These figures have been confirmed by other investigators.[9] Beginning thus early after puberty, sexual intercourse on the male's part ranges more or less widely prior to marriage and is none too severely constrained by custom even afterwards. Its practical universality, with the rare exceptions explicable on religious or ethical grounds, is substantiated by the wide prevalence of venereal complaints. "Roughly speaking," remarked a distinguished specialist, whose opinion, when quoted by me to his confrères has rarely been strongly overruled,— " roughly speaking, one may say that most German men have had gonorrhœa, and about one in five syphilis." [10]

No wonder that where practice is so general, theory has accommodated itself so far as to assume that sexual intercourse on the male's part is necessary and wholesome. Up to recent times this has been almost undisputed dogma. The practically universal demand was for centuries regarded fatalistically as inevitable and incontestable; in the Middle Ages, a sufficient supply of women was imported by way of entertaining the delegates to church congresses.[11] A change of attitude and opinion is, however, undoubtedly taking place. The universality

[8] *Zeitschrift* XII, p. 34.
[9] See Blaschko, *Zeitschrift* XIII, pp. 154-5.
[10] " The incidence of gonorrhea is estimated at over 100% ; i. e., on the average, every man has had it. This does not mean that actually every man has had gonorrhea, for if one person has had it six times, that would absolve several others." F. Pinkus: *Die Verhütung der Geschlechtskrankheiten* (Freiburg, 1912) p. 21.
[11] Bloch, *loc. cit.*, Vol. I, pp. 710–712 gives details and authorities.

of demand has been condoned on the assumption that it represented an irresistible physiological impulse. A good deal of attention has been latterly expended in the effort to resolve this so-called physiological impulse into its constituent elements, with the following results. In the first place, however strong the spontaneous sex-impulse may be, it is like any other impulse — capable of restraint through the cultivation of inhibitions. Except for the futile precepts of the church, European society has for centuries been singularly free from any such effort. Women have been regarded as inferior creatures and have contentedly accepted the status assigned to them. They have therefore failed to resent masculine immorality; the self-restraint that might thereby have been imposed on men — be it much or little — has been generally lacking. Europe has been a man's world,— managed by men and largely for men,— for cynical men, at that,— men inured to the sight of human inequalities, callous as to the value of lower-class life, and distinctly lacking in respect for womanhood, especially that of the working-classes. The military, the aristocracy, the student, are all conceded their fling. " Dem Studenten ist ja alles erlaubt — To the student everything is allowed." Where soldier and scholar freely indulge themselves without reprobation, it is too much to expect the artisan to refrain.

Not only has there been — up to recently, at least — no social inhibition: there has been a strong social compulsion. Men swim with the current; they fall in with accepted habits and customs, in order to escape being ridiculous, and custom established in this way is prac-

The Demand

tically imposed on successive generations. Certain forms of venereal experience have been popularly treated as marks of maturity. Dr. Magnus Möller tells of a club of military officers existing in Stockholm in the early nineties to which no one was eligible until he could prove that he had had syphilis.[12] Quite as flagrantly, boys have been practically coerced into sowing wild oats. Women, whose influence might have been exerted restrainingly, have been trained not to pry into the prematrimonial records of their husbands; fathers fashion their sons, as a rule, after their own image. Indulgence brought about in this way cannot fairly be characterized or excused as physiological, even though, once experienced, it soon gathers intensity enough to operate on its own account and to play the ominous rôle of suggestion to others.

Finally, we may not overlook the part played by deliberate excitation on the part of the woman or those in whose interests she works. Prostitution is not merely a matter between man and woman,— the former overtaken by a periodic impulse demanding gratification, the latter supporting herself through the passionless sacrifice of the sexual function. Over and above this, it is an industry, deliberately cultivated by third parties for their own profit: and the instinct readily lends itself to artificial exploitation. A very large constituent in what has been called the irresistible demand of natural instinct is nothing but suggestion and stimulation associated with alcohol,[13] late hours, and sensuous amusements, and de-

---

[12] *Zeitschrift* VIII, p. 4.
[13] The rôle of alcohol is described by O. Rosenthal: *Alkoholismus und Prostitution* (with bibliography) (Berlin, 1905). See

Prostitution in Europe

liberately worked up for the profit of third parties,—pimps, tavern-keepers, bordell-proprietors, etc. Street-walking, with the pimp across the way ready to ply the lash; the Animierkneipe, in which the earnings of the prostitute barmaid are wholly dependent upon the extent to which she overmasters her guest through liquor and otherwise; the bordell, in which heavy charges and her small proportional share force her to find an extensive trade,— these are the most obvious examples of supply deliberately and resourcefully engaged in creating demand. Amid conditions as they exist in Paris, Berlin, and Vienna, and the smaller towns like Geneva which aspire to be world cities by being licentious, growing youth is characterized not by a normal, healthy, and natural sexual development, but by an over-stimulated and premature sex activity — a purely artificial excitation of instinct. An artificial supply of prostitutes is deliberately created; forced upon the market under appropriate conditions, an artificial demand is worked up to consume it. Every tolerated focus, through the existence of which third parties benefit, thus soon becomes a vested interest, actively engaged in whipping up demand and supply, reacting upon each other. Supply, everywhere greater than spontaneous demand, is utilized to create a secondary demand. A striking example of deliberate business organization along these lines is to be found in Paris where, closely adjoining one another in the rue Figal are found a dance hall, a café and an assignation house said to form a plant under one management.

also M. Hirschfeld: *Die Gurgel von Berlin* (Berlin, no date) pp. 43, etc.

46

The Demand

The sex impulse, however formidable it may be, is thus on close investigation discovered to be not the single powerful physiological force which it has been represented to be, resistlessly pushing towards an instinctive object, but rather a combination of forces of very different quality as respects both origin and intensity. Taking prostitution and resort to prostitution as they exist in any great city today, three distinct factors are readily distinguished: sex impulse, pure and simple; social instigation or compulsion; sheer artificial excitation. Not improbably, instinct plays a decidedly less important part than is commonly supposed; much of what has been viewed as physiological is undoubtedly social. Less than half of Neisser's cases attributed their lapse to their own impulse,— and even this impulse is not necessarily of really spontaneous origin; of the others, 28.8% blamed comrades for dragging them into trouble; 18.6% acted under alcoholic excitement. In another set of 129 cases cited, less than half acted on native impulse; alcohol figures with 23.6%; comrades, with 29.4%.[14] Nor is native impulse itself any longer regarded as a constant or spasmodically irresistible force; it can be checked, diverted, modified, or stimulated. It becomes stronger with indulgence; weaker through continued repression.

For the reasons above given, demand is no longer spoken of as if it were a constant quantity determined at any given time and place by the ultimate constitution of human nature and unalterable except by transformation of the character of the race; just as it is equally absurd to speak in fatalistic terms of the supply. Not a

[14] *Zeitschrift* XI, pp. 6 and 60.

Prostitution in Europe

single factor in either demand or supply bears this rigid elemental stamp; every factor is capable of mitigation or aggravation by human decisions, institutions, habits,—some of them, indeed, more or less readily so. " Human nature "— so-called — is not the whole of it, in the sense in which the expression is commonly used. Indeed, human nature itself may be made better or worse by opinion, inhibition, suggestion, example. Unquestionably, do what we will, a problem — a vast problem — will remain; but it is an enormous gain to have learned that a considerable volume of prostitution and of the demand for prostitution is the product of conditions that, however difficult the task, are within limits socially controllable.

One must not, of course, overlook the fact that demand does not simply take the form of the male seeking or being induced to seek the female. The seeker is sometimes the woman herself, bent upon her own gratification. Her own effort may thus succeed in increasing demand. It is impossible to say with what frequency male irregularity is thus provoked. Of Meirowsky's 102 first offenders, 29.4% attributed their lapse to the seductive influence of comrades, part of whom were girls; of 28 physicians whose first offence occurred while still at school, over one-half blamed themselves wholly; three of them threw the initial blame on girls, all of whom were servants. But the overwhelming majority of women involved in provocation are open or concealed prostitutes.

The fact just stated throws an interesting light on the possibility of reducing immorality through the cultiva-

The Demand

tion of social inhibitions. We learned in the preceding chapter that under the natural conditions that obtain in the country and in certain sections of the urban working-classes, girls are sometimes equally responsible partners in sexual irregularity. Clan morality does not forbid; we may assume, therefore, that not infrequently the woman indulges her passion precisely as the man indulges his. But the moment that improved social or economic position brings her under the range of more exacting ideals, she checks herself. The first consciousness of the higher requirement results in decidedly reducing the scope which she allows to her impulse. It is perhaps true that self-restraint is actually easier for women than for men; [15] but it is at any rate not achieved without effort. It is therefore not without significance that the social sanction, as yet but slightly operative among men, is among women of the higher classes very generally powerful enough to reverse the animal engine. Unhappy consequences to health are alleged, and doubtless sometimes occur; but they are a lesser evil than disgrace, disease or pregnancy and are endured as such.

The analysis of demand as above outlined has already borne consequences both theoretical and practical. In the first place, it has accomplished a striking change in medical opinion as to the necessity of sexual intercourse and the supposedly unfavorable results of continence. Recent medical literature abounds in strong and authoritative expressions utterly at variance with the traditional position. Cases of irrepressible desire are

[15] See Iwan Bloch: *Das Sexualleben unserer Zeit* (Berlin, 1909) p. 91.

Prostitution in Europe

stamped as pathological, rather than normal; as relatively rare, rather than usual or even frequent. Continence is, in general, increasingly regarded as both feasible and wholesome. " I am convinced that the overwhelming majority of persons are not in the least injured by continuous continence whether during youth or afterwards," writes Moll. " The longer one is continent, the more readily is continence borne, the less is one annoyed by the sexual impulse." [16] Moll insists that, even in cases where neurotic disturbances occur, these are not comparable to the damage, corporal and moral, which attends irregular intercourse — and of course it always remains to be proven that the disturbances in question really result from abstinence. Pinkus, conceding that occasionally depressing symptoms attend self-restraint, points out that " the annoyances arising from abstinence are far from being such serious psychic disturbances as are produced by the knowledge that one has contracted venereal disease: under which conditions abstinence must be practised anyway." [17] " There is not a shadow of proof to show that continence is damaging to health.— To the continent, continence becomes progressively easier,"[18] " Whatever disturbances are attributable to sexual abstinence, they are usually non-progressive and are for the most part remediable through hygienic and therapeutic measures. On the other hand, the damages done through intimacy with prostitutes far overshoot in number and gravity any harm attributable to continence." [19] Exceed-

[16] Moll, *loc. cit.*, p. 887. See also pp. 945, etc.
[17] Felix Pinkus, *loc. cit.*, p. 177.
[18] M. von Gruber, *Die Prostitution* (Wien, 1905) p. 40, etc.
[19] *Zeitschrift* XIII, p. 46; see also III, p. 255.

The Demand

ingly cogent is Touton's curt summary: "In short, all the talk about manifestations due to abstinence is thus far with few exceptions a hodge-podge of superficial observations and uncritical interpretations." [20] Again: "Altogether healthy men, sexually normal, can, without danger of illness, for the most part get along far into maturity without sexual intercourse, if they do not purposely excite themselves or if temptation is not pressed upon them, especially so, if, instead of such stimulation, they resort to moderate exercises and adequate mental employment. The idler cannot remain continent." [21] Johansson urges that through the cultivation of an inhibitory mechanism, the impulse can be limited, and subordinated to the welfare of the individual and of society. [22]

There is no livelier topic under discussion in connection with prostitution than that of the methods to be pursued in order to minimize demand, in accordance with the modern scientific view that irregular sexual intercourse is a reducible evil. The fact that "appetite grows by what it feeds on" pleads strongly for timely action. Instruction, with special reference to sex-physiology, has therefore been widely and confidently urged as the means of acquainting childhood and, later, youth, with the essential facts of sex-physiology, so as to deprive the facts of morbid interest and to warn the child of the dangers

[20] Touton, quoting Troemner's report at the Dresden Conference, 1911, *Zeitschrift* XII, p. 412. See also X, p. 211; for the opposite point of view, see *Zeitschrift* XIII, pp. 82, etc., 92, etc.; also, Max Marcuse, *Das Liebesleben des deutschen Studenten* (*Sexual-Probleme* Nov. 1908); also, *Zeitschrift* XI, pp. 81 and 129.

[21] *Zeitschrift* XIII, p. 70.

[22] *Report, Swedish Commission,* Vol. III, loc. cit., p. 214.

attending uncleanliness.   It will be worth while to give
a brief account of what has taken place in this direction in Europe and to consider what benefit is likely to
be derived from this source.

Despite the prevalent notion to the contrary, the subject of sex-education is as yet very largely in the realm
of theory or controversy.   As to this point, a strange
misconception obtains.   In England, one hears that great
progress has been made in this field in Germany; in
Germany one is referred with equal positiveness to
Scandinavia; in Scandinavia to Finland, whither, however, I did not pursue the will-o'-the wisp.   The facts are
these:

No recognition is given to sex-instruction in English
schools at all.[23]   The head-masters and house-masters in
some of the great public schools,— notably Eton,— endeavor, however, to gain the confidence of the boys individually, to put them on their guard and to assist
them if in distress.   A series of leaflets has been issued
by the church schools for the guidance of parents, who
are urged to open the subject with their sons at the
proper time.[24]   In Prussia, which is representative of
the States of the German Empire, sex-instruction of any
kind is very rarely given at the popular schools;[25] in
the Gymnasien,— the nine-year secondary schools open-

[23] "In this grave matter, so timid and divided is public opinion,
that I have to be practically silent, 'letting I dare not, wait upon I
would.'"   John Russell, in "Can the School Prepare for Parent-
hood?" (Eugenics Education Society, 1909) p. 4.

[24] "Papers for Boys," with a preface by the Archbishop of Can-
terbury (To be had through the Editor, the Headmaster of Dover
College, Dover, for 6d.).

[25] Frankfort-on-the-Oder is one of the few places.

The Demand

ing into the University,— a lecture on the subject may be given to the last year class [26] by the School Director, a teacher or a physician; [27] attendance on the part of the students is optional. The lectures deal with the feasibility of continence, which is strongly urged, the dangers attending sexual irregularity or abnormality, and the misuse of alcohol; at times they are printed and circulated. During the school year 1911, such lectures were given at 76 Gymnasien out of a total of almost 800. Similar talks are given at institutions for the training of teachers. Occasionally pupils before leaving school are presented with books dealing with the topic in a wholesome manner. This represents the sum total of school instruction on the subject in Prussia; additional lectures, of an occasional character are provided for parents, artisans, etc., by local branches of the German Society for the Suppression of Venereal Disease. In Denmark and Norway, nothing either of a general or a compulsory character exists; Sweden practically repeats Prussia, offering no instruction in popular schools, an optional lecture to last year students in the higher secondary schools, particularly those for girls, in the discretion of the head-master or head-mistress. Systematic or general instruction has developed as yet nowhere in Europe. The educational officials of both Prussia and Sweden distinctly hold that under existing conditions the problem is one for the home, not the school. France is at

[26] The so-called "Abiturienten," who are about to enter the University. Whatever these addresses accomplish, the amount of venereal disease found among Gymnasium students would show that the efforts are too late.

[27] It has been objected to physicians that they over-emphasize prophylaxis.

the same stage of development. A memorandum on the subject has been submitted to the ministry of education, but no official action has been taken.

In view of the paucity of our experience, much of the literature on the subject strikes the observer as perhaps promising too much from mere diffusion of knowledge. Undoubtedly it is beyond all question that no boy or girl ought to be permitted to err through sheer ignorance. But it does not follow that fuller and clearer knowledge on the part of the growing boy and girl will itself effectively restrain; not only knowledge, but knowledge suffused with ethical emotion is requisite.[28] By prematurely creating images and stimulating curiosity both of which go further than the immediate communications on the topic, knowledge alone may either originate or increase the danger. Inhibition is unquestionably possible and it must be educationally brought about; but it involves not only a certain amount of intelligence on the child's part, but control of impulse through loyalty — instinctive or deliberate — to precept and example. As the boy matures, the actual dangers involved in immorality may be so depicted as to exert a deterrent effect;

[28] Among the German writers who have emphasized this point are F. W. Foerster, *Sexualethik und Sexualpädagogik* (Munich, 1910), and Julian Marcuse, *Grundzüge einer sexuellen Pädagogik* (Munich, 1908). The latter says with great vigor: "It were a disastrous blunder to suppose that intellectual enlightenment in reference to matters of sex is alone capable of preventing error and damage; the natural impulse is far too forceful to be mastered by mere knowledge of these things. Nay, helpful knowledge must be accompanied by training of the feelings, discipline of the will, things of infinitely greater importance than sheer enlightenment, both of which are foundations for sexual instruction that must be provided for." p. 38.

The Demand

but the main reliance must continue to be upon the higher motivation.

The importance of emotional and ethical training suggests the importance of the home in this connection. Foreign opinion is well-nigh unanimous in recommending that parents initiate the subject at the psychological moment,— a moment that is rarely the same for two individuals; subsequently the school can make its contribution, though there is as yet no agreement as to the form or the time.[29]   Some urge that it be the natural outgrowth of general biological instruction;[30] some favor class teaching, others individual instruction; an occasioual writer contends that, while boys should be urged to continence, they should also be taught the use of preventives since it is well known in advance that they will not obey![31]

The practical difficulties are, however, very great. The researches of Moll and others indicate that sexual instinct and curiosity awaken at different stages in different children; something depends on the constitution of the individual child, something on the environment. Moreover, the parents of the children most dangerously exposed are very often those who are most incapable of managing the situation.   A little later, when the school

[29] "In my judgment, the friends of sexual enlightenment have not yet succeeded in devising a satisfactory way of approaching children."   P. Groebel, *Sexualpädagogik* (Hamburg, 1909) p. 1.   As an example of what is proposed for German schools, see Konrad Hoeller: *Die Sexualfrage und die Schule* (Leipzig, 1907) pp. 45, etc.

[30] Expressly forbidden in Prussia.

[31] "I regard it as best to mention the safety devices in school, because I cannot hope that my injunctions to continence will be heeded by all my pupils." Groebel, *loc. cit.*, p. 15.

might intervene, the difficulty due to individual differences has not disappeared and additional problems have also arisen. Class instruction disregards individual variations and requires the greatest tact and skill in presentation; the teachers are as yet incompetent;[32] physicians lay as a rule too much stress on disease and on mere knowledge, and are as a rule clumsy and ineffective or skeptical respecting the ethical side, without which such understanding of the subject as may be brought about is apt to be of slight value. The danger that lurks in tabooing or avoiding the subject has been clearly demonstrated; but there is danger, too, in breaking down reserve. The more explicit the intellectual aspects of the matter are made, the more important does it become to insist that the mere communication of the facts cannot possibly alone attain the end toward which the movement looks. The girl must develop character enough to resist easy demoralization; the boy, character enough to subdue rebellious impulse.

Still later, when boys are about to leave the Gymnasium — and therewith their homes — in order to enter upon the freedom of University life in strange towns, candid talks to whole classes, laying particular stress upon the penalties attached to immorality, can be indeed given, as from time to time they are. But, unless effective training on higher lines has begun long before, the good to be achieved is of dubious extent: witness the prevalence of venereal disease among last year Gymnasium

[32] A textbook for use in training teachers to give sex-instruction has recently appeared in Swedish: Julia Kinberg och Alma Sundquist—*Handledning i Sexuell Undervisning och Uppfostran* (Stockholm, 1910).

The Demand

and first year University students, and the rapid, even if passing, demoralization characteristic of the latter.

The educational situation in reference to sex hygiene may then be concisely put as follows: little progress has been anywhere made in actual instruction; decided benefit is to be hoped for only where increase of knowledge is accompanied by increase of self-control — by loyalty, conscious and unconscious, to higher ideals of personal behavior.

I have mentioned above the factors and influences that tend artificially to develop demand. Whatever makes prostitution prominent, easy, attractive, seductive, unquestionably operates to increase demand. By the same token, measures that deprive prostitution of prominence, facility, attractiveness, seductiveness, reduce demand, or, — what amounts to the same thing — hinder its artificial increase. In the modern city, many conditions make, some purposely, some incidentally, for the stimulus of sex appetite: glitter, luxury, the mad rush for amusement, the stage, the café, the tavern,— all assist in the early maturity of the sex function, the exercise of which they also facilitate. With many of the artifices that have been employed to develop prostitution as a business conducted for the profit mainly of third parties, I shall deal in other chapters.[33] But certain of them may properly be considered in this connection.

A by no means negligible factor in stimulating appetite are erotic books, prints, etc. Obscene objects of this character are frequently circulated in secret in schools, — girls' as well as boys'; occasionally they are even ad-

[33] E. g., pimp, pp. 95, etc.; bordells, chap. VI; alcohol, pp. 98, etc.

57

vertised under more or less deceptive titles. In recent
years active efforts have been made to stamp out this
nefarious trade. An international agreement has been
arrived at, according to the terms of which the police departments of the nations who are parties thereto co-
operate in ferreting out publishers and importers of immoral publications and in endeavoring to bring them
to justice. In France,[34] Germany,[35] Austria and elsewhere popular societies have been formed for the purpose
of making war on pornography; laws have been strengthened and ministerial decrees emitted, establishing special
police bureaux to handle offenders.[36] The kinemato-
graph is the most recent invention open to abuse in this
direction; to forestall which, inspection of films has already been introduced at police headquarters in Berlin.
Many congresses, national and international, held in recent years, are evidence of a growing determination to
stop the artificial and premature excitation of sex demand through immoral books, pictures, plays and other
representations. The total laxity which once prevailed
has been checked and increasing restraint may be looked
for, as public opinion is educated to require and to sustain it.[37] For even where laws exist, their enforcement

[34] *Fédération francaise des Sociétés antipornographiques.*
[35] *Volksbund zur Bekämpfung des Schmutzes in Wort und Bild.*
[36] In Austria, July 31, 1912; in Bavaria, March 6, 1906, supplemented June 3, 1912; in Prussia, December 28, 1911.
[37] The literature on the subject in German is already very extensive. As containing data of all kinds, I may specify the following: Bohn, *Materialien zur Bekämpfung der unsittlichen Literatur
— ein kulturgeschichtliches Denkmal für die deutsche Presse,*
(Berlin, 1905). *Berichte der ausserdeutschen und deutschen Be-
richterstatten,* (Congress held at Cologne, 1904) (Berlin, 1905). E.
Schultze, *Die Schundliteratur* (Halle, 1911). A monthly periodical dealing with the problem in all its aspects is issued in Berlin;
it is called *Die Hochwacht,* is edited by Professor Karl Brunner

The Demand

depends on the vigor and sympathy of police officials and magistrates, who, in the interpretation of the statute, in some measure take their cue from the newspapers and popular opinion. In a recent London case, a Bow Street Magistrate convicted a bookseller for disposing of a book, of which, in imposing punishment, he stated that nothing "more foul or filthy" had been found in London in a long time. Subsequently another case, involving the same book, was brought into court; and in the latter instance, the culprit was acquitted.[38] In Germany, the laws — long since fairly adequate — were for years a dead-letter; but recent agitation has already had a noticeable effect. Curiously enough, the most decisive action on the part of the authorities is feasible only in countries where the liberty of the press is most firmly established: for only in countries thoroughly free in spirit will the public deliberately impose limitations on itself without fear that such restrictions may ultimately be abused to serve other ends than those originally intended.

Though no quantitative evidence of improving morality can be given, the various movements above touched on supply proof that opinion is undergoing a change which must in the end affect conduct. I was indeed

and published by the Ulrich Meyer Verlagsbuchhandlung. Summaries of all legislation bearing on the topic are found in: *Bekämpfung der Schundliteratur — Flugschrift der Zentralstelle für Volkswohlfahrt* (Berlin, 1911). Roeren, *Die Gesetzgebung gegen die unsittliche Literatur in den verschiedenen Ländern* (Berlin, 1905.) A Blue book on the subject has also been issued by the English government. It is called: *Report from the Joint Select Committee on Lotteries and Indecent Advertisements* (London, 1908).

[38] Some explanation is found in the fact that the statute does not define indecency.

Prostitution in Europe

assured that a change is already perceptible to those whose knowledge spans a sufficiently great period of time. Custom once practically constrained the French student in the Latin quarter to swim with the current; now it has become possible to lead a blameless life without incurring contempt for his idiosyncrasy; an impassioned literature appealing to the German student has made its appearance.[39] The woman's movement will uuquestionably destroy the passivity of German women in respect to masculine irregularities. The task of developing continence in nations habituated to indulgence is one of inexpressible difficulty; but it may be fairly said that now for the first time it has been deliberately faced on the Continent by a small, but earnest band of men and women bent upon the purification of the sexual life.

[39] For example: Hans Wegener, *Wir jungen Männer* (Dusseldorf, 1906).

CHAPTER III

THE SUPPLY

Relation of demand and supply.— Demand increased by forcing supply.— Supply derived mainly from lower working classes.— Occupations of parents.— Occupations of women themselves.— Is the prostitute a born degenerate?— Importance of the milieu.— Effect of loosening home ties.— Broken homes.— Demoralization of minors.— Unmarried mothers.— Influence of bad example.— Economic pressure.— Low and irregular wages.— Perilous employments.— Efforts to improve conditions.— Rescue work.— Volume of supply.— Forced supply.— White slavery.— Employment agencies.— The pimp, bars, variety theaters, etc.— Rescue and preventive work.— Supply capable of modification through laws and social conditions.

THE supply, which after a fashion responds to the demand just described, must be considered from three distinct points of view: its sources, its volume, its reaction on demand itself. On the face of it, the general relation of demand and supply appears simple and mechanical: a demand exists; somehow, thereupon, a supply springs up to meet it. The demand thus recognized, a moving equilibrium is established. Unquestionably, as the situation now stands, prostitution to a certain extent illustrates this purely mechanical conception. There is a demand of such strength and upon such terms that a supply is forthcoming: in so far as this particular demand is concerned, outright efforts simply to deny its satisfaction would for the most part lead to higher bidding or to circuitous methods of gratification. Demand itself must be affected before this sit-

Prostitution in Europe

uation can be essentially or fundamentally altered. There is also a supply on hand, which will employ a high degree of ingenuity to bring itself into relation with actual or potential demand. But, after all, however important, this is only one aspect of the problem. The modern merchant, in whatever commodity he may deal, is a practical, if not a trained, psychologist. He knows that appetite not only exists, but may be both created and developed: that, in the absence of strong restraint, supply can be worked up to almost any extent; and that there is no more efficient way to manufacture and to develop demand than to crowd supply in an attractive form upon the possible buyer's attention, when he is most amenable to suggestion of the requisite kind. True of every article of commerce, be the need for it native or acquired, this principle is nowhere more valid than in respect of a vice that starts with a tremendously powerful momentum, and is easily susceptible of still further stimulation. The volume of the business is, moreover, not only a question of the number of women engaged in it, but of the intensity with which the vocation is plied. A thousand women may consort with a thousand men in the course of a night; or, conditions favoring, they may entertain five or ten times that number. The definition adopted in the preceding chapter looked ahead to precisely this fact,— a fact that will become increasingly important as we proceed. For prostitution represents not only the periodic coming together of demand and supply; it represents also the exploitation of artificial, instigated appetite and overworked supply. The prostitute may indeed satisfy her

The Supply

own or another's passion; but there is no passion in the sexual drudgery which as a rule she performs. So far then from dealing with a simple natural or mechanical process of satisfaction, demand and supply in this matter tend to display rather more than the complications and interrelations characteristic of enterprise in general.

The most striking fact in connection with the source of supply is its practically total derivation from the lower working-classes, and mainly the unmarried women of those classes.[1] The victims come in a highly preponderant ratio from this definitely circumscribed milieu. Half a century ago, Parent-Duchatelet, studying their social origins, found that Parisian prostitutes are recruited well nigh exclusively from artisan families; among 828 fathers, there was a bare sprinkling of better-conditioned men.[2] These conditions still obtain. Of 11,413 women prisoners incarcerated during several years in Milbank prison, 10,646 were the daughters of working-men, or the equivalent; 544, of small shop-keepers; 128, of professional men; 82, of small officials; 13, of gentlemen.[3] Of 565 Stuttgart women, the fathers were, in 172 instances, artisans; in 84 instances, day laborers; in 60 instances, peasants; in 31 instances, small shopkeepers. Skilled occupations were barely represented.[4] Of 173 registered women in Munich, 95 of

---

[1] Adele Schreiber has calculated that 57% of German women between 20 and 30 years old are unmarried. *Loc. cit.*, p. 459.

[2] *Loc. cit.*, Vol. I, pp. 67–68.

[3] G. P. Merrick, *Work Among the Fallen* (London, 1890) pp. 23–24.

[4] *Zeitschrift* XII, pp. 18, 19. Similar results appear in statistics given by Meher: *Die geheime und öffentliche Prostitution in Stuttgart, Karlsruhe und München* (Paderborn, 1912) pp. 221–222.

thè fathers were artisans; 46, day laborers; 17, peasants. Of 2,574 so-called clandestines in the same city, the fathers were: artisans, 1,147; laborers, 944; peasants, 248; under-officials, 140.[5] Two thousand one hundred and three women appeared on the inscription lists of the Stockholm police between 1885 and 1904: in 179 cases, the fathers were small landowners and lease-holders; in 42 cases, merchants; in 14 cases, national or municipal officials: the rest were gardeners, peasants, fishermen, mechanics, publicans, unskilled laborers, etc.[6]

The occupations of the women themselves suggest the same conclusions. They are the unskilled daughters of the unskilled classes. Out of 1,327 street-women of Geneva examined between 1907 and 1911, 503 had been servants; 236, tailoresses and laundresses; 120, factory workers;[7] of 173 registered Munich prostitutes (1911), 52 had been barmaids;[8] 29, domestic servants; 29, factory workers; 15, seamstresses; 8 had no particular employment. Of 2,574 clandestines in the same city, 721 had been servants; 608, barmaids; 255, factory hands; 60, stage-dancers or singers; 170, without definite calling.[9] Of 1,200 women enrolled in Berlin 1909–10, 431 had been servants; 445, factory operatives; 479, seamstresses and laundresses; 145 were without vocation.[10] One thousand five hundred women who were sent to the hospital

[5] Statistics kindly contributed by the Chief of the Sittenpolizei.
[6] *Report, Swedish Commission,* Vol. III, *loc. cit.,* p. 77.
[7] Manuscript communication, based on private investigation.
[8] Kellnerinnen.
[9] For these figures, I am indebted to the courtesy of the Chief of the Sittenabteilung.
[10] F. Pinkus, in *Archiv für Dermatologie u. Syphilis* CVII 1–3, p. 147.

The Supply

on account of venereal disease show the same voca-
tions: 431 were servants; 445, factory hands; 112 without special employment. Of 2,275 inscribed Viennese
women, 44.52% were servants; 20.55%, factory workers; 16% without calling.[11] Of 427 admitted to a London Reformatory, 275 were servants, 25 laundry workers; 20, factory hands; 11, dressmakers; 6, barmaids;
33, without a vocation.[12] Of 675 cases included in another study, 283 were servants; 114 without occupation; 52, factory girls; 12, barmaids.[13] Another London list of 168 girls shows 2 described as " typist and
clerk,"— all the others engaged in unskilled domestic,
industrial, or mercantile labor.[14] Among Merrick's
thousands, already referred to, one-half had been servants; one-tenth each, laundresses, charwomen, factory
hands and seamstresses; another large contingent were
barmaids: a few described themselves as governesses.[15]
In the Stockholm cases, the facts are identical: 996 were
servants; 395, unskilled workers; 266, sewing-girls; 57
were shop girls; 6 connected with the stage.[16] Almost
7,000 Paris women, inscribed between 1878 and 1887
illustrate the same principle.[17]

Merrick's data as to the educational opportunities enjoyed are also generally sustained: less than one-tenth

[11] Baumgarten in *Zeitschrift* IX, p. 135.
[12] Figures courteously communicated by the Secretary of the institution.
[13] *Ditto.*
[14] *Ditto.*
[15] Merrick: *loc. cit.,* pp. 25–26.
[16] *Report, Swedish Commission,* Vol. III, *loc. cit.,* p. 75. Dr.
Lindblad, studying 800 hospital cases, reaches the same conclusion.
Ibid, p. 12.
[17] Analyzed by Commenge, *loc. cit.,* p. 336.

of his cases had had anything beyond the most rudi-
mentary training; [18] the German prostitutes show at the
most only the compulsory " Volksschule " education. Of
the minors apprehended during the year 1901, only 36%
of those over 12 years of age had completed the popular
elementary schools; only one-fifth of 1% had advanced
further.[19] Very few indeed have acquired in any direction a substantial degree of skill. They belong to the
intellectual as well as to the social proletariat. And this
is just as true of the elaborately dressed denizens of the
Palais de Dance as of the unpretending street-walker
of Potsdamer Platz: they are, generally speaking, all of
the same origin and the same capacity.

The foregoing statistics are obviously, however, not
fully representative, derived as they are mainly from the
records of the hospital, the police, the prison, and the
rescue home. Professionals of low grade and failures
are perhaps too largely included,— the women of the
street and the brothel; the dull drudges, who are most
likely to fall into the hands of the law; the stupid, who
most readily give up in despair. The vocational desig-
nations are also in one respect somewhat deceptive: the
women involved not infrequently describe themselves in
terms not of an habitual vocation or of a position held
at the moment, but of perhaps their last occupation, or
some occupation capriciously selected from the various
jobs on which they have been more or less transiently employed. Low grade help is as a rule thus variable and
casual. For instance: 1,689 women were inscribed by

[18] Merrick, *loc. cit.*, pp. 49–50.
[19] Schiller in *Zeitschrift* II, p. 304.

The Supply

the police of Berlin in twelve months following March
1900; all declared some sort of employment; yet only
352 had work at the moment.[20]   The returns are therefore not precisely accurate; yet from the standpoint of
our interest in them, they do more than justice to the
quality of the women, for to the extent of implying preference or capacity for one kind of work rather than indicating aimless shifting from one to another and then
again to nothing, the impression created is more favorable than the facts warrant.   In any case, the economic
competency of the prostitute is not higher than the
statistics indicate and may be lower.   Exceptions, of
course, are bound to occur.   One finds here and there a
stenographer, an elementary teacher, a former actress;[21]
but in most of these cases, the woman is, socially speaking, of inferior origin and intellectually not more pre-
possessing than others of her type.   Very rarely indeed
a person of some education, social standing, and personal
charm is met with.   A Parisian woman to whom this
description is fairly applicable was asked as to the possibility of finding others like herself.   " I am one in a
million," she proudly — and truthfully — answered.

The particular features of the milieu that involve peril
I shall discuss in a moment.   Meanwhile, the fact that
prostitution recruits itself from a single social class is
itself fatal to the contention that the prostitute is necessarily a born degenerate; for if prostitution involved
born degeneracy; and if, vice versa, congenital degeneracy

[20] Statistics quoted by Grotjahn, *loc. cit.*, p. 153.
[21] Some confidential London statistics name a few music teachers, school teachers, trained nurses, etc.   But the percentage is very
small.

Prostitution in Europe

made straight for prostitution, a single milieu would not furnish practically the total supply. The definiteness of the type is, of course, indisputable. Characteristic traits, external and internal, mark the scarlet woman; she has a distinct gait, smile, leer; she is lazy, unveracious, pleasure-loving, easily led, fond of liquor, heedless of the future, and usually devoid of moral sense. Defect undoubtedly accounts for certain cases, and especially so where a psychopathic family strain is continuously implicated. Of 21 girls recently admitted into a newly-established observation home in Berlin, 5 were reported as mentally below par; of Mrs. Booth's 150 cases discussed below,[22] 12% were feeble-minded. In the case of prostitutes committed under the British Inebriate Acts, the percentage naturally runs much higher: in 1909, out of 219 such immoral women, only 70 are described as of "good" mental state; 118 were "defective"; 23, "very defective"; 8, "insane"; i. e., almost 70% were below normal. "There is," writes Dr. Branthwaite, "almost consistent evidence here of some causative relationship between mental defect and prostitution; but the evidence is by no means overwhelming enough to justify more than a general conclusion that mental defect is one of many causes for its prevalence." [23] Bonhöffer, studying 190 prostitutes incarcerated in prison at Breslau, found that one hundred came from alcoholic families and that two-thirds of them were mentally defective — hysterical, epileptic or feeble-minded; his judgment is ad-

[22] Page 80.
[23] Report of the Inspector under the Inebriate Acts, 1879 to 1900, for year 1909 (London, 1911) p. 24.

The Supply

verse to the existence of the " born prostitute," but in favor of congenital defect as providing soil favorable to immorality.[24]   One hundred and fifty-five Berlin cases between 12 and 21 years of age, yield an equally striking result; 30% are reported as "intact," 23%, as feeble; 43%, as psychopathic; 66% are therefore abnormal.[25] Premature development on the sex side is also frequently encountered.   Among Lindblad's 800 cases, 52 had had sexual intercourse before they were 15 years old; 111 more, before they were sixteen.[26]   In these instances there was presumably a lack of self-control, but not necessarily always a lack of the very possibility of acquiring it, such as the degeneration argument requires.   How far these statistics are reliable, representative, or significant, it is impossible to determine.   Expert scientific study of large numbers of women from each of the different strata of prostitution, without as well as within prisons, reformatories, hospitals and refuges is needed in order to clear up the question.   For though degeneracy and native depravity may account for the prostitute alone or in connection with other facts, her conduct and qualities are also otherwise explicable.   The women involved have, as we have learned, undeveloped intelligence to begin with; riotous sex-indulgence, the loss of shame,

[24] Quoted by P. Pollitz, *Die Psychologie des Verbrechers* (Leipzig, 1909) p. 89.   It must be observed that just as Branthwaite's high percentage is due to complication with inebriacy, so Bonhöffer's must be regarded as complicated by criminality.   A similar investigation dealing with the tramps and beggars of Breslau has been made by Bonhöffer; see "*Ein Beitrag zur Kenntnis des grossstädtischen Bettel- und Vagabondentums.*" (Berlin, 1900.)
[25] Helene F. Stelzner, *Gibt es geborene Prostituierte?* (Dresden, 1911) p. 9.
[26] *Report, Swedish Commission*, Vol. III, p. 10.

Prostitution in Europe

alcohol, irregular hours, disease, combine to bring about speedy and far-reaching demoralization. Moral idiocy, covetousness, aversion to work, vanity, inclination to steal, libidinousness, may be acquired as well as native traits; they may be qualities exaggerated, even if not altogether bred in the course of the career. "The personality of the prostitute," Bloch contends, "is the result rather than the reason of her occupation."[27] Branthwaite holds that even the so-called "temperamental prostitute," with morbidly violent sexual desire, is apt to be the product of her way of life: in the majority of his cases he believes the symptom to be a "characteristic acquired by habit."[28] Undoubtedly personal or anthropological factors are usually involved: for if it were a question of milieu alone, all affected by it would succumb. But the exact extent to which the anthropological factor is congenital defect or only imperfect education and protection remains as yet to be settled.

However this may turn out, the peril of the milieu remains. It increases in geometric ratio with the feebleness of the girl, to whatever cause that feebleness be due. The reason of this may best be comprehended, if the question is approached from the opposite end. Let us ask, not why some women fall, but why others go straight. A certain number, undoubtedly, because of sheer character; these are the women who lead righteous lives under all circumstances whatsoever; for they are made of the hardy fiber that withstands any kind of

[27] "*Die Prostitution,*" Vol. I, p. 331. Parent-Duchatelet describes the type excellently: *loc. cit.,* Chapter II.
[28] *Report,* 1909, *loc. cit.,* p. 24.

wear and tear. A proportion, one has no way of knowing how large, keep straight for the mere lack of sufficient temptation to do otherwise: "The happy accident of the absence of opportunity has helped to the
rescue of many eminent virgins at critical moments,"
George Meredith caustically remarks.[29] But a still
larger number, though doubtless persuaded of their own
ethical superiority, attribute to positive character what is
really due to the unnoticed pressure of clan opinion, and
the imperceptible barriers by which they are completely
surrounded. The certain disapproval of family and
friends, the sure ostracism that attends a serious departure from the accepted code of behavior consciously or
unconsciously act as powerful deterrents; the esteem we
are taught to crave, the warnings, expostulations, and demands of family and friends constantly on the lookout,
keep the growing child within a well-marked path; established habit, position, responsibility for others, and
ripe reason ultimately approving the same — these function in many cases as a substitute for fundamentally
hardy character. The superiority in such instances is
trained, not inherent; and not so much narrowly educational as widely social. The whole organization of certain strata of society supports those who pass their lives
securely within it.

In many cases — we have as yet no way of knowing how many — the girls who fall differ from those who
go straight in lacking precisely these supports; they are
born in a stratum in which no strong supporting bulwark
of opinion and habit has been developed; or the bulwark,

[29] Letters (2 Vols., New York, 1912) Vol. II, p. 532.

such as it is, has been in one way or another broken down. The strong characters — and they are immensely more abundant than is usually supposed — do without it; the weaker too often succumb. Even so, their collapse is rarely sudden. It is a hopeful fact that decency is often only gradually and cunningly undermined. The buyer dealing with the seasoned prostitute may go straight to his object; his purpose must be veiled in negotiations with the beginner, who is led on by pretty clothes, amusements, wine and glitter. There is no reason to believe that, as a rule, promiscuity is congenial to the woman from the start; it is sometimes increasingly odious. Low as the barrier may be, the prostitute has rarely once and for all deliberately stepped across it. Her demoralization is a progressive, not a summary, process. With her, the sex instinct is, for reasons already given, less apt to be valued at its real worth, or to be properly safeguarded by deference to exacting opinion; less apt, too, to be reduced in comparative urgency by the volume and abundance of other satisfactions. The girl has, however, no notion in the first place of becoming a prostitute. She begins by giving away what ultimately she learns to sell.

From the above discussion, it appears that, as far as we now know, it may be not so much individuals as environments, that are superior. Danger lies where the environment puts up no high barrier; still more so when the low barrier, the strong temptation, and the weak resistance, coincide. How completely the untrained daughters of the proletariat lack the positive protections and supports by means of which better-conditioned girls are,

The Supply

even in default of their own strength, held upright, a somewhat closer study of the facts will soon show.

There is, in the first place, no quicker way of evading the immaterial forces that assist in maintaining an approved line of conduct than abrupt transplantation of an immature person into an environment within which no such forces operate on the individual in question. Accordingly, a heavy percentage of urban prostitutes are girls who have left home: of 168 girls in a London rescue home, 85 were born abroad; not all the 83 English girls were London born.[30] "The servants in Manchester," I was told, "come almost invariably from remote counties; they have been familiar at home with the men, with whom they walk out." In a strange city, without work, or with hard work, they obtain through the too lightly prized sex-function, at least for the moment, what their lot otherwise lacks. Out of 12,707 women inscribed in Paris, two-thirds were born outside the department of the Seine.[31] Only 213 out of 781 girls newly enrolled in Paris in a single year were natives of the city.[32] Of 1,376 inscribed prostitutes of Stockholm (1890-1904), only 21.1% were natives of that city; the same proportion were born in other Swedish cities; 57% were country girls; the rest, foreigners.[33] Many of the prostitutes of Vienna were born in the poor districts of Galicia and Poland. The studies of Lindblad

[30] Private communication.
[31] Parent-Duchatelet: *loc. cit.,* I, p. 44. Of 6,842 clandestines, two-thirds were born outside the department of the Seine. Commenge, *loc. cit.,* p. 304.
[32] M. Talmeyr, *Das Ende einer Gesellschaft* (Berlin, no date) p. 256.
[33] *Report, Swedish Commission,* Vol. III, p. 74.

and Welander in Stockholm show how closely immorality has followed detachment from home in hundreds of instances.[34]

The home barrier is itself often so low as to constitute little or no obstacle to demoralization,— often indeed, demoralization is of domestic origin. Sidney and Beatrice Webb, dealing with London destitution, describe a situation existing in all crowded European cities: " The herding together, by day and by night, of men and women, of young and old, of boys and girls, of all degrees of relationship or no relationship, not only destroys health, but makes, to the ordinary human being, the particular virtue upon which the integrity of the family depends, wholly impracticable. Any person who has dwelt among the denizens of the slums, cannot fail to have brought home to him the existence of a stratum of society of no inconsiderable magnitude in which children part with their innocence long before puberty, in which personal chastity is virtually unknown, and in which ' to have a baby by your father ' is laughed at as a comic mishap." [35] In a close in High Street, Edinburg, I visited with the city physician a family consisting of father, mother, grandmother, daughter of 13, and two younger children, all of whom slept in a single bed. Professor Blaschko declares that " what Robert Koch once said of tuberculosis, viz., that it is a question of living conditions, holds equally of prostitution. Living conditions are responsible for the fact that children learn all forms of evil

[34] *Report, Swedish Commission,* Vol. III, p. 28.
[35] *The Prevention of Destitution* (London, 1912) p. 306 (slightly abridged).

The Supply

prematurely and forego all natural enjoyments." [36]   Of the inhabitants in Berlin in 1900, 73.7% lived in dwellings of two rooms or less; 785,000 lived in single rooms; 561,000 in two rooms; 5,450 in one unheated room; 7,759 in a kitchen.[37]   Too frequently, the home, such as it is, is broken besides.   Not infrequently, necessity drives the mother herself to become a wage-earner. Something above 2,000,000 German women are engaged in factories, one-third of whom are married, widowed or divorced.   The children of these families,— boys and girls alike,— lack the rearing which would be their most important safeguard.   Unfortunately, too, the tide is rising: the married women workers of Bavaria increased absolutely in number 72% from 1895 to 1907; [38] throughout Germany a similiar rise is taking place.[39] As this increase involves especially women between 30 and 50 years of age, it is clear that they are driven into factories in order to support children whose welfare requires that the mother should stay at home.   In other instances, the home is fractured by death, desertion or immorality: of 565 Stuttgart prostitutes, 64.2% were

[36] *Mitteilungen der deutschen Gesellschaft zur Bekämpfung der Geschlechtskrankheiten* (Leipzig, 1912) X, 6, p. 129.

[37] Münsterberg, *Prostitution und Staat* (Leipzig, 1911) p. 13. The subject is discussed at length, with bibliography, in *Zeitschrift* I, pp. 134–162; and III, p. 165.

[38] Rosa Kempf, *Die Industriearbeiterin als Mutter,* in Adele Schreiber's *Mutterschaft* (Munich, 1912) pp. 230–243.

[39] Marcuse, *Beschränkung der Geburtenzahl,* pp. 57–58. The proportional increase looks less startling; the figures were 34.8% of the entire female population in 1882, 38.3% in 1907.   For further details, see: Helene Simon, *Der Anteil der Frau an der deutschen Industrie nach den Ergebnissen der Berufszählung von 1907* (Jena, 1907) also: Robert and Lisbeth Wilbrandt, *Die deutsche Frau im Beruf.* (Part IV of *"Handbuch der Frauenbewegung"* (Berlin, 1902).

wholly or partially orphaned;[40] of 384 London cases, only 24% had both parents alive.[41] In Lindblad's cases, 219 out of 772 homes are classified as "bad" or "very bad."[42] Ominous is the rôle played by alcohol in dissolving the home and in undermining the constitution of the children.[43]

The inordinately large contingent of servants is partially accounted for on these lines; for the servant has given up her own home and does not always make for herself another in the house she serves. She has come from the landless country proletariat, where sexual intercourse is either customary or not forbidden; in the city, exposure and weak resistance make her a frequent victim. Servants between 16 and 30 years old form one-fourth of the female population of Berlin; they bear one-third of the illegitimate children of the population. Of the registered prostitutes of Berlin in 1900, 60% had traveled this road.[44] In Paris, of 6,842 clandestine prostitutes arrested and found ill within the decade 1878–1887, 2,681 — i. e., 39.18% — were domestics.[45] Two hundred and eighty-four of Lind-

[40] *Zeitschrift* XII, p. 19.
[41] The details are: 124 had lost both parents
147 had lost one parent
20 did not know if parents were living or dead
93 had both parents alive
384
Report, London Female Preventive and Reformatory Institution 1910–11. Merrick, *loc. cit.*, p. 31 gives additional statistics to the same effect. See also: Othmar Spann,— *Untersuchungen über die uneheliche Bevölkerung in Frankfort-a. M.* (Dresden, 1905).
[42] *Report, Swedish Commission*, Vol. III, *loc. cit.*, p. 30.
[43] Branthwaite, *Report, 1909*, p. 24.
[44] Wilbrandt, *loc. cit.*, pp. 147, 148.
[45] Commenge, *loc, cit.*, p. 337.

The Supply

blad's 800 patients were servants, 80 more were attendants on little children, 170 charwomen.[46]

If the urban home often leaves its girls defenceless [47] or demoralized, the daughters of the rural proletariat fare even worse. The children of the landless peasant are a sheer drain — they have no economic value to the family. I recall a characteristic instance of a girl of 27, one of fourteen children belonging to a peasant family, eleven of whom had died in infancy. She herself had had no rearing whatsoever. Drifting from pillar to post, she had come to Munich, where at 17 she had a child; since then, five others, of whom one survives, maintained by her on her illicit earnings.[48]

It is early demoralization that is most dangerous, and it is precisely to early demoralization that the bad or broken home most surely leads. In all great European cities the rapid increase of the prostitution of minors has been noted. Without domestic protection, the girl seeks her amusement on the streets and wittingly or unwittingly is led to her fall. Between 1880 and 1903 the average number of minors annually arrested for prostitution by the Paris police was 1,370,— the total, 32,-885.[40] Nine hundred and seventy-five minors were arrested there for this offence 1,638 times in 1908,— 91 of them under 16; 988 minors were arrested 1,739 times

[46] *Report, Swedish Commission,* Vol III, *loc. cit.,* p. 12.
[47] It is of course impossible to give an exhaustive account in the text. The living-in system in vogue in English shops affords another example of the demoralizing outcome of the broken or unnatural home. See *Report of the Truck Committee* (London, 1900) Vol. I, pp. 70, 71.
[48] See also Adele Schreiber, *loc. cit.,* pp. 243–256.
[49] Fiaux, *loc. cit.,* Vol. III, p. 608. See also his *L'Intégrité intersexuelle des peuples et les Gouvernements* (Paris, 1910) p. 206.

the next year,— 221 under eighteen.[50] In general it
has been estimated that one-half of the minors arrested
have not yet finished their seventeenth year.[51] The
Viennese authorities declare that "clandestine prostitution in its varied forms is made up for the most part of
youthful persons. Clandestine prostitutes, especially in
so far as they are incidentally engaged as waitresses in
"Animierkneipen" and restaurants, singers and dancers, are usually young, since, among other reasons, youth
is a condition *sine qua non* of employment. While out
of 1,000 inscribed prostitutes only 16% were under 21
years of age, among the same number of non-inscribed arrested on the streets, over 57% were minors."[52] In the
year 1910, of 1,319 arrests, 823 were minors whose utter
isolation is proved by the fact that efforts to preserve
some sort of family guardianship failed in 802 instances.[53] In Cologne, 1,626 arrests were made in 1911,
— 1,296 of them minors,— 79 under 18 years of age.
German authorities hold in general that the danger period
lies between the 12th and the 21st year: "only a small
percentage go wrong after the 21st year."[54] Among 846
newly inscribed prostitutes in Berlin in 1898, 229 were
minors, despite a settled policy in favor of registering
adults only. There is perhaps no better proof of the
extent of demoralization during girlhood: seven of these

[50] *Rapport de M. Georges Honnorat,* Chef de la Première Division
de la Préfecture de Police, presented to the VIII Congrès national
du Patronage, 1910 (pp. 6, 7).
[51] Eugène Prévost, *De la Prostitution des Enfants.* (Paris, 1909)
p. 215.
[52] E. Finger und A. Baumgarten, *Referat über die Regelung der
Prostitution in Oesterreich* (Wien, 1909) p. 88 (abridged).
[53] Personal communication from officials.
[54] Stelzner, *loc. cit.,* p. 8; also Pollitz, *loc. cit.,* p. 89.

The Supply

were mere children,— 15 years old; 21 were 16 years old; and 33, seventeen years of age.[55] Nor are conditions any better in smaller towns. Bendig, studying prostitution in Stuttgart from 1894 to 1908, finds 55% of the women deflowered under seventeen years of age; 70%, between sixteen and eighteen; 97.3%, between fourteen and twenty-five.[56] Over one-half were under twenty years of age at the time of their registration as professional prostitutes by the police. Through some English Rescue Homes, 745 children between eight and fifteen years of age passed in the course of three years.[57] The confidential memorandum dealing with 168 cases already referred to shows that all but 30 were under twenty-one years of age. So, of 92 girls admitted to a London Rescue Home, 50 were less than twenty-one years old. Of 1,882 prostitutes arrested on the streets of Glasgow for drunkenness or soliciting, seven were between fourteen and sixteen; and 314 between sixteen and twenty-one.[58] Of this type are usually the white-slave cases,— young girls for the most part enticed from poor rural or urban homes by the promise of employment or marriage in a great city; as also instances not altogether unknown in which mothers sell their own children. A brisk de-

[55] Schiller, *Zeitschrift II*, p. 309.
[56] *Zeitschrift* XII, pp. 19, 22.
[57] T. G. Cree, *The Need of Rescue Work Among Children.* (London, Church Penitentiary Association) p. 3; Merrick's data on the same subject are given, *loc. cit.,* p. 34.
[58] *Report of the Chief Constable* for the year ending December 31, 1909. An even more unfavorable account is contained in the *Memorandum on a Social Evil in Glasgow* previously referred to. The Chief Constable in reply holds that the memorandum exaggerates.

mand for the child prostitute constitutes a strong inducement.[59]

Exposure sometimes originates otherwise. Sometimes
the seduced servant or shop girl, or the pregnant
country lass, may lose position or caste, and, besides,
find herself responsible for the maintenance of herself
and her child, law and custom bearing all too lightly on
her partner. In point of character the girl has no longer
anything to lose; meanwhile, need presses. Eighty-
three out of the 168 London cases already discussed were
of this type. In Berlin, 1,531 girls were newly inscribed
in the years 1908–9–10; of these, 636 — i. e., over 41%,
had borne children.[60] Mrs. Bramwell Booth furnished
me a detailed study of 150 cases, out of which 11%
were believed to be attributable to pregnancy following
seduction. Lindblad found that 62 of 800 women —
7¾% — insisted that they had become prostitutes in order to support children: of these 10 were widowed or
divorced; 34 were unmarried, but confessed to a succession of lovers; 18 were unmarried and with but one
child.[61] Children born under such conditions represent
at times the most aggravated form of the broken home,
and not a few of the girls afterwards take to irregular
lives: nevertheless, by no means universally. For, as
Adele Schreiber has forcibly pointed out, illegitimacy is
a complicated phenomenon, by no means universally involving recklessness and irresponsibility.[62] The premarital intercourse of European boy and girl may result in

[59] Moll, *loc. cit.*, pp. 383–4.
[60] Moll, *loc. cit.*, p. 390.
[61] *Report, Swedish Commission*, Vol. III, *loc. cit.*, p. 24.
[62] Adele Schreiber, *loc. cit.*, pp. 257, 501, etc.

The Supply

an illegitimate birth which is either preliminary to marriage or is regarded as equivalent thereto. This fact enables us to understand why the researches of Johansson in Stockholm[63] and Pinkus in Berlin appear to indicate that illegitimate children contribute somewhat less than their expected quota to the recruiting of the prostitute army. While 17.3% of the births in Berlin during certain specified years were illegitimate, only 13.7% of the inscribed prostitutes in the same period were of illegitimate origin.[64] Johansson calculated that one would expect to find 12% to 14% of the enrolled women of Stockholm to be illegitimates: they make up only 9% to 11% of the entries.[65] Meanwhile the situation is charged with danger, unless the father meets his responsibility. Too often this is not the case; and a relationship that perhaps began in passion deteriorates — the man seeking other women, the women turning to prostitution.

One more consideration ought to be separately mentioned, because it is mainly and most fatally operative in the milieu with which we are dealing,— the influence of evil example. From vicious suggestion practically no child is free; but the children to whom our attention has been directed may be so loosely anchored that they are easily carried away. The ruined girl, glancing back over the path she has come, overlooks the fundamental facts of environment and disposition and sees only the older comrade or chance acquaintance, whose easy at-

[63] *Report, Swedish Commission*, Vol. III, *loc. cit.*, p. 79.
[64] Pinkus, *Archiv. loc. cit.*, p. 415.
[65] *Report, Swedish Commission*, Vol. III, p. 79.

Prostitution in Europe

tainment of fun, clothes, trinkets, she envies. Of the 800 Stockholm cases to which I have already frequently referred, 71% attributed their final decision to advice from tainted sources; 217, from professional prostitutes; 215, from clandestines; 81, from immoral girls; 4, from their own mothers.[66]

I need hardly call attention to what the reader will already have observed, viz., that I have frequently cited the same statistics in different connections: for the same girl may appear as orphaned, as servant, as ignorant, as illegitimate, as badly advised. No one circumstance can be regarded as alone fatal; the complicated skein of influences and associations cannot be completely disentangled. The facts that have been adduced,— broken homes, bad homes, exposure,— do not then act directly as causes, in the sense that the girls involved take to prostitution "as the sparks fly upward." Of several sisters, all placed in precisely the same situation, only one may succumb; personal or anthropological forces may successfully defend all the others, despite their apparently identical position. The environment is, however, not thus freed of responsibility,— it is merely freed of direct, simple or sole responsibility. It does not cause prostitution; but the huge proletariat is the reservoir from which victims can be readily drawn. Nor are single factors characteristic of the proletariat causally responsible; but the phenomenon attaches itself to a chain of factors belonging in their totality to this milieu alone. Bad fathers, loose mothers, alcoholism, poor associations,

[66] *Report, Swedish Commission,* Vol. III, *loc. cit.,* p. 81. See also Moll, *loc. cit.,* pp. 393-4.

The Supply

physical defect, occur sporadically in every social stratum; but all together combined with defective education, low economic capacity, absence of oversight and restraint, rampant desires and meager satisfactions occur only in the proletariat.

We are in position now to judge the part played by economic pressure. The preponderance of servants suggests the proper interpretation: for the servant does not lack food or shelter, and her services are everywhere in demand. She does not therefore resort to prostitution as an alternative to starvation. Animated by a natural desire to excuse their conduct, as most human beings are, the direct pressure of need is rarely assigned by prostitutes in exculpation of their conduct. Mrs. Bramwell Booth, than whom there is no more competent or sympathetic authority, found among 150 successive and unusually varied cases only 2% who explained their prostitution by inability to earn a livelihood; Ströhmberg discovered among 462 enrolled women at Dorpat only one who protested poverty as her justification;[67] Pinkus, [68] studying the incomes of 1,550 Berlin women before embarking on the life, decides that 1,389 had earned enough for self-support.[69] But it would be obviously unfair to say of these 1,389 women capable of earning a living that social-economic conditions had nothing to do with their fall; for precisely these conditions create a situation capable of being exploited. Undeveloped moral character, early and careless infringement of the sex func-

[67] *Loc. cit.,* p. 81.   [68] *Archiv. loc. cit.,* p. 149.
[69] Lindblad studies his Swedish cases from this point of view; *Report, Swedish Commission,* Vol. III, *loc cit.,,* pp. 41, etc.

tion, drudgery, on the one hand, unsatisfied and uncontrolled cravings, on the other,— these are all largely social-economic in their origin and scope. It happens all too often that girls born perhaps to pull canal boats, and with education and intelligence hardly above their lot, possess some little fancy, or love of pleasure, or taste in dress, without the strength of will or ideals to content themselves with an existence of mere endurance in a world full of enjoyment. They end by exploiting the sex function in order to obtain the satisfactions not otherwise accessible, or to escape difficulties and drudgeries from which they can contrive no other exit.

Prostitution is thus of economic origin and significance in so far as the region of economic pressure is mainly the region from which the prostitute comes. Whether or not the family lives in this region is primarily a question of the father's income. The region is, however, not statistically definable: a specified income may keep a given family or a given individual under dangerous pressure; the same income may release from pressure another family or another individual. Severest, of course, where actual poverty exists, all those whose needs, desires and protests beat vainly against the limits imposed by their resources, live within the area of economic pressure. But the mere fact of living within the area, whether in its darkest tract or elsewhere, is not of itself conclusive. For the prostitute is, in the last resort, to use a biological phrase, "individually selected" in the manner already sketched.

The menace of unfavorable economic conditions can be clearly discerned in certain directions. Prostitution fluctuates with seasonal and casual labor; in certain employments it is looked upon as a regular source of incidental income to women workers; in other employments it offers to girls not living at home the readiest recourse. As bearing on the part played by casual and seasonal labor, it is important to note that the proportion of their female help permanently employed by certain London shops often falls as low as 25% of their maximum help; it rarely rises above 75% :[70] that is to say, something between one-quarter and three-quarters of the women employees of the London shops are casual hands, turned adrift in increasing numbers as the trade barometer falls. Charles Booth notes in addition to the "more regular members of this varied group of women, some who take to the life occasionally; tailoresses or dressmakers who return to their trade in busy times; girls from low neighborhoods, who eke out a living in this way."[71] "It is true," writes Wilbrandt of the irregularly employed girls in Germany, "that when out of work, many of them succeed from time to time in sewing more or less for private customers, or the lodging-house keepers give them credit ('give food to the unfortunate also at times'), but for the majority this is no remedy. Even more than the isolated factory workers, these girls are fairly forced to prostitution. Where there is no serious obstacle, hardly one of this type, if isolated, but is given to occasional prostitution."[72] The vagrant class in trade and

[70] Statement made to me by Miss Maud Bondfield.
[71] *Loc. cit.*, p. 127.
[72] *Loc. cit.*, p. 123, with note (2). To the same effect, Hans Ostwald, *Das Berliner Dirnentum*, 8 Abteilung — *Gelegenheitsdirnen,*- among whom he reckons "a great mass of women and girls" more or

industry and those dependent upon them are necessarily restless, improvident and irresponsible.[73]

Practically in the same category are the workers whose wages suffice only if they live at home, in which case part of their support is borne by other members of the family; where — as so often happens with those who come to the city to earn a living,— this is impossible, occasional or incidental immorality is a perilous temptation. Immorality may thus by low or irregular wages be almost woven into the very tissue of their lives. I was told, for example, that in certain English manufacturing towns, such as Bradford and Sheffield, a sliding-scale is accepted among some of the girl operatives; when wages rise above a certain point, a virtuous life is required by public opinion; when they fall below, the source of supplementary earnings is not scrutinized. The minimum wages of the sewing-women, factory hands, laundresses throughout Europe do not support the most meager sort of decent independence.[74] An official report states that out of 226 inscribed women at Frankfort-on-the-Main, 98 were laundresses and shop-help, earning from 1.50 marks to 1.80 marks a day,— less, that is, than 50 cents.[75]

less occupied as singers, dancers, waitresses, shophands, models, maids, laundresses, nurses, etc.

[73] Cadbury, Matheson, & Shann: *Women's Work and Wages* (London, 1909) pp. 246, 247.

[74] The literature on this topic is abundant. I give by way of illustration a few references to Munich, where the conditions have been well investigated: Dr. Rosa Kempf, *Das Leben der jungen Fabrikmädchen* (Leipzig, 1911). Dr. Elizabeth Hell, *Jugendliche Schneiderinnen und Näherinnen in München* (Berlin, 1911). Meher, *loc. cit.*, pp. 110–148. Also, *Handbuch der Frauenbewegung*, already mentioned, passim.

[75] P. Hirsch, *Verbrechen und Prostitution* (Berlin, 1907, pp. 101–102.

The Supply

The same holds true of superior help — dressmakers, shop-assistants, whose standards are necessarily higher: "these girls accept wages which would not be enough to support them if they had not a friend to help them." [76]

There remain the employments in which only prostitutes engage or in which the perils are so enormous that a girl who has not fallen, soon will fall. Irregular earnings are tacitly assumed as the major or sole consideration in bargaining for a position. The chorus, ballet, or cabaret girl can usually afford "'the stage'" because she is already immoral and the glamor of the footlights increases her earning capacity; the same conditions of course tend to force into immorality a girl who has hitherto been honest. A monthly salary of 10 marks ($2.50) is paid the dancers at the Court Theater in Hanover; the leading lady at Eisenach draws 15 marks ($3.75) a month for a six months' season; a prominent soubrette at Munich states that she received an annual salary of 3,600 marks, from which the outlay for wardrobe was 1,500 marks; one reads of salaries of 1,200 marks conjoined with wardrobe expenses of 2,-000 marks; incomes of 5,400 marks and expenses of 8,000 marks. [77] If a decent girl objects to a salary of 20 marks a week ($5.00) on the ground that it will not supply her necessities — living, wardrobe, etc. — the Director retorts: "Why should you want any salary? You are a pretty girl." [78] The maelstrom thus tends

[76] C. E. Collett, *Educated Working Women* (London, 1902) p. 51. As to conditions in Paris, see *Revue d'Economie Politique*, Aug. 1911.
[77] *The German Stage and its Members*, by Dr. Charlotte Engel-Reimers (Leipzig, 1911).
[78] Wilbrandt, *loc. cit.*, p. 355. The whole section is most valuable.

87

powerfully to suck in those not previously tainted. The English barmaids and continental waitresses [79] are not infrequently virtuous women, leading decent lives; but they are also often selected for the lively manners so certain to lead, if they have not already led, to extra remuneration, that only a nominal wage attaches to their posts. The 37,000 waitresses in Germany are recruited from among the country or urban proletariat, whose invaded chastity has already been noticed. Their wages are nominal — or less; one-fourth of them are under 20 years of age.[80] It is not surprising to find a Berlin insurance fund reporting that waitresses make up one-half of those of its numbers venereally afflicted.[81] In England and Wales, of 27,707 barmaids in the Census of 1901, 18,251 were under 25 years of age.[82] Their wages range from 5 to 15 shillings a week.[83] Mrs. Booth concludes that of the prostitutes in the West End of London, one-fourth were originally barmaids and a still higher estimate has been made.[84] In many establishments, irregularity either precedes employment or is common enough to be taken into account in determining the conditions of employment.

Nothing would be gained by going into the foregoing matters more thoroughly. Enough has been said to show why in the presence of the demand previously characterized, an ample supply is forthcoming, and why it is almost totally derived from a single social stratum. It is de-

[79] Meher, *loc. cit.,* pp. 133, etc. Also: Wilbrandt, *loc. cit.,* pp. 272, etc., and the *Denkschrift* previously cited.
[80] *Denkschrift,* p. 12.
[81] *Ibid,* p. 12.
[82] *Women as Barmaids* (London, 1905), p. 8.
[83] *Ibid,* p. 4.
[84] *Ibid.,* p. 33.

rived, of course, with all sorts and degrees of difficulty. Sometimes demoralization has set in so early, or there has been so little development of intelligence or character, that the girl is herself from the start not only willing, but the main instigator; in other cases, with intelligence too undeveloped and character too unformed to urge her away from temptation, a vague but profound instinct holds her back until her dumb resistance has been overcome by other inducements or weakened by alcohol, pretended affection or interest. Despite this dark picture, however, most girls in the various stations described do resist like a stone wall. Of all those marked at any time by a given characteristic, the number engaged in prostitution is rarely high. The huge total is to be ascribed to the variety of paths and cross-cuts by which the morass may be reached.

So much for the source of supply: let us turn for a moment to its volume. Prostitution is an urban phenomenon; its volume increases even more rapidly than population. For as the demand seeks particularly younger women, the older tend to become a drug on the market. It is therefore inevitable that, while there is a comparative dearth of the youthful, the total supply should be in excess of the requirements. This situation, of course, favors the exploiter; for he procures without difficulty and on easy terms the commodity which he pushes on the street, in the bar, the dancing hall, the café, and the brothel.

In the case of supply, as in the case of demand, two different problems present themselves. In so far as individual reasons alone lead a girl of mature years to prostitution or deliberately to persist in prostitution, preventive action is both practically and theoretically difficult; prostitution of this kind is a reply to demand or an invitation thereto, taken in its simplest, even if not purely physiological form. Very different is the situation as respects supply arbitrarily developed to satisfy a specialized or artificial appetite. The girls thus involved are forced into prostitution; demand in the sense just mentioned has not been brought to bear upon them. Once violently ruined, however, they become part of the army requiring that the mass of immorality be increased so as to sustain them. Of this type are the white slave cases, and those led into ruin through employment agencies. In both instances, innocent girls are lured into strange places, deceived with promises that fail to materialize, and coerced into an immoral life, which holds them easily enough after their demoralization is completed. How much of the present supply is of this forced character it is obviously impossible to say. Stead's revelations in the *Pall Mall Gazette* in 1885 and such incidents as the " Process Riehl " [85] at Vienna disclosed the existence of a large and active trade in innocent girls of tender years.

We found that there is no reason to regard demand as a fixed quantity. The same is obviously true of supply. Girls may be forced into prostitution; they can also be kept out. To some extent, as they are kept out, demand also shrinks; for the provocation is thereby reduced. It must be altogether obvious that all social amelioration tends thus to reduce the supply, by diminishing exposure

[85] See p. 185.

and strain. Within the scope of this volume it is impossible even to mention briefly the steps that have been taken in this direction in different European countries during recent years. Suffice it to say that every effort in social and economic reform, education, and sanitation has tended to reduce the number of prostitutes and to strengthen the resistance of those exposed to danger.

In addition to indirect and slow-working processes of this kind, the problem has been directly and in some respects effectively grappled with. Of these efforts, the international movement for suppression of the White Slave Traffic is the most conspicuous. There is no question that not many years ago an extensive, though but loosely organized, traffic in girls was carried on in large European cities. The bordells were thus recruited with young and attractive inmates. The subject was first brought to public notice in 1877; but little attention was paid to it until the *Pall Mall Gazette* published a complete exposure in 1885. Shortly thereafter the British Vigilance Society was formed; similar organizations were then organized in other countries and in 1899 an international congress was held in London. Annual congresses now meet to review progress and to suggest legislation; societies are everywhere engaged in watching at steamboat landings and railroad stations in order to assist unaccompanied travelers or to locate suspicious couples; and associations in different countries endeavor by correspondence to run down offenders and to release their victims.

Successful prosecution is, however, as a rule, surrounded by many technicalities. In Germany the statute provides that any one who induces a female to leave the country for the purpose of prostitution by means of concealment of his object is liable to penal servitude for five years, to loss of citizenship and a fine of 150 to 6,000 marks.[86]   But as a rule the culprit, if arrested, has made an attempt only, and thus escapes the severe penalty here imposed.   To avoid this pitfall, the congress of 1910 urged as a model provision the following: " Whoever procures a female for purposes of prostitution, abducts, carries off, or leads her into prostitution, even if the steps thereto occur in different countries, shall be punished, etc."   Several countries have proceeded on this line, notably Hungary, in a law passed in 1908.   The most advanced legislation is, however, the recent amendment of the British Criminal Law by a provision empowering a police officer to arrest a procurer caught with a suspected victim without the delay involved in procuring a warrant.

This legislation indicates the form to which the White Slave Traffic has been largely reduced in Europe. Beyond question an innocent girl might be entrapped, enticed, and immured in a European brothel; but if so, the instance would be an isolated crime, like a mysterious murder or robbery.   Under existing conditions, there is absolutely no reason to think that such cases occur frequently, though there are those who would be quick to take advantage of any relaxation of vigilance on the part of governments, the police, and the private organizations constantly on the alert.   In the cases to which from time to time attention has been sensationally called, the women

[86] *Reichsgesetzbuch,* sec. 236, 237: *Auswanderergesetz,* sec. 48.

The Supply

involved are neither innocent nor deceived. On the other hand, there is evidence to suggest that European cities and ports are utilized for purposes of transit to South American ports where the trade still flourishes. A trafficker may entice a girl from Poland and Galicia on the promise of marriage or work; indeed every police office in Europe has a list of men thus engaged. The countries from which women are procured are believed to be mainly Hungary, Galicia, Poland, and Roumania; the countries to which they are carried, Brazil, Argentina, South Africa and the Levant.[87] The pair steal through Vienna and Berlin and appear at the dock in Hamburg, Rotterdam, London, or some less prominent port just as the boat sails for Rio Janeiro, Buenos Aires or a South African harbor — too late to procure a warrant or detailed proof. The new English law above mentioned is calculated to deal with just this emergency: for it authorizes the detention and arrest of such couples without warrant, on suspicion, and throws the burden of proof upon them.[88] The entire White Slave movement is thus forcible interference with the making of prostitutes.[89]

[87] E. Wulffen, *Der Sexualverbrecher* (Berlin, 1910) p. 700.
[88] *Criminal Law Amendment Act 1912.* Section 1 provides: A constable may take into custody without a warrant any person whom he shall have good cause to suspect of having committed or of attempting to commit, any offence against section two of the Criminal Law Amendment Act 1885 (which relates to procuration and attempted procuration). Section No. 3. Any male person convicted may, in addition to imprisonment, be sentenced to be once privately whipped, and the number of strokes and the instrument shall be specified by the court. Section No. 7 deals with the "bully."
[89] The most recent discussion of conditions in Germany is by Polizeirat Dr. Robert Heindl in No. 298, *Berliner Tageblatt.* Dr. Heindl proves the following points: (1) White Slave Traffic in innocent German girls into foreign lands is of the utmost rarity. (2) It is even questionable whether German ports are utilized for pur-

Prostitution in Europe

While the traffic in young girls has been thus greatly restricted, there is no question that a trade in already ruined women is still carried on. Prostitution is, as I have repeatedly insisted, a business,— a business, too, in which novelty is an important item. Deprived of a supply of fresh young girls, the bordell keeper, the proprietor of cabaret, dance-hall or Animierkneipe must at least have variety. The trafficker scours the market for the most attractive women he can procure and women are thus kept in circulation through his efforts. He carries on his business in European cities, in the Levant and in the large cities of South America.

The employment agency has been similarly employed as a means of forcibly increasing supply. Girls are sent out as servants into disreputable places, in the activities of which they have been induced or compelled to take part; or, they are sent out of the country as dancers or singers, only to find themselves, on reaching their destination, consigned to cabarets in which theatrical entertainment is but a cloak for the exploitation of prostitution. Newspaper advertisements and the *poste restante* are deceptively employed for the same purposes. Of the numbers thus victimized no accurate statement can be given. But preventive measures are being taken. The London County Council has undertaken a strict regulation of the employment agency: establishments must be annually licensed, their records must be kept according

poses of transit. (3) No single case of genuine White Slavery has been discovered in Saxony in the last ten years. The General Secretary of the German Evangelical League for the Promotion of Decency endorses these statements. Pastor Bohn, in *Zeitschrift des deutsch-evangelischen Vereins*, etc., July 15, 1913, p. 49.

to a specified form, inspectors are free to examine them at will. Agents are prohibited to arrange for the employment of females abroad unless the satisfactory nature of the employment has been clearly established; nor even then shall an agent arrange for the employment abroad of a girl under sixteen unless with the written consent of her parents or lawful guardian.[90] The worst of the agencies abandoned the business as soon as the new regulations went into effect.[91] In Austria, the Employment Agency is regulated by the trade ordinance; the establishment must be licensed, those conducting it must be sufficiently educated, and the business is subject to the inspection of the safety, health and morals police.[92] A special license must be obtained if international operations are contemplated. Books must be kept according to a prescribed form; girls under 18 years of age can in no case be sent out of the country except with the permission of the Court of Chancery; precautions are taken to insure good faith in the case of older girls; the license can be canceled by the government without notice.[93] There is a marked tendency to limit the business to societies or the commune.

The pimp is connected with the supply of prostitutes in two ways: he cultivates intimacies with the ultimate purpose of putting his victims or associates on the street;

[90] *London County Council: Public Control Department; General Powers Act 1910.* Part V.

[91] Up to Oct. 1911, 1,033 applications for license had been made, 1,000 had been granted, 8 refused, 23 withdrawn, 2 adjourned. Report of Public Control Committee.

[92] Gesetz, Feb. 5, 1907: *Gewerbsmässige Dienst und Stellenvermittlung.* Sec. 21a.

[93] *Verordnung des Handelsministers,* May 7, 1908.

Prostitution in Europe

he then drives them to the utmost, forcing them to ply their trade with all possible intensity. He is thus an important factor in increasing the number of prostitutes and the volume of prostitution. How formidable an element he becomes is evident from the fact that nowhere less than 50% and in most cities as many as 90% of the professional prostitutes are declared by the police to support their lovers. In Paris the proportion is given as 80% to 90%; in London at 90%. Of 93 foreign prostitutes in Zurich 85 were proved to be working for souteneurs; of 204 at Rotterdam, 130 were known to be supporting their lovers.[94] In form they vary; now appearing as base hangers-on, now as paramours, again as husbands. No European city has, however, successfully coped with the system. During September and October 1891, 350 arrests were made in Paris with only 14 convictions.[95] In London, the numbers convicted have increased, though they are still almost negligible: in 1902, there were 132 arrests, with 105 convictions; in 1905, 123 arrests and 95 convictions, in 1909, 201 and 167 respectively, in 1910, 185 and 151.[96] Glasgow shows 25 successful convictions for the same offence in 1911.[97] The present Dutch law has been in operation since June, 1911; up to November 15, 1912, there were 39 arrests and 30 convictions. In Vienna there were 30 convictions in 1912. Wulffen has carefully compiled the statistics showing the extent to which panders of all kinds — the pimp, the owner of disorderly houses, hotels, etc.—

[94] Limburg, *loc. cit.,* p. 17.
[95] Commenge, *loc. cit.,* p. 90.
[96] *Reports of the Commissioner of the Police of the Metropolis.*
[97] *Criminal Returns, City of Glasgow Police, 1911.*

The Supply

have been prosecuted in Germany. Very striking are two points, viz.: that the number of convictions has risen, as public opinion has developed, and that the total represents even yet only a small fraction of the guilty. In the entire Empire, between 1883 and 1887, convictions were obtained in only 5.18% of the cases; in the period 1898–1902, this figure had risen to 7.37%, an increase of 50%. Meanwhile local differences are enormous: Berlin convicted 565,— 43.92% of the accused; Cologne, 507,— 39.36% of the accused; Hamburg, 193,— 15.01% of the accused; Frankfort 26,— 2.03% of the accused.[1] The statutes differ somewhat in principle and detail, but the difficulty arises partly from varying interest on the part of the authorities, partly — nay largely, from the inherent reluctance of the woman to testify. Perhaps this vilest on-hanger of prostitution is the most difficult to lay hold of.

Of the various forms which prostitution takes the bordell plays a peculiar part in creating and intensively working supply; but, for reasons that will appear, the bordell requires special treatment and will occupy a separate chapter.[2] It would carry us far afield to describe fully here the other establishments that cater to prostitutes, directly or indirectly inducing girls to enter the life or furnishing facilities for the intensive pursuit of the vocation. The Animierkneipe, the Variety Theater, the café and other establishments largely derive their profit, direct or indirect, through affording an ever

[1] Wulffen, *loc. cit.*, p. 282. See also *Zeitschrift* XII, pp. 6, 7, for statistics of many German cities.
[2] Chapter VI.

increasing supply an abundant opportunity to work up a demand, that will overtake it. Prostitution in these forms doubtless answers in part what I have loosely termed the physiological craving: that is to say, men bent on gratifying appetite sometimes betake themselves to the Animierkneipe, in the absence of which they would betake themselves elsewhere. Beyond all doubt, however, a fair, perhaps a very large, share of the immorality connected with these establishments is incited in them.

In London, license to sell liquor was formerly granted to music halls; no further licenses of this kind are granted, and one by one licenses formerly granted are being canceled. A few well known establishments, however, still remain, in which prostitutes loiter about the bar and in the promenade. Regular dance-halls where liquor is sold — as is the case everywhere on the Continent — do not exist in London, though special permits for dances in hotels and elsewhere where liquor is sold are obtainable. A determined effort has however been made in Great Britain to break up the close connection between prostitution and the sale of drink. The licensing act forbids an unaccompanied woman to remain in a café or public house longer than a reasonable time to consume her drink. In the provincial towns this law is vigorously enforced; saloons which violate it may be deprived of their license on the charge of harboring prostitutes. The danger to the proprietor is a real one, for the government takes advantage of every legitimate pretext for reducing the number of liquor establishments. In London the law is less consistently enforced than in

The Supply

the provinces: certain notorious resorts in and about Leicester Square remind one of the continental café.

On the Continent, however, little has been done to hinder the exploitation of prostitution in connection with drinking, dancing, and the theater. "In Paris, cafés, balls and theaters are from this point of view, not the object of any particular restriction." [3] In German cities, these establishments fall under the regulations applicable to business establishments and, for practical purposes, are not molested as long as outer decency is preserved, — the term being as a rule rather broadly interpreted. Public dance-halls where liquor is freely dispensed abound everywhere. A Zurich law sought to improve conditions by forbidding waiters to work beyond midnight; but the law is evaded by engaging a second set to work in the early morning hours! Stockholm closes all public dance-halls, cafés, etc., at midnight. The police could proceed against a vicious establishment only by inducing the license bureau to revoke the permit, a step very rarely taken. Meanwhile of the pernicious character of these places in wrecking innocent girls and facilitating the operations of prostitute and pimp, there is nowhere any question. "Legitimate trade is not large enough to keep them going," remarked the head of the Zurich police. "The women make them pay by

[3] Statement of Prefect of Police. On the other hand the following provision is found in the police regulations touching clandestine prostitution: "Police commissaries may freely enter cabarets or cafés where clandestine prostitutes are notoriously harbored, up to the hour of closing or later if the resorts are open contrary to police ordinance." Annexes au rapport général de la commission extraparlementaire (Melun, 1908), p. 3. This document in two volumes (Procès-Verbaux and Annexes) will be referred to as Report, French Commission.

increasing the amount that each customer drinks. They
thus win customers for themselves." The difficulty in
dealing with problems of this sort arises from several
factors — the overlapping of the legitimate and illegitimate purposes which they serve, the lack of a definite
public opinion, and the dispersion of authority among
various detached departments.

An increasingly active interference with the making
and forcing of supply is represented by rescue and protective work. Religious and philanthropic societies
maintain street workers who endeavor to reclaim fallen
women, and homes in which those in distress are received
and rehabilitated. These institutions are more highly
developed in England than on the Continent; nevertheless attractive and wholesome retreats have been established in Paris, Berlin, Copenhagen and elsewhere.
Nowhere, however, is the capacity equal to the demand or
the opportunity. Of the outcome of rescue work, the police are naturally skeptical; but it is a striking fact that
those who have been longest engaged are the most hopeful.

There is, however, no difference of opinion at all
as to the superior importance of prevention. Children
immediately exposed to demoralization must be removed
from danger and trained to some useful and profitable
avocation,— for the girl who possesses some form of industrial skill is least likely to err and most likely to recover herself. The French government has recently provided for homes answering this purpose, but the machinery by means of which children are to be got into
them is so clumsy that the legislation has proved ineffective. The recent Prussian " Fürsorge Gesetz " of 1901

The Supply

(Law on Guardianship) is much more satisfactory. The procedure is applicable to children under 18, but guardianship continues until the age of 21. In less serious cases, children are placed in families under supervision; if the situation warrants, they are interned in institutions. In Prussia, about 6,000 children are yearly cared for on these lines, ⅓ of them girls, of whom about 40% have already gone wrong. For the most part their domestic environment was bad,— their birth illegitimate, the father alcoholic, the mother immoral, etc. This law is a fair sample of modern effort on the part of the state to control the conditions under which imperiled children are reared.[4] Energy expended at this stage attacks the problem of supply at its very source.

Our consideration of demand and supply has shown the complicated character of modern prostitution. The important point to remember, from the standpoint of practical policy, is this. Supply is to some extent artificially created and demand is to some extent artificially forced; whatever may be true of minimum supply and demand, the artificial processes in question are in greater or less degree socially controllable or modifiable. This is, of course, not to say that powerful commercial interests and social habits would not resist interference; for the abnormalities in question are at once the product and for thousands the attraction of metropolitan life. The fascination and the curse of the great city lie thus close together,— perhaps inextricably so, as is so effectively portrayed in the concluding scene of Char-

[4] The English Statute bearing on the subject is the Children Act of 1908.

Prostitution in Europe

pentier's "Louise." With this local pride to be a great city through forcing the sensual pace, modern Europe is fairly mad. Berlin and Vienna are rich and gay; the idle and curious throng thither from all quarters of the world. Smaller towns like Geneva, smitten with envy, struggle to imitate the license of those great capitals. In so far, prostitution is in the broadest sense a social problem,— the problem of rationalizing human life, and only indirectly to be grappled with.

Precisely therefore as there is nothing absolutely fixed, predetermined, and inevitable about the strength of demand, so there is nothing fatalistic about supply. In general, the two move together, one — either one — provoking the other. In the end, they have to be solved together; but within limits, effective action attacking one can itself ameliorate the other. Human nature is indeed weak enough on the sexual side; but the mass of existing vice is out of all proportion to what would exist on that account alone; and one way to abridge demand is to abridge supply, as it is being abridged by white slave legislation, by control of employment agencies, by care of the unprotected young and by rational management of the drink and amusement traffic. Moreover, whatever interferes with intensive exploitation virtually reduces supply. As forced supply increases demand, so diminished and hampered supply to some extent checks it.

Note.— Since the above was written the Report of the Fifth International Congress on the White Slave Traffic has appeared. It contains a complete account of the various movements and efforts above described. It is published by the National Vigilance Association, London.

CHAPTER IV

PROSTITUTION AND THE LAW

Apparent acquiescence of European communities.— Indications of scientific study and action.— Opinion more homogenous than laws.— Is prostitution in itself a vice or a crime?— Its exploitation a crime.

DESPITE the evidence to the contrary produced at the close of the preceding chapter, the notion is prevalent that the conscience of Europe has been and is, to put it euphemistically, philosophic in its attitude towards this ancient evil; that on the Continent at least the " oldest of professions " is simply acquiesced in, on the theory that " what can not be cured must be endured." Certain external appearances seem to give countenance to this view: the prostitute walks the highway apparently unmolested; she waits in the café and music hall for her prey; in some cities the licensed bordell furnishes a notorious market for the buying and selling of sensual gratification. The situation, however, is less simple than thus appears. Society has never, as a matter of fact, for any great length of time contentedly accepted prostitution as an unavoidable evil. Periods of harsh and unintelligent repression have alternated with periods of comparative but never complete indifference, consequent upon previous failure. Recently much intelligent effort has been directed to the comprehension of the evil and of the phenomena contributing to and contingent upon it. An era of scientific study may be fairly said to

Prostitution in Europe

have set in. Wholesale and traditional methods of attack have been discredited and are being discarded. Frank discussion of the subject as a social problem is common on the Continent and is beginning to take place in Great Britain, where it was long tabooed.

I have pointed out that prostitution appears as an almost uniform phenomenon in different European countries. The same uniformity in the main characterizes public opinion in reference to it. I mean, not that every nation is a unit, but that the general trend of opinion is much the same and that the same shades of opinion exist in all countries. For the most part, the attitude is indulgent towards the man, severe towards the woman; on the other hand, the single moral standard has never been so vigorously advocated in Europe as it is to-day.

While public opinion in regard to prostitution is thus fairly uniform, laws differ considerably; but this is of less importance than might be supposed, because the general attitude of the authorities conforms to sentiment rather than to statute. Laws passed under strong but transient emotional excitement are simply not enforced, or are enforced so capriciously that they do not affect the situation. Similarly, laws are sometimes outlived rather than repealed. In the long run policy is in this matter determined by dominant opinion. In France, as we shall see, a very definite policy is pursued, not because it is laid down in the law, but because it is in harmony with tradition and general sentiment; in Germany public opinion not only sustains the authorities in ignoring certain laws, but actually compels them to ignore them; in

Prostitution and the Law

England, policy, law and opinion are more nearly in unison. It is important therefore to ascertain what the general substratum of foreign opinion is, for unless harmonious therewith laws are a dead letter; judges and juries will not convict, prosecutors and police will not act consistently.

We must, in the first place, recur to a point already made. Prostitution is not a single and simple phenomenon. Certain distinctions must be made. In one case, prostitution may be the voluntary and unobtrusive act of two mature individuals presumably in full possession of their senses; in the next, it may involve the exploitation under duress or otherwise of women for the benefit of third parties; in the next case, its salient feature may be offensive provocation by the woman for the purpose of inducing men to indulge in immorality. From the standpoint of law, public opinion and police policy these different phases or aspects of the practice of prostitution present different problems. For the moment it is only the first of these varieties with which we deal. In reference to prostitution thus taken in its simplest form as the voluntary and unobtrusive act of two adults, the practical and fundamental question which confronts law-maker and administrator is this: Is the mere act of prostitution, is prostitution taken by and in itself, a vice or a crime?

In general the line between vice and crime can not be clearly drawn, for the question is one for the publicist, not one of abstract ethics. It lies now here, now there, according to circumstances.[1] Crimes are

[1] An interesting example of just such shifting is afforded by

Prostitution in Europe

such acts as are reprobated by unified opinion and as such punishable by the crude process of the law; vices are repugnant to the cultivated instincts of society. An act — prostitution, for example, may have all the disastrous consequences of crime, and yet in a given society not be reachable as such. Whether it is or not depends partly on public opinion, partly on the difficulty and the consequences of applying penal methods.

Whatever be the legal theory, public opinion in Europe to-day regards the prostitution of mature individuals in the first of the senses above characterized as in itself a vice, not a crime. We shall shortly hear that under certain conditions professional prostitution is penalized; but it will appear on closer examination that the penalty in so far as it is actually sustained by opinion and enforced by the courts or otherwise attaches not to prostitution in and for itself, and not to the prostitute as a person, but only to certain overt acts and to certain surrounding or attendant conditions. There is indeed a distinct tendency against the extension of the conception of criminality to the act itself. In other words, opinion is plainly in favor of viewing prostitution as a vice, not as a crime, wherever the criminal view is not forced by conditions extraneous to the person or to the mere act of immorality.

This can not be for the reason that prostitution is a less serious evil than was formerly supposed: on the

the opium traffic. The smoking of opium in China had long been looked upon as at most a harmful vice; according to E. A. Ross (*The Changing Chinese*, p. 140) it has at length become possible to treat it as a crime and vigorous action looking to the suppression of opium smoking is said to be in successful operation. Public opinion had, however, first to undergo a complete transformation.

Prostitution and the Law

contrary, never before have its disastrous consequences been so clearly and fully apprehended; nor because the law is indifferent as to the form which sex relationship takes, for it expressly declares in favor of the monogamous married state. An explanation must be sought in an entirely different direction.

I have previously pointed out the fact that prostitution is a conception necessarily involving two factors, both equally essential. It so far resembles slavery: if there are slaves, there must be slaveholders; if slavery is a disgrace, then the slaveholder must bear his full portion of obloquy. If prostitution is a vice, both parties are vicious; if it be a crime, both parties are criminals. Now as a matter of history, no proposition aiming at punishment has ever involved both participants. The harlot has been branded as an outcast and flung to the wolves: she alone,— never the man, her equal partner in responsibility. And, indeed, not even the harlot uniformly. The poor and stupid have been the victims; the showy courtesan, pursuing roundabout methods, has never been molested. Something more than justice has thus been violated; the very objects of punitive policy have been sacrificed. For prostitution must be punished if at all, because its consequences are bad. Yet so long as the woman alone suffers, these consequences are not abated. In defining prostitution we recognized certain criteria as accounting for society's objection to its existence — the waste it involves, the disease it spreads, the demoralization it entails. Punishment of the woman in any particular case stops none of the these; the man simply wastes his substance upon others; contracts disease from other women and carries it elsewhere, even into his own family; corrupts others, in case a previous associate has been put out of reach by the law. To make prostitution a crime for the woman alone is therefore at once inequitable and futile. It is likewise becoming progressively more difficult. As long as societies were organized on the theory of male superiority, the woman could perhaps be singled out to bear alone the burden of a dual offence. But that day is past. Theoretically, the equal ethical responsibility of both sexes in every relation in life is already recognized; it is rapidly becoming incorporated in law. With the probable advent of woman suffrage, it will become operative in fact. The stigma and consequence of crime must therefore be either removed from the woman or affixed to the man.

As to the latter, certain difficulties interpose. The professional prostitute being a social outcast may be periodically punished without disturbing the usual course of society: no one misses her while she is serving out her turn — no one, at least, about whom society has any concern. The man, however, is something more than partner in an immoral act: he discharges important social and business relations, is as father or brother responsible for the maintenance of others, has commercial or industrial duties to meet. He can not be imprisoned without deranging society. Is the offence of such a nature as to make this advisable or feasible?

Assuredly, as matters now stand, it is not feasible. It is not feasible for men; it is not really feasible for the women either; indeed in the case of many women, the same difficulty arises that I have just pointed out in the

Prostitution and the Law

case of men. We have long since learned that the bulk of women engaged in prostitution are also more or less otherwise employed. They may be aiding to support their families, by their legitimate as well as by their illegitimate earnings. Are these women to be plucked from their employments under conditions not enforced against their male partners? No society in which prostitution is held to implicate two parties will tolerate it. Moreover, if the criminal charge is to lie against the professional prostitute alone, how is the line to be drawn? The women concerned are, as we learned, professionals one day, incidentals the next; at some other time they may be leading an immoral life, yet not that of a prostitute. Finally, in view of the tendency of women to leave the life, is it wise to coerce them to cling to it by branding them as criminals? The attempt to view prostitution as in itself a crime is therefore inexpedient as well as unjust.

"When society declares a certain act punishable" says Johansson, "a general feeling of equity requires that all actions of similar nature performed under similar circumstances be likewise declared punishable. If it appears to be a matter of insuperable difficulty to apply the punishment to an extent in some way satisfying the demand of the public for a wide and equal application of the law, it is better to refrain from any application of punishment at all. There is no reason to fear that moral indignation and its beneficent effects on individuals will therefore cease, for it is not the punishment that produces the indignation." [2]

[2] *Reglementeringsfragan, loc cit.,* p. 51.

Prostitution in Europe

There is still another aspect of the problem. Investigation shows that irregular sex intercourse on the part of the male is practically universal on the Continent. That some of it is casual and unpaid, the rest purely mercenary, only aggravates the difficulty; for no one proposes to treat mere immorality as a crime and in concrete cases it may be technically impossible to make out whether a specific act is prostitution or immorality. An act universally indulged in by men may be universally deplored as a weakness; it cannot be universally punished as criminal unless all men join in penalizing one another.

Other difficulties also arise to prevent the acceptance of the crime concept. Prostitution and commerce therewith are indeed deplorable, but whence, it is asked, does the State derive the right to interfere with the voluntary exercise of personal liberty by mature individuals, so long as no one else is disturbed thereby? We touch here the root of the European view of the matter. The English urge that personal liberty in this realm can be infringed only to prevent scandal,— that is, only when something beyond mere prostitution is involved. " A woman may become mistress or paramour," said a high police official to me, " she may indulge in occasional immorality as she pleases,— why not in prostitution? She is only using her personal freedom." Still more plain-spoken was a Dutch authority: " A grown girl may do what she likes with her own body." No one hopes successfully to interfere by means of penal legislation with the occasional immorality of two individuals; laws aiming to punish fornication and adultery are therefore practically dead letters, not only because proof is

Prostitution and the Law

difficult, but because it is commonly held to be no concern of the State, provided both parties to the acts are willing. They are vices, therefore, not crimes, as societies are now constituted. In the same category, contemporary opinion in Europe is more and more inclined to place prostitution. The unanimous enunciation of the French Extra-Parliamentary Commission fairly expresses present day feeling: " The prostitution of women does not constitute a crime and does not fall under the application of the penal law." [3] This dictum, be it noted, applies only to prostitution in so far as it involves only two adults without annoyance or profit to others. Nor is it to be understood as implying that society is either indifferent or helpless. Denied the use of the criminal arm it still possesses all the paraphernalia of education, hygiene, and social reform. Our previous discussion of demand and supply will have suggested that in the end enlightenment is of broader scope perhaps than punishment,— even though, as we shall discover, the latter has its place.

The foregoing interpretation of the present state of opinion is confirmed by the fact that, with the qualification to be shortly mentioned, prostitution is on the whole practically regarded in the same light by all European nations. The qualification in question has reference to controlled or inscribed prostitutes — who form a class apart, are indulged or punished on lines peculiar to themselves and for reasons, ostensible and actual, that will be fully discussed later.[4] The point I now wish to empha-

[3] Fiaux, *loc. cit.*, II, p. 873.
[4] See Chapters V, VI, VII, VIII.

Prostitution in Europe

size is this: that the general attitude of the European authorities towards prostitution in its totality is practically the same, though the laws differ; and it is the same, because public opinion is so nearly homogeneous.

In England, Italy, Norway, Holland, and Switzerland,[5] there is no penal enactment against prostitution as such. "Immorality in itself is not an offence against the law,"[6] declares the Chief Constable of Glasgow in a memorandum to the Corporation. A woman therefore runs no risk of prosecution if quietly and inoffensively she receives men in her room or house for the purpose of paid sexual intercourse.[7] In France the ancient laws against immorality were swept away by the Code Napoleon. Since then, an inoffensive prostitute has been absolutely free to ply her trade without danger of molestation by the police. We shall later learn that the police have indeed laid hands on several thousand prostitutes whom they require to comply with certain regulations; but we shall also see that this is but a negligible portion of the army engaged in prostitution, that there exist peculiar reasons for singling them out for attention, that they are not thus distinguished merely because they are prostitutes, and that even so the police position in reference to them is becoming increasingly untenable.

A more complicated legal situation in Germany works out in much the same way. On its face the penal code

[5] The situation in the Swiss Cantons is fully dealt with by Theodor Weiss: *Die Prostitutionsfrage in der Schweiz und das schweizerische Gesetzbuch* (Bern, 1906).
[6] Under date, Nov. 20, 1911.
[7] The subject is more fully discussed in Chap. IX.

punishes professional prostitution for money,[8]— i.e.,
prostitution is itself a crime. The section reads: "Any
woman shall be punished with imprisonment, who having been placed under police control on account of professional prostitution, violates regulations adopted by the
police for the protection of health, order and decency,
or any woman, who, not having been placed under such
control, carries on prostitution for pay."[9] A certain
number of women have been placed under police control;
so long as these obey police regulations affecting "health,
order and decency," their professional prostitution is
free from interference; in so far as they are concerned,
professional prostitution is not a crime. But the great
majority of German prostitutes are not under police control; they are therefore liable to criminal prosecution as
being professional prostitutes. It is, however, a notorious fact that prosecution simply on this score is not
attempted. In Germany as in France, the inoffensive
prostitute is not molested. Practically, prostitution for
money, called a crime by the law, is treated as a vice by the
authorities.[10] Women are indeed sentenced to prison
terms in accordance with provisions quoted; but on investigation it will be discovered that they are arrested not

---

[8] It will be noted that two things are punishable: Prostitution for
money; violation of regulations by enrolled women.

[9] *Strafgesetzbuch für das Deutsche Reich*: 361, 6.

[10] This subject will be much more fully discussed in the ensuing
chapters. An additional word may be here added for the sake
of clearness. The police can at any moment arrest a prostitute as a
criminal; but, as a matter of fact, they do not do so unless she is
guilty of something besides prostitution. If, for example, a
woman restricts her operations inconspicuously to her own room,
she is no less a prostitute amenable to the letter of the law; but
the authorities would not interfere. If, on the other hand, she
made a nuisance of herself; arrest would follow. Robbery is in

for prostitution, but for disorder, though they are nominally punished as prostitutes.

The statutory provisions respecting the prostitute's domicile are similarly interpreted. The law is very explicit: " Whoever habitually or for profit assists prostitution by countenancing or affording facilities for it, is to be punished with imprisonment for not less than one month, and is liable to fine, besides, of from 150 to 6,000 marks, and to loss of franchise. In case of mitigating circumstances, imprisonment can be reduced to one day." [11] Under the terms of this statute, the keeper of a licensed bordell, the hotel proprietor who lets rooms for purposes of assignation, the landlord who knows that his lodger is a prostitute, are all guilty of crime. Nay, it has been held that merely renting a room to a woman for the purpose is criminal even though criminal use is not actually made of it; further, that the words " for profit" do not mean that money must be received; food, drink, sexual gratification may form the profit. By another section of the same law, the definition of pandering is still further extended.[12]

A small section of the German people would undoubtedly like to see the enforcement of these laws attempted; but generally speaking, people realize that suppression on such lines is unfair and impossible and that the undertaking would be disastrous to the police. For the laws bear on the woman and the renter, wholly passing over

Germany a crime and is treated as such no matter how it takes place; prostitution is a crime if additional circumstances make it worth while to treat it as such. That is to say, in itself it is practically not a crime, but a vice.

[11] *Ibid.*, Sections 180-1.
[12] *Ibid*, Sec. 181.

the man, who is at least the accomplice and perhaps instigator. As a matter of fact, therefore, no steps are taken against the keepers of such bordells as are conducted on lines sanctioned by the police; inoffensively conducted *rendezvous* hotels are not molested; and women rent rooms freely wherever they please, without danger to themselves or their landlords, so long as all external proprieties are observed. That is to say, the law to the contrary notwithstanding, prostitution is for all practical purposes a vice, not a crime. Once more, the court calendars show more or less numerous prosecutions for "pandering," i. e., for infractions of the paragraphs in question. Between 1903 and 1907, the prosecutions averaged 343 annually in Cologne; in Frankfort, 373; in Stuttgart, 57.[13] These figures tell the tale; landlords are punished if attention is drawn to them by scandal or otherwise; but the letter of the law, requiring wholesale eviction, is ignored, because — among other reasons — it is unsupported by public opinion. " Simple experience teaches that the standpoint cannot be maintained." [14] " The penal code proposes to punish any one who rents a home to the prostitute," writes Blaschko. " That is an insupportable condition. Excessive severity leads to arbitrary punishment of a few individuals, while the mass go unpunished. The prostitute pays a higher rent to offset the landlord's risk." [15] To the same effect writes Schmölder: " According to the law, a prostitute

[13] *Zeitschrift*, XII, p. 6, where statistics for other German cities are also given.
[14] Wulffen, *loc. cit.*, p. 682.
[15] Blaschko, Art. *Prostitution*, in *Handwörterbuch der Staatswissenschaften* (Jena, 1910) p. 1239.

Prostitution in Europe

is not entitled to have a domicile at all; — in practice they do anyway." [16]

What has long been a dead letter, the newly projected criminal code proposes now frankly to omit. If the present draft is adopted the law will henceforth read: "Whoever habitually or for profit furnishes facilities for prostitution shall be punished with imprisonment. This provision is not to be applied to the renting of lodgings unless the landlord undertakes to get a higher price through permitting prostitution on the premises." [17] The new paragraph thus seeks to free prostitution as such from prosecution by enabling the prostitute to live wherever a landlord is willing to rent her a room on the same basis as anyone else; but a landlord who becomes a pander to the extent of encouraging prostitution for the sake of obtaining high rentals remains amenable to the law. A subsequent paragraph still further frees the prostitute as such from punishment; it reads: "A person shall be punished by arrest or imprisonment, who is a professional prostitute, provided he or she violates the regulations set up for the protection of health, order and decency." [18] That is, the penalties are attached not to the prostitute as such, but in so far as she oversteps limits imposed by the police for the maintenance of health and order. Thus the law will be squared with practice. In one respect also the proposed statute registers an advance in public opinion, for it substitutes "person" for

[16] R. Schmölder, *Die Prostituierten und das Strafrecht* (Munich, 1911), p. 19.
[17] *Vorentwurf zu einem deutschen Strafgesetzbuch* (Berlin, 1909) Section 251.
[18] *Ibid,* Section 305, 4.

" woman " and thus opens the way for a more equal treatment of the sexes.

To the foregoing discussion, the theory and practice of other countries add very little. A general conviction that prostitution is an evil not to be tamely endured has led lawmakers from time to time to endeavor to stamp it out on penal lines; but invariably the considerations previously adduced have undermined the legislation in question. Thereupon much ingenuity has been expended in some places in the effort to gain another foothold. Granted,— say the lawmakers in Hungary and Denmark — that prostitution in itself cannot be treated as a crime; at any rate, the prostitute is a vagrant, in that she is without legitimate means of support. She can therefore be put to hard labor as a public menace, not because she is a prostitute, but because she is a parasite. And in this determination,— it is argued — there is no unfairness, since male tramps and vagrants are similarly disposed of.

This indirect and disingenuous method of treating prostitution as a crime has had, in practice, precisely the same fate as has befallen more candid legislation. In the first place, it is dishonest: a vagrant is homeless; the prostitute is a vagrant, therefore, only if she is without a domicile. Fairness requires, therefore, that only homeless prostitutes be taken up as vagrants and for that no special legislation is needed! The statute will obviously not be invoked against prostitutes generally; public opinion sustains its application only when there are other objections than prostitution,— viz., homelessness, intoxication, etc., and such offences can be otherwise reached.

Prostitution in Europe

Moreover, in so far as the prostitute is in reality aimed at through the subterfuge of vagabondage, the man-accomplice once more escapes — an intolerable condition, as I have already shown.[19] It remains then generally true that, despite all legislation and endeavor to the contrary, prostitution in its elemental form is regarded as a vice, not a crime.

The situation as respects public opinion alters decidedly, however, the moment the act involves others beside the two participants. As soon as order, decency, the contamination of minors, or the interest of an exploiter is involved, a totally different question arises. A man and a woman may be permitted unobtrusively to arrange and carry out a *rendezvous*. So far there appears to be no police method of dealing with them effectively and impartially. Public sentiment is not ready; efficient agencies have not been created; fundamental questions of personal liberty may be raised. But when the streets are used to carry on negotiations and thereby others are drawn into the maelstrom; when third parties, — be they pimps, bordell keepers, venders of liquor and entertainment, or others,— endeavor to develop prostitution for their own profit; when disease is communicated, not infrequently to innocent persons: in all such cases a third party is concerned; and a public that was more or less indifferent as to what took place between two mature individuals has become increasingly clear as to its interest and duty. The measures which were explained in the preceding chapter are required and justified on this ground. The state prohibits the manufacture of

[19] The subject is more fully treated in Chapter IX, p. 334.

prostitutes by heavily penalizing the white slave traffic; it attacks the pimp system on the score of its inhumanity and because it seeks to widen artificially the scope of the prostitute's operations; the bordell, the liquor shop, the low cabaret are in the same category. Wherever a case can be made out against a third party, the law tends to become increasingly explicit and severe, for the reason that, even though prostitution itself be only a vice, its exploitation for the benefit of others violates every conception of humanity and needlessly extends the range of demoralization and disease.

The general European attitude may then be summed up as follows. The two participants in every immoral act are more and more coming to be viewed as of equal responsibility. Their conduct is as between themselves and themselves alone, vicious and not criminal. It becomes criminal the moment it becomes open, involving annoyance to others. In still higher degree does criminality attach to any third party who profits by promoting, stimulating, or countenancing the immorality of others. The differentiation here indicated has by no means been consistently carried out anywhere in practice or in theory; the laws lack codification, and authority is more or less dispersed; but opinion is traveling in the direction indicated, and law and administration are taking their cue from it.

The change of opinion from the crime concept to the vice concept of prostitution accompanies and denotes not less, but greater, public concern on the subject. For it betokens a critical and discriminating study of the problem,— a reduction of its vast total into constituent elements, each to be met by its own appropriate procedure. The societies whose laws indiscriminately denounced all immorality as crime are conspicuous for the futility of most of the steps which they took in dealing with it. Results have appeared coincidentally with discrimination. The scientific attitude has also introduced a mature and deliberate, though not of course facile, hopefulness. A highly learned German authority disputes even the necessity of prostitution: "What is evil in prostitution is not necessary and what is necessary is not evil." [20]

The situation as now characterized is, however, retarded and confused by legislation, police regulations and habits of thought that represent mere survivals from a standpoint now becoming obsolete. They are tenaciously held to because, whatever view may be entertained as to far-reaching policies, prostitution still exists as an evil to be managed as part of the day's work. Most conspicuous among the traditional policies of the Continent is Regulation, to the examination of which the following chapters will be devoted.

[20] Bloch, *Die Prostitution*, Vol. I, *loc. cit.*, p. 3. It is interesting and suggestive to encounter the same attitude in the writings of a police commissioner. Limburg (*loc. cit.*, p. 16), protesting against the view that prostitution is a permanent necessity, writes: "Whoever undertakes to fight vice, either by individual labor or, where the authoritites are concerned, by legal or other measures, is by no means entering upon a hopeless cause and, with judicious choice of weapons, has some chances of success."

CHAPTER V

REGULATION AND ORDER — THE STREETS

Regulation defined.— General description of the system.— Regulation in Berlin.— Compulsory and voluntary inscription.— The Sittenpolizei (Morals Police).— Variations from the Berlin system.— The Paris system.— Additional variations.— Lack of legal sanction.— Administrative punishment.— Liberality of regulation in Vienna.— Varying size of the morals police division.— No approved system of regulation.— All alike arbitrary in character.— Inscription lists relatively small.—General tendency downwards.—Objections to regulation from standpoint of rescue and preventive effort.— Objections to summary police process.— The inscription of minors.— So-called clandestine prostitution.— Omissions.— Disappearances.— External order in regulated cities.— Failure of regulation to affect conditions.— Regulation inconsistent with strict order on streets.—Arrests for infraction of rules.

I HAVE thus far endeavored to convey some notion of the complexity and extent of modern prostitution and to point out the peculiar difficulties that attend an effort to deal with it on simple lines. I have described the measures now beginning to be taken to diminish demand, to abridge supply, and to interfere with efforts to exploit the existing supply. Endeavor in these various directions looks to gradual amelioration of the situation now generally existing in large cities. Meanwhile, prostitution is a phenomenon that must be dealt with by every municipal government. What are the methods employed in Europe and with what results?

Generally speaking, two opposite policies are employed: regulation and abolition. The former endeavors to handle prostitution by inducing it to submit to certain rules; it urges that as a matter of fact prostitution exists, is a social pest, and cannot be summarily wiped out; something will, however, be gained for decency, health, and order, if the phenomenon can be forced to conform to conditions laid down by the police authorities. These conditions form the regulations from which the policy in question derives its name.

The opposing party — the abolitionists — agree as to the mischief due to prostitution, as to the impossibility of extirpating it, as to the difficulty of repressing it, as to the unwisdom of allowing it to flourish rampant. They insist, however, that regulation fails to achieve its purpose; worse still, as they argue, the moment prostitution is accepted provided it submits to certain rules, the state is placed in the position of authorizing, legalizing, or privileging the practice of vice. While the regulationists claim that the privileges conferred do not embody the license to do an immoral and illegal thing, but merely involve common sense acceptance of the inevitable, the abolitionists retort that, verbal quibbles to the contrary notwithstanding, regulation is a compact with vice. In the present and succeeding chapters these two opposing policies will be described and the effort will be made to decide the issues raised by them.

To describe regulation is by no means an easy or simple task; for the systems in vogue in different places vary fundamentally and essentially. They agree in stipulating that prostitutes registered with the police must heed certain restrictions placed upon their conduct in the interest of public order and decency, and that they must present themselves at regular intervals for medical examination in the interest of public health. They agree, that is, in their avowed objects. There is, however, no general agreement whatsoever as to what is feasible or necessary in order to attain the objects in question. The more thoroughly one examines European practice and theory in the matter, the more one is perplexed as to precisely what that practice and theory essentially are. The general term " Regulation" covers up difficulties and inconsistencies respecting which even the partisans of control are still widely at variance. This will become clear, if, after describing the rules in force at one place, I point out the divergencies from these that obtain elsewhere.

For the sake of simplicity, I shall divide the discussion into two parts: the first dealing with registration and with regulation in so far only as they touch the preservation of order and decency; the second, dealing with regulation in so far as it touches the question of venereal disease. Berlin shall furnish the basis of our discussion.[1]

The Berlin prostitute almost invariably first comes into contact with the police in consequence of street soliciting.[2] The plain-clothes morals police, shortly to be de-

---

[1] The Berlin regulations are translated into English and printed in full on pp. 415–419.

[2] The attention of the police is occasionally called by letters, usually anonymous, to women accused of professional prostitution. In these instances the police proceed with great caution, investigating fully all the persons involved before taking any action whatsoever. "Experience teaches that totally erroneous misconceptions of what constitutes the offence in question usually characterize charges made by private individuals, or that the charges spring from revenge, envy, or gossip." Inspector Penzig, head of *Sittenabteilung*, Berlin.

scribed, are charged with the duty of watching not only registered women — to see that they respect the regulations — but also unregistered women whose actions arouse the suspicion that they are seeking to practise prostitution for money,— the offence which is alone obnoxious to German law.[3]   We are concerned to trace the course of the latter.

A woman whose behavior is suspicious is, in the first instance, warned by the officer — not arrested; if warning is unavailing, arrest follows.   Should she prove to the examining officer before whom she is taken that she has a proper dwelling place, she is released on undertaking to appear next day before the morals police; if she is without dwelling or resources, she is taken there at once.   In any case, she has at police headquarters no contact whatsoever with inscribed women, who may happen to be under arrest at the same time.   Whatever may happen elsewhere, contamination does not occur there. Henceforth the procedure varies, according as the girl is under 18 years of age, between 18 and 21, or over 21.   If under 18, she can nowadays in no event be inscribed; she must be turned over to her natural or legal guardian or to the juvenile court in order to bring her under proper conditions either in her own home or in an institution of the required type.   If the girl is between 18 and 21, the same preliminary steps are taken; the morals police communicate with parent or guardian, as previously mentioned; and an endeavor is made to secure wholesome conditions for her at home, in some other family or in

---

[3] "*Gewerbsunzucht*" (professional prostitution) involves "geschlechtliche Hingabe gegen Entgelt" (sexual intercourse for pay).

an institution.[4]   If these efforts are unsuccessful,— and the facilities are so far in arrears of the requirements that successful placing is possible for only a small fraction of the cases,— the girl, despite the fact that she is a minor, may be inscribed, should she be rearrested for the same offence and adjudged guilty in court.[5]   Women over 21 are at once turned over to the courts upon arrest and after conviction may be summarily enrolled.   In addition to such enrolment by compulsion, women over 21 are also enrolled upon their own application.

Up to the moment of inscription, prostitution for money or its equivalent is an offence punishable by imprisonment and hard labor; after inscription, the state withdraws its objection.   The woman is permitted or authorized to earn her living by prostitution, provided she obey the following directions.[6]

She must not loiter offensively in streets and public places, nor solicit, nor be found in the company of prostitutes or pimps;[7] except in case of urgent need, she must not walk in the following streets and places, viz., The Zoological Garden, Unter den Linden, Friedrichstrasse, Potsdamer Platz, etc.;[8] she is forbidden to linger in the vicinity of schools, churches or royal buildings, or to attend the theater, circus, expositions, museums, or concert gardens attached thereto;[9] she is to have no in-

[4] The procedure is based on the Prussian law respecting the care of minors, of July 2, 1900, already mentioned, p. 100.
[5] In conformity with *ministerial decree,* December 11, 1907.
[6] It will be understood that the stipulations bearing on health are reserved for a subsequent chapter.
[7] *Polizeiliche Vorschriften* (Berlin) Section 4.
[8] Sixty-three streets and places are enumerated, Section 6.
[9] *Ibid.* Section 7.

tercourse of any kind with minors;[10] she must admit police officers at any time into her dwelling, day or night, and give information about any person discovered with her;[11] she must keep police headquarters constantly informed of her address;[12] she may not reside in the vicinity of schools, churches, or public buildings and must change her dwelling on peremptory notice from the police.[13] Any infraction of these regulations is punishable by imprisonment for not longer than six weeks; but the condemned woman may also be remanded to the police, on expiration of this sentence, for a workhouse term imposed by the police of not exceeding two years, in their discretion.

I have said that inscription at Berlin may be either compulsory or voluntary; that is, an unregistered woman arrested for practising prostitution without authorization in the shape of police registration and thereafter either warned in vain or punished, may be inscribed by the police, even though she protest against it; thenceforth she is compelled to comply with the regulations above named as well as those to be hereafter described in dealing with the sanitary aspect of police control. This is compulsory inscription. Or, without waiting to be forcibly inscribed, she may appear and herself request to be inscribed, whereby she voluntarily undertakes to respect the obligations that inscription imposes upon her.

[10] *Ibid.* Section 9.
[11] *Ibid.* Section 11.
[12] Registration of addresses is so generally required that this provision is not offensive to the European sense; but the prostitute is compelled to notify a change of address more promptly than other persons.
[13] *Ibid.* Section 15.

Regulation and Order — the Streets

It is apparently easy to understand why a police force, believing in the necessity of regulation as a means of preserving decorum, and in its efficacy as a means of promoting sanitation, should favor compulsory inscription; but why should a prostitute herself, without pressure from the police, ever ask to be subjected to its régime? A complete explanation will gradually emerge as we proceed with the description and discussion of regulation; but a partial account must be given at once. I remarked in the foregoing chapter that prostitution for gain is in itself a crime according to the letter of the German law; the prostitute is liable to arrest, punishment, eviction, whenever it can be proved that she earns money through immorality, whether she have other occupation or not.[14] Voluntary inscription is an open confession of irregular life as a business. Instead, however, of leading to her immediate punishment for admitted violation of the law, confession and inscription operate in precisely the contrary way; they relieve the woman of molestation provided she agrees to carry on her illegal business in compliance with police formulæ. Once inscribed, she is free to seek and to entertain patrons as long as she does so without scandal. Inscription — voluntary or compulsory — thus involves her submission to certain conditions, more or less restrictive and capable of somewhat disturbing her business opera-

[14] It is sometimes stated that according to the German law, professional prostitution is not punishable if the woman is registered by the police. It is therefore argued by many jurists that technically it is not prostitution that is punishable, but non-registration. The offence is not, so it is said, that the woman is a prostitute, but that she is an unregistered prostitute. I have purposely avoided verbal technicalities of this kind in order to bring the reader face to face with the real issue.

tions; but it has the great advantage of relieving the prostitute of vague dread of police interference in general. How far the conditions to which she subscribes when registered are enforced we shall learn later.

The characteristic features of the Berlin regulations are then as follows: either voluntary or compulsory inscription; arbitrary and additional police sentence following judicial sentence, in case the court so orders; interdiction to prostitutes of prominent thoroughfares, amusement, and other resorts; non-inscription of minors under 18; possible inscription of minors between 18 and 21; and complete control of dwelling-places. As the local police are opposed to bordells and brothels, it follows that the legalized prostitution of Berlin is scattered through the city.

For the enforcement of the Berlin regulations a specialized police division, known as the Sittenpolizei or morals police, exists. Its head is an Inspector; he is assisted by five assistants, called Commissioners; and he commands a force of 200 patrolmen, who, in plain clothes, walk the streets in pairs. These men have sole and complete charge of the vice problem; the uniformed police have no duty or responsibility in connection with prostitutes or prostitution, intervening only in case of an emergency — a street brawl, for example, when there are no morals police in sight. The duty of the morals force is twofold. First, they observe the inscribed women, in order to prevent infractions of the regulations. If a medical visit — to be described in a subsequent chapter [14a]— is missed, a morals patrolman searches

[14a] See pp. 235-6.

for and produces the offender; if a registered woman otherwise notoriously transgresses her bargain, it is left to the morals policeman to take her in hand. Secondly, the morals force is charged with the duty of watching the uninscribed — usually called clandestine — prostitutes. I have already told how these women are observed, warned, and if they continue to be objectionable, arrested; — in all these steps, the morals patrolman is the agent who deals with the prostitute. His judgment and discretion determine who shall be warned, who shall be arrested, and thus, in the long run, who shall be forcibly inscribed. I shall shortly explain more fully the working of the system, but it is important at the outset to show the reader the nature and extent of the responsibility laid on the morals police.

Regardless, for the moment, of the manner in which the above mentioned regulations are executed, or the results thereby attained, it is interesting to note that in no two German cities is the same system in vogue. Nor do the differences touch mere matters of detail; they go to the very root of the whole matter. Berlin has, as we have seen, in addition to voluntary, also compulsory inscription, with scattered prostitution; that is to say, a prostitute detected in the practice of her vocation may be inscribed against her will; thereafter she is forced to reside in a place approved by the police,— which place will in no event be a brothel or a bordell. Bremen, proceeding on the basis of the same statute, has only voluntary inscription, and women who thus offer themselves for inscription are compelled to occupy quarters in a single street in houses which, whatever the theory, are prac-

Prostitution in Europe

tically bordells;[15] that is, no woman is inscribed except
on her own application and a woman so inscribed may
remove her name from the list at her pleasure; the sole
condition being that she live in Helenenstrasse during inscription, and remove from it to some other part of the
city whenever she cancels her enrolment; of course, cancellation of her inscription and removal to another part
of town do not necessarily involve any change in her occupation. Therefore a small number of Bremen prostitutes are inscribed and corralled; the rest — all non-
registered — live as and where they will. Bremen and
Berlin are therefore decidedly dissimilar. Other cities
differ from them both and from each other. Munich,
for example, has, like Bremen, only voluntary inscription, but, unlike Bremen and like Berlin, only scattered prostitution. Stuttgart adds another variation:
for, unlike Bremen, Munich, and Berlin, the inscribed
women live in scattered bordells, and in them only.
Hamburg is again different: for, like Berlin, it has both
compulsory and voluntary inscription, while, contrary to
all the above examples, the inscribed women live partly
in bordells on a number of different streets and partly in
approved but scattered lodgings on the Berlin plan. Nor
are the possible combinations even yet exhausted: for
Dresden, Cologne, Frankfort, and other cities have each
its own idiosyncrasies.

Substantially the same variations are found in the
other countries and cities that I visited. For example, in
Paris, inscription is, as in Berlin, both voluntary and compulsory; the inscribed prostitute dwells in a bordell or

[15] See below, pp. 177–8.

not, as she pleases; she may, however, instead of living in a bordell, leave her name and address with the keeper of an authorized *rendezvous* house, to which she regularly repairs or may be summoned between certain hours; these houses, like the bordells, are found in many sections of the city; meanwhile no part of the town is exempt from prostitutes occupying scattered lodgings. Though they are thickest in certain well-known sections of Montmartre and the left bank of the Seine, they are also found in the Avenue Victor Hugo and the fashionable streets radiating from the Arc de Triomphe. In Vienna, once more, only voluntary inscription prevails: no woman is enrolled against her will. But if a woman carries on professional prostitution, the regulations make it her duty to enroll herself voluntarily; if she fails in this duty, she may suffer seriously! The rules expressly provide that the police shall handle the non-registered women more severely than the registered.[16] The woman's freedom to enroll or not as she pleases is thus ostensible rather than actual. It is assuredly a bit casuistical to maintain that the prostitute may inscribe herself or not — only she will be relentlessly pursued if she fails to exercise her option in the desired direction. Once registered, however, she may live in a bordell, or, as all but a mere handful do, privately. At Budapest, the girl is first turned over to a social worker who pleads with her to desist from her evil ways. If her efforts prove unavailing, registration follows. Meanwhile, unregistered prostitution is harried with great severity. The Stockholm regulations also make it the woman's duty

[16] Regulations, Section 51; see p. 441.

to register; [17] but, as the chief of the division is authorized to observe non-registered women " suspected of immorality," [18] it is clear that compulsory enrolment is not
impossible.

Divergencies touch other points also: as for example,
the circumstances that lead to arrest; the registration of
minors; of married women; of women with other means
of livelihood; the employment of non-judicial administrative punishment; the cancellation of inscription; etc.
Married women can be forcibly enrolled in Paris and
Berlin and, with the husband's consent, in Budapest.
They are not even at their own request permitted to enroll in Munich or Vienna. In one place it is argued that
marriage is often a mere form, for the husband is only
the woman's pimp; if regulation is efficacious, or meant
to be efficacious, it cannot allow itself to be defeated by
such a technicality. Elsewhere it is argued that the institution of marriage is degraded, if a married woman
is expressly authorized by the law to practise prostitution for her livelihood, and by inscription allowed to gain
immunity for an otherwise intolerable and illegal line of
behavior. Again, in the matter of other employment:
the Berlin and Paris rules proceed on the assumption that
many occupations are either cloaks for the practice of
professional prostitution, or do not affect the character
of the woman concerned. The whole intent of inscription can therefore be defeated if the mere fact that a
woman follows some sort of occupation necessarily ex-
empts her from inscription. Hence women so engaged

[17] *Regulations of Stockholm*, Section 3.
[18] *Ibid*, Section 10, h.

may be enrolled if they are professional prostitutes. Indeed, the rules of some cities give these women a certain leeway in the matter of reporting to the police so that their other occupation may not be interfered with. The point is that Paris, Berlin, and other North German towns see no inconsistency between registration as a professional prostitute and simultaneous employment as barmaid or otherwise. Bremen, Stuttgart, Munich, and Budapest take a very different view. They regard any kind of employment as the beginning or possibility of salvation; as soon as a girl begins to earn something honestly, there is hope that she may clamber out of the mire; to enroll her would be to brand her and thus to bar the road to betterment. Finally, as to punishment: at Paris administrative punishment is regarded as the very core of regulation. A registered woman has no legal rights. She is absolutely in the hands of the police inspector, who, on hearing the morals patrolman's complaint against her, pronounces sentence upon her. She may, of course, protest her innocence, but she is allowed neither attorney to represent nor witnesses to support her. Nor can the action of the police be reviewed by any regularly constituted court of justice. The Paris police regard regulation as unworkable without this summary administrative power. The Prussian police partly disagree. They prefer that the courts should act in the first instance. Only after the courts declare the woman guilty of professional prostitution does she fall to the jurisdiction of the police. Once there, however, she is absolutely without legal rights. At Hamburg and Dresden it is likewise argued that prompt action, unhampered by technicalities, is the only way to deal with such culprits, and administrative punishment is accordingly still in vogue. The women may without judicial trial be sent to jail on sentences running from 7 to 14 days, with 6 months more in the workhouse if without home or occupation.

Finally, in the matter of withdrawal from the police lists: Bremen, Stuttgart, Vienna, and Budapest cancel inscription on request; they regard every request as the possibility of a return to decency, and fearful of ever interfering with such a desire, however faint, never interpose an objection. Hamburg and Berlin, on the contrary, cancel no inscription until the police are satisfied that the woman is in earnest; an applicant is therefore secretly watched and on the report of an ordinary patrolman embodying his interpretation of her comings and goings, the ability of a prostitute to get a fresh start wholly depends. Stockholm removes a woman from the list " until further notice " in case she announces her decision to return to a decent life, proves to the inspector that she has an honorable occupation or other means of support, and after three months' surveillance, is favorably regarded.

In one respect, Vienna differs at least in the letter of the regulations from all other cities. The reader will have remarked the effort of the Berlin stipulations to remove the prostitute from human associations. She is barred from certain streets; she is forbidden certain places of amusement. These restrictions are not conditioned upon her conduct, but upon the fact that she is a prostitute, and they form an important part of the regulations not only of Berlin, but of Paris, Munich, Brussels,

and other cities.   We shall have something to say later of
the enforcement of these, as well as other, rules.   But,
as showing once more the total failure of any agreement as to the details, the new Vienna regulation entirely
abandons even the attempt to make the prostitute an outcast in this sense; she is only only forbidden to appear in a
group of immoral women or with a pimp.   As to the
rest, it is expressly declared: "In respect to her behavior she is liable only to the same rules as to order
and decency that apply to all other persons." [19]

Divergencies might be still further multiplied.   I
might point out that there is no agreement as to what
constitutes the sort of prostitution which must be amenable to regulation, if regulation is successfully to achieve
its purpose in preserving order and health.   Germany
holds that regulation need apply to prostitution only in
so far as money passes; and the actual passing of a material consideration must be either admitted or proved.
Austria urges that no headway can be made against such
a technicality; the Vienna police, therefore, after watching and vainly warning, arrest on suspicion.   Berlin
acts most rigorously when the girl is without a definite
home; [20]   Stuttgart and Bremen enroll only when the
girl has a definite home, and in a bordell [21] at that.   It is
clear that the variations mentioned seriously involve the
nature, scope, and applicability of the system.   I shall,
as I proceed, discuss them on their merits.   But I want

[19] *Das neue Wiener Prostitutionsrealement*, June 1, 1911. Section 26.   An English translation of the Vienna regulations is given
pp. 429–444.
[20] "*Feste Wohnung:*" the significance of this is explained below,
p. 275.
[21] Or its equivalent: see below, p. 178.

for the present simply to call attention to the fact that,
what at long range is called a system, or the system, of
regulation, proves on fuller knowledge to be a very large
number of systems,— a confusion of systems, inconsistent with one another in viewpoint and diverse in organization, range, operation, and even purpose. Confusion
in structure may be taken to indicate that a satisfactory
technique of regulation remains to be worked out. It
becomes, therefore, important to accompany any discussion of the merits or demerits of regulation with a
bill of particulars specifying the precise form of regulation in question; for the variations above noted are not
immaterial or accidental. Their number and importance
at once introduce grave suspicion into the mind of the
disinterested observer.

Though systems of regulation differ thus in practically every respect, they are singularly alike in one
highly important regard: they have been generally developed by more or less arbitrary action on the part of
the police and without the deliberate and express sanction of a competent legislative authority. From this
statement, the British Contagious Disease Act — long
since repealed — must be excepted; to the extent that
that legislation introduced regulation into Great Britain,
adequate legislative authority could not be said to be lacking in any respect; the Belgian system, too, reposing on
communal law,[22] is apparently well authorized; such is
also the case in Hungary, where two statutes — one passed
in 1876, the other in 1899,— authorize the police regulation of prostitution. Elsewhere this is not, and never

[22] Of date, March 30, 1836.

has been, the case. But continental tradition accords to the police an extensive jurisdiction and initiative in regard to matters more or less loosely left within their province. In dealing with certain matters, the police are therefore in the habit of taking summary and arbitrary action on the basis of custom or on the warrant of ancient degrees of dubious validity. The courts usually decline to interfere, even though, as I shall show, they do not hesitate to impugn the adequacy of the legal basis. The police have everywhere become acutely uncomfortable on the subject. They cling to the powers; but they crave explicit legislative warrant such as will place their authority beyond suspicion. This legislative reassurance they have nowhere obtained; neither in France, nor Germany, nor Austria has the national legislature deliberately and unambiguously created or even sustained by statutory enactment the police regulation of prostitution, as now carried on in those three countries: nay, more, in certain important respects, regulation has been practised by the police only by subterfuge in more or less plain disregard of the letter of the statutes.

The questions here involved are obviously of highly technical character. The statement above made would not be greatly strengthened by the citation of even weighty authorities, who are opposed to regulation on principle; it would be easy to point out that their interpretation of the law may unconsciously and even unintentionally have been influenced by their position in reference to the policy itself. I propose therefore to quote only jurists who are favorable to regulation, men whose interest lies in making out the strongest possible case for its legal warrant.

Prostitution in Europe

As to Paris, I shall follow M. Lépine, to whom I have previously referred as an extraordinarily able official.[23] The powers there exercised by the police in respect to prostitution are derived from a royal ordinance of 1684 appointing the Salpétrière for the reception of prostitutes and vaguely prescribing that final sentences in respect to them may be imposed by the police; by two subsequent ordinances of 1778 and 1780 forbidding the renting of rooms to prostitutes; and by a law of the year VIII (1799) authorizing the police to watch prostitution, to provide for the security of the streets and to check epidemics and infectious disease. From these general directions to the minute specifications and exemptions of the Paris regulatory system is indeed a far call. It is impossible seriously to maintain that they warrant or were ever intended to warrant the procedure ostensibly derived from them. The police themselves are so conscious of the uncertain footing on which their system rests, that they have again and again sought its validation through express legislation. In the year IV (1795) of the Republic, the directory vainly asked that the legislative body define prostitution and " give judicial proceedings a special form "; subsequent failures to obtain explicit legislative sanction are recorded in 1798 and in 1810,— the latter being the date of the recasting of the penal code; legislators were at that time not prepared to

[23] *Rapport de M. Lépine sur la règlementation, etc.*, in *Annexes; Report, French Commission.* The extract is abridged, so as to raise no question at this point except as to the legal basis of regulation. For a discussion of the topic by a German jurist opposed to regulation, see Schmölder — *Die Bestrafung und polizeiliche Behandlung der gewerbsmässigen Unzucht* (Düsseldorf, 1892) p. 11, etc.

forbid regulation, but they refused to write it explicitly on the statute book. In 1811, 1816, 1822, 1848, 1877, and 1895 similar efforts met with the same failure. Reviewing these unavailing endeavors to establish regulation on a secure legal basis, M. Lépine declared before the Extra-Parliamentary Commission: " In these conditions the Police Prefect has had no other resource but to cling to old methods which, even if not converted into laws, have been tolerated and approved by all governments." [24]

The situation is no better in the rest of France. Regulation in the provincial cities is based on certain paragraphs of a law of April 5, 1884,[25] in reference to which M. Hennequin, of the Ministry of the Interior, a pronounced regulationist, admits: " Without doubt, the law does not speak expressly of morals, and prostitution is not referred to by name in article 97: "[26] that is, the comparatively recent statute, on which provincial regulation in France rests, does not venture to mention the policy in defense of which it is now invoked. The Austrian regulations are likewise a creation of the police, ostensibly pursuant to a general statutory provision that vaguely leaves the " punishment of professional prostitutes to the police authority." [27] But regulation con-

[24] *Report, French Commission*, Annexes p. 5.
[25] Section 91, " The mayor has charge of the municipal police;" Section 94, " he has the right to make arrests, to ordain local measures in respect to objects confided to his vigilance and authority;" Section 97, " it is his duty, above all, to assure order, security, and the public health."
[26] *Annexes, loc. cit.*, p. 36. For a severe criticism of M. Hennequin's stretching of the law, see Fiaux, *Police de Moeurs*, Vol. I, pp. 41, etc.
[27] *Oesterreichisches Strafgesetzbuch* Section 509, and *Gesetz*, May 24, 1885.

sists not in *punishing,* but in *condoning* prostitution, provided certain police stipulations be complied with.   Like
its French prototype, the Austrian system thus lacks statutory basis as well as express legislative sanction; and
precisely as the French defect is admitted by M. Lépine,
regulationist, so the corresponding Austrian flaw is confessed by Dr. Baumgarten, the capable, humane and
cultivated official who presided over the morals police
of Vienna: " The legal basis upon which the present
system of police regulation reposes is throughout vulner-
able." [28]   The law must be so amended, he urges, that
the police are charged, not with *punishing* prostitution,
but with *watching* and *controlling* it, on lines to be devised by themselves.   Only if so amended would the
present system rest on an unequivocal legal basis.   Needless to say, no such amendment has yet been carried,[29]
and the regulation system in vogue in Austria stands,
because, as in France, lacking the protection of the *habeas
corpus* writ, the outcast can obtain no footing in court.

The foundation of regulation in Germany is equally
dubious.   Paragraph 180 of the Criminal Code makes it
a punishable offence to rent a room to a prostitute.   Now
the moment the police inscribe a prostitute, they register
her dwelling-place; and they bear with particular severity
on prostitutes who are " without a definite domicile." [30]
Regulation [31] begins, therefore, by flying in the face of

[28] *Zeitschrift* IX, p. 217.
[29] *Ibid.,* pp. 156–160.   Dr. Baumgarten urges the substituting of
the word " Ueberwachung " (watching over) for " Bestrafung "
(punishment) in the statute.
[30] *Ohne feste Wohnung.*
[31] It is, of course, also true that Section 361, 6 conflicts with
Section 180.

the statute: whether regulated prostitutes live scattered, as in Berlin, or interned, as the Hamburg police prefer, regulation in so far as it involves their inhabiting dwelling-places approved by the police is inconsistent with the section quoted. Grave doubt exists further as to whether in any event compulsory inscription is legally defensible. The present Imperial Chancellor admitted that the law is " illogical and confused; " [32] and the most recent decision of the Reichsgericht, involving the interpretation of the statute, concedes that " the competency of the police in the matter of compulsory inscription is not uncontested." [33] A recent ministerial instruction [34] endeavors to break the force of objection, as far as possible without amendment of the statute, by insisting that, though the police still retain the power of forcible registration, it is not to be exercised in Prussia until the woman has been regularly convicted of professional prostitution. A recent defence of the adequacy of the legal basis pursues a line of argument itself calculated to deepen mistrust: " The police are competent to do whatsoever follows from the general nature of their business; they are entitled to take such measures as are naturally dictated by their objects. They are therefore competent to take such measures in reference to prostitution as contribute to the achievement of police purposes. Now the regulations governing prostitution aim to protect order

[32] *A Speech* in Prussian House of Representatives, February 21, 1907.
[33] See a review of the Court's judgment in *Mitteilungen der deutschen Gesellschaft zur Bekämpfung der Geschlechtskrankheiten* X, pp. 49–51.
[34] Dated December 11, 1907. It will be observed that this safeguard applies only to Prussia, and there only to women who have not previously been inscribed.

Prostitution in Europe

and health. Regulation is therefore a function that follows from the general competency of the police. That is true in Prussia as in France. The stipulations of the police regulations have therefore the force of law." [35] It will be observed that this author makes no pretense of higher warrant than that of necessity as judged by a police authority making its own rules. But perhaps still stronger evidence of the legal insecurity of the existing systems is furnished by the radical changes proposed in the draft of a new criminal code. Conceding that prostitution as such is not to be punishable as a crime, it takes the position that " it is necessary to watch prostitution " and empowers the police to issue the necessary regulations, subject to prior enactments on the part of the state legislatures; but these regulations may not distinguish between controlled and non-controlled prostitutes,— they must be applicable to all alike.[36]

The most striking fact in connection with the operation of all systems of regulation is the small inscription

[35] Dr. Jur. Kurt Wolzendorff, *Polizei und Prostitution* (Tübingen, 1911) pp. 57–59, abridged. Schmölder's writings, already cited, argue strongly against the sufficiency of the statutory basis relied on by Wolzendorff. Blaschko points out that the other states of the Empire have less legal warrant for regulation than Prussia (Art. on *Prostitution, loc. cit.,* p. 1236).

[36] *Vorentwurf, loc. cit. Begründung,* pp. 850–853. High authorities question even then whether the proposed changes are sufficiently explicit to put the systems of regulation beyond all question. Lindenau suggests a definite declaration, but there is no likelihood of its adoption (*Die strafrechtliche Bekämpfung der Gewerbsunzucht,* in Prof. von Liszt's *Festschrift*).

I am informed by a member of the Swedish Commission that regulation in Stockholm is based on a set of instructions issued by the Grand Governor, but never signed by him, as is regularly the custom. The official in question is described as having been unwilling to affix his signature to such a document; the police overlook the technical defect.

142

Regulation and Order — the Streets

list. There are, it is true, variations: but the largest list, that of Paris, probably includes hardly more than one prostitute in eight, from which maximum the lists in other cities decline rapidly to utter insignificance. The following table exhibits the size of the inscription lists, the population of the towns in question, and the ratio between the two.[37]

The facts that stand out are the fractional nature of enrolment at its very best, and the enormous variations in ratio. I shall point out the reasons for this and later inquire for the effects.[38]

RATIO OF INSCRIBED WOMEN TO POPULATION

	Population	Number of inscribed women	Ratio of latter to former
Paris	2,888,110	6,000 (Approx.)	1 to 481
Marseilles [39]	550,619	639	1 to 861
Bordeaux	261,678	410	1 to 638
Lille	217,807	108	1 to 2,016
Nantes	170,535	125	1 to 1,364
Le Havre	136,159	136	1 to 1,001
Toulon	104,582	325	1 to 322
Berlin	2,071,257	3,559	1 to 582
Hamburg	931,035	935	1 to 995

[37] For table showing numbers inscribed in German cities, as compared with population, see A. Blaschko, *Hygiene der Prostitution* (Jena, 1901) p. 55. Since this date, the disproportion has been aggravated, rather than mended. Valuable statistical tables showing date of installation of sanitary control, number of inscribed women, their ages, etc., are given by Dufour: *Geschichte der Prostitution* (translated from the French, Berlin, 5th Edition, no date) Vol. III, part 2, pp. 38–49.

[38] The disproportion is practically greater than the ratios show; for the populations given take no account of suburbs or transients; adding the former alone, Berlin had an estimated population of 3,400,000 in 1910. The populations given are taken from the *Statesman's Year-Book* 1913; the number of inscribed women as given does not always represent the same year as the population, but the difference is negligible.

[39] For the French statistics I am indebted to M. Victor Augagneur, Député du Rhône, and to Dr. Louis Fiaux.

143

Prostitution in Europe

RATIO OF INSCRIBED WOMEN TO POPULATION

	Population	Number of inscribed women	Ratio of latter to former
Munich	596,467	173	1 to 3,441
Dresden	548,308	293	1 to 1,871
Cologne [40]	516,527	600	1 to 828
Frankfort	414,576	300	1 to 1,382
Stuttgart	286,218	22	1 to 13,010
Bremen	247,437	75	1 to 3,299
Mannheim	193,902	14	1 to 13,850
Augsburg	102,487	6	1 to 17,081
Munster	90,254	1	1 to 90,254
Vienna	2,031,498	1,689	1 to 1,203
Budapest	880,371	2,000 (Approx.)	1 to 440
Rome	542,123	225	1 to 2,409
Stockholm [41]	346,599	554	1 to 625
Brussels	659,000	182	1 to 3,621
Geneva	154,159	86	1 to 1,793

Different years show a considerable fluctuation in the above totals, but the general tendency is markedly downward. Paris, for instance, inscribed 4,519 in the year 1830, when its population was 800,000;[42] in 1873, the registration was practically the same, 4,603; thenceforth it declined steadily to 2,816 a decade later; since that time a progressive rise brings it in 1903 to 6,418;[43] a decline is again in progress, for 1910 does not exceed 6,000. At Berlin there was a steady rise from 1886 to 1896: the

[40] Accuracy is more difficult in dealing with Cologne than elsewhere, because a fresh list is compiled annually and no names are removed in the course of the year though many women disappear. A list that at the close of the year contains 1,500 names probably amounts at no time to more than 600, of whom about one-half regularly report to the police. This statement is based on personal information, confirmed by Zinnser, *Zeitschrift* V, p. 202.

[41] Enrolment for year 1912.

[42] Moll, *loc. cit.*, p. 371.

[43] *Rapport, Conseil Munic. loc. cit.*, p. 29. These and other statistics may be found in Fiaux, *Police des Moeurs*, III, pp. 907, etc.; R. Degante, *La Lutte contre la Prostitution* (Paris, 1909) p. 109; Talmeyr, *loc. cit.*, pp. 246-7.

list stood at 3,006 in the former year, 5,098 in the latter; since which time, despite increased population, the enrolment declined to 3,115 in 1905; [44] i. e., almost 40%. The last figures obtainable show a registration of 3,559. In Vienna, 1,780 stood on the books in 1900, decreasing year by year until only 1,441 remained in 1910; since the revision of the rules in that year, increased vigor has brought about an increase to 1,689.[45] Hamburg has receded from 1,266 in 1903 to 935 in 1910.[46] Breslau dropped from 1,856 in 1889 to 1,045 just five years later; [47] Mannheim from 60 in 1890 to 13 in 1902.[48] Stockholm reached practically the same high water mark at different intervals, showing the inevitable fluctuations with which, there as everywhere else, inscription has been pursued. In 1903 the number stood at 936,— the figure which it had also reached over a quarter of a century before. Thereupon there came a decided drop: 119 women had been newly enrolled in 1903; 67 were enrolled in 1904. By the year 1912, the total enrolment — itself considerably larger than the effective enrolment — had sunk to 554.[49]

In most cities — as the figures above given show — regulation is moribund, and in many quite dead. As compared with the total volume of prostitution, the enrolment is at the best unimportant, and at the worst, altogether negligible. Paris, as I have said, registers per-

[44] P. Hirsch, *Verbrechen und Prostitution* (Berlin, 1907) p. 11.
[45] For these and all other Austrian statistics I am indebted to Dr. Anton Baumgarten.
[46] Official figures obtained through American Consulate.
[47] *Zeitschrift* I, p. 197.
[48] *Ibid*, II, p. 96.
[49] Johansson, *loc. cit.*, p. 14.

haps one in eight. If, as is estimated, there are 30,000
prostitutes in Vienna,[50] the maximum inscription is
barely 5%. As opposed to a registration of 225 in
Rome, the police records show 5,000 women under observation at one time or another.[51] In the year 1909,
140 women were inscribed at Munich; during the same
year, the police were keeping track of 2,076 clandestine
prostitutes: the enrolment was thus less than 7% of
those actually known,— and they were only part of the
whole;[52] in 1911, with 173 women inscribed, 2,574
clandestines were under police observation, the former
about 7% of the latter.[53]

The inexperienced outsider may jump to the conclusion that an active and efficient police administration
could easily enough gather into its net most — or at
least many — of those who now slip through. As a matter of fact, there has been in some towns no lack of endeavor to accomplish this very thing; but it does not,
and cannot, succeed for reasons that will be explained.
And this quite regardless of the existence of any strong
sentiment adverse to regulation as such.

Nowhere, of course, is forcible inscription possible, unless a clear case can be made out. The police agents
are therefore bound to proceed with great circumspec-
tion. They are indeed instructed that a hundred omissions are preferable to a single error, or apparent error.
The agent may lay hands on the poor and friendless
street-walker without danger of exciting hostile crit-

[50] *Zeitschrift* IX, p. 217.
[51] From official data exhibited to me at headquarters.
[52] P. Bruns, *Geheime Prostitution* (Dresden, 1911) p. 6.
[53] Officially communicated.

icism; but for several reasons the more sophisticated forms of prostitution he dare not touch. Proof is harder; the woman has friends; the public resents interference with personal liberty. Forcible enrolment, therefore, very quickly encounters limits beyond which it cannot be pushed. The mere size of the force at the disposal of the police inspectors makes little difference; Berlin has a relatively large body of agents, Vienna a very small one. Yet the latter achieves almost as much as the former, because neither can forcibly detain any but the most obvious and flagrant offenders.

But there is another difficulty, connected with the size of the morals division. Berlin sets aside 200 men for the service; Paris 240; Vienna 6; Brussels 6; Dresden 18; Frankfort 14; Hamburg 24; Budapest 32; Bremen 3. It is complained at Berlin that 200 are inadequate; clearly then six cannot suffice for Vienna. Yet to any proposition to increase the force materially the objection is made that only a small body of men can be protected against corruption or defilement. The morals police are thus on the horns of a dilemma; if numerous enough to be aggressive they are exposed to corruption; if few, they are inadequate. For, be it remembered, wherever enforced inscription is in vogue, the morals police have enormous power. It practically lies with them to say whether the clandestine prostitute walking the streets is to be cited before the division head for punishment and enrolment; whether the registered woman is to be permitted with impunity to violate the stipulations above given, or to be punished for infraction thereof. In general, the perils to which a large force is exposed have decided the authorities in favor of a small one; with the result that thorough and consistent action is impossible.

A somewhat apologetic attitude has resulted from the general failure of even forcible inscription to make a better showing: one is told that the police do not desire a large list; that registration is purposely limited, etc. The concrete evidence in favor of this purpose is the presence at the larger police establishments of a social worker who endeavors to dissuade women from the pursuit of a vicious life; but this explanation is not convincing. Of course, regulation has no interest in keeping in prostitution women who can be induced to leave it; but in the case of women who are prostitutes and who cannot be dissuaded to desist, regulation, if effective, must certainly enroll them. Regulation has no desire to swell the ranks; but it cannot succeed unless it has a complete list of those really in the ranks. The police apology is an indirect admission that under modern conditions prostitution by reason of its protean nature cannot be catalogued.

From the impossibility of cataloguing prostitution, other disastrous consequences to which I have already adverted, inevitably flow. Wherever a certain number of individuals are guilty of an offence, and but an inconsiderable proportion of the guilty are punished, the favoritism of the law leads inevitably into blackmail and corruption, by which it is still further defeated. I shall discuss this aspect of the problem somewhat more fully later on; [54] but at this point it is important to note

[54] In Chapters VII and X.

Regulation and Order — the Streets

that, despite the unimpeachable character of the police heads, and the splendid quality of the general force, wherever forcible inscription is practised, that portion of the police force which comes into contact with prostitution, viz., the morals police, is widely believed to be contaminated. Whether with money or favors, the women buy immunity from inscription; the patrolman, warned by his superiors that it is better to let a hundred guilty women escape than to make one mistake, easily conceals corruption beneath the pretense of caution.

Forcible inscription is therefore predestined to failure. But there are weighty objections to it even in the limited form in which it is still employed in a few places. For it traverses at right angles the modern spirit. Our discussion of the nature of prostitution indicated that it is frequently only a phase through which thousands of women pass; their individual interest and the interest of society require that every facility for exit and oblivion should be furnished. Regulation does precisely the reverse: it brands the scarlet letter upon the woman's forehead. The heedless victim of an escapade may be thus converted into a life-long outcast; society may be saddled with her and the harm she spreads as a permanent burden, hardly to be got rid of, so long as she lives. And this power, which once for all deprives her of the aspiration to improve, is ultimately lodged in the hands of an ordinary patrolman: *his* observation, *his* judgment, *his* interpretation, *his* assertion determine whether or not she is to be pushed across the dividing line into the abyss: his word against the girl's. Bad though she may be, her reluctance to request inscription

149

is the faint voice of her better self, not yet completely
silenced; assuredly it is the function of a society, whose
arrangements are by no means guiltless of her fate, not
to extinguish, but to foster the feeble flicker of en-
dangered personality. It must not be forgotten that in
every city there are at this moment thousands of women
technically liable to inscription who will in their middle
twenties and later emerge from immorality and prostitution;[55] they can for the most part emerge, precisely
because they are not inscribed; successful inscription
would in most cases finally rupture the tie that will ultimately rescue them. It may be questioned whether a
mature woman ought to be permitted by society even
voluntarily to brand herself a professional prostitute:
there is no shadow of doubt that no modern society
can afford to compel her to do so.[56]

The essentially medieval character of forcible inscription, by which alone, I repeat, any showing at all can
be made, is most clearly illustrated by its connection
with summary police power. No system of inscription
can achieve even the fractional success of the Paris and
Berlin systems if it allows the accused girl counsel and
witnesses. For the lists are kept at their present minimal
size only because the police can by summary action build
them up as fast as they melt away.[57] Frightful mis-
carriages of justice are bound to occur in consequence
of arbitrary action: for example, a woman leaving her

[55] See Chap. I, pp. 21, etc.
[56] It is true that registered women sometimes return to a decent life. But registration enormously increases the difficulty and
lessens the probability of her doing so.
[57] How disappearance affects the problem is explained below.

wretched home in the Rue des Cordiers is arrested by a morals policeman, in spite of her protestations that she is on her way to procure medicine for a sick child; while she is detained in prison, the child dies in the course of the night.[58] Following her arbitrary detention, the Paris suspect is brought before a police bureaucrat, who hears the accusing patrolman, asks the girl or woman, perhaps terrified and certainly undefended, a few questions and summarily orders her enrolment, if he so please: thenceforth she is not only a social, but a legal outcast. She can by no legal ingenuity be brought before a regularly constituted court; she is amenable to police authority alone. Should she break, or be accused of breaking, the stipulations to which she is now compulsorily subordinated, she must accept the penalties imposed by the bureau chief, without protest. Utter helplessness is her lot; and that too amid conditions that conspire to bring about not improvement but further degradation. For the accessories to Paris regulation, the depot at police headquarters, the hospital and prison at St. Lazare are sheer survivals into our day of the barbarous dungeons of the middle ages. Whoso enters them may be said with truth to leave all hope behind. The present presiding officer endeavors to impart a more or less humane spirit to his decisions; but the conditions under which his power is exercised would overtax the wisdom of Solomon. The task is itself wholly out of keeping with the modern spirit.

Essentially, the objections to summary police action

[58] Meunier, *Annexes,* pp. 271–2; also *Ibid, passim.* See also *Rapport de Dr. Lucas, Ibid.*

are equally strong in Germany. Dr. Lindenau argues that the woman is technically somewhat protected against police tyranny; but, he adds: "One must none the less grant that the procedure in question is not well known to them. Moreover, at best it procures only a police decision reached on the basis of the police officer's personal impressions."

Insuperable difficulties thus confront a vigorous regulatory policy. If regulation is needed to protect order and health and to prevent scandal, then it is obviously impossible to leave it optional with the prostitute whether she will be inscribed or not; force is absolutely necessary to success. But to force there is at once the objection that it can be applied to but relatively few cases at all; that it cannot be applied to these without suspending all legal guarantees, and that, once these are suspended, the way is open to corruption and oppression that are to a modern community utterly intolerable.

But we have not yet recounted all the difficulties that beset regulation. Not even forcible enrolment can greatly swell the lists unless the inscription of minors is allowed. That the duty of the state towards defenceless or erring children is custodial would appear to be a principle on which modern society had already agreed; for a minor, at any rate, there is always at least a ray of hope. Experience already touched on shows, further, that though prostitution is commonest in the teens and early twenties, large numbers of those who give way in these years recover their self-possession afterwards. Hence, forcible or even permissible inscription of girls under twenty-one is the very acme of unwisdom and inhuman-

Regulation and Order — the Streets

ity. Yet, without it, a substantial inscription list is impossible. Had the Paris police refused to enroll minors their list, already relatively small, would have almost collapsed: between 1888 and 1903, 12,471 women were inscribed at Paris, 38% of whom were minors at the time.[59] In the year 1901, 635 women over 21 years old and 660 minors were forcibly enrolled,— more minors than adults![60] The same monstrous practice prevails elsewhere. The Stockholm regulations state that as a rule girls under 17 are not to be inscribed; yet of 4,651 new registrations between 1859 and 1904, 1,353 were under twenty years of age;[61] of 338 women enrolled in 1905, 196 (i. e., 58%) had been registered during their minority.[62] In Germany minors are inscribed in Bonn, Danzig, Dessau ("but not under sixteen years of age!"), Frankfort, where 43 were between sixteen and nineteen years of age, Mannheim, Rostock, Wiesbaden, etc. In the small Munich enrolment — 143 in 1909 — there were six minors,— Munich-born.[63] Dufour's tables show the age of the youngest inscribed prostitute in the various German cities, up to 1885: in East Prussia, she was fourteen years old; in the Rhine province, Schlesien, Posen, West Prussia, Bavaria, fifteen; in eight others over fifteen and under sixteen.[64] Berlin

[59] *Annexes, Report, French Com.*, p 388. See also Fiaux, *Police des Moeurs* I, pp. 196, etc.; ditto *L'Integrité intersexuelle des peuples et les Gouvernments* (Paris, 1910) pp. 205, etc.; *Rapports, Conseil Munic. loc cit.*, pp. 31, etc. Commenge, *loc. cit.*, pp. 599, etc.

[60] Fiaux, *Police des Moeurs* I, p. 38; III, p. 609. Eee also Eugéne Prévost, *De la Prostitution des Enfants.*

[61] *Report, Swedish Commission III*, p. 63.

[62] Welander in *Zeitschrift XI*, p. 395.

[63] Meher, *loc. cit.*, p. 215.

[64] *Loc. cit.*, pp. 41-49.

now refuses inscription below eighteen and acts cautiously in case of girls between eighteen and twenty-one; but in 1898 — before the adoption of the present policy — out of 846 newly inscribed women, 229 were minors of whom seven were fifteen years old, twenty-one sixteen years old. But the evidence afforded by Vienna is even more telling. The inscribed list there is on the most favorable interpretation absurdly small: even so, 16% of those inscribed are minors; meanwhile of non-registered prostitutes arrested on the streets — prostitutes who, be it noted, must be enrolled if the system is to be even fairly adequate to its intention — over 57% are minors.[65] It is thus evident that in this essential matter, the system is also on the horns of a dilemma: if minors are not enrolled, the system collapses; if minors are enrolled, society perpetrates an infamy.

A further weakness inherent in forced inscription has already been alluded to: it is like pouring water into a sieve. When once the obvious cases have been gathered, the total can hardly be increased, no matter how great the pressure. Women disappear on the one hand as fast as they are registered on the other. In a single month in Berlin sixty dropped out; at Cologne, though 1,200 are registered in the course of the year, the active list is hardly half that number. So at Vienna, while 2,600 stand on the books at the close of the year, 1,000 have vanished in the same period, so that the effective inscription is about 1,600. Johansson's careful studies of the 2,442 women enrolled in Stockholm between 1859

[65] Finger and Baumgarten, *Die Regelung der Prostitution in Oesterreich* (Reprinted) from the *Wiener Medizinische Wochenschrift* No's. 35 etc., 1909).

and 1884 show that 23% leave in the first year after inscription.[66]   With a total enrolment of 3,582 at Paris in 1880, 1,757 women disappeared,— 46 by death, one by marriage, six to return to a decent life, the rest simply dropped out, eluding police control in one way or another. The following table exhibits the status there in other years selected at random:[67]

Year	Total Number of Inscribed Women	Disappeared in the course of the Year	Died	Married	Returned to Decent Life
1881	3,160	1,524	34	2	27
1884	2,917	985	39	13	6
1887	4,681	2,503	18	8	22
1893	4,793	1,121	9	8	17
1897	5,233	1,599	14	27	43
1900	6,222	823	26	39	57

Finally during the year 1901, 1,574 women were newly enrolled, while 1,880 dropped out; of the latter, 52 died, 34 married, 77 found other means of subsistence, and 1,717 " disappeared."[68]   A certain point once reached, the structure topples as fast as it is built up.   At Dresden I was frankly told: " Compulsion is useless; it only increases hiding and disappearing."   Forcible inscription therefore cannot be operated.

On the other hand, as I have said, if inscription is voluntary, the whole thing goes to pieces.   The size of the enrolment at Bremen, Stuttgart and Munich, where the girl decides for herself, is absurdly small.   The inducements offered are very substantial, for if a woman complies with the regulations the police guarantee her

[66] *Loc. cit.*, p. 10.
[67] Fiaux, *Police des Moeurs* III, p. 658.
[68] Lépine, *in Report, French Com., Annexes* p. 25.

the unhampered prosecution of her business. Yet even
so, a vestige of surviving decency intervenes to keep
far the greater number from voluntarily branding themselves. In Paris, out of 1,574 enrolments in 1901, only
52 were voluntary; out of 737 in 1908, only 36 were
voluntary.[69]

Meanwhile, neither forced inscription, inscription of
minors nor inscription of working girls can build up a list
that is at all commensurate with the magnitude of the
evil. The showy women of the cafés, the boulevards,
the variety theaters are absolutely free from molestation. The Paris police " do not arrest, do not disturb,
do not even watch the well-to-do courtesans who frequent the Bois de Boulogne, driving a fast pair of
horses; who live luxuriously near the Parc Monceau;
who frequent theaters, concerts and balls,— in a word
the aristocracy of the underworld. Nor do they concern
themselves with the elegant women who in the afternoon
or evening promenade on the main thoroughfares. These
have friends among the journalists,— so it is said; they
go scot-free, for fear of scandal. A third class is also
immune: the grisettes of the Latin Quarter. The de-
moiselles of the Boulevard St. Michel are the faithful
friends of the students: they are respected by the
police! " [70] These women are all technically called
" clandestine,"— an absurd misnomer, for their way of
living is as notorious as that of any registered prostitute
in the city. A little shrewdness enables them readily to
avoid giving offence. The brunt of the system falls

[69] Fiaux, *Police des Moeurs* III, p. 663.
[70] Meunier in *Annexes, Report French Com.* p. 313.

upon the friendless and the stupid. The truth is that
no effort is made to secure thorough inscription,—
partly because it is foredoomed to failure, partly because it could be too easily balked by corruption and in-
trigue, and partly for another reason that will appear in
due course. And this is just as true in other cities as in
Paris. Everywhere the police get hold of the dull and
abandoned only. I recall the indignant rejoinder of a
Berlin street-walker, on my asking whether she was inscribed: " No, indeed, only the stupid are inscribed." [71]

Let us now address ourselves to ascertaining the results of regulation. I have stated that in favor of the
system two reasons are urged,— first, that it is necessary
to the preservation of order; second, that it promotes
the public health. The two must be separately investigated.

In respect to order on the streets, European cities
of approximately the same size are, with few exceptions,
practically alike. I have pointed out that the street-
walker seeks by preference the main channels of retail
trade; there she is found in the late afternoon and evening hours, noticeable by reason of slow gait, furtive expression, and more or less striking garb. Her demeanor
is usually restrained. If no response is made to the
invitation conveyed in a glance, she passes on; doubtful or encouraged, she stops at a show-window or turns
off into a café or a side street. Only in the late hours
of night, does she become more aggressively provocative.
This description applies to all the great capitals — London, Paris, Berlin and Vienna; some fluctuation may

[71] " Nur die Dummen werden inscribiert."

157

Prostitution in Europe

be noticed from time to time, according as police pressure relaxes or increases; but this is also equally true of all alike. In general, it may be said that external appearances in no one of them differ so markedly from external appearances in the others as to imply a different policy in reference to the phenomenon. Public opinion objects to scandal without requiring complete suppression; to this attitude prostitution has everywhere accommodated itself. The streets of London, in which, as we shall see, no particular action is taken in reference to the prostitute, are not to be distinguished essentially from those of Paris and Berlin, in both of which minute specifications aim to exclude the evil from prominent thoroughfares; nor are Paris and Berlin distinguishable from Vienna, in which no such stipulations are made. External conditions have everywhere ameliorated; the general police attitude is everywhere understood and is everywhere much the same: hence London without regulation, Paris with a fairly large inscription, Berlin with a moderate one, and Vienna with a small one reach substantially the same result.

The same general description holds of smaller cities. To this group belong Hamburg, Cologne, Frankfort, Munich, Rome, Budapest, Copenhagen, Stockholm, Lyons, Glasgow, Manchester, and Rotterdam. Roughly speaking these cities vary in population from one-half to three-quarters of a million inhabitants. On the main thoroughfares of their retail trade, a certain number of prostitutes stroll during the accustomed hours; in the intervals of patrolling the streets, the women are to be found in cafés, coffee-houses, variety theaters, in which they are for the most part as little aggressive as when on the streets. A glance, a half whispered invitation and a smile form the usual preliminaries, rarely carried further, unless an encouraging response is returned. From time to time, increased pressure on the part of the police results in perceptible improvement of street conditions; and this happens equally in Liverpool, without regulation, and in Cologne, with it. I visited the latter city at a time of distinct police activity. At eleven o'clock at night the streets on which women used to loiter were practically clear; a solitary street-walker, very suspicious of strangers, explained that conditions had become intolerable and " for her part, she was going back to Frankfort." In general, however, the stranger walking the streets of Hamburg, Rotterdam, or Munich would be entirely unable to conclude from their condition whether regulation was in vogue or not; or, if so, whether it is thoroughly or perfunctorily carried out, and to which type the system belongs. Surely, a factor that does not modify the result cannot be important in bringing it about.

From the preceding it may, I think, be fairly concluded that regulation as it now exists in European cities has failed to improve order on the streets. For, though there has been improvement, it has taken place generally, — in cities that have regulation, in cities without it; in cities where there is a tolerable inscription list, and in cities where the inscription list is merely nominal.

On the other hand particular attention must be called to the fact that regulation itself is an obstacle to thorough cleaning of a city's streets; it prevents the authorities

Prostitution in Europe

from taking vigorous measures in this direction. The law concedes to the inscribed prostitute the privilege of living by immorality. In so far as the women live scattered, they must be permitted to find customers, once the right to earn a livelihood in this way has been granted; for that purpose they must be permitted to show themselves in the streets, in cafés and elsewhere. Street-walking as such is not forbidden and cannot be forbidden in a regulated city unless the same authority that authorizes a woman to practise prostitution sets out to starve her. Hence inscribed prostitutes have the use of the streets excepting only certain thoroughfares and places that are mentioned in the regulations.

But as a matter of fact not even these excepted places are — or can be — protected from the inscribed women. Common sense refuses to consider it a crime to walk on Friedrichstrasse, while patrolling one block below on Charlottenstrasse is harmless; or that a woman, who is free to promenade on Dorotheenstrasse must be fined and imprisoned for promenading on the Linden running parallel thereto. The inscribed woman who conducts herself without scandal on streets in which she is tolerated, soon begins unobtrusively to invade those which are forbidden: and so long as her demeanor is circumspect, no notice is taken. Indeed the streets from which the licensed prostitute has agreed to withdraw are not infrequently those where she is most at home; and a large loophole for police favor and corruption is thus created by the existence of rules only occasionally and capriciously enforced. But other consequences follow. What is allowed to the inscribed woman cannot be

Regulation and Order — the Streets

forbidden to the uninscribed: it is not in human nature to forbid to the one what is so freely allowed to the other. The very fact that 6,000 inscribed women are legally entitled to patrol most streets in Paris and are suffered to patrol the others, makes it impossible for the police to act vigorously and continuously against six or eight times as many clandestines who avail themselves of the same privilege. "What effect do the street restrictions have?" I inquired of a Paris police functionary. "None," he replied, "they are a dead letter." It practically results that the police do not systematically interfere unless scandal arises; in which event they would interfere anyhow, whether regulation existed or not.

In respect to street order, regulation is, therefore, in my judgment, a hindrance, not a help, for it is at war with its own avowed object. Regulation is asked for that the women may be kept under control,— else, it is argued, they will overrun the streets. Once under control, they must be permitted to walk the streets; and if they, responsible to the police, are permitted, how can others, not so obligated, be prevented? Hence a measure designed to clean the streets ends by tying the hands of the police, so that the streets cannot be vigorously cleaned. Consequently no regulated city possesses streets as free from scandal as the streets of Amsterdam, Zurich, and Liverpool,— all non-regulated cities, in which a consistent and thoroughgoing course of action bearing on all women alike is feasible.

That regulation, so far from cleaning the streets, is inconsistent with that effort is not only evidenced by one's senses; it is further proved by police reports. If

Prostitution in Europe

regulation succeeded, the inscribed women would give the
police the least trouble: as a matter of experience, they
give them the most. Paris affords the best proof of
this statement. In the year 1903, 55,641 arrests were
made among inscribed women for street offences.
Meanwhile, among the far more numerous non-inscribed
only 2,821 arrests were made. In Stockholm, against
413 enrolled women in 1903, 9,908 complaints were noted
and 1,273 arrests made; three years later against 241
women, 7,515 complaints are recorded, 1,246 arrests
made. In the years 1900–1904, 34.7% of the enrolled
women received hard labor sentences.[72] So, also, in Germany: the enrolled prostitutes of Breslau and the number of them arrested in the course of the same year were
as follows.[73]

	1890	1891	1892	1893	1894
Enrolled	1,630	1,209	1,162	1,064	1,045
Arrested	1,336	1,570	1,707	1,768	1,995

I shall recur to these figures for the purpose of showing
later the true inwardness of regulation. Meanwhile it
is obvious that it does not effectually prevent trouble.

Attention should also be called to the ineffectiveness of
regulation in dealing with offences. The women are arrested,— sentenced now to prison for a few days, now for
longer periods or set free at once,— only to resume the
way of life that led to their apprehension. Of the 55,-
641 arrests made in Paris, above mentioned, 41,719 resulted in immediate dismissal. I watched the "trial"
of a group of them,— several of whom had been released

[72] *Report, Swedish Com.* III, pp. 54 and 59.
[73] *Zeitschrift* I, p. 298.

from prison but a few hours before they were re-arrested; one of them had spent 28 days out of the last month in St. Lazare; others had been " sent-up " more times than they could recall. The less hardened are so leniently dealt with that the restrictions are ignored on the chance that nothing will come of an offence against them.

The offence on account of which arrests are made is usually disorder in consequence of drink; occasionally, some more serious breach has been committed. But with these problems ordinary police and judicial methods are surely quite competent to deal. As much has been admitted to me by high officials in both Paris and Berlin. One of the latter indeed has publicly proposed to drop the order function from the duties of the morals police and to secure the health function by attaching the work to the health department; and the new regulations of Vienna to some extent reflect this attitude.

Indeed, it seems somewhat absurd to hold that the regular police is competent to cope with thieves, murderers, counterfeiters, and all other irregular characters, crude and subtle, that are attracted like moths to the great cities, while they lack the wit or courage to deal with the crime and disorder in which prostitution is implicated; or that the ordinary process of law and rules of evidence suffice for the former, but must be waived in case of the latter! The fact is that the state of the streets depends on the vigor of the police, the sensitiveness of the public, the management of the drink and amusement traffic and the attitude of the courts. An unfavorable judicial decision as to what constitutes a nuisance may change the entire aspect of things, with or without regulation. In Copenhagen, for example, after the abolition of regulation, the courts held that standing about the streets was not illegal: since which event, the main thoroughfares abound with women. The Acting Recorder of Liverpool held in 1908 that solicitation to be punishable under the Vagrant Act of 1854 must include actual indecency; whereupon the Chief Constable reports that " we are going back somewhat in keeping the streets clear of this nuisance." [74]

If the inscription of several thousand women in large capitals is practically without effect in controlling the streets, it is needless to discuss the effect of the smaller or only nominal inscription lists of other cities. The registration of a few hundred women in Frankfort, and of still more insignificant numbers in Dresden, Munich, Stuttgart, Brussels, Geneva, Lille can cut absolutely no figure at all; its sole outcome is to tie the hands of the authorities.

So much for the streets; and in cities where prostitution is scattered, as in Munich and Berlin, the value of regulation in respect to order depends altogether on what it achieves in keeping the streets free from scandal. There are those who say, however, that it is not fair to arrive at an unfavorable verdict on this basis alone; they urge that the regulation of scattered prostitution may fail, while the regulation of interned prostitution may succeed. That opens up the question of bordells to which the next chapter will be devoted.

[74] *Report* on the Police Establishment and State of Crime. (Liverpool, 1910) p. 63.

CHAPTER VI

REGULATION AND ORDER — BORDELLS AND SEGRE-
GATION

The bordell defined.— Proprietor and inmate.— Licensing of bordells increasingly rare.— Subterfuge adopted in Germany.— Rules
governing the conduct of bordells.— Number of bordells in Europe.—
Insignificant as compared with the volume of prostitution.— Europe
knows nothing of "segregation."— Segregation never successful.—
Why the bordell is dying out.— Houses of prostitution dependent on
White Slave Traffic.— Shameless exploitation of inmates.— Effort in
Vienna to prevent exploitation.— The bordell favorable to abnormality.— The bordell and crime.— The bordell and street conditions.— Does the bordell reduce other forms of prostitution?— The
prostitute's domicile.

STRICTLY speaking, the bordell is a licensed or recognized house of prostitution, the proprietor of which is entitled to carry on the business for which the establishment
is set up. At Brussels such houses are licensed on payment
of specific fees;[1] at Paris and Vienna they are merely

[1] The following schedule is in operation (*Règlement* Sections 35,
36) :

Houses of 1st Class

1 to 5 girls..........100 francs monthly
6 to 10 girls..........150 francs monthly

Houses of 2nd Class

1 to 5 girls.......... 50 francs monthly
6 to 10 girls.......... 75 francs monthly

Houses of the 3rd Class

1 to 5 girls.......... 25 francs monthly
6 to 10 girls.......... 37 francs monthly

The fees are payable to the "receveur communal."

Prostitution in Europe

authorized — tolerated by the police, nominally as long as they comply with certain stipulations; actually, as a rule, until the property is demolished or the business becomes unprofitable.[2] The inmates of the bordell are employees working on a percentage basis. The proprietor boards and lodges them and requires of them practically any service — normal or abnormal — that the whim of a patron may demand; in return they receive — or are credited with — part of the receipts, usually fifty per cent. Against this sum, theoretically theirs, are usually charged clothing, perfumery, medicines, and other extras. Their cash receipts are therefore a diminishing quantity. Exploitation of this sort, though nowadays generally forbidden by the police regulations, it is practically impossible to prevent, as we shall subsequently see; in most instances, the authorities do not even try to prevent it.

To the licensing or toleration of outright houses of prostitution public opinion in Europe has become increasingly hostile; at the present time, it is permitted in France, Belgium, Austria-Hungary, and Italy; it is forbidden in the German Empire, Holland, Switzerland,[3] Denmark, Norway, Sweden, and Great Britain. In France and Austria, no further concessions will under any circumstances be granted; whenever, and for whatever reason, a bordell closes, the institution is by so much nearer to extinction. The bordell is therefore not co-extensive with regulation and the area open to it is constantly shrinking. On the other hand, it is, as a

[2] In rare cases a bordell has been suppressed on account of criminal or too scandalous occurrences.
[3] Excepting only the city of Geneva.

166

Regulation and Order — Bordells

matter of fact, more widespread than official accounts lead one to suppose. For in many German cities, through the connivance or compulsion of the police, establishments are found which are bordells in everything but name. The statutes, indeed, expressly forbid their existence in language the purport of which is unmistakable: "Whoever furnishes an opportunity for immorality shall be punished as a pander."[4] This provision makes the outright licensing or recognition of the bordell impossible, since the keeper would be at once liable to criminal prosecution. In police jargon,[5] therefore, licensed or authorized houses conducted by proprietors are non-existent in Germany. They exist nevertheless. I have pointed out that the police dictate the dwelling-houses of registered prostitutes; they thereby condone the technical violation of law by the landlords or mistresses of those dwellings where registered prostitutes are authorized or ordered by them to live. If then several women are permitted or ordered to "board" at a particular house, an establishment is set up that is a bordell in all but name. Technically, the girls are boarders, going through the form of paying a certain sum for food and lodging, while conducting their business affairs as they please; as a matter of fact little effort is made by the mistress or the inmates to keep up the make-believe. In reference to this matter the police or other authorities vary in candor and straightforwardness. "We have in Cologne no bordells and no bordell streets,"[6] says one; a similar declaration was made in

[4] *Imperial Penal Code*, Section 180.
[5] "In polizeitechnischem Sinne."
[6] *Zeitschrift* V, p. 209.

Prostitution in Europe

Parliament by the member for Hamburg. But in their less technical moments the police admit the practical truth; a high police official in Cologne stated to me that while some of the houses are really boarding-houses, others are really bordells; a similar admission was made in Frankfort.[7] The author quoted above as declaring that there are no bordells in Cologne, subsequently gives a list of streets in which " bordells are found."[8] A questionnaire was addressed by Frau Katharina Scheven to the municipal authorities of 235 German cities in 1904, fourteen of which frankly admitted, and about 200 denied, the existence of bordells: but of the latter, twenty admit that there are so-called " bordell streets," i. e., streets in various parts of the city in which bordells are found, despite the fact that technically there are claimed to be none at all.[9] Hamburg and Bremen are the most prominent examples of the subterfuge practised by the police of certain German cities in this matter. In different sections of the former there are " boarding-places " to which the registered prostitute is " referred "; nor will she be permitted to remain in the city unless she " boards " in one or another of them, provided the police so require. Her " mistress " charges her for rent and food. Nominally, the girl's earnings are her own and the mistress does not command her services.[10] As a matter of fact, the visitor is greeted on entering by the madame and her girls,—

[7] "Es giebt doch Bordelle." The distinction, if existent, is between "Kasernierung" and "Bordellierung" (the enforced boardinghouse and the bordell).

[8] *Ibid*, p. 212. "Es bestehen Bordelle in," etc.

[9] *Denkschrift über die Verthältnisse in Bezug auf das Bordellwesen* by Katharina Scheven: Dresden, 1904 (Tables).

[10] Ich kümmere mich nicht weiter," said one to me.

precisely as in a bordell; the place is notorious as a bordell; liquor is pressed upon the guest's attention and all partake,— just as in a bordell. The girls exercise no freedom in selecting or submitting to their patrons. They may be supposed to retain their earnings, paying only for what they get; but in practice they have to use every possible device to conceal from the mistress the amount received from their patrons — an unnecessary precaution if the police theory were correct. Finally, the sums ostensibly belonging to them are wiped out for the most part by "extras" which they require or are cajoled into purchasing from or through the so-called "landlady." Similar establishments exist in Dresden, Cologne, and Frankfort.[11]

In Bremen, the mistress on the premises is eliminated and the women maintain a certain measure of independence. The twenty-five houses of Helenenstrasse are divided into small flats, each of which is occupied as a housekeeping apartment by a prostitute and her servant. The places differ from bordells in the absence of a landlady, and of a general meeting and drinking-room. But meeting, drinking, and indirect exploitation take place nevertheless. The Bremen establishments differ little in operation or, as we shall see, in outcome from the conventional bordell. Despite this very common violation of the spirit and intent of the law in Germany, it is interesting to observe that the courts have by no means always protected the police in their disingenuous procedure. In Heidelberg in the year 1907 three houses of prosti-

[11] It will be noted that Berlin is not in this list; the law is there observed in both letter and spirit.

tution were closed, the court holding that the connivance of the police did not affect the punishable character of the landlord's offence.[12]

Regulation applied to bordells or quasi-bordells aims to govern their location, the number, age and medical inspection of inmates, the sale of liquor, the money relations of mistress and girls, the maintenance of order, and the extent to which inmates are privileged to appear on the streets. We shall, for the present, omit everything pertaining to the sanitary side, which will be discussed in the next chapter. On other points, the stipulations are usually of a quite obvious character. The maximum number of inmates, an accurate roll of whom must be kept, may not exceed the police allowance; minors may not be employed as servants; schoolboys are not to be admitted; police officers are to have entrance at all times. In Vienna, bordell women are not allowed to seek patrons on the street; the keepers are forbidden to sell liquor or to provide music.[13] The proprietress in Paris is specifically warned of the precarious tenure of her privilege, which will be terminated in case of abuse, scandal, or infraction of the regulations;[14] she is also pledged to enforce police regulations respecting the hours during which inmates, being registered women, may patrol the streets, and to give prompt information to inspectors regarding unusual occurrences.[15] Inmates are forbidden

[12] Adele Schreiber in *Die Kritische Tribüne* I, p. 114.
[13] Baumgarten in *Zeitschrift* IX, p. 174.
[14] Lépine in *Annexes, loc. cit.,* p. 20. For a much more exhaustive account, however, see, in the same volume, the *Report* of M. Meunier, pp. 289–467, especially pp. 418–430.
[15] Préfecture de Police, *Service des Moeurs, Règlement* II (Maisons de Tolérance), p. 6.

to solicit at windows;[16] no attempt is made to regulate
the sale of alcohol or to prevent exploitation; nor can an
inmate decline to put herself at the disposal of any customer who selects her, whatever his condition.[17]   At
Hamburg the authorities are theoretically concerned to
prohibit exploitation.   On the second page of the health
record book, given to every inmate, the following an-
nouncement is printed: "Should the 'landlady'[18] endeavor to detain an inmate on the ground of debts or
loans, the girl is to make a complaint to the physician
who conducts the medical examination, in case she cannot
report to headquarters."   It is further provided that
women must promptly notify the police of change of residence or of absence from town, permanent or transient; that they must not live or spend the night in any
house not approved by the police, consort with minors,
appear at doors or windows, or be found anywhere but in
their dwellings from 11 P. M. to 6 A. M.   The Vienna
stipulations concern themselves particularly with the
prevention of exploitation.   Personal inspection on the
part of the district officer quarterly, on the part of the
central authorities semi-annually, is required.   The inspection concerns itself with the physical condition of the
bordell, with its business conduct, and other possible
subjects of complaint.[19]   The Budapest regulations aim
mainly to obstruct exploitation and to procure a measure

[16] *Obligations et Défenses imposées aux filles publiques.*
[17] Meunier quotes the Prefect of Police as follows: "In a house
of ill-fame a woman is unable to refuse any man who presents himself." *Loc. cit.,* p. 420.
[18] "Zimmervermieterin." This word keeps up the fiction that the
establishment is a boarding-house, not a bordell.
[19] Regulations, Section 16.

of personal freedom. It is explicitly stated that not less than one-fourth of the girl's earnings must belong to her and that the keeper may under no circumstances involve her in debt for either necessaries or luxuries; that she must be allowed to walk abroad " independently and alone " during at least three hours a day, and an extra half day once a week; finally, no hindrance must be placed in the way of her going to church.[20]   The Brussels regulation — to take one more example — applicable to tolerated houses provides that no married woman shall be permitted to open such an establishment without her husband's consent; [21] that such houses must not be located in busy streets or in proximity to schools, public buildings, or " edifices consecrated to worship "; [22] "that there must be no common hall or room for the sale of liquor; [23] that an inventory of the girl's possessions be made in duplicate on her entrance, to the end that she may know what she is entitled to on leaving.[24]

The following table portrays the present European situation in respect to the existence of bordells or quasi-bordells,— their number, location, number of inmates in connection with the number of inscribed prostitutes, and the estimated number of non-inscribed prostitutes; it includes only those cities which I myself visited.

[20] A German translation of the Budapest regulations is given in *Zeitschrift* XII, pp. 437, etc. For the provisions above cited, see pp. 439, 440.
[21] *Règlement sur la Prostitution* (1904), Section 19.
[22] *Ibid.* Section 21.
[23] *Ibid.* Section 25.
[24] *Ibid.* Section 33.

City	No. houses of prostitution	How located	No. of inmates	No. inscribed prostitutes not living in houses of prostitution	Estimated total number of prostitutes
Paris 47		Scattered	387	6,000	50,000–60,000
Vienna 6		Scattered	50–60	1,630	30,000
Hamburg ...113		On 8 scattered streets	780	155	....
Budapest 13		Scattered	260–300	2,000	....
Dresden 81		On 32 different streets	293[25]	Few	....
Frankfort ... 10		Scattered	100 (about)	188	....
Cologne[26] ... 98		Scattered	194	500	6,000[27]
Geneva 17		Scattered	86	None	....
Rome 22		Scattered	125	100	Over 5,000 known to police
Brussels 6		Scattered	37	145	Over 3,000 known to police
Stuttgart 10		Scattered	22	None	....
Bremen 25		One street	75	None	..........[28]
Stockholm .. 30		On 6 scattered streets[29]	98	228	....

Other towns make the same kind of showing:[30]

City	Population	No. of Bordells	No. of inmates
Augsburg 89,770		3	12
Fürth 54,882		4	16
Reichenbach 28,498		2	7
Worms 28,624		2	14–16

[25] A few live scattered, namely, those on probation.
[26] *Mitteilungen der Deutschen Gesellschaft, etc.*, VII. p. 2.
[27] Polizeikommissar Rump, *Ibid.*, p. 3.
[28] Several years ago the police began to compile statistics which soon reached 1,000, "und die lange nicht alle," the Inspector remarked.
[29] In 1904, of these thirty houses the number on each of these streets were as follows: 3, 4, 4, 7, 11, 1.
[30] The figures are taken from Frau Scheven's *Denkschrift.*

Prostitution in Europe

A careful study of the data above given discloses a number of important points. In the first place, omissions are significant. The bordell is altogether non-existent in certain countries, and has been suppressed in many large cities, though other towns in the same countries still permit its existence. In Germany, for example, Berlin and Munich have no bordells such as are found elsewhere in Germany. But the most striking fact is the insignificance of the number of bordell inmates as compared with the number of professional prostitutes. The number is on its face too small to play any part in the management of the general problem. Indeed, it is trifling even as compared with the number of inscribed prostitutes, except in the few towns that actually or practically limit inscription to bordell inmates.[31] The vast majority of prostitutes live untouched by police control; the vast majority of the inscribed prostitutes in Europe live scattered, not in houses of prostitution. Some 40,000 prostitutes in Paris are wholly free of police control; of the 6,000 registered women of the city, 5,575 live with police consent as individuals here, there, and everywhere; the remaining 387 live in forty bordells situated in almost as many different streets. Of 1,689 women inscribed in Vienna, 1,630 live where they please, the regulations expressly stating: "In so far as a prostitute possesses a dwelling-place not shared by other prostitutes, she is not to be restricted in her choice of a location any more than is absolutely necessary;"[32] the remainder, something between 50 and 60, occupy six bor-

[31] E. g., Hamburg, Bremen, and Stuttgart.
[32] Règlement, Section 12. She must only avoid the vicinity of schools, public buildings, and churches.

dells located in different sections of the city; less than
one-third of Stockholm's registered prostitutes are quar-
tered in its scattered bordells, and the registered prostitutes are as everywhere else but a fraction of the whole
number. The limitation of inscription to bordell inmates
at Stuttgart and Bremen is of course a step on the way
to complete abandonment of regulation. Only rarely
do even the police put forward a more favorable interpretation, as, e. g., in Geneva, where, with 86 women interned in bordells, I was gravely assured that not above
forty non-inscribed women strolled the streets. In company with an English physician, I counted twenty unmistakable women between the acts at the Kursaal that
evening; at midnight, standing at a corner of the Place
des Alpes, we observed forty more in the course of a few
minutes.

The table above given disposes once and for all of
" segregation." Segregation in the sense of an attempt
to confine the prostitutes of a city or even the majority
of them to a single locality or even to a few definite
localities is not undertaken in any European city from
Budapest to Glasgow. Waiving all objections and assuming plenary and summary police power such as exists, it is obviously easier to inscribe them than to confine them. If, as is the case, they cannot be caught and
inscribed, how are they to be caught and segregated?
European cities, having universally failed in the attempt
to inscribe prostitution, necessarily refrain from any endeavor to segregate any considerable part of it. Nay,
more, no European city succeeds even so far as to confine to bordells or bordell quarters even the inscribed part

Prostitution in Europe

of the prostitute army which has been expressly ordered
to stay there. "They do not succeed in Hamburg, Nürn-
berg, Altona, Mainz, and Leipzig, in confining prostitutes
to houses or to a row of streets. Even inscribed prostitution breaks away from the streets and the houses to
which it is directed by the police," [33]—a police, be it
added, with summary power to have its way.

Segregation is therefore impracticable; more than
this, any attempt to bring it about is also recognized to be
inadvisable. In the first place, the impossibility of thor-
oughness creates an obvious opportunity for police corruption; a woman who objects to being segregated may
for an adequate consideration induce the police to overlook her; and as hundreds are bound to be overlooked
anyway, the chances of detecting fraud are slender.
Again, a segregated quarter would give to vice the greatest possible prominence. Finally, it would expose to
moral contagion those who are already most imperilled
and whom every consideration of interest and decency
should impel society to protect — the children of the
poor. For the segregated quarter will inevitably be located where rents are low and where the neighbors have
least influence. Objection to bordells on the part of those
living in the vicinity is, moreover, becoming increasingly
louder: "Urgent requests on the part of the public for
the closing of the houses are becoming more frequent,"
says the head of the morals police of Budapest in his last

[33] Kampffmeyer, in *Zeitschrift* III, 215. The article is an exhaustive study of the living conditions of prostitution in Germany
and completely sustains the position taken in the text,—that the
most arbitrary police procedure is incapable of segregating prostitution, if segregation is construed as in the text.

report. A few months ago, the police of Frankfort endeavored to placate neighborhood sentiment by ordering the transfer of certain scattered bordells to a single street adjoining the railroad. A storm of public indignation led to the speedy abandonment of the proposal, although fifteen houses had already been bought on speculation for the purpose.[34]

To what is said above as to the non-existence of segregation in Europe, Hamburg and Bremen are sometimes said to be exceptions; not infrequently they are described as having segregated prostitution. Such is not the case. In both these cities inscribed prostitution is — as everywhere else — limited, and decreasing in relative importance. In Hamburg the bordells forced into existence by the police are found, not in a segregated quarter, but in at least eight different streets scattered through the town; and six of the eight streets contain houses in which prostitutes do not reside and are not permitted to reside. But the case is less favorable to segregation than even the foregoing statement represents; for not even all inscribed prostitutes live on the eight streets in question; and the non-inscribed do in Hamburg what they do everywhere else,— quarter themselves wherever they can.

Nor is the example of Bremen any more favorable to

[34] An account of the public meeting, which I was fortunate enough to attend, is given in *Die Kritische Tribüne,* I, 10, in two articles: Adele Schreiber. "*Zur Prostitutions — und Kasernierungsfrage;* Henrietta Fürth, "*Bordellstrasse?*" The same situation has just arisen in Hamburg. The progress of the city makes it necessary to raze certain of the houses mentioned in the text. There is vigorous opposition to the proposal to allow the proprietors to locate themselves elsewhere.

Prostitution in Europe

the feasibility of segregation. There the entire registered
list is indeed confined to one street,— Helenenstrasse;
but the separation of seventy-five women or less in a
seaport town in which hundreds of prostitutes live scattered through the city is assuredly not "segregation."
Nor was Helenenstrasse itself a deliberate move towards
segregation. A contractor had built up the street with
twenty-six little apartment houses as a speculation in
1878,— the year of a panic in the building trade. Fac-
ing ruin, as the houses could not be rented, he accepted
the chance suggestion of a police official that the rooms
be let to prostitutes. The historian of the incident
writes: "Since that time,— more than thirty years —
notwithstanding many efforts, this step has never been
repeated. As every inhabitant knows, only a fraction of
the prostitution of Bremen utilizes this street,— altogether insufficient for the existing volume of the
traffic." [35] Helenenstrasse is therefore perhaps the
strongest argument in Europe against the feasibility of
the policy in support of which it is mistakenly cited.

In passing, it is interesting and significant to observe
that the impracticability of effective segregation is not
new. Medieval regulation ordered the prostitute into a
bordell or forced her to wear a costume which proclaimed her occupation. The bordells were preferably located on the periphery of the town in the vicinity of the
city gate, i. e., in what purported to be a segregated district. Now, medieval prostitution was indeed character-
istically a bordell prostitution: a hamlet of from two to
four hundred inhabitants had its bordell; and the number

[35] *Mitteilungen der deutschen Gesellschaft, etc.*, VII, I, p. 7.

of licensed bordells kept pace with the increase of population. We may be sure that, having undertaken to force prostitution into bordells, and having undertaken to force bordells into a localized quarter, medieval authority was none too tenderly or cautiously applied; fear of error did not paralyze the official arm. Yet the policy failed! The researches of Bloch leave absolutely no doubt on this point.[36] "Despite the fact that municipal authorities endeavored to confine prostitution to municipally controlled and administered bordells and legislated severely against prostitutes living elsewhere, nevertheless the number of scattered prostitutes was very large,— perhaps larger than of those living in houses. In contrast with the bordell women, they were called clandestine,— but this does not mean that there was the least doubt as to their trade."[37] At times the clandestines — in the sense here indicated — lived on the very streets on which bordells were situated, yet refused to be coerced into them; again, they lodged — sometimes several together — with a landlady who operated a brothel which the authorities were unable to change into a controlled bordell. A policy that failed in the relatively small medieval town, where it encountered no hostile sentiment and could ride rough-shod over personal privilege, can hardly be successfully carried out in a modern metropolis, in the face of strong ethical objection and exaggerated sensitiveness at any invasion of individual liberty,— not to mention the complications created by mere quantitative increase.

If the table — to which we now return — is examined

[36] *Die Prostitution*, Vol. I, pp. 731–791.   [37] *Ibid.*, p. 780.

from an historic point of view, it becomes clear that the
bordell is rapidly losing ground. The bordell is at this
date illegal in Great Britain, Switzerland (except Geneva), Holland, Denmark, Norway, and the German Empire, though in many German towns, as I have pointed
out, a subterfuge exists; in almost all these countries it
was once an acknowledged institution. In towns in
which its existence does not violate law, it is rapidly disappearing, even though in some places the authorities
favor its maintenance and extension. Neither Paris,
Vienna, Stuttgart, nor Frankfort will authorize the opening of a new bordell; they all look forward to a time in
the near future when those still surviving will succumb
to adverse sentiment and decreasing receipts,— the
causes of which I shall shortly explain. Hamburg, where
the police still strongly favor the bordell and utilize all
their tremendous power in its favor, has seen the total
number of inmates decrease from 1,050 in 1876 to 780
in 1910,— despite the doubling of population in the
same period; three houses authorized to contain 12
girls apiece were found to harbor 2, 3, and 6 respectively. Budapest,[38] like Hamburg, prefers the bordell,
and once maintained from 50 to 60 bordells, with 600 to
700 women; only 13, with 250 inmates, survive, despite
the encouraging attitude of the authorities. The most
elaborate establishment in the city, authorized to receive
21 girls, had at the date of my visit only 7. In Brussels
there were 7 bordells, containing 66 women, in 1890; six
houses, with 37 inmates, in 1910.[39] But most striking

[38] This was also formerly true of Vienna, where the regulations
of 1900 favored bordells, but failed to increase their number.
[39] Other Belgian towns show the same conditions: Antwerp had

Regulation and Order — Bordells

of all are the Paris records: with 235 bordells, containing 1,450 women in 1841 (population 1,200,000), as recently as 1888 there were 69 tolerated houses, with 772 inmates; in 1903 there remained 47 houses, with 387 inmates [40] population had meanwhile increased to 2,800,000. At the last named date, 6,031 inscribed women were living in scattered lodgings. The following table exhibits the relation between inscribed prostitutes living in lodgings and those interned in the bordells of Paris:

Year	Enrolled	Living in bordells	Living scattered
1872	4,242	1,126	3,116
1882	2,839	1,116	1,723
1892	5,004	596	4,408
1903	6,418	387	6,031

The rest of France shows the same development in progress: Amiens had 13 houses of prostitution in 1880 none in 1895; Havre 34 in 1875, 9 in 1895; 75 bordells in Lyons in 1840 shrank to 17 in 1895; 125 in Marseilles in 1873 were reduced to 12 in 1899; 31 in Nantes (1855) to 12 in 1896; 60 at Bordeaux (1869) to 16 in 1906.[41] At Rome, the 22 authorized houses were said at the time of my visit to contain some 125 inmates; none had its full authorized complement: a huge establishment, with a capacity of 18, had 5 inmates; another, with capacity of 12, had 7; others, authorized to harbor 10 women, contained 4, 5, and 6 respectively.[42]

29 houses in 1882, 3 in 1885; Liège 33 in 1881, 20 in 1895; Charleroi 10 in 1872, 3 in 1895.

[40] Fiaux, *Police des Moeurs*, I, p. 211. Also Vol. II, pp. 907–8; Vol. III, p. 664.

[41] Felix Regnault, *L'Evolution de la Prostitution* (Paris, 1907) p. 142.

[42] Von Düring (*Zeitschrift* IV, p. 113) quotes Ströhmberg as stating that the same evolution is in progress at St. Petersburg,

Prostitution in Europe

The causes responsible for the decay of the bordell will explain why the bordell cannot be re-introduced, even though it were an efficacious device for the maintenance of public order and decency and for the diminution of disease,— points that still remain to be discussed. The bordell prospered as long as its management was uncontrolled; its decay set in the moment public sentiment required the slightest deference to the dictates of humanity. For, in the first place, the bordell can be tenanted only through the exertions of the trafficker. A few hopeless wretches, whose independent career is over, may of their own accord seek its food and shelter; but these are precisely the women whom the management accepts only under pressure of necessity. Young and attractive inmates are desired,— innocent, or, at least, beginners. Prior to their suppression in Zurich, 60% of the inmates of its 18 bordells had not completed their seventeenth year![43] The fact that there are more bordells in Hamburg than experience elsewhere would lead us to expect may be due not only to police preference, but to the fact that inscribed minors are permitted — perhaps even forced — to enter them. Now these eagerly desired youthful recruits are procurable as a rule only through traffickers; the bordell therefore prospers only where trafficking prospers. In the heyday of this infamous business, victims were brought into the large European cities by every species of fraud and imposition,

where 206 bordells in 1879 decreased to 65 in 1888. Similarly, Baumgarten (*Zeitschrift* IX, pp 174-5) states that Prague, which had in 1903, 48 bordells with 220 inmates, has (1908) 26, with 100 inmates.

[43] *Die Prostitutionsfrage in der Schweiz* (Zurich, 1913) p. 10.

only to find themselves imprisoned in bordells until thoroughly broken to the trade. Thus the houses of Paris were filled with girls enticed from their homes in the departments of the Somme and the Rhône, or Paris itself; the bordells of Vienna and Budapest with victims from Posen and Galicia. The local traffic in young girls, as I have already explained, has now been largely broken up; the European police, responding to the quick and vigorous development of humane interest characteristic of recent years, have taken steps which practically deprive the bordell of youth,— its most attractive asset. Girls under 21 are as a rule no longer permitted to become inmates; at Budapest even the bordell servant must have reached the age of forty. The mistress whose memory goes back to a less scrupulous era is in no doubt as to the main causes of the hard times on which her lot has now fallen: " Something young and fresh is nowadays no longer to be had," [44] remarked the candid madame of a Budapest bordell.

An outside proof that the bordell is necessarily associated with trafficking in girls may not be amiss in this connection. The trafficker, avoiding the aroused continental police, seeks a remote and less perilous market. The great European cities, in which he can no longer carry on with impunity a trade in young or innocent girls, can at the most be utilized as way stations on the journey to Rio Janeiro or Buenos Aires; in the latter city, 192 well-known bordells, with 1,022 inmates of different nationalities, are found; 95 of them Russian establishments with 532 girls, 17 Italian establishments with 92

[44] " Etwas junges und frisches ist überhaupt nicht zu kriegen."

Prostitution in Europe

inmates, 22 French houses with 136 girls.[45]   The victims whose obscure trail is traceable from Galicia through Vienna and Berlin to Hamburg, Rotterdam, or London, are nowadays discovered in the brothels of a South American city, instead of in those of Hamburg, Brussels, or Paris.

Meanwhile, though the European bordell can no longer be recruited with the young, the trafficker's business has not been completely stamped out; nor can it be until the last recognized bordell is exterminated.   The reduced scope within which madame and trafficker operate makes it all the more important to do the best possible under the circumstances,— to make as attractive a showing as possible and to keep the women moving: hence, redoubled efforts to fill orders for women of the various types required by the different establishments and to conduct a chain of houses so that a certain amount of novelty can be introduced into the trade.   An inspection of police records discloses the fact that women remain on the average only a few weeks in a given house. Through the 13 bordells of Teplitz-Schönau, Bohemia, between January 1, 1909 and July 30, 1910, 550 inmates passed: one of the bordells, operating with two girls, had 65 different inmates during this period of 18 months.[46] In the Zurich bordells, 85% of the inmates changed within 5 months, 63% within 2 months.[47]   In the white slave bureau of one large European police establishment, I was shown a huge list of persons suspected or already convicted of trafficking in girls.   The traffic in youth has

---

[45] For these figures I am indebted to official courtesy.
[46] Meher, *loc. cit.*, p. 150.
[47] *Prostitutionsfrage in der Schweiz*, p. 11.

been hampered; but a traffic in women still remains — a traffic which, though it will not restore prosperity to the bordell, is absolutely dependent for its existence on the prolonged life of the house of prostitution. I have repeatedly quoted with respect the words of Dr. Baumgarten of Vienna; on this point, his opinion is absolutely unmistakable: "The bordell is inseparable from the traffic in girls," he declared to me. Bloch's investigations are tersely summarized: "Without bordells, no white slave traffic." [48]

A notorious instance of the manner in which alone a bordell can be successfully conducted is furnished by the so-called "Riehl case" uncovered in Vienna in 1906. The woman conducted an establishment containing 20 girls and paid an annual rental of 10,000 kronen ($2,000). A large number of persons were employed to procure recruits,— old women and young boys, offering good places in domestic service to young girls who, having come to Vienna, found difficulty in securing work. Employment agencies directed to Madame ·Riehl young and friendless applicants. Suspicion was never aroused in the victim's mind, for the door bore a plate marked "Riehl's Dressmaking Salon." The behavior of the madame varied: now, she made no concealment of the nature of her business; again, she hired the newcomer as a servant, certain that before long she would yield to the demoralization of the place. Minors were registered at police headquarters as of full age, or forged documents testified to the consent of the parents or guardians. The girls lived as prisoners, so cowed by the treatment they

[48] "*Ohne Bordelle, kein Mädchenhandel.*" Bloch, *Sexualleben*, p. 377.

received and so utterly demoralized by their way of life that they made no effort to recover their freedom even if opportunity offered.[49]

The conscience of those authorities who are still willing to tolerate bordells, provided girls are not involuntarily forced into them, has revolted on another point, viz., the exploitation of the women by the keepers. For the bordell is a business. Though theoretically only a convenient place for the gratification of uncontrollable desire, it is practically an establishment so conducted as to fill the pockets of the owners, the inmates being forced to receive the maximum number of guests that can be obtained, after which they are victimized out of their earnings on every conceivable pretext.[50]

Recent alterations in the police regulations seek to protect the bordell women against exploitation; but no amount of menace or oversight suffices to procure the enforcement of the simplest precautionary regulations. One of the most disgusting aspects of bordell life is the forced consumption of alcohol; the customer on entering is plied with drink, and of course the inmates share; conviviality is procured by general and continuous indulgence in beer, wine, and champagne. In order to prevent complete physical disorganization on the part of the women and to restrict the commerce in volume, the sale or use of liquor is forbidden in the bordells of Brussels, Altona, Hamburg, Stuttgart, Bremen, and other cities. But it goes on openly and flagrantly, nevertheless. An Al-

[49] Schneider, loc. cit., pp. 171-2.
[50] See p. 257. For a detailed account of the exploitation of inmates in Paris, see Fiaux, Les Maisons de Tolérance (Third Edition, Paris, 1896) Chapter VII.

Regulation and Order — Bordells

tona madame candidly admitted to me the reason: "The business couldn't be carried on otherwise." [51] In the bordells of Stockholm, champagne costing 2½ crowns a bottle is sold to guests for 15 and the "girls are made to aid in the consumption as much as possible, so as to increase the profits." [52]

The fact is that if the police wish or are willing to maintain bordells, they cannot refuse to tolerate some of the conditions on which alone it is worth while for the keepers to conduct them. In Vienna, Budapest, Dresden, and elsewhere, minute specifications attempt to regulate the charges which may be levied on the girls by the keepers. But the girl is completely exploited nevertheless: for exorbitant prices are charged for necessities, and extras — forbidden or not — usually swallow the remainder. In the most wretched establishments of Altona, the minimum charge for board and lodging is reckoned at 75 marks a week; at Stockholm, a girl pays 5 crowns a day for board,— and various sums for "extras,"— an "unreasonable sum," [53] in Johansson's judgment. The Dresden police name 8 to 15 marks a day — the latter sum itself enough to procure accommodations at a first-rate hotel; the girl is actually charged 15 to 18, and if anything is left to her credit it is absorbed by way of paying for cosmetics, clothes, shoes, etc. The kind landlady is the intermediary between girls and merchants in a series of transactions which somehow always leave the girls penniless and amply reimburse the landlady for her intervention. Frau Scheven related to me the story

[51] "Ohne Trinken ging es nicht."
[52] Linblad in *Report, Swedish Commission*, Vol. III, p. 65.
[53] *Report, Swedish Commission*, Vol. III, p. 176.

of a young girl for whom she had procured admission to
a hospital, where in the course of her recovery the girl
decided to abandon her licentious life. When her bene-
factress applied to the bordell for her clothes, she was informed that there were none; and only threats of calling
the police extorted a few meager rags — the sole asset
after months of service, despite the minute prescriptions
of the authorities, aiming to check the rapacity of the
keepers.

At Vienna a more serious effort in this direction is
now made. A periodical survey by the ranking officials
of the morals bureau is required,— the director himself as a rule being one of the party. I possess tran-
scripts of two reports made on a Vienna bordell. The in-
specting party included the division chief, the head of the
medical service, and one or two others of lower rank.
The roll was called and every inmate accounted for;
thereupon the inmates were separately interviewed, especially with a view to ascertaining whether their personal freedom had been interfered with or whether they
had complaints to make in respect to exploitation. On
the first inspection, the women unanimously declared and
proved, that despite the prospect of this official review,
they had been swindled out of all their earnings, even
including such incidental gratuities as they had received
from visitors; that their food was inedible, and that bed-
linen was changed only once a month. The authorities
thereupon threatened the closing of the establishment unless conditions were at once improved. Revised regulations became effective before the next inspection, at which
time it appeared that each inmate paid something over

Regulation and Order — Bordells

five dollars a day for board and lodging (26 kronen), beyond which their earnings belonged to them; the earnings of the preceding night ran from $10 (50 kronen) to $30 (150 kronen) apiece. The food had improved in quality, but the condition of the linen and towels still left much to be desired. Three of the inmates were badly bruised. The keeper was again warned that sanitary conditions must be improved. To hinder the crassest exploitation and to secure the most elemental cleanliness, the highest officials,— physicians and jurists of university training — had to make a personal inspection; even then, 6 brothels, containing from 50 to 60 women, could not be kept entirely acceptable. Were brothels more numerous in Vienna, it would be absolutely impossible to utilize officers of high rank and spotless personal and professional character for this sordid duty; if delegated to others, a source of corruption and abuse would be created. Hence, though rules against exploitation and in favor of decency are promulgated, successful efforts to enforce them are practically nowhere encountered.

Though its heyday is over, the bordell can, however, still be made to pay, if the authorities are disposed to condone exploitation. At the bare suggestion that a new bordell street would be created in Frankfort, 15 houses in the proposed street were promptly bought up at extravagant prices;[54] the houses in Helenenstrasse, Bremen, valued at 327,000 marks, cost their present owner 585,-000 marks;[55] a tumbledown medieval hovel, long util-

[54] *Kritische Tribüne, loc. cit.*, p. 114.
[55] Schneider, *loc. cit.*, p. 168.

ized as a bordell in Stuttgart, was recently sold for 60,-
000 marks to a "dummy" purchaser. Shortly after
the transaction, the police, heeding neighborhood complaints, decreed the closing of the establishment; whereupon they were bitterly reproached for summary violation of an implied contract.[56] Paris transactions are
naturally on a far higher scale: 200,000 and 300,000
francs have changed hands for a single business.[57] Another establishment earned 70,000 francs for its owners
in a single year. Like all profitable enterprise in this
generation, efficiency and economy have been still more
highly developed through organization; of 31 immoral resorts " situated in the zone of the Champs-Elysées, near
the Arc, the majority belong to the same managers." [58]

Fortunately other causes conspire with the suppression of the white slave traffic and increased control over
the internal management of the bordell to bring about its
decline. Taste has changed. "The public has lost its
appetite for officially designated resorts, with their large
numbers, closed shutters, colored windows, visited nowadays usually by strangers, provincials, and soldiers; the
trade inclines rather to houses of rendezvous, where
greater discretion is practised and where, with a little
imagination, one is conscious of an air of adventure." [59]
The women, too, are filled with the desire to enjoy their
own freedom. They prefer the reckless abandon of the

[56] " The renter of these buildings charges the inscribed prostitute 8 to 10 marks a day for a room so that the owner gets from
each inmate something like 4,000 marks a year." Bendig in
Zeitschrift XII, pp. 11, 12. (Abridged.)
[57] *Annexes, loc. cit.,* pp. 424-5. See also Fiaux, *Police des
Moeurs,* I, 213-217.
[58] Fiaux, *Ibid,* p. 220.
[59] Lépine in *Annexes, loc. cit.,* p. 21.

Regulation and Order — Bordells

streets, the cafés, and the theaters. Under these circumstances, the girls who are still found in bordells are as a rule the failures and the wrecks, with too little spirit or attractiveness to make an independent success.

In accounting for the decline of the bordell, I have inevitably touched on the objections to be urged against its further tolerance. The European bordell has in the first place declined because its recruitment through young victims has been largely broken up, and because the most flagrant forms of exploitation no longer prevail entirely unhindered. But other equally good reasons for the suppression of the bordell may be cited. The bordell is a veritable school of abnormality. The Paris bordells are elaborately equipped for every conceivable form of perverse indulgence. The inmates compete with one another in forcing upon the youthful customer the knowledge of unnatural and artificial forms of sexual gratification.[60] Similar excesses are practised elsewhere,— indeed wherever the bordell is found. The Swedish women told Dr. Lindblad that " the girl-house is the main seat of perversity; soon," they added, " Stockholm will be as bad as Paris."[61] The infamous implements employed are in full view as one enters the apartments in Helenenstrasse. The degradation of the bordell inmate is total;[62] her rehabilitation well-nigh impossible. She fares far worse than the street-walker, who sometimes returns to an orderly manner of life.

Finally, cautious as the keeper may be not to deserve

[60] See Fiaux *Maisons de Tolérance,* Chapter X, etc.
[61] *Report, Swedish Commission, III,* p. 66.
[62] See Meunier's detailed account in *Annexes, loc. cit.,* pp. 420, etc.

the suspicion of the police, the bordells, especially those of lower grade, are everywhere in close touch with certain classes of criminals. Between the lowest class of criminals and the corresponding class of prostitutes intimate relations subsist.[63] To the low class resort the law-breaker betakes himself; there the outlaw receives sympathy and shelter. It is occasionally alleged that the reverse is true: that the bordell keepers turn the law-breaker over to the police, assisting the authorities in discovering criminals. But the Dutch police, who have tried and discarded the bordell system and who, like other police with the same experience, would under no conditions countenance its reintroduction, are of a different mind. "Did the bordell keepers assist you in the detection of criminals?" I asked. "Oh, yes," was the reply, "after they realized that we already knew."

So much for the inner side of the bordell; it remains to inquire into its influence on external order.

It is claimed that the bordell, by providing an ascertainable, if not well known, resort for immoral women and their customers removes scandal and suggestion from the public highways. Let us consider the argument in the light of the table already given. The bordell can at most interfere with the promenading and soliciting of the women interned in it; it cannot reduce the prominence of non-inscribed women, or of inscribed women living at large and expressly authorized by the police to walk all but a few streets. The existence of 47 bordells, with 387 inmates, in Paris does not interfere with

[63] See Moll, *loc. cit.*, p. 366: Ostwald, *Schlupfwinkel der Prostitution* in *Das Berliner Dirnentum*, Vol. II.

Regulation and Order — Bordells

the promenading of perhaps 50,000 unregistered prostitutes or of 6,000 registered, but scattered, prostitutes;
the existence at Brussels of six brothels, with 37 inmates,
does not restrain 145 other registered prostitutes, resident elsewhere, nor the several thousand non-registered
women who live where they please.   The facts thus show
that the pressure on the streets is nowhere relieved by the
herding of a few women — and the herding of more
is impracticable.   Between Paris and Berlin there is no
difference observable: the former has bordells, the latter
lacks them.   The streets of Hamburg with bordells
are no better than those of Rotterdam without them,
and are distinctly inferior to those of Liverpool and
Amsterdam, both without them.   Zurich without bordells is externally much more orderly than Geneva
with them.   If the bordell played any part in the maintenance of decent street conditions, cities like Berlin,
Munich, and Zurich — where there are no bordells —
would be worse off than Paris, Hamburg, or Stuttgart;
or the former would require some extraordinary agency
not needed where bordells exist; as a matter of fact,
the cities in question are not worse and they neither require nor possess any unusual machinery.

What can be more clearly decisive on this point than
the fact that just at the time of my visit to Geneva, the
chief of the department of justice and police, in consequence of " frequent complaints, named a special committee charged with the duty of devising means to put
an end " [64] to the sort of vagabondage we are consider-

[64] *Tribune de Genève*, March 30, 1912.   See also A. Guillot, *La
Lutte contre l'Exploitation et la Règlementation du Vice à Genève*
(Geneva, 1899) pp. 138–9.

Prostitution in Europe

ing? As a matter of fact, coincidentally with the gradual extinction of the bordell, general street conditions have improved throughout Europe; and the few towns whose streets are strikingly free from prostitutes are without exception towns in which neither regulation nor the bordell exists. The bordell is not the controlling factor; police, courts, public opinion. decide; and police, courts, and public opinion are likely to be most vigorously in favor of clean streets in communities that do not recognize prostitution as a legitimate livelihood.

But, more: the bordell does not necessarily or usually remove its own inmates from the streets! The women cannot be caged; current tendency is in just the reverse direction. The Budapest authorities, for example, regard with horror the " inhumanity " of the Bremen restrictions. Bordell women are becoming more and more free to come and go as they please; on other terms they are increasingly reluctant to enter the bordell at all. Moreover, when business lags — as indeed it tends to do — they go forth to find patrons on the streets,— for grist must be provided for the ever active mill. At Dresden, the courteous official who escorted me through the bordells, explained that it would be useless to start on our round of visits before midnight,— for the women would all be " out." I walked through several of the 32 streets on which bordells exist in the earlier hours of the evening; from some houses the inmates were just emerging in striking costumes, to others women were already returning, accompanied by the prey picked up on the streets, in the cafés, and elsewhere. The bordell does not, therefore, reduce street scandal even to the extent of the number of its inmates.

Meanwhile, though the bordell does not relieve the general thoroughfares, it tends strongly to local scandal and disorder in its own quarter. The eight bordell streets of Hamburg lie for the most part close to busy streets in the heart of the city. Except in the forenoon, when the women are sleeping off the dissipation of the previous night, shocking scenes are observed. The pedestrian who in the afternoon inadvertently stumbles into the Schwiegergasse is greeted from window, vestibule, and doorstep by a volley of invitations; scantily clad women solicit his attention from the street door in broad daylight. The dark narrow passages in Cologne, notorious for brothels, are filled with a procession of reckless boys and half-intoxicated men on the verge of surrender to temptation. A beating rain did not empty the bordell streets of Altona, or drive indoors the lightly clad women who called out the superior attractions of their competing establishments; at Bremen, in the summer evening, the interned women forbidden to solicit on the street, approached all passersby and endeavored in every imaginable way to entice them into their barracks,—"just for a glass of beer," if nothing else. A recent writer, describing conditions in Frankfort, remarks that "the presence of the policeman does not hinder even unmistakable and utterly shameless prostitution of minors in the Rosengasse and Metzgergasse," [65]— two of the streets in which bordells are found. In a few instances only,— Budapest and

[65] *Mitteilungen, etc.,* X, 5 p. 96.

Prostitution in Europe

Rome, for example, I encountered no street disorder in the vicinity of recognized houses of prostitution.

From the preceding account, it is clear that the case for regulation on the side of public order is not strengthened by the bordell. Not infrequently, however, it is argued that, whatever be the situation in inland towns, the seaport has reasons of its own for requiring the existence of bordells; without it, drunken sailors of many nationalities will throng the highways, insulting women and imperilling children. This kind of argument is not new; I was told by a high official in Paris that no woman was safe from insult in the streets of Zurich, now that the bordells had been suppressed. Both statements are equally without basis. Rotterdam is well-nigh as important a seaport as Hamburg; its streets suffer nothing by comparison; the streets of Liverpool are at the moment the cleanest of all. Once more, the bordell is, to say the best for it, immaterial.

Nor can it even be claimed for the bordell that it lessens other forms of prostitution. Side by side with it flourish the " Animierkneipe," advertising " weekly change of service," the cabaret, dance hall, café, cheap lodging-house, the concealed bordell, the *rendezvous,* the *maison de passe,*— all engaged, as the bordell is engaged, not in satisfying normal desire, but in arousing, inflaming, and perverting lust, while at the same time thrusting upon the victim's attention accessible means for its gratification. Rome possesses besides 20-odd authorized bordells, 235 — perhaps more — unauthorized houses of prostitution, well known to the police. I was escorted by an officer to houses of both types and observed no difference beyond a somewhat greater nervousness on the part of the keepers of the latter; Geneva abounds in irregular lodging-houses and *maisons de passe*, lists of which have been even furnished by anti-regulationists to the police, without result; Amsterdam reports that it had more clandestine brothels during the time when bordells were licensed than are to be found now that they have been suppressed. At Paris, with bordells — as in London, without them — every imaginable subterfuge is employed in the effort to carry on surreptitious prostitution: chambers are advertised, foreign language lessons announced, art objects, pearls, dressmaking, massage, bibelots employed as baits for the curious.[66] The bordell does not really affect this situation at all.

Discovering, however, that bordell prostitution is disappearing, the police of Paris and Budapest are endeavoring to maintain their grip by authorizing or permitting *rendezvous* establishments. At Paris, these establishments may be opened without police permit and will not be disturbed as long as they comply with a few simple police orders, e. g., admitting only inscribed women or at least women regularly examined by a physician agreeable to the police.[67] They have increased in number from 64, with 235 women regularly in attendance, in 1900, to 243, with 770 women attached, in 1908.[68] A somewhat similar policy is pursued in Budapest, where

[66] See, for example, *Annexes, loc. cit.,* pp. 433–435.
[67] A detailed account of the terms is given by M. Lépine in *Annexes loc. cit.* pp. 22–24. M. Paul Meunier (*Ibid,* 428–430) discusses these houses and gives particulars concerning a raid on one of them in which he himself took part.
[68] Fiaux, *Police des Moeurs,* III, p. 664.

the police tolerate without interference the " hotel garni " with 20 to 50 rooms, which admits only inscribed women on showing their certificates, sells no alcoholic beverages, provides every room with water, towels, etc., and allows no guest to remain longer than twelve hours; these hotels are regularly visited and inspected by the authorities. Similarly, the *maison de passe* is recognized,— usually an apartment of five to eight rooms, where towards six in the evening one finds 5 to 10 girls seated around the dining-room table, sewing or rouging while waiting for customers to drop in. But these substitutes for the bordell are as futile as the bordell itself; police recognition of authorized places of *rendezvous* does not diminish in any wise the number of hotels surreptitiously utilized for the same purpose. In Budapest, despite the vigorous police policy, there are as many unauthorized hotels engaged in the business as there have ever been; and Paris is notorious for the abundance of uncontrolled resorts. The explanation is easy. Neither the girl nor her customer desires to submit to the stigma and notoriety involved in resorting to an authorized house of any kind; the same motive that leads them to avoid the bordell leads them to evade the authorized *rendezvous*. In any event, only controlled women can resort to a controlled establishment; uncontrolled establishments continue to command the trade of non-inscribed women,— who always and everywhere enormously preponderate.

Could the futility and impossibility of regulation be more clearly exhibited? The police of Paris, Budapest, and Vienna offer the woman every facility for the easy and unimpeded prosecution of her trade, provided only

Regulation and Order — Bordells

she will submit to inscription: bordells, if she pleases; a private lodging, if she prefers; or, if neither of these is agreeable, hotels discreetly conducted in accessible localities, where the police will never trouble her or her customers. In return, the authorities ask only that she register her name, nominally submit to a few restrictions, and undergo medical examination at intervals. Yet not even on these favorable terms can a considerable body of women be induced to submit. Meanwhile, whatever may be said for the bordell as a possible way of removing prostitutes from the street, the *rendezvous* house, now cultivated to take its place, operates in the directly contrary fashion; for the couples resorting to it generally meet and strike their bargains in the streets.

There is perhaps another point of view from which the bordell must be considered. Whatever opinion one may form as to the ultimate fate of prostitution in civilized society, unquestionably it must, like certain other social evils, be reckoned with as a phenomenon to be dealt with as part of the day's work. I have pointed out that European opinion is moving towards the conclusion that, for the present, third party exploitation, overt and offensive manifestation, are aspects with which our social and governmental instrumentalities are most likely to cope effectively. The pimp, the bordell keeper, the prostitute herself — when her conduct scandalizes — with these the ordinary resources of a well-managed municipality are increasingly competent to deal. Clearly, however, we are thus left with the prostitute herself on our hands,— with the prostitute, I mean, who is vicious, not criminal, leading her own life, reprehensible of course, but without unnecessary offence to others. In reference to this type of woman — the type, in other words, that survives even a successful war on third parties — the first question that arises is this: where shall she live? For even the inconspicuous and well-behaved prostitute is a peril, inasmuch as she is a constant and inevitable source of moral contagion,— particularly objectionable, of course, in close contact with children and working-girls. The bordell represents one effort to solve the domicile problem, by isolation, just as infectious disease is isolated. The analogy to disease fails, however, for two reasons: first, because isolation is usually resisted by the prostitute; second, because the prominence that vice obtains through bordells — be they many or few — far outweighs any good attainable through the forced isolation of those who can be interned. Other positive efforts to regulate the domicile of the prostitute have also been made,— so far, without success. The German law, as I have already stated, forbids the professional prostitute any lodging at all; but the law has broken down, first, because the vagrant prostitute is most objectionable of all; second, because the statute is enforced only in flagrant cases of abuse; third, because it is in conflict with the regulation system in common use.

Budapest approaches the problem differently. There bordells house a fair number; the rest are free to live where they please, provided they give no offence. Authorized places of *rendezvous* are provided as above stated, in the hope that women will thus be induced to transact business elsewhere than in their homes. In the

event, however, that a woman persists in bringing customers to her apartment, decent tenants are in position
to protect themselves through the following enactment:
" Any tenant has the right to forbid a prostitute to continue to occupy rooms in the house where he lives, if,
before he himself moved in, he was not told that prostitutes live in the same house; should prostitutes move in
subsequently, the tenant may dislodge them by complain-
ing to the police. No tenant need endure the presence
of prostitutes in the building where he resides; no tenant
can be obligated to remain in a house where prostitutes
live unless he knew the fact when he made his lease.
The landlord is obligated to tell prospective tenants the
truth without being asked. If the landlord on the tenant's demand does not evict a prostitute, the tenant may
break the lease and demand damages. These provisions
apply also to apartments used for *rendezvous.*" [69]

How far this excellent law has affected the situation it
is difficult to tell. Its enforcement against non-registered women is difficult, to say the least. Besides, the
poor can easily be quieted by favors or concessions. I
was therefore not surprised to see children playing in
the courtyard and on the steps of houses in Budapest
to which prostitutes could be observed to be returning
in the company of men; prominent *rendezvous* apartments were visited in large buildings tenanted mainly
by families of the working-class. Neither regulation in
general nor the bordell in particular has thus succeeded
in solving the dwelling problem. This has been frankly
recognized in the revised Vienna regulations which aban-

[69] *Dwelling and Rent Statute,* Section 6.

don all effort to deal with the question; paragraph 12, previously quoted, enjoining the least possible interference with the free choice of a dwelling place on the part of a prostitute who lives alone.[70]

I have throughout this chapter considered the bordell mainly as a factor in the program of regulation. It is from the standpoint of order evidently futile. But from another standpoint it is worse than futile. The bordell gives to sexual vice its most prominent advertisement. By working on the curiosity of the young and of strangers — its main patrons, by the way — it substantially increases demand; by requiring constant service of its inmates, it virtually increases supply. It is therefore absolutely at war with sound public policy which aims to reduce both — certainly to avoid their gratuitous increase. Finally, the bordell is the most flagrant instance of exploitation for the benefit of third parties, which modern feeling and legislation are emphatically determined to prevent. For the keeper's profit men waste their sub-

---

[70] The only exhaustive statistical study of the living problem that I found is that made by Johansson for the Swedish Commission (*Report*, Vol III, pp. 175, etc.) and this deals only with the registered women, relatively few in number. Johansson divides the 400 inscribed women of Stockholm into 5 groups as follows:

I	Living in lodgings where they receive customers	16
II	Living in girl-houses	98
III	Living in families and utilizing hotels	232
IV	Living in suburbs and utilizing hotels	23
V	Vagrants	31

Of course a girl does not permanently belong to any one group, but may vary from time to time. Group III is most important. At the close of 1904, the police had listed 34 hotels with 405 rooms, utilized by these women. He states that the hotel is conducted "like a factory," the women being practically in the employ of the proprietors. That is, the enrolled women are operated for third-party profit; less than 4% of them work for themselves.

stance and are — to what extent the ensuing chapter will tell — infected with disease; while women are dragged down to the lowest depths of degradation and excess. The bordell is therefore something more than futile, something more than inhuman.[71]

---

[71] It is often said that this opinion is held only by sentimentalists and religious persons. As a matter of fact, it is the conclusion of police officers all over the Continent, many of whom are still administering the system. Prominent among these is Baumgarten of Vienna, for whose views see *Zeitschrift* IX, pp. 183–4. The literature attacking the bordell in a strictly scientific spirit is enormous. See Bloch, *Sexualleben.* Index, *"Bordelle."* For a view favorable to the bordell, see G. Roscher, *Gross-Stadtpolizei* (Hamburg, 1912) pp. 257–8. Dr. Roscher is the able and accomplished head of the Hamburg police.

CHAPTER VII

REGULATION AND DISEASE

Regulation nowadays concerned chiefly with sanitation.— Variety of methods employed.— Berlin system.— Equipment and procedure. — Equipment in Paris, Vienna, Brussels, etc.— Quality of medical inspection in Berlin,— in Budapest,— in other cities,— in Paris.— Effect of medical inspection on male indulgence.— Peculiar characteristics of syphilis,— of gonorrhœa.— Amount of disease detected among inscribed women.— Clinical methods inaccurate.—Deceptions practised.— Flux in inspected body.— Failures to report.— Periods of hospital detention brief.— Minors, usually non-inscribed, most infectious.—Inspection and disease among clandestines.—System conceded to have accomplished nothing hitherto.— Its possibilities remain to be proved.— No basis for favorable expectation.— Insuperable difficulties in the way of successful medical regulation. —Does isolation of even a small number of infected women achieve some good?— Amount of disease depends on amount of irregular intercourse.— The bordell and disease.— Absurdity of linking disease and crime.— System illogical and inequitable.

THE preceding chapters have presumably shown that regulation is not necessary to the maintenance of public order; indeed, even the pretense that it is needed for that purpose is now in a fair way to be generally discarded. As I have pointed out, the traveler is rarely aware of differences in external conditions that suggest different police methods of restraining or controlling prostitution. Prostitution may be described as perhaps equally prominent in Berlin and London,— one a regulated, the other a non-regulated city. Regulation is therefore not a factor that, from this point of view, needs to be taken into ac-

count. Moreover, as we shall see later, the few cities
in which the underworld is distinctly inconspicuous are
without regulation. For the rest, cities long without
regulation and cities that have recently dispensed with it
are at least as quiet as those that still adhere to it; nay
more, to find a really disorderly section one must resort
to the bordell quarters of regulated towns. As far as
order goes, therefore, it is impossible to make out a case
favorable to regulation.

As the argument in behalf of regulation on the score of
public decency loses force, the maintenance of the system
depends more and more on the assertion of its sanitary efficacy; and on this aspect increasing emphasis is laid. A
prominent official of the Berlin morals police, tracing the
history of the institution for me, remarked: "The
historical function of .the *Sittenpolizei* was to deal with
decency; but under present conditions the sanitary object has come to the fore. The morals police could be
dispensed with, if only their original business were in
question. They should certainly now be called the
health police." The recent reconstruction of the Vienna
system was undertaken in execution of just such a program: " Conversion of the morals police control into
a sanitary control, and its extension as far as possible
over clandestine prostitution." [1] The main effort to save
regulation through readjustment to modern knowledge
has thus been made on the sanitary side. In the present
chapter I shall endeavor to describe regulation as a sani-

---

[1] Finger and Baumgarten, *Referat*, p. 82. It must be noted, however, that this health function is lodged with the police, not the
health authorities,— a fact which will be explained in the next
chapter.

tary policy and to determine what it achieves in that direction.

The diversity previously commented on in connection with regulation prevails also in respect to its sanitary details. Between the worst and the best organized systems on the medical side, there is perhaps an even greater discrepancy than between the worst and the best systems on the side of police methods. Thus far experience has worked out no accepted sanitary model. Important variations will be noted in reference to the method of inspection, its quality, its frequency, the disposition made of disease when discovered, the payment of physicians, and the extent to which free choice of physicians is still allowed.[2]

Berlin, where the bureau has been completely reorganized in recent years, may serve as a point of departure. Women under control are required to report to police headquarters for examination twice weekly, if under 24 years of age; once a week, if between 24 and 34 years of age; and fortnightly, if over 34. In addition, the inscribed or controlled prostitute is re-examined whenever arrested for any offence, regardless of the date of her last or her next regular examination.[3] Clandestine prostitutes may be subjected to compulsory examination at the discretion of the bureau chief,— the examination being conducted by a woman physician attached to the division for this purpose.[4] By special re-

[2] In respect to the last two items, a tendency towards a uniform policy is discernible.
[3] Inscribed women are examined by men physicians.
[4] That is, non-inscribed prostitutes. As previously pointed out, "clandestine" prostitutes may be just as notorious as inscribed ones.

quest, an examination by an approved private physician may be substituted. In either event, the woman is herself at no expense for the examination.

A staff of eight police physicians and four microscopists are occupied with medical inspection, of whom four are on duty at one time; the work goes on daily, except Sunday,[5] from nine to twelve o'clock and from twelve to three. The examination consists of a clinical inspection and the use of the speculum. For the detection of gonorrhœa, microscopic examinations of the secretions are made fortnightly in case of women under 34; monthly, in case of older women. At any time, however, when appearances are suspicious, the physician is instructed to ask for a microscopic examination without waiting for the regular day. Female assistants are provided for this work; the word of the assistant is sufficient in case the microscopic preparation is found to be negative; the physician must by his own observation confirm a positive result. The medical policy of the police department is directed by a physician who holds the rank of commissary,— the sole instance in all Europe of expert medical control of what is admittedly a sanitary matter.[6]

Inscribed women discovered to be infected are confined under duress in a municipal hospital, on the theory that, being professional prostitutes, who can maintain themselves only by plying their business, they must be in-

---

[5] Inscribed prostitutes who also hold positions or who are on probation looking to release from the rolls may by special arrangement come on Sunday for examination.

[6] The present incumbent is Dr. Med. Georg Güth, Kriminalkommissar und medizinizch-technischer Dezernent in der Verwaltung der Berliner Sittenpolizei.

terned in order that the carrying on of their business may be temporarily suspended. In very rare cases, however, even when found to be diseased, they are permitted to retain their freedom provided an approved physician makes himself responsible for their systematic treatment, and provided, further, that there is reliable evidence to show the possession of resources which will enable the women in question to keep their engagement to refrain from plying their vocation for the time being. Women are also at times released from the hospital on condition that they report at intervals for further treatment; should this understanding be violated, they are once more interned.

Clandestine and occasional prostitutes if found diseased on being arrested are somewhat differently managed. If without resources, they are sent to the hospital; but the bureau chief may, in his discretion, permit them to remain at large on condition that they place themselves in charge of a competent physician. It is, however, admitted that pledges, whether given by clandestine or registered women, are not to be relied on.

At both hospital and police headquarters in Berlin conscientious and intelligent efforts have been made to provide satisfactory arrangements. Registered and non-registered women are scrupulously separated at every stage, on the ground that the latter group may contain young, innocent or, at least, not yet hardened persons, who should not be further contaminated by the carelessness of the state. Premises not adapted to this end have, therefore, been extensively remodeled. The rooms utilized for the medical examinations at the police headquarters are light and equipped with a modern examining-chair, hot and cold water, and electric light; the microscopic-room has the necessary equipment for clean and accurate work.[7] The hospital, though old and small, has been latterly renovated and its staff reorganized. The present medical chief of the police division in charge of venereal disease is a specialist of distinction, who has made important contributions to the literature of the subject on both medical and sociological sides. The division possesses an excellent laboratory manned with trained assistants; and it is properly equipped with microscopes, culture-ovens, animals for experimental purposes, etc. Patients are examined separately in a clean, well-lighted room, containing all necessary paraphernalia. Women at different stages of demoralization,— registered, non-registered, first offenders,— are scrupulously kept apart; clean and orderly as the women are in appearance, there is nothing in their demeanor or surroundings to suggest prison confinement.[8]

In many other towns, two examinations per week for the youngest class of inscribed prostitutes are also required; but by no means everywhere. In Paris, for example, women in bordells are examined weekly, those at large at least fortnightly; in Dresden examinations take place once a week. In Hamburg, women under " light control " are examined only once a month, and even for this examination a certificate from a private physician

---

[7] Güth, *loc. cit.*, p. 13, gives details of equipment.

[8] The preceding account is based on personal inspection and interviews, on the leaflet issued by the bureau, entitled " *Dienstanweisung für die bei der Sittenpolizei beschäftigten Aerzte,*" and on Penzig's " *Die Bekämpfung der Gewerbsunzucht durch die Sittenpolizei,*" previously referred to.

may be substituted; the same is true in Cologne, where enrolled women discovered to be diseased are permitted to obtain treatment privately, provided they keep the police informed of their progress.[9]   At Stockholm most women report twice a week; some thirty older women, once a week.

Examination and treatment are not always free.   Dresden requires every inscribed woman to contribute to a sick insurance fund, paying four marks as initiation fee, and two and a half marks weekly dues; she is thereby entitled to 13 weeks' hospital care if ill.[10]   A sick fund, out of which the cost of the weekly examination is also paid, is similarly supported in Hamburg; in Bremen, the women bear the expense of the medical inspection; Brussels permits examination to take place in the rooms of the women on payment of five francs monthly; Stockholm allows a woman to appear for examination privately on payment of a crown; at Stuttgart, the examination is free at police headquarters, paid for, if at home; in Geneva, the girls pay two francs for each examination; in Rome the bordell stands the expense, and also, subject to the approval of the health authorities, selects the physician.   In Vienna, girls were formerly required to pay one crown if examined at headquarters, two crowns if examined in their rooms; but since January 1912, a system of free examination has been gradually introduced.   It is universally conceded that abuses creep in wherever the physician derives his income in whole or in part from the women or the bordells.

[9] This was the practice at Budapest also, until the regulations were reformed in 1908.
[10] Schneider, *loc. cit.*, p. 21, gives additional instances.

Regulation and Disease

Much greater and more significant diversity exists in respect to the equipment of the examining-rooms at police headquarters and the method of conducting the examinations. Facilities as good as those of Berlin exist only in Dresden, Bremen and Budapest. In the last named city, twenty-two physicians, eight of whom come daily, are employed. Unlike Vienna, where a physician usually examines the same woman from week to week, the women are purposely sent to different physicians for successive examinations,— a policy adopted in order the better to prevent deceit, bargaining, etc. A bacteriologist is on hand to make microscopic tests in suspicious cases.

In all other cities the appointments are meager and antiquated, conducing to mistaken diagnosis, on the part of even honest physicians, and to fraud, on the part of the women. In Paris, for example, bordell women are examined in their own quarters, where no facilities for good work can possibly exist, where imposition is easily practised by the women, and where the environment is apt to interfere with the seriousness of the occasion. Examinations so conducted need not be seriously discussed. Inscribed Parisian prostitutes living at large and non-inscribed women who are arrested, are examined at police headquarters, where the equipment consists of two rude chairs, an ancient sterilizer in which a few specula are boiling, and a glass of sterilized water in which the spatulæ used in holding down the tongue are hastily dipped from time to time. Arrested women — whether registered, clandestines, or mere suspects — are huddled indiscriminately with all other varieties of female of-

fenders, into a dark and ill-ventilated " dépôt," not in-
aptly called the " human pound."

In Vienna, as in Paris, the medical examination is
still conducted either at headquarters or at the dwellings
of the women, though the tendency is in the direction of
concentrating work at the former. The Viennese accommodations and facilities are distinctly better than
those of Paris, even though the establishment does not
yet boast a microscope. At Hamburg, girls arrested are
clinically examined at headquarters; inscribed women are
examined in the bordells,— a convenient bordell being
selected in each neighborhood,— but beyond a deal table,
and the spoon and speculum which each girl brings, no
equipment whatever is provided.

Elsewhere facilities answer the same general description. In Brussels a plain table is carried into the reception room of the bordell. Rome is no better; in one
establishment, on asking to see the facilities for medical
examination, I was shown a filthy old metal table and
a few dirty basins; in another, a tattered leather chair;
in a third, a small table.

Of hospitals provided for the reception of diseased
women, Budapest possesses perhaps the best that I visited anywhere; the service contains three hundred beds,
excellent laboratories, operating and treatment rooms of
the most modern pattern. Cologne provides a satisfactory, renovated building, with one hundred and twenty
beds, equally divided between controlled and uncontrolled
women. The appointments are modern in character,
attractive in appearance. Hamburg possesses similar
facilities with one hundred and thirteen beds; Frank-

Regulation and Disease

fort sets apart eighty beds in an excellent institution; Bremen, forty-four; Stockholm, sixty in an attractive building situated in a pleasant garden. In most of these establishments a deliberate effort is nowadays made to efface the impression of enforced detention. The Stockholm clinic, among others, has no locked doors or barred windows, in consequence of which the girls are rarely refractory.[11] Though the subject lies outside our present inquiry, it should be added in passing that all continental cities make, in addition to the above mentioned facilities, more or less liberal provision for other venereal patients.[12]

Conditions are less favorable in Vienna, where there is no special hospital for diseased prostitutes; they must be distributed between the three skin clinics of the city. Even so, there is such a scarcity of beds that they are often kept waiting in prison several days before they can be placed and then are dismissed too soon. But for really disgraceful accommodations one must cite Paris. The infected Parisian prostitute is interned in a medieval prison — St. Lazare — a name, at the mere sound of which, the most hardened offender blanches with terror. In this bleak dungeon, young and old, the new offender and the hopeless hag, mingle freely; they sleep in the same huge dormitory, meet in the same dark corridors, and get their brief airing in the same narrow court-yard.[13]

[11] This point will be referred to again in Chapter X.
[12] An exhaustive study of Swedish conditions in regard to hospital accommodations for venereal patients was made by Johansson and is printed in Vol. III of the *Report of the Swedish Com.* For Germany, see A. Guttstadt, *Krankhenhaus-Lexikon für das Deutsche Reich* (Berlin, 1900), passim.
[13] See Eugène Pottet, *Histoire de Saint-Lazare* (1122–1912), Paris, 1912.

The quality of the examination varies widely. At Berlin, typical of the four best, clinical inspection is made of the mouth, hands, feet, and other external surfaces; the genitalia are invariably explored with the speculum; microscopic examination for gonococci are made fortnightly, or oftener in suspicious cases. The magnitude of the work may be roughly indicated as follows: On the basis of 3,500 inscribed women, each examined twice weekly, 28,000 clinical examinations would be made monthly,— 3,500 by each of the eight physicians. As a matter of fact, the figures are smaller, since bi-weekly examinations are required only of women under 24. It would be nearer the truth to estimate that each physician makes from 1,500 to 2,000 clinical examinations monthly. In August 1911, each of the four assistants made 2,646 microscopic examinations for gonococci,— an average of 98 for each working-day.[14] It is estimated that on the average three minutes are available for the examination: but as this takes no account of time lost, the actual duration of the operation is much less.[15] Women sent to the hospital are discharged only after three successive negative microscopic findings, followed by an examination at police headquarters confirming this result.[16]

The Budapest system is modeled on that in use in

[14] Güth in *Zeitschrift* XIV, p. 11.
[15] Güth, *loc. cit.*, p. 10.
[16] Non-registered prostitutes, if arrested, are also liable to medical examination; the microscope is utilized in suspicious cases. The police procedure is described by Inspector Penzig (*loc. cit.*) as follows: "After the usual questions have been asked of the accused woman, the Inspector decides whether a medical examination shall take place. The woman assistant (social worker) also expresses her opinion on this point. If decided on, the examination is made by a woman physician. As a rule the women make no objection."

Regulation and Disease

Berlin. Inscribed prostitutes are card-indexed at police headquarters, according to the days of the week on which they are scheduled for examination. Their cards are removed as they appear; the cards remaining over at the close of the day form thus a list of those who have failed to keep their appointment. Every girl carries her own spatula. The examination does not materially differ from the Berlin pattern, above described, except that the microscope is utilized only whenever suspicion is aroused, — not at regular intervals regardless of suspicion.[17] Between 600 and 700 girls are examined daily between the hours of 9 and 2. In the month of August 1912, 341 specimens were subjected to microscopic examination; had the 2,200 enrolled girls been subjected on each inspection to microscopic examination, 17,600 specimens would have been required.[18]

Vienna is the most favorable example of the large group by no member of which the microscope is employed at all. The women appear stripped for the examination, which consists of a cursory clinical inspection, always including the vagina. A wooden spatula — discarded after a single use — is the only distinctive feature. The examination is very brief,— a matter of seconds, not minutes.

In the remaining cities, the examination is still less thorough. At Hamburg, for example, the women convene in a bordell, as many as can be accommodated crowding into the room in which batches are examined.

[17] So also at Bremen; at Stockholm a microscopic slide is made at each examination.
[18] The Dresden procedure is not essentially different from that of Berlin and Budapest.

Prostitution in Europe

The physician takes a hasty look into their mouths in succession, and then glances at the genitalia, with only occasional use of the speculum. His hands are not cleansed before he proceeds from one girl to the next. Only a few seconds are devoted to each case. In Cologne it is frankly admitted that the medical examination is not "intensive." In Geneva the clinical inspection is confined to the mouth and the genitalia. In Rome the examining physician assured me that "if the woman is sound, he (I) could tell it at the first glance; he is more circumspect, if the case is suspicious."

The Paris examination deserves a paragraph to itself. All day long a dismal succession of groups of abandoned women file into the rudely-equipped rooms in which two physicians ply their repellent task perfunctorily. A line is formed; with open jaws and protruding tongue they march rapidly past; the doctor uses one spatula for all, wiping it hastily on a soiled towel from time to time. This finished, the same group in quick succession ascends two surgical chairs to permit a cursory vaginal inspection; the physician, stationing himself between them, loses no time, for one woman is assuming the recumbent position while he is engaged in the examination of another; he switches back and forth as rapidly as the women can get up and down,— indulging in good-humored and sometimes unseemly jocularity as the work proceeds. Of the two physicians employed on the occasion of one of my visits, one used a rubber glove, the other a rubber finger,— in both cases the same for all; though wiped on a towel from time to time, neither was changed or cleansed. On one occasion I observed one

Regulation and Disease

of the physicians examine 25 or 30 girls without changing, washing, or wiping the rubber fingers he wore; and
a number of those examined were adjudged "diseased."
The speculum was rarely used. In one instance, pressure
by the finger on the urethra discharged an abundant suspicious secretion; the same finger, unwashed, was used
in examining the next case; in another instance, the
same rubber finger was used on the genitalia and about
the mouth. The inspections consumed from 15 to 30
seconds each; "for vaginal examinations," so read my
notes made on the spot, "it takes less time to examine one
woman than it takes another to mount the examining
chair and offer herself for examination, despite the fact
that her clothing has been adjusted before entering the
room."

The printed accounts give the impression that the medical inspections are more deliberately carried on. Bettmann, for example, publishes a table in which it is stated
that each examination averages 1½ minutes in Paris, 5
minutes in Vienna;[19] to the same effect is Blaschko's calculation, though he himself says that even so, "the
length of time devoted to the examination is too brief."[20]
I feel sure, however, that these and other similar estimates were arrived at by dividing the entire time at the
disposal of the physicians by the number of women to be
inspected,—a fallacious method of getting at the facts.
The truth can be learned only by observation registered
on the spot. At Paris, and elsewhere as well, much time
is lost in making ready for a task which is subsequently

[19] Bettmann, *Die ärztliche Ueberwachung der Prostitution*, (Jena,
1905), p. 50.
[20] *Hygiene der Prost.*, pp. 83, etc.

rushed, so that the nominal period is by no means entirely devoted to the business in hand.

What is the value of each of the types of medical inspection above described? The question must be subdivided for answer; we must inquire as to the general effect of sanitary inspection of women on participation in irregular sexual indulgence on the part of men; as to the utility of each of the methods in reference to the women subjected to them, respectively; as to the effect of police control of inscribed women on the sanitary habits of the non-inscribed; finally, as to the incidence of venereal disease, its fluctuations and their relation to sanitary control of prostitutes.

Continental Europe, as I have pointed out in a previous chapter, traditionally condones incontinence on the part of the male sex. No single cause accounts for this phenomenon; but certainly among the most important factors is not only the existence of a powerful instinct in man, but also the extent to which its indulgence is facilitated by the low social status of woman. This attitude was incorporated in, not originally due to, regulatory systems of dealing with prostitution. The continental attitude towards prostitution and all the machinery developed in connection with handling it, both from the police and the sanitary sides, were undoubtedly not orginally the cause, but the result, of an indulgent attitude towards the male sex, on the one hand, and a disregard of woman's dignity, on the other.

Once instituted, however, the system itself became a factor in perpetuating the conditions out of which it sprang. The existence of regulation amounts to a concession by the state that a vast volume of prcmiscuous intercourse is to be accepted as a fact;[21] that for this purpose professional prostitution is recognized and, despite verbal quibbles, authorized. For the prosecution of what is thus treated as an essential and in a sense legitimate traffic, these women obtain a privileged position on the streets or in quarters notorious for the use to which they are put. The prominence thus given to immorality operates psychologically as an incitement to it. The complacent attitude towards indulgence implied in the mild effort made by the state to remove or reduce its dangers indubitably diminishes internal inhibition on the part of the male. Nothing is more certain in the domain of effort and ethics than that good conduct is largely the response of the individual to the expectation of society: men "can because they think they can."[22] Social stigma is a most powerful deterrent; social assent a powerful stimulus. Regulation implies the absence of any expectation of male self-restraint; it is society's tacit assent to laxity.[23] Nay more, it is an invitation to laxity in so far as it deprives dissipation of one of its terrors, for the existence of medical regulation must be interpreted as implying a certain degree of efficacy in the attainment of its object. There can, therefore, be no ques-

[21] It is perhaps hardly necessary for me to state that I do not mean to imply that if the State made no such concession, prostitution would either vanish or at once be greatly diminished; the point is that the attitude involved in regulation interferes with a vigorous or a general struggle in the direction of self-restraint.

[22] Vergil, *Aeneid*, Book V, line 231, Conington's version of " Possunt, quia posse videntur."

[23] " Still more objectionable must be considered the fact that society helps in this way to maintain the belief among many persons that prostitution is a necessity." Johansson, *loc. cit.*, p. 130.

Prostitution in Europe

tion that state regulation of vice increases the volume of irregular intercourse and the number of those who participate in it. Certain it is that the notion that male self-control is both possible and wholesome has spread "pari passu" with the attack on regulation and with the elevation of the status of woman that invariably accompanies this movement.

The utility of regulation is thus opened to serious question not only on ethical but on hygienic grounds. For the present, I take no position as to the hygienic condition of the woman examined; I am looking at the problem more broadly. Regulation tends to increase miscellaneous sexual congress. Such congress takes place in the long-run with both inscribed and non-inscribed women. Irregularity craves variety; and infection is the wellnigh inevitable penalty of sexual promiscuity. To whatever extent regulation tends to increase irregular commerce by diminishing individual and social resistance, to that extent it tends to increase the amount of venereal disease. Therefore, even if regulation should be found to be more or less effective, its sanitary achievement has to be offset against the increased amount of congress to which it indubitably conduces; one has to ask whether more congress with regulation is not likely to result in more disease than would result from less congress without any regulation at all.

It is occasionally denied that the mere existence of regulation tends to develop recklessness on the basis of assumed security. Blaschko, for example, a distinguished authority, while conceding that here and there an individual is misled, does not believe that the problem as a

whole is appreciably affected.[24]   But Blaschko starts with
the assumption that things have always been as they are
and will never be much different.   My own impressions
are, however, distinctly opposed to Blaschko's view: I
have, I think, observed unmistakable evidence that regulation is itself one of the factors in demoralization, by reason of the prominence it gives to prostitution, the undermining of the forces that make for good conduct, and the
illusions of safety that it creates.   My notes contain
many random conversations which cannot be wholly without representative significance as to the last-named
point.   I happened, for example, to call on one of the
most eminent of French dermatologists at the time when
he was consulted by a wealthy Mexican gentleman who
was passing the winter in the gay capital.   A prompt
diagnosis of syphilis was made.   " Impossible! " rejoined
the perturbed patient.   " I have had nothing to do with
any woman except an inmate of a well known resort of
high character (he named the house and street), who
possesses a certificate of good health.   For this security
I pay 100 francs."   " You could purchase equal security
much cheaper on the streets," replied the French savant.
Communications of precisely the same tenor have been
made to me by intelligent men — foreigners as well as
Americans — in Paris, Berlin, Rome, and Stockholm.
Schneider, an exceptionally candid witness as to the well-
to-do German youth, declares: " A very large propor-

[24] *Hygiene der Prostitution,* p. 88. In view of the fact that
within a few pages I have twice ventured to differ with Prof.
Blaschko, it is perhaps proper for me to state that he is one of the
foremost and one of the soundest of European authorities on the
entire subject.

tion of men who hunt out official prostitutes live in the belief that sexual intercourse with inscribed women is, in consequence of medical control, practically without danger. In my earlier years I myself held to this view, and only after I had taken pains to study the subject thoroughly, did I perceive that there was no safety at all. Alas, too late! And the same thing happens to thousands of others, who are lulled into a false sense of security and whose moral scruples are also weakened." [25]   If such is the state of mind among the intelligent, is it not probable that the uneducated make the same assumption? Experienced physicians can be quoted in support of this view. " The public is fooled. The laity is led to believe that it is possible to distinguish diseased from healthy prostitutes. As all the diseased ones are sent to the hospital, relations with controlled prostitutes are free from danger. This is the popular conclusion." [26]   The official rules themselves practically concede the point. For the police are now at pains to disavow the natural consequence of their own policy. The Paris regulations state in bold type that " the card delivered to inscribed women must not be regarded as an incentive to debauch; " and the public is commonly warned that the medical examination is not to be interpreted as a guarantee of safety.

Regulation may therefore be regarded as calculated to increase the volume of irregular intercourse: what does it accomplish by way of rendering such intercourse harmless?

Medical control is concerned chiefly with two diseases,

[25] *Loc. cit.,* p. 107 (slightly abridged).
[26] *Zeitschrift* VIII, p. 399.

syphilis and gonorrhœa,[27] in reference to both of which its object is not primarily to heal the woman, but rather to protect her patrons from infection. It is therefore not essential, from the standpoint of regulation, that prostitutes who have contracted syphilis should be interned during the several years during which the disease runs its regular course; it is only essential that the woman be kept under lock and key during the infectious stages of that tedious process. And the same is true, theoretically at least, of gonorrhœa.

The salient points in connection with these diseases are, for our purposes, these. Both are contracted early in the prostitute's career. Syphilis is a protracted affair, but the girl who has run the entire gamut of a single infection is subsequently immune; she does not herself freshly contract the disease. She may, of course, at any time, act as a carrier, receiving the germ from one patron and conveying it to another, even while herself not becoming actively infected. Having herself, however, contracted the disease, she is highly infectious during the primary stage, calculable in weeks, and during the secondary stage, usually occupying from two to three years, but sometimes lasting from five to ten. During this time, fresh manifestations, indicative of danger, appear from time to time; but infection may also be communicated when no signs of disease are visible. It is very important at the very outset to get clear notions as to these points. Syphilis is highly infectious during the entire duration

[27] I have paid little attention to soft chancre because it is of so much less consequence than the two diseases on which the argument turns.

of the primary local lesion. In the secondary stage, it is highly infectious when florid; probably not infectious, when really latent;— that is, when the disease is active only in liver, brain, and other internal organs or tissues. But the difficulty is that syphilis is often regarded as latent when it is actually florid,— the signs escaping observation. At any time, infection may take place not only in sexual intercourse, but also through the mouth, saliva, and other secretions and contacts.[28] Relapses are also very common. Of 722 prostitutes with secondary syphilis, 529 relapsed 1,601 times in the first year, 204 relapsed 303 times in the second year, 90 relapsed 120 times in the third year, 53 relapsed 73 times in the fourth year.[29] Often the symptoms are almost unnoticeable, at times escaping the vigilance of a careful observer. The clinical history of a syphilitic woman is by no means a sufficient assurance that she is no longer a source of peril to her patrons.

Gonorrhœa is wholly incalculable. No matter how frequent its attacks, no immunity results. Prostitutes, it is true, appear to contract acute infections less often as they grow older; but this is probably due, not to an acquired immunity, but to toughening of the tissues and decreased exposure to infection through falling off in business. Clinical appearances as to the presence or cure of the disease are entirely unreliable. Of the elements on which such judgments rest — the color, odor, and consistency of the secretions — Güth declares: " No criterion could be more arbitrary or deceptive, for, on the one hand, the clinical character of the gonorrhœal excretion varies so

[28] M. v. Gruber, *loc. cit.,* p. 6.   [29] *Ibid,* p. 26.

Regulation and Disease

often and so suddenly, that a person who appears suspicious to-day may be free of secretion to-morrow, and subsequently again show suspicious symptoms. An apparently innocent manifestation may be infectious; a transparent vaginal secretion may be infectious; a purulent discharge may be non-communicable."[30] Whether even a microscopical examination is competent to decide the question involved is open to grave doubt. Unquestionably the microscope can note the decrease in the number of gonococci; but it is not yet proved that their virulence diminishes in the same ratio. Moreover, a secretion relatively poor in gonococci may still transmit infection, even though the secretion is so poor in them that successive slides fail to indicate their presence.[31] Finally, gonococci of diminished virulence quickly recover their full virulence when transferred to a favorable membrane.

What does regulation, as we have described it, accomplish, first, with those examined, next, with respect to the general situation? It needs little argument to show that the crude clinical procedures of which Paris is typical achieve little in the way of isolating infected foci. In the first place, the examination is so rapidly and carelessly conducted that, if the truth were known, it might well be found to communicate more infection than it detects, (as, for example, when a finger, used to separate actively diseased parts, is applied uncleansed to the same parts of others). In ascertaining clinical conditions the

[30] Güth, *loc. cit.,* p. 3.
[31] In the preceding account I have followed Blaschko, "*Hygiene der Prostitution,* etc.," pp. 1-19; Pinkus, "*Die Verhütung der Geschlechtskrankheiten*" and Güth, *loc. cit.*

commonest precautions are by no means invariably employed. One physician examined in my presence 30 girls,
using the speculum only three or four times; all were
pronounced well; his neighbor, who used the speculum
regularly found a few infected cases, such as the former
must have missed. The examining physicians realize the
slipshod nature of their work. A suspicious secretion
having been noted by a bystander in the case of a woman
pronounced "well," the physician was asked how he
knew. He shrugged his shoulders: "I don't know; but
there's no way to tell. If we kept cases like that, we'd
keep over half." Another of the examining physicians
disposed of a similar case in the same way: "We can't
keep them, we haven't space, though we aren't sure that
they are well." Still another: "Accurate diagnosis is
impossible; under these conditions, gonorrhœa, unless
virulent, is ignored; our real effort is to detect syphilis."
In another case, a woman pronounced "well" was leaving the chair when, on a bystander's skeptical remark, the
physician reversed his opinion and sent the unfortunate
to St. Lazare. The total number of women incarcerated
at any one time on the score of venereal infection is
negligibly small. On the occasion of my visit to St.
Lazare, 170 venereal women were confined there, and I
was informed by the chief clerk that this was a fair average; these are the scapegoats for the venereal disease
in circulation among the prostitutes of the French capital!
Assuredly the temporary withdrawal of 170 infected
women from the thousands with whom Paris teems is
utterly without influence in the long-run; more especially
as these women are themselves turned adrift before their

infectiousness has passed. Regulation of this type has less effect in reducing disease than a rainy night or a spurt of police activity,— both temporarily diminishing the accessibility of supply to demand and its provocative character.

The medical examination at Geneva, Brussels, and Rome is of the same general type and works in the same way. The City Physician of Geneva explained to me that it required only " about an hour or so " to examine the 86 inscribed women of that city. To my comment " this is pretty quick work," he replied, " Yes, but I know them! " I asked how often disease is found. " Very, very rarely," he candidly replied. Elsewhere I learned that as a rule the hospital of Geneva is free of women in so far as this source of supply is concerned. The conditions under which the examinations are made in Brussels and Rome preclude anything beyond primitive work. The provincial health officer at Rome declared that the official examinations by the police physicians disclosed " very little disease "; subsequently one of the latter conceded that " the examination is good enough to detect primary syphilis; it is of little value otherwise. Of course virulent gonorrhœa would be observed. But it is absurd to suppose the others safe,— in so far as gonorrhœa is concerned, no public woman is ever safe." At Brussels, during the two years preceding my visit, a total of 26 prostitutes had received hospital treatment,— inscribed and non-inscribed. The year before — 1910 — nine inscribed prostitutes and 27 clandestine were pronounced " diseased." [32]

[32] *Rapport Annuel, Ville de Bruxelles, Année*, 1910, p. 65. In

Prostitution in Europe

"The real harmlessness of the registered prostitute," says Dr. Baget, head of the hospital division at Brussels, "consists in this,—that she is practically non-existent. My clinic at Hospital St.-Pierre contains four beds for prostitutes, and even these are almost always empty." [33]

The above description has dealt with regulation at its worst. In reply, it may be fairly urged that, though showing how regulation has worked in the past, it does not prove that better results are either unattainable or unattained. Let us see, therefore, what happens in Vienna and most German cities in which a more conscientious type of clinical examination obtains. In these, at least, the examination is not in itself a direct factor in spreading infection; for individual spatulæ and individual specula are commonly used. If not, the instruments employed are as a rule properly cleansed. The overburdened physicians have, however, neither time nor facilities to make proper observations. I was present at Hamburg at the examination of 42 women in a bordell; the whole process occupied less than 20 minutes. These women are supposed to be "under strict control"; [34] on another occasion, I witnessed the examination of 50 women, some under "light control," [35] others, clandestine; the speculum was not generally used and the entire transaction, including the writing of the protocol, occupied less than a quarter of an hour. All were pronounced well.[36] The

1898 — at a time when 172 women were enrolled — 7 patients were sent to the hospital in the course of the year (*Compte Rendu des Séances, IIᵉ Conférence Internationale*, Bruxelles, 1903, pp. 185-6).

[33] *Zeitschrift* VIII, p. 291.

[34] "Strenge Kontrolle."

[35] "Leichte Kontrolle."

[36] The hands of the physician were uncovered and were not washed until all the examinations were completed.

Regulation and Disease

medical service in Cologne suffers — as it suffers in all great cities — on account of the inadequacy of the staff. " A thorough hygienic examination is impossible. Syphilis especially in its most infectious forms can be quickly recognized by an experienced observer; but chronic gonorrhœa can be made out only after accurate scrutiny: the preparation and study of a microscopic specimen demands more time than a police surgeon can give." [37] In consequence, the number of women who are isolated is everywhere inconsiderable; at Cologne, on the day of my visit to the police hospital, 30 registered women were confined for treatment; in the course of January, 1912, 75 women were found to be suffering with disease in Hamburg; in February, 67; in April, 53. In Vienna, the total found diseased during five successive years was as follows:

	1906	1907	1908	1909	1910
Soft Chancre	129	97	82	80	70
Gonorrhœa	127	87	107	70	94
Syphilis	224	162	185	206	168
Total	480	346	374	356	332

In Berlin, during the vogue of the clinical examination, the average number of women interned ranged from 260 in 1895–6, to 157 in 1903–4.[38] In Stockholm, for all causes, 522 enrolled prostitutes were sent into the hospital 955 times in the year 1904.[39]

It is obvious that among the registered prostitutes of a city there are at every moment many more diseased women than any of the above figures indicate. Why are

[37] Zinnser in *Zeitschrift* V, pp. 204–5 (abridged).
[38] Communicated by Prof. Pinkus.
[39] Johansson, *loc. cit.*, p. 36.

they not detected? The doctors are overburdened with work, which is of such a nature as to make severe and uniform scrutiny impossible. Enormous fluctuations therefore occur, fluctuations which cannot possibly be due to sudden improvement or sudden deterioration in the condition of the women. For instance, in Vienna, with an enrolment of 2,569 in 1901, 1,185 women were found to be diseased; of 2,380 enrolled in 1905, 543 were diseased; with 2,329 in 1910, 332 were diseased. At Stockholm, between 1890 and 1904, the annual number committed to the hospital ranged from 523 to 1,026.[40] Sixty-seven girls were sent to the police hospital of Berlin in December, 1907; under the same system, 349 were sent in May 1911; 230 in December of the same year. The average daily hospital roll numbered 262 in 1897-8, 184 in 1900-1, and 122 in 1908-9. A change of doctors is invariably followed by an increase in the amount of disease detected,— surely not in an increase in the amount of disease existing. Thus in 1903-4, 1,258 cases of venereal disease were discovered in women, both inscribed and uninscribed; a new medical staff found 1,845 cases the next year.[41]

The utter baselessness of any confidence placed by the patron on the fact of medical inspection is thus obvious: inspected women may not only be diseased at the moment they are sent to the streets and bordells to do business as sound,— but, as we shall also see, if found diseased, they are, as a rule, even after treatment, allowed to return to their avocation while still highly dangerous.

[40] Johansson, *loc. cit.*, p. 36.
[41] Figures given by Professor Pinkus.

Regulation and Disease

But aside from such variations, the clinical method is utterly incompetent to detect any considerable portion of infectious disease.[42] I have already quoted Güth on the difficulty attending a clinical diagnosis in gonorrhœa; his position can be fully sustained by both figures and opinions. Güth himself tells of a series of cases, 35% of which showed clinical symptoms of gonorrhœa; the microscope showed 90%.[43] The figures for three years at Budapest are highly instructive,— those for 1907 the result of clinical examination, those of 1909 and 1911 the result of clinical assisted by some microscopic work:

Year	Number of enrolled prostitutes	Total cases venereal disease	Gonorrhœa	Syphilis	Bubo
1907	1,717	884	328	105	451
1909	1,914	2,775	1,112	897	766
1911	2,097	2,100	839	697	564

Between 1907 and 1909 the number of prostitutes increased 22%; the amount of ascertained disease increased 137% — gonorrhœa, 156%, syphilis, 25%. So at Berlin, the number of cases detected leaped from 1,258 in 1903-4 to 3,721 in 1911-12, with change of personnel of the medical staff and the introduction of partial use of the microscope; consider the amount of misplaced confidence and resultant disease that medical inspection had previously made itself responsible for! Dr. Möller of Stockholm gives confirmatory statistics; in 1874, 19

[42] Though this book deals only with prostitution in Europe, I venture for the purpose of conclusively establishing the uselessness of the clinical method to refer to the researches of Dr. Archibald McNeil of New York City. Of 647 girls examined, 20.56% had clinical manifestations of disease; of 466 of these same girls, microscopic and other tests showed 89.3% to be venereally infected. See Kneeland, "Commercialized Prostitution in New York City (New York, 1913), pp. 188-190.

[43] Loc. cit., p. 4.

cases of gonorrhœa were found among 298 prostitutes by clinical methods (6 per cent.); in 1884, 64 among 431 women (15 per cent.); in 1894, 141 among 464 (30 per cent.); partial use of the microscope in 1904 with 408 registered women revealed 749 cases, i. e., 174 per cent. in the course of the year.[44] Baermann at Breslau concludes after long experience that "without the use of the microscope the question as to whether an exudate from the urethra or cervix is infectious or harmful cannot be decided." This being the result of incomplete use of the microscope, to how much infection did the privileges conferred by regulation lead in Cologne in the year 1905, when among 2,048 prostitutes examined in the course of the year, 148 (i. e., 7.2 per cent.) were pronounced venereally diseased?[45] Or at Vienna, when, out of 2,116 enrolled women, 87 were found to be suffering with gonorrhœa and 162 with syphilis in the course of the year 1907?[46] The following table[47] shows the absurdly inadequate amount of disease detected by clinical methods in the prostitutes of those German cities that I visited.[48]

City	No. inscribed women			No. found diseased		
	1903	1905	1907	1903	1905	1907
Berlin [49]	2,231	2,663	2,272	620	576	733
Hamburg	1,266	1,291	920	759	719	791
Munich	248	215	175	165	46	36
Dresden [49]	277	394	281	248	333	426
Cologne	500	500	500	312	212	336
Frankfort a/M	*449	*412	*512	341	529	493
Stuttgart	23	16	22	22	18	28

* About.

[44] *Zeitschrift* VI, pp. 232 etc.
[45] *Zeitschrift* V, p. 205.
[46] *Zeitschrift* IX, p. 172.
[47] *Zeitschrift* XIII, p. 6.
[48] Bremen not included.
[49] This refers to a date preceding the reform of system to be next discussed.

Regulation and Disease

The women themselves have learnt the trick of defeating the examination. So crude an examination for gonorrhœa as that with which we are now dealing can be eluded by thorough irrigation before examination. Güth specifies various devices by which clinical inspection may be deceived and declares that there are " in the large cities persons who make a business of undertaking these manipulations for controlled women." [50] The more careful type of clinical examination can also be eluded: " If one remembers that especially women who are regularly examined are highly expert in concealing the traces of disease, one realizes that the medical examination has after all only a relative value," [52] writes Professor Zinnser, who calls himself a regulationist. The bacteriologist of the Budapest police regards these practices as serious obstacles even to the more refined methods practised in that city. " The visible symptoms of disease are rendered either invisible or misleading. These disreputable physicians perform antiluetic cures and treat the urethra with injections, thus enabling the prostitute to ply her trade." [52]

The actual scope of regulation is, however, less than its apparent scope; for an inscription list of 6,000 at Paris or 3,000 at Berlin or 25 at Stuttgart does not mean that the number of prostitutes in question is in each city under continuous, even if periodic, inspection, so that there is a more or less stable body of approved women. No system of inspection can be effective if it is discontinuous; hence a large subtraction from even the possible

[50] *Loc. cit.,* p. 3.
[51] *Zeitschrift* V, p. 205.
[52] Translation from police journal " *Public Safety,*" May 29, 1912.

efficacy of a limited and imperfect system must be made on the score of irregularity. Though 6,000 women are registered at Paris, the number who continue for a considerable period and who come regularly to inspection is relatively small. In a few instances, a withered hag reports for examination and one is told that she has been under observation for 25 years or longer; but far the greater number are constantly shifting. For example, in 1884, 1,006 women were newly inscribed, 1,089 disappeared from the rolls; in 1886, 1,145 were inscribed, 2,283 dropped out; in 1902, 1,574 and 1,717, respectively.[53] Some of these are, of course, restored to the list, but as a rule only to slip away again. Of 629 women newly inscribed in Breslau during the year 1886, 147 dropped out in the first year, 94 in the second, 80 in the third.[54] In Vienna, as already shown, the number of disappearances and the number of enrolments keep close together. A small body of older women are more or less stationary; the remainder are in perpetual transit, — and this remainder includes the younger and more aggressive, whom effective regulation would have to keep under continuous observation. The same is true at Berlin; additions and disappearances from the list are as follows:[55]

Year	1902	1903	1904	1905	1906
Newly inscribed	538	590	683	917	1,207
Dropped out	699	696	1,105	1,069	824

Whether even the humane spirit of the new regulations

[53] *Report, French Com., Annexes,* p. 259.
[54] See Bettmann, *loc. cit.,* pp. 177–180 for additional illustrations. Also *Zeitschrift* I, p. 298.
[55] Pinkus, *loc. cit.,* p. 71; of course some withdrawals are due to death, change of occupation, etc. See also *Zeitschrift* VIII, p. 59.

will greatly affect disappearances remains yet to be proved; in a single month, as many as 60 have dropped out; in 1911, 218 disappeared.[56]

In Stockholm, Möller found that of 857 controlled women, 286 were missing after one month; 109 more after two months; 100 more after three; 76 more after four: at the close of the 15th month, i. e., 5% were left.[57] A cursory inspection of police records at Bremen showed me that with few exceptions a woman was rarely on the rolls longer than a few months. Of Stuttgart's small roll of 24, 22 had been inscribed less than a year,— of these, 10 less than a half-year.[58]

In addition, visits are frequently missed, so that those who remain on the rolls are examined less frequently than the regulations require. Under the old Berlin system, more than 50% of the visits from 1888 to 1901 were thus omitted; there should have been 208,000 examinations; 94,000 were actually performed.[59] At Stockholm, out of 6,667 examinations ordered from July to December, 1905, 2,242 were missed on the appointed day.[60] Taking the entire period 1870 to 1912, Johansson finds that fully 40% of the women who ought to appear at least fortnightly for medical inspection fail to remain under regular control. The office records seem to make a more favorable showing only because they note merely the beginning of an interruption in the woman's attendance which may, however, last several weeks.[61]

[56] Personal communication.
[57] *Zeitschrift* VI, p. 275. Also Johansson, *Report, Swedish Commission*, Vol. III, p. 47.
[58] Meher, *loc. cit.*, p. 157.
[59] Schmölder, *Unsere heutige Prostitution* (Munich, 1911) p. 22.
[60] Johansson, *Report, Swedish Commission*, Vol. III, p. 43.
[61] *Reglementeringen* in Stockholm, pp. 78-9.

Prostitution in Europe

The tendency to disappear is of course strongest in the case of women who, knowing themselves diseased, face the prospect of detention. Between 1885 and 1899, for example, Johansson finds 156 inscribed women who stayed away from the medical inspection; of these, 92, i. e., just under 60%, had primary syphilitic sores.[62] In 1904, 31% of the Stockholm women sent to the hospital missed inspection just before their commitment. During that year 9% of the women had to be apprehended on the charge of missing the medical visit; hence, staying away from medical examination was more than three times as frequent among the sick as among the general list.[62a] It appears, further, that of 845 women who between 1885 and 1906 contracted syphilis after enrolment the primary symptoms escaped detection, through interruption of inspection in 656 cases (77.6%).[62b] Inspection is therefore apt to be terminated by the act of the woman just at the moment when it becomes important. The women whom the police find to be ill are therefore largely those who, arrested for infraction of the rules, are subjected to an unexpected examination; women who are deceived as to their condition; and those who have bungled in the attempt to hide it or have not yet learned how to do so. Thus the system is even less effective than the size of the enrolment and the method of conducting the examination themselves indicate.

But the system undermines itself at another point: the women, if found to be diseased, are not detained long enough. Dr. Commenge, head of the Paris bureau, re-

[62] Johansson, *Report, Swedish Commission* Vol. III, p. 168.
[62a] *Reglementeringen* in Stockholm, p. 41.
[62b] *Ibid*, p. 43.

ported to the Brussels conference that in the two decades between 1877 and 1897, 15,095 syphilitic prostitutes were confined in St. Lazare an average of 30 days each.[63] In Vienna, between 1893 and 1896, cases of gonorrhœa were detained from 18 to 21 days, cases of syphilis from 21 to 27 days.[64] The police bacteriologist of Budapest states: "One and the same prostitute might come into the hospital repeatedly for the same infection. We know that syphilis lasts for years; it is undeniable that, since the hospitals are crowded and the beds therefore insufficient in number, prostitutes are obliged to leave before they are cured;" syphilis is there kept "at least three weeks," gonorrhœa "at least two."[65] At Stockholm, 174 women with primary symptoms were detained an average of 48 days each; 140 with secondary symptoms an average of 35 days each.[66] Partially in consequence of premature dismissal, partially in consequence of re-infection or recrudescence, women often alternate for years between freedom and hospital detention. Of 498 Stockholm inscribed prostitutes, 81 escaped the hospital altogether while on the lists. The following table shows the experience of the others:[67]

	Once	Twice	Three times	Four times	Five times	6–10 times	11–15 times	16–20 times	21–25 times	26–30 times	31–50 times
No. in hospital	71	42	42	41	37	98	42	29	7	6	2

[63] Quoted by Schmölder, *loc. cit.*, p. 17.
[64] Gruber, *loc. cit.*, p. 28.
[65] "*Public Safety.*" May 29, 1912, etc.
[66] Johansson, *loc. cit.*, p. 155.
[67] *Ibid*, p. 124; *ditto*, p. 37.

Prostitution in Europe

In Bremen it is now the practice to detain gonorrhœal patients from three to six weeks; syphilitics were receiving at the time of my visit[68] two injections of Salvarsan and were discharged at the end of a fortnight. Finally, at Berlin the average length of the hospital stay of venereally diseased prostitutes has tended steadily to decline as the following figures indicate:[69]

Year	Average stay of each prostitute
1895–6	36.4 days
1896–7	32.2 days
1897–8	36.8 days
1898–9	36.4 days
1900–1	39.5 days
1901–2	48.8 days
1902–3	36.7 days
1903–4	41.0 days
1908–9	23.0 days
1909–10	19.91 days
1910–11	19.6 days
1911–12	22.0 days

The sudden drop since 1907 follows the introduction on a considerable scale of ambulatory treatment, allowed theoretically on condition that the women refrain from the prosecution of their business,— an obviously unsafe calculation. It is clear therefore that at all times the period of detention is too brief; hospital care goes far enough to remove the obvious evidence of disease,— the evidence that might, if left untouched, itself deter a more or less cautious patron. Disease being once rendered latent, or apparently latent,[70] the customer presumes, at

[68] June, 1912.

[69] For these valuable statistics I am again indebted to the courtesy of Professor Pinkus.

[70] If gonorrhœa, it is not the less dangerous on that account; in case of syphilis, as I have previously remarked, if actually latent it is not infectious; if just supposedly latent, as is apt to be the case, the danger is extreme.

238

Regulation and Disease

his own sure cost, on the supposed safety of the woman whom medical regulation has just discharged from the hospital as fit to prosecute her calling.

Even if we take regulation at its word and assume that it is fairly successful in isolating disease, it still remains true that it arrests more healthy than diseased prostitutes and thus increases the commerce of the undetected sick,— professional or clandestine. For the number of supposedly well prostitutes arrested for trifling violations of the rules is always larger, indeed much larger, than the number of ill ones. In Paris, 35,625 such arrests were made in 1897, 32,122 in 1898. The culprits, most of them well according to police standards, were sent to prison to serve short sentences, for "racolage" (soliciting). I observed the handling of a group of such cases: a girl found in the Avenue Wagram at 1.30 A. M. pronounced "well," got 4 days in prison; the next had just four hours previously finished a four-day sentence; re-arrested last night for loitering and sent back for four days more. The others were of the same type: all were "well" and all were sent to prison. Blaschko found the same conditions prevailing in Berlin under the old régime: 13,591 healthy prostitutes were imprisoned for "ridiculous trifles" in the years 1897–98, while 1,998 diseased prostitutes were under compulsory treatment:[71] that is, regulation removed seven times as many healthy prostitutes as diseased. In 1909, 1,122 different registered women were arrested for violation of rules, 327 different registered women were detained on the score of illness; in 1910 and 1911 the figures were

[71] *Loc. cit.*, p. 89.

239

1,984 and 434 respectively.[72] In Stockholm, at the close of 1911, 28 women were in the hospital, 127 — supposedly well — in prison. In Cologne, 438 registered prostitutes were detained on the score of disease, 1,334 for violation of rules, in 1906; in 1911, 272 for disease, 2,066 for infraction of regulations.[73]

I have thus far dealt with registered prostitution alone: in reference to it, I believe we are justified in asserting that the numbers treated have nowhere been relatively large and that the methods of conducting the examinations and their actual working greatly reduce even the apparent efficacy of the system. In Stockholm it has been calculated that three-fourths of the disease current escapes detection.[74] It is therefore an incontrovertible fact that only a small part of the disease in existence among inscribed women has been isolated and that these diseased women have been discharged before they are very much safer: in consequence of which, men consorting with medically inspected prostitutes are the victims of misplaced confidence. If, then, regulation, on account of the general attitude it encourages and on account of the feeling of security it must logically create, has at all enlarged the volume of irregular intercourse, it has operated to increase, not to decrease, the volume of venereal disease.

So much for regulation taken fairly and strictly on its own ground. But the case against it is greatly strengthened when the remaining factors of the situation are taken into account. Regulation has always had to be

[72] Police report, 1911, p. 72.
[73] Personal communications by officials.
[74] *Report, Swedish Commission*, Vol III, p. 132.

Regulation and Disease

cautious in the inscription of minors and nowadays tends more and more to omit them altogether. It is held — and of course rightly — that no civilized society can permit a minor to brand herself as a professional prostitute, authorized by the community to earn her livelihood as such. Now, immoral girls still in their minority are at once the most attractive and the most dangerous prostitutes; ignorant and reckless, they are quickly infected and their infection is distributed to a larger clientele. How many infecting foci escape sanitary control by the exclusion of minors a few figures will make clear. Out of 4,341 cases of obviously infectious syphilis in Viennese prostitutes, 44.9 per cent. were between 15 and 20 years of age, 38.1 per cent. between 21 and 25.[75] The chief physician of the Vienna police in 1908 gave a most striking proof of the collapse brought about by excepting minors from regulation,— as he admitted must be the case: in 1900, 329 prostitutes were newly enrolled, 303 of whom (92.2%) were between 15 and 25 years of age: in that year, 2,686 cases of venereal disease were detected among inscribed women. In 1907, 83 prostitutes were newly enrolled, of whom 63 were between 15 and 25 years old: 426 venereal cases were discovered in that year. "In the same measure as the enrolment of minors declines, the total amount of disease discovered declines correspondingly."[76] In the relatively few instances in which minors are still inscribed at Berlin, the percentage of active gonorrhœa detected by the micro-

[75] Neisser in *Zeitschrift* I, p. 255.
[76] *Zeitschrift* IX, p. 194. The fact is striking even though in my judgment certain factors affecting the result have been overlooked.

scope is very high: of 38 controlled girls between 18 and 20 years of age, 29, i. e., 75% were discovered to have gonorrhœa.[77] Penzig declares that of prostitutes under 18, fully 50% are venereally infected. Pinkus, studying 1,357 inscribed prostitutes at Berlin found that at least 624, i. e., 45.9% had been syphilitically infected before enrolment.[78] Paris statistics teach the same lesson: of 12,615 unregistered minors arrested between 1878 and 1887, 56.26% were syphilitic.[79] More recent statistics sustain this result showing, as is claimed, that active disease is " ten times as common " among the unregistered minors as among the older women who are inscribed.[80] In Zurich, 39.7% of the syphilitics described by Müller and Zürcher were between 12 and 17 years of age, 42% between 16 and 21 years old; of those over 26 years old, very few indeed showed active signs of the disease, proving " the well-known saying, that the prostitute becomes syphilitically infected at the very outset of her career." [81] Roget at Brussels verifies this conclusion; he states that most infections occur between 16 and 22.[82] At Munich, of 2,686 clandestines arrested and medically examined, 711 were found diseased, and of these, 326, i. e., over 50% were minors. That is to say, even assuming forcible inscription of adults, over 50% of the diseased would have been missed as the suf-

---

[77] Privately communicated by official physician.
[78] *Loc. cit.,* p. 50.
[79] Commenge, p. 235. These arrests are made on the score of disorder, not of suspected disease. Minors who behave go on with impunity. This is made clear below.
[80] *Zeitschrift* VIII, p. 301.
[81] *Zeitschrift* XIV, pp. 234–5.
[82] *Zeitschrift* X, p. 108.

Regulation and Disease

ferers were ineligible to enrolment on account of age. Of 88 such cases, 55 per cent. of those 15 years old were infected, 61 per cent. of those 16 years old, and 67 per cent. of those 17 years old.[83] A Viennese estimate showed that out of every 1,000 prostitutes arrested for offences, over 57 per cent. were minors,— practically ineligible to inscription and medical control. Infection takes place so early that it is believed that in general " every prostitute who has followed the business a year is infected." [84] Regulation is therefore in the position of creating a certain presumption in favor of the hygienic security of irregular intercourse; even if it could create a monopoly in favor of inscribed women, there would be no reason to believe in its efficacy; but as the appetite that it fosters satisfies itself indiscriminately, the result is that bad is simply rendered worse.

One arrives at the same conclusion from another angle. I have repeatedly pointed out that on any rational definition of prostitution the total army of prostitutes is many times as large as the registered portion. Most of these women ply their business unhindered. Having had precisely the same history as the registered women and conducting their affairs with similar promiscuity, disease is of course equally rife among them. Yet, as long as they conduct themselves with discretion they are free from police interference: in towns where compulsory enrolment takes place (e. g. Berlin and Hamburg, etc.) they must be thrice warned before they are arrested and com-

[83] *Münchener medizinische Wochenschrift*, January 7, 1913, pp. 12, 13.
[84] *Zeitschrift* VIII, pp. 399-400.

pelled to submit to medical examination, with a chance of compulsory registration; elsewhere, as at Bremen, Munich, Stuttgart, etc., they are, if arrested for disorder, medically inspected, but are in no event compelled by forced inscription to submit to regular examination afterwards. Thus only the disorderly clandestine or non-inscribed woman is ever anywhere inspected at all. The cautious street-walker and fashionable and showy women who in Berlin frequent the Palais de Danse [85] are never inscribed, despite their notorious character. Women of the latter type are, in fact, nowhere enrolled; yet they do a large business, dangerous not so much on account of syphilis, which is with them long since a matter of the past, as on account of gonorrhœa, from which they are chronic sufferers. How much disease regulation in one way or another thus permits to go untouched among the non-inscribed is made clear by the amount of disease detected among the small part of clandestine or non-registered prostitution that the police lay hold of. A single clinical examination of each of 12,825 non-inscribed women arrested in Berlin in five successive years (1903–1907 inclusive) showed 17% venereally diseased; [86] of 1,514 arrested in 1909 and 1910, 421 were diseased.[87] At Cologne, the percentage is much higher: 660 non-inscribed women were arrested in 1906, 178 were infected; 1,626 were arrested in 1911, 304 were infected.[88] At Vienna, 1,319 such arrests were made in 1910: 222 cases

[85] It is said that managers of enterprises of this character require the habituées to employ private physicians to keep them advised as to their condition.
[86] Pinkus, *loc. cit.*, p. 71.
[87] Police Report, *loc. cit.*, p. 72.
[88] Personally communicated by officials.

Regulation and Disease

of infection were discovered among them.[89] It must be emphasized that the police surgeons get hold of these women, not because they are diseased, but because they are disorderly. Had they remained sober and quiet, regulation would have permitted them to continue undisturbed in the work of spreading infection, precisely as it does not touch the thousands of others, who, however diseased, are careful to keep the peace. The amount of disease thus surprised is interesting as a symptom of the vastly larger amount that wholly eludes observation; and, finally, the disease thus detected is — like the disease occurring among inscribed women — but a part of that actually existing among those examined; and, like all the rest, is readmitted to circulation while still infectious after an inadequate period of detention. An incident related by Welander may well close this line of argument. "It is superfluous to mention," he writes in his account of venereal disease and prostitution in Sweden, "that the clandestines are the main sources of infection. Recently there has been a small epidemic of soft chancre in Stockholm. Daily, male patients thus afflicted are admitted to the St.-Göran Hospital; but the hospital for prostitutes, during this entire period, has received only five women thus infected. This epidemic cannot be attributed to inscribed women," [90] and, further, he might have added, inscription did not locate or isolate the infecting foci.

[89] For the statistics of arrests of inscribed women and the results of their medical examination in German cities, see *Zeitschrift* XII, p. 7. Also, Pinkus, *loc. cit.*, pp. 72, 73; *Zeitschrift* X, p. 108; *ibid*, XIV, pp. 236–7. For Stockholm, *Report, Swedish Commission*, Vol. III, p. 30.

[90] *Zeitschrift* XI, p. 417.

Prostitution in Europe

I have, at the risk of being tedious, discussed the fore-going points in considerable detail in order that we might be in position to decide whether — whatever may be held theoretically as to the possibilities of regulation — it has in the past operated to reduce the amount of venereal disease. Let it be remembered that, except in three or four cities shortly to be taken up, regulation throughout Europe has been and is of the type above described or worse, and that in the three or four cities in question, improvements are so recent that no effect is as yet noticeable. Whatever, then, one may hold as a matter of theory, it is clear that, as a matter of practice, regulation as it has been carried on during the past century has increased, not decreased, the volume of venereal disease. No successful experience in the past can anywhere be quoted in its behalf. Those who believe in its possibilities are loudest in condemning its actual results. Professor Finger of Vienna, a regulationist, so-called, and one of the authors of the recent improvements there, says of the usual system: "As far as the good of regulation goes, I can speak from experience: the good can't possibly amount to much."[91] Professor Neisser of Breslau, the discoverer of the gonococcus,— a regulationist, too — declares: "If a radical reconstruction cannot be brought about, it is better to drop the entire system. The present system not only does not effect a real sanitary control of the inscribed women,— it rather operates to increase the volume of venereal disease."[92] Professor

[91] *Zeitschrift* IX, p. 230. It is to be remarked that all those quoted above are avowed regulationists and all are men of international eminence.
[92] *Zeitschrift* I, p. 198.

Regulation and Disease

Zinnser, of Cologne, likewise a regulationist, opens a discussion with these words. " The knowledge that the regulation of prostitution as generally conducted heretofore is obsolete, defective and urgently in need of reform, is not new." [93]   The Hamburg system, in the form in which I have above discussed it, is the creation of Dr. Julius Engel-Reimers, whose authority in Hamburg was, during his lifetime, so great as practically to render criticism futile. Nevertheless in a volume of lectures on venereal disease, published in 1908, Dr. Engel-Reimers, at the close of a career identified with regulation, declares: " Medical control of prostitutes has very slight influence on the incidence of syphilis and gonorrhœa among the male population. It is absolutely clear that these diseases are no less common where regulation exists than in places where prostitutes enjoy unrestrained freedom to ply their trade." [95]   This is assuredly candid, as well as startling testimony. As to the point here touched on, viz., the incidence of venereal disease in the general population, as far as it can be made out, I shall have something to say when I discuss conditions in nonregulated countries.[95]   For the present it is enough to note that the authorities above quoted — and the number can be extended — all call themselves regulationists; but it is some new form of regulation, not regulation as it exists historically, that they believe in. Those who defend the system and its results against the regulationist medical authorities above quoted are in the main police

[93] *Zeitschrift* VIII, p. 413.
[94] Julius Engel-Reimers: *Die Geschlechtskrankheiten* (Hamburg, 1908), p. 83.
[95] See Chap. X.

officials, whose favorable judgment will be accounted for in the next chapter.[96]

If regulation has, even in the opinion of authorities theoretically inclined to believe in it, failed in the past, is there any evidence to support an opinion favorable to it in some revised form in the future? In certain cities, the medical examination has been reconstructed on modern lines,— Berlin, Budapest, Bremen and Dresden; the same modifications and improvements could be generally introduced if money and intelligence — both procurable — were provided. Would regulation then be efficacious as a sanitary measure?

Let me call attention at the outset to the peculiar position in which the system is placed the moment one asks this question. It implies that regulation is not a policy more or less approved by experience, but an experiment, the value of which as a possibility has nowhere as yet been demonstrated. So far as history goes, the verdict is against its efficacy; so far as the revised system is concerned, not even those trying it as yet pretend to be able to assert for it any perceptible measure of success. " I must note at the very outset," says the candid police bacteriologist of Budapest as recently as May 29, 1912, " that the time which has elapsed since the new ordinance has been in force is as yet entirely too short for us to render a final opinion concerning its advantages." [97] " There is no telling whether the new regu-

[96] A prominent lay official of the Berlin police, Dr. Lindenau, candidly admits: "A usable set of statistics as to the effect of sanitary regulations is not to be had." (From *"Die strafrechtliche Bekämpfung der Gewerbsunzucht.*)
[97] *Loc. cit.*, p. 2.

Regulation and Disease

lations have accomplished anything," said one of their authors, Dr. Dumitreanu Agoston, to me. Regulation in its historic form is thus something worse than a failure; in its modern form, an experiment, of whose success not even its authors can give any evidence or venture any prediction!

Is there any substantial reason to believe that the improved system will successfully cope with the difficulties fatal to the old? The number that it reaches is less rather than more. Under the clumsy old system, Berlin enrolled 5,098 women in 1896; under the improved new system, 3,559 in 1912,— a decrease of over 30%, despite the city's growth; under the old system, Dresden enrolled 394 in 1905; under the new, 293 in 1912; at Budapest, the numbers are practically unchanged. The increased leniency and humanity of the new system thus decrease enrolment and tend to offset any advantage gained by improved medical methods.

Nor does the new system enjoy any advantage over the old in other important respects. Women continue to miss visits and to disappear: at Budapest, for example, with an enrolment of 2,000, the monthly non-attendance in 1912 ran as follows: [1]

March	293	June	315
April	353	July	414
May	398	August	319

Finally, the sick are not detained for longer periods of time: indeed, ambulatory treatment is more apt to be allowed as the administration of the system becomes more lenient, and thus additional loopholes are created.

[1] Personally communicated by officials.

Prostitution in Europe

These are, however, matters of detail on which it is not worth while to pause longer. The issue turns mainly on the effect of the partial use of the microscope,— at least once in two weeks at Berlin, on suspicion in other places. How far-reaching is the improvement thus wrought among the small number of women affected by it?

In respect to syphilis, the situation is hardly modified at all, except in so far as the general quality of the personnel has unquestionably been improved by the introduction of more modern methods and a more dignified environment. But these factors are not far-reaching. The inscribed women have either had syphilis before inscription, in which event no check was placed on them at the time; or they contract it subsequently, in which case they are interned only until the active ulceration has been converted to more or less latency, without certain termination of the infectious character of the disease. The scope of improved regulation in dealing with inscribed syphilitics is thus practically as limited as that of the older form; it has no definite or reliable effect during the dangerous primary and secondary stages and is, of course, unnecessary in the tertiary stage.

For the reasons just urged, neo-regulation concerns itself mainly with gonorrhœa. Figures already given [2] show that the moment the use of the microscope begins, the amount of gonorrhœa detected increases; indeed, the more slides one prepares in dealing with a group of women at a single inspection, the higher the percent-

[2] Pages 231–2.

age of infectious subjects. Whether gonorrhœa is discovered in a prostitute or not is largely a question of the microscopist's patience: " the oftener microscopical examinations are made, the more girls are found diseased." Lochte examined 172 girls once each, when 19.1 per cent. gave positive evidence of gonococci; on a second trial, twice as many (38.6 per cent.). Different investigators have discovered that from 50 to 65 per cent. of inscribed women carry the gonococcus hidden in glands or folds.[3] Ten successive daily examinations of a former servant gave negative results for 5 days. positive on the fifth and seventh, negative, sixth, eighth, ninth, and tenth. Instances are known in which the disease has been contracted by a patron from a woman in whom the microscope was unable to demonstrate the gonococcus. The explanation is obvious. When the germs are less numerous, it is a matter of chance whether the infinitesimal amount of the secretion examined happens to contain a sample or not; but infectiousness exists none the less. The microscopist may not encounter it; the customer may. In order to reduce chances of error, negative findings on three successive days are required before release; but Professor Pinkus told me of women released from the hospital on these terms in the morning who — without intercourse in the meanwhile — gave positive specimens at the police examination in the afternoon. Besides, under sexual excitement, the gonococcus that has burrowed more deeply

[3] Möller, *"Ist eine Gonorrhöekontrolle möglich?" Zeitschrift* VI, p. 233.

is all the more apt to be exuded. The explanation is simple: "Gonorrhœa in the male is almost invariably curable, if the patient submits to treatment; gonorrhœa in the female is almost never cured at all." [4] And again: "Every prostitute, even though not acutely and violently diseased, is always more or less infectious and not the least confidence in her freedom from gonorrhœa can be justified." [5] A chronic condition supervenes that is always infectious,— and most of all so during intercourse. Professor Havas of Budapest, long the head of the hospital service to which diseased prostitutes were sent, a regulationist at first, and now a strenuous opponent thereof on the basis of experience, refused to certify released women as "well"; he struck the word from the woman's protocol and inserted "improved"; but in the "improved" condition, the danger of communicating infection is always present.

All that I have just urged would be true even if the microscope were constantly used. But, as a matter of fact, even where neo-regulation is most systematically installed, the labor and the time involved are so enormous that it has proved impracticable to institute anything beyond occasional microscopical control.[6] What does the fortnightly microscopic slide in Berlin prove? That at two moments in the course of a month, a random shot failed to elicit positive proof of infectiousness! During two weeks, the utterly incompetent clinical examina-

[4] Pinkus *loc. cit.*, p. 86. Some physicians hold that the latter part of this statement is perhaps too sweeping, but all are agreed that gonorrhœa in the female is infinitely more stubborn than in the male and that gonorrhœa in prostitutes is practically never cured.
[5] *Ibid*, p. 91.
[6] Güth admits this, *loc. cit.*, p. 11. See also *Zeitschrift* II, p. 106.

Regulation and Disease

tion alone threatens the woman's withdrawal from business; should she be even palpably infected, she may easily be allowed to continue the distribution of gonococci during this period. At the close of two weeks, her chances of detention momentarily increase. Yet, even so, the numbers at any time interned show the inadequacy of the method to reach and to isolate any considerable volume of infection. During four months — December 1910; January February and March 1911 — 809 cases of gonorrhœal infection were discovered among the registered prostitutes at Berlin:[7] that is, on the average, the number of women in circulation was reduced about 200 per month. On the last day of four successive years (1908-9-10-11) the total number of interned prostitutes was as follows: 98, 105, 140, 242.[8] In the other towns where the improved system is in use, its inadequacy is equally striking. At the time of my visit to Dresden (June 19, 1912), 9 inscribed and 27 non-inscribed women were in the venereal hospital ward; at Bremen there is an average of 18 to 20 patients of all kinds. All this is well-nigh negligible even when compared only with the total inscription; when viewed in connection with the total amount of prostitution and disease, it is not worth mention.

It is, of course, urged that, be the number removed and temporarily confined ever so small, infection is at least reduced by that amount. The argument holds only in case the number removed is large enough to affect the accessibility of temptation. Ten women in a

[7] Privately communicated at headquarters.
[8] Personally communicated by officials.

bordell will, for example, satisfy all the customers who come; if one is withdrawn — and the percentage withdrawn by medical inspection is by no means so large — the remaining nine will dispose of the same volume of trade. The amount of congress is therefore hardly affected: is the amount of disease reduced? That depends on the condition of the nine with whom the business is transacted. Similarly, on the streets: two hundred women are withdrawn from the streets of Berlin, on which every evening thousands of others roam. The provocation is not perceptibly influenced. Let us follow what happens to a prospective customer. A woman — Marie, let us say — to whose solicitations some man would have succumbed, is in the hospital. Is her clientele so attached to her that they will abstain until she is released? If so, undoubtedly, there being less congress, there is less disease in that interval. But the traffic is not organized in that way. Marie's customers are picked up by Gretchen or by some one else. Does the withdrawal of 250 women reduce disease, if it involves only redistributing business so that what would have been intercourse with the interned Marie is transferred to others?

That depends on the condition of the other women. Are they safe? The vast clandestine army not hygienically supervised is no safer than it would be if there were no medical regulation; and this army is so large a proportion of the whole that we may declare at once that the effect of removing a controlled prostitute is to force her business largely upon prostitutes who are uncontrolled; and the latter are so numerous and prom-

Regulation and Disease

incut that the business is kept to the maximum permitted by general conditions, regardless of the forced isolation of an inconsiderable number. Those of Marie's customers who fall to controlled prostitutes are hardly likely to fare better,— for the controlled prostitute is suffering with a chronic cervical gonorrhœa which any customer may contract. When 150 inscribed women are withdrawn from the roll of 3,000, all having gonorrhœa in some form, when 70 women are withdrawn from the uninscribed thousands, mostly infected, the good luck of a patron may save him once or twice with or without regulation, but sooner or later he will fall a victim.

The amount of disease communicated and contracted is, therefore, in the long run, dependent not on the existence or the non-existence of medical inspection, but on the frequency and amount of irregular intercourse. Professor Havas, in discussing with me the Budapest situation, urged vehemently that there is but one factor to be reckoned with, viz., the amount of promiscuous coitus. Whatsoever reduces such coitus, reduces disease: a rainy night, driving women and men from the streets, an outburst of police repression, do more to check disease than any system of regulation; on the other hand, regulation, by making controlled — and in consequence uncontrolled — prostitution prominent, by weakening the inhibitions, social, individual and hygienic, increases the amount of coitus and thereby increases the amount of disease. It is surely not without significance that Professor Pinkus, head of the hospital for venereally infected prostitutes, has published a book,

Prostitution in Europe

called the "Prevention of Venereal Disease," in which
he emphasizes the infectiousness of all prostitutes, controlled as well as uncontrolled, and bids his readers refrain
or utilize mechanical preventives for their protection!

It is therefore not surprising to find how frequently
afflicted men in regulated cities refer their infection to
professional prostitutes. Pinkus, inquiring of 2,512
male patients, traced 1,571 cases (62.54 per cent.) to
prostitutes, of whom 1,350 (52.74 per cent.) were professionals.[9] Of 661 infections in Stockholm, 297 could
be traced to their sources: 151, or over 50 per cent.,
were known to come from inscribed women.[10] Dealing with 102 infected gymnasial students, Meirowski
traced little less than half to registered women.[11]

Does the foregoing condemnation of sanitary control
apply to the bordell inmates as well as to scattered prostitutes? Or does the medically regulated bordell offer an
increasing measure of hygienic protection? Assuredly
not on the score of more thorough medical examination.
In so far as the inspection takes place in the bordell,
as is the case in Paris, Hamburg, Rome, Geneva, and
Brussels, the situation is aggravated rather than improved; for nowhere are there proper facilities, and the
women may all the more readily practise imposition.[12]
Disease is therefore not more likely to be discovered.

[9] *Loc. cit.*, p. 89.
[10] *Zeitschrift* V, p. 286.
[11] *Zeitschrift* XI, p. 6. See also articles by Loeb referred to
under Chapter I.
[12] This would appear the more charitable explanation of the fact
that 429 inmates of Paris bordells showed one case of syphilis in
1902; 312 showed none in 1903. Turot, *loc. cit.*, p. 70. In the
Roman brothels, "not oftener than once in three or four months
is a girl discovered who is diseased and forced to withdraw from

Regulation and Disease

On the other hand, it is more likely by far to be widely distributed: for the bordell prostitute entertains, as we have learned, a stream of patrons. Schrank estimated that the Vienna women averaged three to ten visitors daily; but the number is known on occasions to have risen to thirty or higher.[13] An authentic instance of 57 visitors in one day is recorded;[14] the city physician of Rome vouched for a case of 60 visitors; the mayor of Bordeaux told the French commission of a woman who had received 82 clients in a single day.[15] The sale of alcohol in the bordell markedly increases the range of infection, for it provokes recklessness and banishes caution. It has been estimated that one-third of the gonorrhœal infections are incurred while the victim is in liquor.[16] If then, the woman is herself infected, she has enlarged facilities for distributing disease; even if not herself infected, she may be the carrier of disease from one of her patrons to others of the series. The chief physician of the Vienna police remarked in a public discussion of this point: "The prostitute is often only the carrier of an infection. It is nothing new to find a man who has contracted disease from a woman whom the most careful examination pronounces 'healthy.' These things happen with all infectious diseases."[17]

Statistics favorable to this contention can be submit-

the house!" In one establishment it was declared that no girl had been disbarred for years on account of disease: an instance was however recalled — "four years ago."

[13] Schrank, *loc. cit.*, Vol. II, p. 209.

[14] *Zeitschrift* I, p. 375.

[15] *Report, French Commission*, p. 110.

[16] Pinkus, *loc. cit.*, p. 108, with notes. In Möller's cases at Stockholm, 67.7% of the infected men admitted intoxication. *Zeitschrift* V., p. 301.

[17] *Zeitschrift* IX, p. 103.

Prostitution in Europe

ted; but in view of the liability of the patient to error [18] in locating the source of his infection, the argument is perhaps more conclusive than the figures. A single set of statistics from Bremen that appears to prove the reverse will be presently accounted for. More significant, however, is the contrast between the amount of disease discovered in the bordell inmates of Hamburg and the scattered prostitutes of Berlin: [19]

Number inscribed women

Year	1903	1904	1905	1906	1907
Berlin	3,709	3,287	3,135	3,518	3,692
Hamburg	1,266	1,258	1,291	1,039	920

Number found diseased

Year	1903	1904	1905	1906	1907
Berlin	620	505	576	660	732
Hamburg	759	843	719	721	791

Percentage diseased

Year	1903	1904	1905	1906	1907
Berlin	16.7	15.3	18.3	18.7	19.8
Hamburg	59.9	67.0	55.7	69.3	85.9

When the comparison is made in terms of examinations rather than individuals, the result is similarly to the disadvantage of the bordell. Of 1,000 examinations made of bordell inmates in Brussels between 1881 and 1885, 2.71 per cent. showed disease; of the same number of examinations of scattered women 2.51 per cent.[20] But perhaps the best statistical proof is derived from Vienna, where substantially the same methods — if poor, at any

[18] This is well discussed by Oppenheim and Neugebauer in *Zeitschrift* XII, pp 306-7. One-half of the men interrogated were unable to give definite answers. *Ditto*, p. 314.
[19] *Zeitschrift* XII, pp.6-7.
[20] *Ditto*. It is, of course, clear that these figures are vitiated by the poor quality of the examinations; but undoubtedly, whatever her own condition, the bordell prostitute can contaminate more men, if she is herself diseased — as our argument proves her to be — and, in any event, she is so situated as to act as a passive carrier more largely.

rate consistently poor — were applied to both sets of registered women, the bordell women making regularly the worse record: [21]

| Year | 1888 | Percentage diseased | | | | |
		1889	1890	1891	1892	1893
Bordell inmates 13		12	15	13.5	13.5	12
Scattered prostitutes. 2		3.6	5.3	4.7	6.5	5.8

The bordell is particularly dangerous to youth, whose curiosity it excites; and recklessness and ignorance characteristic of that period results in an exceptionally high ratio of infection. Pinkus gives some statistics collected at Kiel, showing that of 100 boys under 20, 33.75 per cent. had been infected in the bordells of that city; of 100 men over 20, the bordells were held responsible in only 19.75 per cent.[22] Hecht, discussing the experience of Prague, points out the " relatively greater frequency of infection in bordells " and attributes it confidently to the " greater volume of their business in consequence of their readier accessibility." [23]

Against the position above taken, the experience of Bremen has recently been cited. There the percentage of infection discovered among bordell women has been steadily reduced by the system of regulation in vogue. In 1900, the 50 inhabitants of Helenenstrasse averaged 1.4 infections each; in 1905, the seventy-odd women there averaged .73 infections each; in 1910, .38 apiece.[24]

Can it be fairly inferred that a strictly supervised bordell system will thus greatly diminish danger? As a matter of fact, there is no pretense that the total

[21] Referat, *loc. cit.*, p. 104.
[22] *Loc. cit.*, p. 69.
[23] *Zeitschrift* VIII, p. 399.
[24] The system is fully described by Weidanz in *Zeitschrift* XIV, pp. 88, etc. It is to be observed that nothing is said as to the amount of disease contracted by men.

amount of venereal disease in Bremen has been perceptibly influenced by the bordell control. The business of
the bordells is steadily shrinking; the clandestine prostitute — uncontrolled and unregulated — thrives. Hence,
even if effective, the Bremen remedy is impossible. Seventy women can be drilled to exercise all kinds of precaution,— but the moment the number is largely increased,
supervision collapses. The smaller number of women
here interned can be forced to provide their guests with
mechanical devices — and themselves to utilize strong an-
tiseptic douches.[25]   But it by no means follows that the
same policy could be operated wholesale. The figures are
themselves, however, without the significance attributed
to them. In the first place because, as the oft-infected
prostitute suffers from chronic gonorrhœa, she is always
a menace, most of all so during coition (let the examination say what it will); strong douches simply wash
away accessible evidence. In the second place, because
the membership of the little colony is so constantly
changing that the figures do not speak for the condition
of a definite set of women. The following table brings
this point out clearly:

Year	Enrolment Jan. 1st	Added during year	Withdrawn
1902	47	33	28
1903	52	59	41
1904	68	78	72

There was thus a constant entrance and exit, the entire membership being transformed in a short space of
time.[26]   Looking through the police records, I ascertained that one woman had been resident six years, one

[25] It is stated that 22,000 sublimate of mercury pastilles were used
by them last year.
[26] *Zeitschrift* IV, p. 81.

or two others one and a half years; all the rest were recent additions.

There is therefore no basis in experience for a verdict favorable to bordells on the ground that they conduce to a form of medical inspection that tends to diminish disease. The fact is that, though infection can be lessened by the use of mechanical devices, the recklessness developed in bordells consequent on alcoholic indulgence operates to prevent rather than to encourage precautionary measures. The women never cease to be dangerous; and as they transact an amount of business impossible outside, the actual amount of infection is enormously increased.

On the medical side, therefore, regulation is even weaker than on the side of order. There is a connection between prostitution and disorder, in such wise that some sort of police control of disorderly or criminal prostitution might conceivably be a useful way of keeping them in easy reach. Experience proves that the same object can indeed be otherwise attained, and without granting enrolled prostitutes privileges which are themselves damaging to the public and straightway involve the extension of similar privileges to the uncontrolled. But there is still a grain of truth at the bottom, namely, that the low-grade prostitute tends to align herself with crime and for that reason may be properly made a constant object of police surveillance.

It is absurd, however, to infer that machinery devised in the interest of order is equally applicable to sanitation. On the score of order, the police are interested in criminal and semi-criminal prostitutes. The discreet

Prostitution in Europe

women who ply their vocation inconspicuously and in a businesslike spirit give no trouble and are therefore never inscribed. Disease however, is an altogether different matter. From that there is for the prostitute no exemption whatsoever. She contracts it irrespective of her outward demeanor; and she communicates it, regardless of the general decorousness of her behavior. The criminal law runs against a part of the prostitute army; the bacteriological law against all. A form of control adequate to the former is therefore entirely inadequate to the latter.

There is then on the sanitary side no support whatever for the theory of police regulation. It assumes that those dangerous to order are the ones most dangerous to health; that crime and disease go together; that if the police inscribe women inclined to join prostitution and crime, they will thus get hold of the main sources of infection. But the truth is far otherwise. The non-criminal prostitute is at least as dangerous to health as the criminal prostitute. The young, who cannot be inscribed; the older, more cautious and more showy who take care not to annoy the police; the occasionals and incidentals, who oscillate between or mingle prostitution and work; — these are perhaps even more active agents in spreading disease than the utterly repulsive women whose thieving or drinking propensities make them the peculiar objects of police care on the score of order.

There is another objection to identifying disease and crime, as the association of medical inspection with the police inevitably does. The infected prostitute has been taught that the consequences of disease resemble the

262

consequences of crime; they lead to arrest and condemnation,— even though condemnation means only a hospital ward. This ward is in some places still a prison; in others, prison associations cling to it. In consequence, the woman's first impulse on realizing her condition is to flee or to hide. She resorts to a quack, she employs superficial remedies to conceal the ravages and signs of infection; and she plies her business. Hence a few wretched or foolish girls and women who are in ignorance of their condition or who have been suddenly apprehended find themselves pronounced " diseased." One sees them at St. Lazare and other less hideous places,— all alike poor and friendless. The more clever of the inscribed women, if diseased, disappear into remote lodgings or to other towns; the fear of the prison hospital leads them to conceal and to scatter infection. Nor is there any hope of breaking off the association in the woman's mind so long as a pretended sanitary function is lodged in police hands.

The women have thus completely penetrated the sanitary insincerity of regulation. They know that they are not regulated simply because they are prostitutes,— not even because they are diseased prostitutes. Too many mere prostitutes are never touched; the diseased prostitute is too rarely apprehended just on that account. A woman is inscribed because, being a prostitute, with or without disease, she has incurred,— justly enough, doubtless, as a rule — the suspicion and displeasure of the police. The hygienic motive did not and does not start the machinery to move, and its connection with ordinary police functions, methods and spirit results in its own discredit and defeat.

Prostitution in Europe

A final absurdity remains to be pointed out. What can it avail to incarcerate for brief periods a few unhappy women, if meanwhile the manufacture of fresh foci of infection proceeds unhampered? As long as regulation completely omits men,[27] new sources of infection are produced far more rapidly than by any known method they can be eradicated. A vicious circle exists. Men infect the beginners — themselves at the time out of reach — who in their turn infect other men. I pointed out in the opening chapter that prostitution is a concept involving two persons. Logic and justice alike require that both parties be considered as equal partners in the act; and in no respect is it more completely impossible to omit either of the two essential factors from the reckoning than in the matter of disease. Society has chosen to overlook the man; but nature has righted the balance by impartially distributing disease and suffering; nor will she permit herself to be outwitted by any one-sided scheme, even though it be far more extensive and efficient than regulation has thus far anywhere been.

Regulation, needless on the score of order, is thus seen to be positively harmful in its bearing on disease. As a system, therefore, it runs counter to the modern spirit in ethics, in politics, and in hygiene. Why then should it still exist in places, why should it fight so stubbornly for survival? To the answering of this question, the last chapter dealing with the subject will be devoted.

[27] The absurdity of ignoring the male factor in any endeavor to lessen disease is clearly shown by the following incident: In Christiania, in 1910, among those applying for free treatment of venereal disease, were 21 women who named their husbands as the source of infection, 6 men who named their wives.

CHAPTER VIII

THE REAL INWARDNESS OF REGULATION

Reasons for partial survival of regulation.— Policy rapidly losing ground.— Ignorance of its details.— Political and social conservatism. — Vested interests.—Regulation and police corruption.— Ulterior motives.— Final objection to regulation.

In the course of the last three chapters I have been at pains to discuss in detail the continental regulation of vice. I have shown that the term regulation denotes no uniform system, but that, on the contrary, marked variations of system exist, explicable in the main, as different attempts to stop a gap, to prevent further collapse, or to effect a readjustment somewhat less repugnant to modern feeling. Two reasons continue to be advanced officially in support of the system: that it is necessary to the police authorities for the maintenance of order, and that it contributes to the reduction of venereal disease. The former contention has been shown to lack substantial basis; the latter is assuredly in most cases either insincere or mistaken,—insincere, I take it, in Paris, where the most elementary sanitary precautions are neglected, where the administration of the hygienic features is so notoriously bad that one cannot but suspect the entire sanitary object; mistaken at Vienna, where a conscientious administration continues to labor at the task with implements and methods already obsolete. I have shown, further, that, futile at its best,

Prostitution in Europe

regulation is at its worst when associated with recognized or tolerated bordells, for the bordell is itself the scene of disorder and the hotbed of exploitation, excess, and disease. Of the ethical argument against regulation little has thus far been made, for it seemed better in the first place to examine the system on its own chosen ground. Nevertheless, it must be admitted that the ethical argument has played a part in discrediting a system, which has suffered alike from its own obvious failure as well as from the growing disgust of society.

For the reasons just summarized, regulation has lost and is still rapidly losing ground. As recently as a quarter of a century ago it was in vogue throughout the Continent of Europe; in the seventies it enjoyed a brief currency in Great Britain as well. It is decaying in France where, of 695 communes having over 5,000 inhabitants, it has entirely disappeared from 250[1] and practically from many others. In Germany, of 162 cities, 48 have dispensed with it,[2] while it is moribund in others. In Switzerland it survives only in Geneva; it has been wholly abandoned in Denmark, Norway and Great Britain. A special commission has recommended its total abolition in France; and a similar body in Sweden, far from unanimous at the start, has unanimously come to the same conclusion. Partisans of regulation sometimes endeavor to explain away this general movement on the ground that in it ethics and sentimentality have simply prevailed over science and commonsense. But the facts lie far otherwise. Religious bodies have indeed taken a

[1] *Report, French Commission, Annexes,* p. 54.
[2] Scheven, *loc. cit.,* p. 11.

The Real Inwardness of Regulation

prominent part; but there has been no lack of facts contributed and vouched for by physicians and scientists of distinction. Among the most prominent opponents of regulation are publicists, who have observed its futility from the standpoint of order, and medical specialists who have become convinced of its uselessness from the standpoint of sanitation.[3]

For its partial survival thus far in France, Germany, and Austria-Hungary there is no single or simple explanation; several considerations combine to retard what is unmistakably a general movement destined to efface the system in all its forms. Let us briefly consider the factors in question.

Ignorance is partially responsible. The general public is uninformed; many intelligent people have only the vaguest ideas as to what is taking place in the name of regulation; even the police have rarely studied the problem except shortsightedly in relation to their own daily necessities. In Paris, the principles involved have been indeed the subject of acrimonious discussion for many years; but I recall the utter amazement with which a distinguished politician, to whom I had been referred as one keenly interested in the topic, heard that at that moment only one hundred and seventy women were interned on the score of disease. Other similar incidents could be given. The Budapest officials had studied and adopted the revised Berlin procedure; the Vienna officials had studied the Budapest and Berlin bureaus on the ground; but other instances of painstaking examina-

[3] Lack of space makes a fuller historical account impossible in this volume. The reader will find the details in " *The Social Evil: a Report* " (New York, 1912) pp. 163-196.

Prostitution in Europe

tion of the workings and the effects of regulation even on the part of those charged with its enforcement were very rare indeed. I learned to my surprise that the police of one town knew of other systems only what was printed,— an inadequate basis for judgment, because the official accounts are too favorable and quite fragmentary, conveying no accurate idea of conditions and events; the abundant outside literature is so uneven and so conflicting that the bureaucrat, reading it in his office, and not knowing what to believe, neglects it almost altogether. Partisans of retention, reform, and abolition alike fight more or less largely with lame weapons,— reports, hearsay, and newspaper clippings. The Paris police, for example, urge that if the morals patrol were abolished, respectable women would not be free from molestation on the streets; and a high official cited Zurich as a striking example. Inquiry and observation on my part at Zurich failed to discover the slightest basis for the statement. Non-existent statistics are frequently referred to, to show the dreadful things that have followed in the wake of abolition in England. Under these conditions the emotional fervor with which the ethical argument has been pushed has had at times an effect just opposite to that intended. The police official sees a conflict between facts and ethics where, had the facts been dispassionately and comparatively presented, he might remark that religious zeal was merely sweeping away in righteous indignation the fallen timbers of a structure condemned by its own results.

The political and social conservatism of Europe doubtless also operates to stay the reforming hand.

The Real Inwardness of Regulation

Regulation of some kind has existed time out of mind, — in classical and medieval, as in modern times. Prostitutes have formed a class apart; and societies which respect class differentiations readily enough transmit an institution which appears to be founded simply on the frank acceptance of what has been, is, and will continue to be. That much more than this is implied in and countenanced by regulation is a consideration, the force of which is not appreciated until the critical and inquiring spirit becomes active.

Regulation enjoys, however, more positive and more formidable protection than would be afforded by either ignorance or tradition. It is identified with powerful vested interests. Of European office-holders — as of all others — it is true that "officials rarely resign and never die." The officials — lay and medical — and the patrolmen directly and indirectly connected with the morals bureau form a place-holding interest, magnifying its own importance, stating its own case in the way that is most likely to carry conviction and resisting interference with all the strength of the instinct that struggles for existence. The destruction of the system would sweep away a more or less numerous official apparatus: commissaries and inspectors for whom there might be no other places; examining physicians to whom the official stipend is perhaps an important item.

Less creditable motives are also alleged. The European police [4] bear, on the whole, an excellent reputation. As to the capacity, intelligence and integrity of the offi-

[4] This topic will be exhaustively considered in Mr. Raymond B. Fosdick's forthcoming volume *The European Police* in this same series. I touch it briefly here for the reason that appears in the text.

cials one hears no question raised. The administration of the police furnishes a legitimate and honorable career, comparable in prominence and dignity with that of the army or the bench. The police president is usually a jurist of university training who has risen to his post by promotion on the basis of merit. His appointment has no connection with politics, and he holds office for life or good behavior. The very patrolmen are selected with scrupulous care. In Germany no man is appointed unless he has served as an under-officer during his military service; in England, fresh men are taken from the country and small towns in order to avoid connections and associations possibly prejudicial to disinterested service. The rank and file therefore are trustworthy and respected. Exceptions occur, but it is nowhere believed that they are frequent or serious.

But this exemplary reputation does not belong to the morals police. Once more, the head officials are nowhere involved; charges of corruption and grave impropriety on the part of the patrolmen in the morals service are, however, all too common. The situation created by regulation is indeed an impossible one. Prostitution is treated as inevitable; it is authorized and " regulated " on the ground that men will indulge themselves. And yet the morals police who are closest to it are expected to hold aloof! Again, women are exploited by pimps, by liquor-dealers, by bordell-keepers; yet regulation assumes that the morals police who are every moment in position to sell favors, exemptions and privileges will refrain from doing so.[5]

[5] Lindenau grants this by implication. He argues for a change

The Real Inwardness of Regulation

In truth, such oversight as would insure an honest morals police adequate to the need in point of number cannot possibly be instituted. The task would be difficult enough if all prostitutes were treated alike; for public opinion and official supervision could then enforce a consistent policy. But public opinion and official supervision cannot enforce a policy abounding in exceptions. The moment exceptions occur, an opportunity for trading, for corruption, for collusion is created; hence the danger arising from measures applicable to part only of the offenders. If at the most one prostitute in six or eight or ten is to be registered, who is to know on what basis the others escape through the net? Who is to tell whether an officer refrains from making an arrest, because he lacks proof, or has been bought off with money or favors? It can occasion no surprise therefore to find it freely asserted that among the stronger forces working for the retention of regulation must be reckoned the personal interest of corrupt placemen, and of liquor-dealers, dance-hall-owners, and bordell-keepers who through regulation come into possession of a group of women whom they can exploit. The effort to dislodge regulation in Geneva — the sole Swiss town in which it survives — has been so far successfully resisted by a combination of bordell-keepers, liquor-dealers, gamblers and high livers, who proclaim Geneva as a "smaller Paris," and urge that the miniature should be characterized by all the gaiety and frivolity of the prototype. In Paris it is charged that morals policemen have acted as

of law on the ground that thus "an end will be put to the reproach that controlled prostitutes are exposed to the caprice of subaltern police officers on account of the details of the rules." *Loc. cit.*, p. 27.

" go-betweens " in negotiations between brothel-keepers
and street women; that they have in some instances under
threat of arrest forced girls from the street into houses
needing recruits; and that they have been bribed to
overlook infractions of the age-limit. These are not
the irresponsible charges of unknown journalists; they
are made on the authority of some of the ablest publicists in France,— a former prime minister among them.
I have in my possession a copy of a letter written by a
morals policeman to a street prostitute working for him
as a pimp! One hears of similar incidents elsewhere.
Shortly before I went to Berlin,— so I was informed —
twelve men had been dismissed from the force for un-
worthy conduct. A similar incident again recently took
place. The Berlin morals patrolmen are permitted to
utilize registered women as spies in order to obtain information for their guidance. A girl thus used turned
upon her employers, denouncing them as " pimps." Of
those accused additional evidence was procured against
only three; and of these one was clearly proved to have
received from her 1,000 marks. At Frankfort I was
told of instances in which it was found that police officers lived in the very houses to which registered
prostitutes were referred. We may conclude, therefore, that the corrupt interest of unprincipled men
inside and outside the force is a factor in the struggle to
retain regulation.

With the difficulties of the police situation in non-
regulated communities I shall deal in subsequent chapters; but it must be remarked at this juncture that the
defects of the morals police above pointed out arise not

The Real Inwardness of Regulation

only from the existence of this specialized force, but from the fact that they are called on to execute a self-contradictory policy; neither superior officers nor the public can know to whom the rules are applicable and to whom not. But in non-regulated towns, with or without a morals police system, the same policy is applied to all. Street-walking is or is not allowed; bordells are or are not tolerated. The opportunity for corruption disappears, not simply because the morals police disappear — this is not always the case — but because an equitable and readily controllable régime is introduced.

There must, of course, be other motives at work to account for the maintenance of regulation; for the police heads being, as I have urged, men of honor and intelligence must be regarded as putting up with, while combatting, the evils just mentioned for the sake of other objects, which they assume to outweigh the disadvantages involved. Certain provisions of the rules governing inscribed women give the clue by means of which the motives in question may be arrived at; and confirmatory evidence can also be found.

I have frequently called attention to the fact that a woman is not registered because she is a prostitute, nor even because she is a diseased prostitute. The women who nightly frequent the cafés, dance halls and variety shows are among the most notorious prostitutes in Europe,— thoroughly well known to the police and to the public,— yet no effort is anywhere made to inscribe them. These women are not overlooked because their health is miraculously protected; as a matter of fact, they have run the gamut of disease, are liable to gon-

orrhœal re-infection, and are by some specialists regarded
as especially dangerous because they appear to rather
better advantage than street-walkers. The same statements apply to hundreds, in the largest cities to thousands,
of prostitutes, far more humble in aspect who ply their
trade quietly and unostentatiously on the streets. From
time to time a few of them, apprehended for drunkenness
or soliciting, are forcibly inscribed in towns permitting
compulsory inscription; but for the most part, these
women do not reach the police rolls and no systematic
effort is anywhere made to place them there. Over a
glass of wine in the cafés of Montmartre or the Latin
quarter one readily elicits the tell-tale facts. The hab-
itués of these resorts know the police and the police
know them. There is not the slightest doubt as to their
status; nightly they appear in their habitat. They are
not inscribed, even though their notoriously promiscuous
relations necessarily result in infection. They are not
inscribed because they behave well. Unaggressive in
demeanor, they engage the passer-by in bantering conversation, disclosing their purpose but rarely pushing it.
Their habits, abode, and associations are known to the
police, but known to involve no open break with order
or with conventional notions of decency. Only when
crime or disorder brings them into suspicion or prominence, do they become objects of police observation,
eventually inscribed and forced to report for medical examination — the device by means of which they are kept
under close surveillance. " The medical visit is only the
excuse made for arbitrary police power." [6]

[6] "La visite est la seule excuse de ce règlement de police arbi-

The Real Inwardness of Regulation

The fact then that notorious prostitutes who give no offence by their actions, associations, or movements easily evade inscription suggests at once that inscription is not due to prostitution as such, or to prostitution complicated by disease, but to prostitution in so far as it is suspected of alliance with criminality or disorder.[7] This interpretation is sustained by many facts; in the first place, by the spy system, which has just been exposed in Berlin The streets abound in prostitutes to detect whom no spies are needed; yet they are for the most part overlooked by the police. Spies are utilized to get hold of prostitutes to whom there is some objection other than their promiscuous sexual life. Again, everywhere in deciding the question as to whether or not a woman should be arrested, enormous importance is attached to her possessing a definite domicile. In Berlin, for example, girls with " feste Wohnung " (definite domicile) are not apprehended on the streets unless irrefragable evidence is at hand; girls who on interrogation prove to be without " feste Wohnung " are taken up promptly. The distinction is obviously not made on the theory that the former is not a prostitute, while the latter is,— both are; nor on the theory that the former is probably infectious, the latter not,— again, both are. The significant difference is that prostitutes with " feste Wohnung " are apt to be law-abiding and can in any case be readily

traire." Reuss: " *La Prostitution au point de vue de l'hygiène et de l'administration.*" Paris, 1889, p. 788. Quoted by Schmölder in "*Staat und Prostitution.*" (Berlin, 1900), p. 13.

[7] There is also an element of luck that ought to be taken into account. Some girls fall into the hands of the morals police because they happen to be caught doing things which others have done and continue to do with impunity.

Prostitution in Europe

laid hold of, while prostitutes without " feste Wohnung "
are apt to be criminal vagabonds of highly elusive
quality.[8] Registration enables the police to pin these
women down and by compelling them to report to headquarters at brief intervals enables the police to keep in
constant touch with a criminal or semi-criminal element.

There is perhaps another point worth mentioning.
The continental police are constantly concerned lest some
possible source of disturbance escape surveillance. For
this reason they keep a close watch on individuals, on
political movements, social agitations, societies, etc.
Prostitution is a potential source of disturbance; the
police therefore need to do something about it, before
anything happens. Fortunately, from time to time experience shows that well-ordered and well-governed
communities may safely be less solicitous about themselves; and cities which have discarded regulation are
surprised to find that the loss of unusual machinery and
the neglect of unusual precautions have been without
baleful consequences.

The above view — that regulation at the present day
is retained because it gives the police an additional arm
in dealing with a certain class of delinquents — is further
sustained by certain explicit provisions of the rules.
For the Berlin regulations stipulate: " Registered
women must at once, at any time, day or night, admit to
their rooms police officers who come to make inspection

---

[8] Vagabondage is elsewhere also the prime factor in registration.
A prominent Belgian publicist said to me in reference to Brussels:
"Only the women who are poor suffer from the law." See also
Chapter IX for the *Danish law on Vagabondage.*

The Real Inwardness of Regulation

respecting persons found with them." [9] Similarly in Hamburg: "Apart from all the regulations affecting registration of addresses required of all inhabitants, registered prostitutes must in person report within twenty-four hours every change of address; further, if they propose to leave the city permanently or transiently, they must in person announce the fact.[10] Police officers wishing to view their premises must be admitted without delay." [11] In Paris, the rules warn women "not to resist the agents of the authorities, nor to report falsely their names or addresses." [12] In Vienna, "the police may without explanation at any time forbid prostitutes to occupy a particular house or to room with a particular madame; the domiciles of prostitutes are to be under constant surveillance and delegates of the police must be admitted on request." [13] Schneider, noting that it "is well known that the police frequently utilize the lowest grade of prostitutes, who are accustomed to consort with criminals, as detectives," and that not seldom bordell-keepers and bordell inmates are required to act as police spies, quotes the following from the regulations in vogue at Eger: "Bordell proprietors are in duty bound to keep close watch on strange customers and to give the police prompt and quiet notice whenever suspicion is aroused." [14] The above regulations apply only to controlled women; uncontrolled prostitutes are amenable only to the rules applicable to all other per-

[9] Rule, 11.
[10] Rule 6.
[11] Rule 7.
[12] *Obligations et Défences inposées aux filles publiques.*
[13] Rules 14, 15.
[14] *Loc. cit.,* pp. 23, 180.

sons. The special provisions above cited are comprehensible if it is understood that a certain class of prostitutes, themselves of doubtful character, consort with and conceal criminal and suspicious characters; and the fact that regulation makes in general no effort to be more extensive than the class in question lends color to the view here taken.

There is, however, other evidence to the same effect. M. Lépine the former Prefect of Paris, has already been quoted as authority for the statement that it is the controlled women who annoy the police. Unless these women are enrolled not because they are prostitutes, but because they are criminals, there would be no reason why arrested prostitutes should prove to be mainly controlled prostitutes. If prostitutes were enrolled without regard to criminality or criminal associates, those arrested would be mainly non-registered women, since the latter are much the more numerous and at least as prominent. Yet the figures everywhere tell the opposite story. In Paris, for instance, in 1903, 55,641 arrests were made among the inscribed women, numbering that year 6,418 women; among the far greater number of unregistered women, 1,426 were arrested once, 1,395 more than once,— a total, almost negligible, of 2,821.[15] The disproportion is less marked at Berlin and the totals smaller, but the same fact emerges: of controlled women in 1909, 1,122 were arrested; of clandestines many times as numerous, 636; in 1910, the figures are 1,984 and 878 respectively.[16] The following table shows for

[15] Turot, *loc. cit.*, pp. 33, 35, See also Commenge, *loc. cit.*, Ch. II.
[16] *Police Report, loc. cit.*, p. 72. I cannot make out whether re-arrests are included in these figures,— probably not.

The Real Inwardness of Regulation

a series of years the number of women arrested by the morals police of Breslau and the quotas contributed thereto, by inscribed, formerly inscribed, and non-inscribed women: [17]

Years	1890	1891	1892	1893	1894
Total arrests	1,336	1,570	1,707	1,768	1,995
Inscribed women	1,197	1,386	1,497	1,560	1,621
Formerly inscribed women..	12	16	22	14	17
Non-inscribed women	127	168	188	194	357

At Stockholm, those imprisoned are always much more numerous than those in the hospital, as e. g., 201 in prison, 23 in the hospital in 1870; 162 as against 30 in 1890; 216 as against 74 in 1904.[18] So, of 979 women punished between 1885 and 1889, 198 were sentenced to hard labor twice, 146 three times, 111 four times, 10 ten times, and 2 thirteen times.[19] That enrolled prostitution and criminal prostitution fairly coincide is thus manifest.

It is absurd, as we shall see when we deal with the preservation of order in non-regulated cities, to argue that either regulation or a special police is required in order to make these arrests. As a matter of fact, not a few of the occasions leading to arrests are attributable to regulation, partly in consequence of the well-nigh inevitable abuse of the privileges extended to the inscribed prostitute, partly because of trivial infractions of liberties enjoyed by non-inscribed and denied to inscribed prostitutes; [20] for just as the inscribed prostitute is au-

[17] *Zeitschrift* I, p. 298.
[18] Johansson in *Report, Swedish Commission*, Vol. III, p. 11.
[19] *Ibid,,* p. 123.
[20] For example, the following table shows number of breaches of

thorized to do certain things without molestation, so she is forbidden to do others that her non-inscribed sister does without interference.[21]   In any case, as disorder and crime are most rife among registered women, it would appear that the women are registered on the ground that they need police oversight and thus get it more effectually.

In the proceedings of the Paris bureau, incidents occur daily, explicable on the theory that I have just set forth, and not otherwise.   The police possess, as I have elsewhere explained, summary power; the girl has no witnesses, no counsel, no appeal.   I watched the following transactions, all suggestive of ulterior motive: a girl released from St. Lazare forty-eight hours before, was brought before the police physicians without charge of definite offence, adjudged diseased, and sent back to prison.   Clearly the police wanted her behind the bars, and regulation enabled them to put her there and keep her there.   Another had left St. Lazare twenty-four hours previously: picked up for disorder, she was sent back for four days.   A third, arrested the previous Friday, spent Saturday and Sunday in prison; re-arrested Monday, she received a six days' sentence.   The fourth was arrested at 2 A. M., after being out of prison one day. The next was asked at my suggestion, " How many terms have you served at St. Lazare? " Her answer: " I don't know,— too many to count."   The prison attendant explained to me that some of these " repeaters "

rules on the part of the few hundred inscribed prostitutes of Stockholm :

1903	1904	1905	1906
9,908	8,191	7,159	7,515

[21] This is the situation above adverted to as leading to corruption and injustice.

The Real Inwardness of Regulation

spend twenty-five nights out of every month there, receiving a constant succession of short sentences. They are hardened cases, whom the medical inspection keeps close to the police,— the police, who, by means of their summary jurisdiction, can put them out of the way whenever their suspicions are aroused! The fact that clandestines thrice arrested for "racolage" (soliciting) are compulsorily inscribed bears witness once more to the fact that registration seeks to get hold of only the disorderly and criminal.

The criminal arm with which the police are thus furnished is a plain-clothes division — a secret body moving noiselessly and armed with summary power. The women and the bordell-owners, where bordells exist, prosecute their business on the sufferance of this body. I have pointed out how this situation may lead to corruption of the rank and file. It is openly and responsibly charged that it has led even the higher authorities in some places — notably Paris — to employ their irresponsible power for political or other purposes. It is alleged that prostitutes and bordell-keepers have been utilized for blackmail and espionage. Concrete cases are always so involved in detail that the charge is hard to substantiate; but the high character of the persons who make it warrants the belief that it is not wholly baseless [22] Only a few months ago, the city of Mainz was profoundly agitated by the charge that the matron at-

[22] This appears to be especially true of Paris, where I was assured of the fact by many persons prominent in public life,— senators, former Cabinet Ministers, economists and physicians. My notes show their names, which are in not a few cases honorably known the world over. I regret that I do not feel warranted in giving them here.

tached to the morals bureau had been utilized illegally by her superiors in this very direction. To one who has taken the time to understand both the letter and the spirit of continental regulation, the point is too clear to require extensive argument. Blaschko's comment is entirely sound: " Hygiene is not the reason why the police so stubbornly hold on to regulation. For reasons that have nothing to do with hygiene the police have a decided interest in keeping under constant observation precisely this group of professional prostitutes. They are the women who stand in intimate relation with the criminal world, the friends of pimps, thieves, and burglars, often enough themselves thieves. Nobody disputes the right of the police to watch this dangerous class. But there is no doubt that the criminal point of view. which is the real basis of existing regulation actually gets in the way of efficient sanitary control." [23]

I shall show in the chapters dealing with abolition, that, in so far as concerns legitimate police control of the criminal element on which Blaschko here touches, there appears to be nothing in the problem that requires an extraordinary instrument vested with extra-legal powers; in so far as the final explanation of the tenacity of the police is espionage, there is no place in any modern society for an agency of this character. Crime can be kept within bounds without giving certain criminals the right to practise prostitution; to use the prostitute and her exploiter as spies and for that purpose to condone or to license their immorality traverses the modern conception of the function of the state.

[23] *Loc. cit.,* p. 83.

The Real Inwardness of Regulation

And here we come upon the final and unanswerable objection to any form of regulation. The modern state — the modern European state — is an organization charged with the positive duty of securing and promoting conditions which make for the welfare, happiness, and usefulness of every member of society. How far it can at any moment travel in the direction of compelling better conditions is a detail to be determined; but certain it is that the fundamental basis of modern statesmanship is violated by the notion that certain members can be sacrificed, body and soul, in order to win a trivial police advantage! Prostitution exists and on a large scale. The state is bound to face the fact, bound to admit its present existence,— its long history in the past, its menace for the future. But, be the outlook for its extermination or reduction good or bad, favorable or unfavorable, at the very least the whole weight of the state's power and influence, direct and indirect, must be thrown against it as wasteful, demoralizing, and infamous. If positive measures are feasible, they must be taken; if social disapproval is even slightly deterrent, it must be proclaimed with all the authority of society. "The law must be a teacher" in so far at least as it embodies an expression of what ought to be. It is absurd to suppose that the state can take this position — whatever its value — and yet authorize prostitution on any ground whatsoever,— absurd to preach continence and to license vice.

True enough, no police officer in Europe admits that regulation licenses vice. But, whatever the legal theory be, it does, nevertheless! The prostitute believes that she is practising a trade regulated by society, that society sim-

283

ply prescribes rules for the conduct of her business. There is, therefore, no more pathetic incongruity than that which is presented in the morals bureau of Berlin, Munich and Budapest, where a social worker is installed for the purpose of dissuasion, while the police officer waits in the adjoining room ready to authorize the career from which well-meaning but ineffective pleading has first endeavored to deter. The permission implied in the existence of regulation is at cross purposes with the sound attitude implied by the effort to persuade the girl to renounce her vicious ways. The social effort under these circumstances is little more than a sop to the popular demand that the state address itself with all its might to prevention and to salvation and under no circumstances to authorization.

This then is the final and weightiest objection to regulation: not that it fails as hygiene, not that it is contemptible as espionage, not that it is unnecessary as a police measure, but that it obstructs and confounds the proper attitude of society towards all social evils, of which prostitution is one. Men can refrain; the state must do nothing to make indulgence easier. Women must be saved, if possible; rescued, if preventive measures have come too feebly or too late. These sentences sum up the simple and entire duty of the state. Society must presume that the human spark has not been utterly quenched in the wrecked soul,— a fact that is not without support from experience. As against all this, inscription entices the girl, offering her a *quid pro quo* if she crosses the line. Thus it snaps the last weak thread that ties her to decent occupation or other

The Real Inwardness of Regulation

associations. In its ultimate effect, therefore, it is a compact with vice, whatever the language employed. It may not intend to encourage vice, but by conceding to vice a privileged position, it discourages all effort to prevent or uproot it.

CHAPTER IX

ABOLITION AND ORDER

Meaning of term " Abolition."— Immediate effect of abolition.—
General distinction between regulation and abolition.— Abolition not
laissez-faire.— Provisions of English law as to street-walking,—
as to brothels.— Legislation in Norway,— in Denmark,— in Holland,
— in Switzerland.— Public opinion an important factor.— Actual conditions as to street-walking in London.— General improvement.—
Actual conditions as to vice resorts.— Effects of London policy.—
Comparison with continental cities.— Abolition and the police.—
Conditions in provincial and Scottish towns.— Conditions in abolition towns on the Continent.— The suppression of bordells.— Street-
walking in Copenhagen,— in Christiania,— in Dutch cities.— No loss
through abolition.— Prostitution and vagabondage.— The domicile
problem.— Prostitution and crime in abolitionist communities.—
Morals police in abolition communities.

THE term abolition is more or less widely misunder-
stood. Not infrequently it is supposed to mean " the
abolition of prostitution," and abolitionists are represented as bent upon summarily abolishing prostitution
through statutory enactment or otherwise. As a matter
of fact, abolition refers only to the abolition of laws and
police ordinances regulating, recognizing, or licensing the
practice of prostitution; [1] and abolitionists are those who
oppose all statutory enactments or police decrees authorizing the inscription or medical examination of prosti-

---

[1] Strictly speaking, no community can be an abolition community
unless it has previously had regulation; but in this chapter — and
indeed generally — the term abolition is also applied to cities that,
without ever having had regulation, are opposed to the adoption of
that or any similar policy; and persons are called abolitionists if they
are opposed to the things implied by regulation.

Abolition and Order

tutes, as well as all laws which bear upon only one of the two parties involved. Still another misconception will be exposed in the course of the present chapter: opponents of abolition (i. e., those favoring regulation) often assume that abolition is identical with *laissez-faire;* they argue that if the regulatory system is swept away no apparatus remains by means of which prostitution can be kept in bounds, and their terrified imaginations at once conjure up pictures of abolitionist communities overwhelmed by the rising tide of immorality and disease. Without at all prejudging the case either in favor of or against abolition, the notion that abolition is a purely negative policy beginning and ending with the ignoring of prostitution may be characterized as baseless. Unquestionably, such might be the case. A community might refuse to recognize prostitution by regulation, and might, like the ostrich, bury its head in the sand, refusing to admit the existence of prostitution as a phenomenon requiring the attention of society. But, to be candid, this is nowhere the case, though one frequently and commonly hears it said. The abolition of regulation has nowhere resulted in a *laissez-faire* policy. Against both the above errors we need therefore to be warned at the outset. Abolition means only the abolition of regulation, not the abolition of prostitution; abolition does not require that prostitution be ignored, overlooked, tabooed, or treated in a spirit of prudery as non-existent: it is entirely consistent with thorough inquiry into the whole phenomenon, and constructive social action aiming to deal with it.

Generally speaking, the immediate effect of abolition

287

Prostitution in Europe

is to place the mere act of prostitution in the same position as any other private vice. The prostitute as such is like the drunkard as such, or the opium-eater. A woman, for example, who prostitutes herself for money is in abolition communities in the eye of the law in precisely the situation of the man whom she has gratified: if the pair give no offence, the State takes no cognizance of the act. The intervention of the law is conditioned not on the act itself, but on certain conditions or results which make it something more than an affair involving two participants. If decency is violated, if disorder is created, if neighbors are scandalized, in some countries if disease is communicated, society considers itself warranted in interfering, just as it interferes in other circumstances to preserve or to promote the peace and health of the community. So far, there would appear to be little difference between what happens in regulated and what happens in unregulated towns. In Paris, as in London, in Budapest, as in Copenhagen, the mere act of irregular copulation is not regarded as a crime, even though money passes; even in Germany, despite the letter of the German law, which brands all non-registered professional prostitution as criminal, inoffensive prostitution for money is treated like ordinary immorality and is not interfered with. On the other hand, everywhere the authorities act whenever the usual order of the community is disturbed by prostitutes or prostitution. So far, then, I say, regulation and non-regulation are alike. There are, however, two distinct differences. In regulated towns, inscribed prostitutes are treated differently from non-inscribed prostitutes; in non-regulated or abo-

Abolition and Order

litionist towns, all prostitutes are regarded as alike. **In** regulated towns, what is an offence if committed by a non-inscribed woman is not an offence if done by an inscribed woman. In non-regulated towns whatsoever constitutes a violation of law on the part of A would constitute a violation of the law on the part of B. If street-walking is forbidden to one, it is forbidden to all; it is not allowed to one sort of prostitute (viz., the registered prostitute) and denied to another (viz., the unregistered, falsely called clandestine) prostitute. If disorderly houses are illegal, they are illegal: they are not legally authorized for one group of women and criminal for another group. From the standpoint of positive policy, this is a significant difference, for it favors the formulation of a general policy applicable to the phenomenon as a whole. Regulation is, as I have pointed out, a policy of exceptions; and wherever a fractional policy is adhered to, the exemptions operate as a drag upon a comprehensive program; the exceptions impede and hamper the conception or the execution of any plan conceived in reference to the entire problem.

The second distinction relates to the legal forms employed in dealing with infractions of public order. I have described the methods employed in regulated towns; by the act of inscription the woman surrenders the rights and privileges of a human being; she makes herself a legal, as she is already a social, pariah. The police may use their arbitrary powers as considerately as they will; their behavior, if humane, comes to the outcast as a matter of grace, not of right; except through the pressure of public opinion, the woman has no assurance of humane treatment,— she has no recourse, no redress, no rights. In abolitionist countries, offences against order, decency, or health committed by prostitutes are handled precisely as are the same offences when committed by other persons. The law operates along established lines for all offenders alike. If summary procedure is prescribed — i. e., a hearing before a magistrate without a jury — it is prescribed for all persons accused of the offences in question. In any event, the accused has every opportunity and facility to make a defense,— attorneys, witnesses, and the right of cross-examination. She can be convicted only by regular processes, based on the explicit law of the land; in England, a writ of habeas corpus would promptly take her before a court of competent jurisdiction, if any ground for arbitrary detention could be made out. I do not say, at this juncture, that the two points just instanced are of themselves enough to justify abolition. The issue between regulation and abolition will in this book be decided by the outcome of a comparison between them in respect to order and disease, — the two aspects of prostitution with which regulation undertakes to deal. Nevertheless, the characteristic differences above touched on cannot be overlooked, if the situation is to be grasped in all its essential bearings.

Though consistent in their indifference to prostitution in itself, the statutes of abolitionist countries provide more or less amply for the phenomena that are its prompt and wellnigh inevitable accompaniments: so prompt and so inevitable indeed, that, for practical purposes, prostitution itself can almost be said to be dealt with. A woman may indeed prostitute herself with impunity; but

Abolition and Order

if without reputable occupation, she may be taken up as a vagabond. She may sell her favors without for that act incurring the penalties of the law; but she may be taken up for street-walking, for solicitation, for keeping a brothel,— for any one, indeed, of the steps by means of which she procures trade enough to keep breath in her wretched body. Abolition is therefore not necessarily crippled in the matter of dealing with nuisances; but the offending woman is prosecuted, not because she is a prostitute, but because she has made herself obnoxious in practising prostitution.

Close as the prostitute thus always is to the clutch of the law, the distinction in principle is broad and clear. The prostitute is an object of police action in abolition countries only when guilty of offences against order and decency. Her business can with difficulty be conducted without such offences. Nevertheless, as long as police interference is conditioned on the offences in question, no novel or dangerous police function is created,— such as would be created if the police were asked to intervene on the ground of immorality. In the latter case, they would be required to discharge an entirely new duty, distinct in quality from anything else they do: they would become "*custodes morum*"— guardians of public morals, instead of guardians of the public peace. To do the latter they are competent, for breaches of the peace are open, obvious, concrete,— perceptible by the ordinary senses of sight and hearing. It is quite different with offences in the forum of morals. These are at times difficult to detect, and involve subtle or problematic distinctions which the police are too crude an instrument to make. Hence, as long as the police deal with the concrete infractions by means of which prostitution tends to bring itself into the net, they can act consistently; should their range be extended so as to cover prostitution as such, a partial policy would result: they could not act, unless guilt were obvious; and this justified failure would create precisely the opportunity for corruption and collusion that originates from regulation. Finally, in so far as disorder leads to police interference with prostitution, both parties to the act may be apprehended. Were prostitution as such made a crime, only the woman would be reached. For all these reasons, abolition legislation has consistently viewed prostitution as a vice, attaching penalties only to its objectionable manifestations.

We have seen in a previous chapter how prostitution tends to certain forms or expressions,— street-walking and brothels, for example; how it tends to associate itself with certain occupations or activities,— the stage, the café, the public dance hall, and a few employments, genuine or otherwise. The present chapter will tell how these various aspects are dealt with in abolitionist communities and will endeavor to decide whether regulation possesses any advantage over abolition in respect thereto.[2]

The English law provides:[3] "Every common prosti-

---

[2] Following the division made in discussing regulation, I shall in this chapter deal with order only; disease is remanded to the succeeding chapter.

[3] A very convenient manual of English Law dealing with all phases of the subject is available: W. A. Bewes, "*A Manual of Vigilance Law*" (2nd Edition by W. F. Crails), London, 1905. The law dealing with solicitation is summarized and luminously discussed in the Report of the Royal Commission upon the duties of the Metropolitan Police, Vol I, p. 323 (London, 1908). This report will be referred to in this chapter as *Report, Roy. Com.*

tute or night-walker loitering and importuning passengers for the purpose of prostitution in any street, to the obstruction, annoyance, or danger of the residents or passengers "[4] may be arrested by a constable[5] without warrant and on summary[6] conviction be fined 40s. or imprisoned fourteen days. In the Metropolitan Police District of London a prostitute is liable to the same penalty, even though actual solicitation is not proved.[7] The English police have therefore full power and authority to clear the streets.[8]

The law is equally clear on the subject of disorderly houses or brothels. A brothel is in England defined as a " place resorted to by persons of both sexes for the purpose of prostitution " ; it need not be a whole house and may be a single room, but it does not include a house that is occupied by one woman who is there visited by many men for the purposes of unlawful intercourse nor a house let out in separate apartments to prostitutes in which the owner does not live and over which he has no control.[9] The English definition is thus broad enough to include not only outright resorts, where prostitutes live and practise their trade, but *rendezvous* houses and

[4] *Towns Police Clauses Act, 1847,* Section 28. The Vagrancy Act of 1824 may also be invoked against a " prostitute wandering in the public street or in any place of public resort and behaving in a riotous or indecent manner." c. 83, Section 3.

[5] *I. e.,* patrolman or policeman.

[6] Summary conviction does not mean that the woman is without witnesses or attorney.

[7] By 2 and 3 Victoria c. 47, subs. 11.

[8] There are no statutory provisions expressly relating to the annoyance of women by men in the streets. The Royal Commission was however of opinion that insults of this kind could be dealt with under the *Metropolitan Police Act,* 1839, Section 54, 13. See *Report,* pp. 33, 118–120.

[9] Manual, p. 8, where cases are cited.

hotels where rooms are let for immoral purposes to transient customers without baggage. The Common Law
viewed the brothel as a nuisance, on the same footing
as a gaming-house or any place frequented by noisy and
disreputable characters. It could be proceeded against
by indictment, because it " endangers the public peace by
drawing together dissolute and detached persons." [10]
Any person might initiate prosecution and recover a re-
ward, if the prosecution were successful. With the passage of the *Criminal Law Amendment Act* of 1885, however, more expeditious procedure was introduced. The
Act penalizes " any person who keeps or manages or acts
or assists in the management of a brothel," permits the
use of premises he controls for the purposes of habitual
prostitution or is a party to such use.[11] Places kept for
public dancing, music, and other forms of entertainment
as well as taverns, lodging-houses, etc., must be licensed;
and, as we shall see, their relations to the practice of
prostitution have been greatly affected by the general
change of policy in this respect.

The statutes governing the provincial and Scottish
cities are not the same in all respects as those applicable
to London, but in the upshot there is little difference.
The *Towns Police Clauses Act* already referred to is the
legal warrant on the basis of which the provincial authorities proceed. Certain towns, however, operate under special acts, not materially different in theory or application. The law of Glasgow, for example, runs as
follows: " Every prostitute or street-walker who on or

[10] Russell on *Crimes* (6th Edition) Vol. I, p. 740.
[11] *Crim. Law Amend. Act*, 1885, c. 49, Section 13.

Abolition and Order

near any street loiters about or importunes passengers
for the purpose of prostitution shall be liable to a penalty." [12] In so far, therefore, as the letter of the law
is concerned, it is clear that abolition in England by no
means involves a policy of *laissez-faire* as respects the
outward manifestations of prostitution. This is perhaps a sufficient refutation of the commonly made statement that the English law " ignores prostitution," " shuts
its eyes to it," " refuses to recognize its existence," etc.
As to all these points, English law exactly corresponds
with that of many continental nations; it deals, not with
prostitution in itself, but with scandal arising in connection therewith. Further, the English law differs from
that of some continental nations in refusing to authorize
or license prostitution, but in so doing it occupies precisely the position of certain other continental nations
that maintain the same position.

At the present time, the abolition legislation of Norway and that of Denmark — largely modeled upon it —
are perhaps the most influential of all statutory enactments dealing with prostitution.[13] In Norway, a severe
penalty is attached to the maintenance of houses of prostitution; the ordinary provisions of the criminal code enable the police to arrest women for intoxication, for solicitation, and for other violations of decency; the prostitute can also be proceeded against on the ground of vagabondage. Persons who for their own profit aid " in the
immoral intercourse of others or take advantage of such

[12] *Report Roy. Com., loc. cit.,* p. 124.
[13] This is especially true in respect to the communication of
venereal contagion; but consideration of this portion of the Scandinavian statutes is postponed to the next chapter.

immoral intercourse" are liable to imprisonment up to
two years.[14]

The Danish law of 1906 follows along the Norwegian
lines. It repeals the law of 1866, by which regulation
had been instituted, and, as Police Inspector Schepelern-
Larsen acutely remarked, the "prostitute's recalcitrancy
was rewarded," for the woman twice punished as a common prostitute had — as elsewhere — been inscribed and
was thereafter privileged to pursue the course for entering upon which she had twice suffered a penalty! The
new law abolishes this privilege; it denounces the common prostitute as a vagabond [15] and renders her amenable
to the consequences of vagabondage; any one who solicits
or invites immorality in such wise as to offend against
the sense of shame, causes public scandal, or annoys a
neighbor is liable to punishment; [16] bordells are expressly
forbidden, and severe penalties are aimed at those conducting places of assignation; the police are empowered
to prevent keepers of hotels, cafés, and restaurants from
utilizing immoral women as waitresses.

The Dutch law of 1911 for the prevention of immorality bears with especial severity on the violation of minors
and the promoting of immorality — the latter intended to
suppress bordells,[17] and to prevent third parties from

[14] All Norwegian laws bearing on this subject have been brought
together in a special pamphlet issued by the Norwegian Law Journal
(*Norsk Lovtidende*). A useful compilation, unfortunately no longer
up to date is: A. Faerden, *Exposé des dispositions pénales con-
cernant les délits contre les moeurs dans divers pays.* (Christiania,
1891.)
[15] Section 1. I utilize a German translation of the Danish law;
it is called, *Gesetz zur Bekämpfung der öffentlichen Unsittlichkeit
und der venerischen Ansteckung* (Berlin, 1907).
[16] *Ibid*, Section 2.
[17] *Staatsblad van het Koninkrijk der Nederlander. No. 130*, Sec-

Abolition and Order

profiting through the demoralization of others. **Local** ordinances in some instances go even further: in Amsterdam, for example, owners and renters are forbidden to " afford others an opportunity for immoral acts, either customarily or in the pursuit of gain " ; after such places have been closed or ordered closed " it is prohibited to visit them." [18]

Street order is a matter of local determination. At Amsterdam the ordinance reads: " Women are forbidden to take their stand on the steps or in the doorways of taverns and beer-houses or other houses accessible to the public, or being within the houses to attract the attention of passers-by to themselves by a deliberate act of communication or exposure." [19] But a more formidable weapon is put in the hands of the authorities by the following proviso: " Women are forbidden to stand in the public streets, in front of or in the vicinity of the places above specified or on the corners of streets in which such places are situated or *to walk up and down* in the vicinity after a police officer has ordered them to move on." [20]

It is perhaps unnecessary to enter into the question at greater length in order to show that abolition does not mean *laissez-faire;* in all the countries that I visited, abolition of regulation is accompanied by definite statutory authority to deal adequately with prostitution in so far as it imperils order and decency. Switzerland,[21] where

tion 250 bis. The sections of the penal code are supplemented by local ordinances.

[18] *Algemeene Politie Verordening* Sections 201, 202.
[19] *Ibid,* Section 205a.
[20] *Ibid.,* Section 205 bis.
[21] The Swiss laws are brought together in Weiss's book already cited.

297

the discussion has thus far been left to cantonal regulation,[22] may serve as a concluding instance. In Zurich, to take a fair representative, persons who provide opportunity for the immorality of others or derive a profit therefrom (i. e., bordell-keepers) are liable to heavy fine and five years of hard labor.[23] For the maintenance of decency in public thoroughfares, it is provided that " women who in public places offer themselves for immoral purposes or tempt thereto may be imprisoned up to eight days." [24]

Clearly, therefore, it does not follow that the laws are silent or ineffective merely because prostitution is in itself regarded as a vice, not as a crime; on the contrary, legislation may in non-regulated countries be at once more comprehensive and more consistent than in regulated communities. I have already instituted a comparison between regulation and abolition in respect to certain points. For the sake of simplicity, it may be well to continue this method, as we proceed. As far, then, as the legislation goes, the police authorities of London, Copenhagen, and Christiania evidently have a simpler, more logical and more thorough-going statutory basis from which to proceed in the protection of the public and of the prostitute herself than is possessed by the police of any regulated town or country. For the London or Copenhagen police can at least go as far as the police of Berlin

[22] This explains the continued existence of regulation in Geneva, where the French influence is still strong. A new Federal Criminal Code is, however, now in preparation. I am informed by jurists of high standing that the new law will surely contain provisions which will forbid cantonal regulation by means of a general Federal enactment.

[23] *Strafgesetzbuch für den Kanton Zürich*, Sections 119, 120, 121.

[24] *Strafgesetzbuch für den Kanton Zürich*, Section 128.

Abolition and Order

or Hamburg and they can act consistently in reference to all prostitutes. They are empowered to deal with the entire phenomenon in so far as it endangers public order; at no point are they balked by the exemptions that regulation makes in favor of women privileged through inscription. This point, however, must not as yet be regarded as decisive of the issue. It still remains to be seen how the competing systems work.

For laws do not enforce themselves. They must be converted into a policy by the attitude of the police, by the interpretations of the courts, by the demand of public opinion. Let us consider briefly how statutory provisions are modified by these factors.

Public opinion is unquestionably the most powerful of influences. Be the letter of the law what it may, actual achievement under it will depend first and foremost on what general sentiment demands and consistently supports. As abolition has been brought about in part by agitation on ethical lines, one would expect a more highly developed public opinion in abolitionist countries. This undoubtedly exists. The suppression of the public bordell is without question an achievement due not only to legislation, but to popular insistence that police and courts enforce the law. In Germany as in England, the bordell is illegal; but public opinion in Germany being less highly developed and less articulate, the law remains in most places a dead letter.

Curiously enough, public opinion in this entire matter is more or less self-contradictory. On the one hand, orderly streets, free of scandal, are required; on the other hand, a blunder made or apparently made by the police is violently resented. The same opinion that demands the former stands ready to burst into flame in the event of the latter. The Royal Commission which, in consequence of a supposed blunder, investigated the London police, declared that " the main difficulty in enforcing the law (as to solicitation) is caused by the over-sensitiveness and impatience of the public whenever there seems ground, however slight, for alleging that there has been a mistake in arresting a woman on a charge of solicitation. Not only the particular constable who effected the arrest, but the police as a whole find themselves suddenly the object of public censure in the press, in society and even in Parliament. These displays of emotion are curious in the case of a law-abiding and law-respecting community such as ours seeing that similar feelings of indignation are rarely aroused in cases where men are acquitted of crime of the greatest gravity. Every one must, however, recognize that it is a very terrible misfortune for an honest woman or girl to be publicly tried on a charge involving an imputation of peculiarly disgraceful unchastity. Whatever may be the causes of, or excuses for, these gusts of popular emotion, there can be no doubt that they tend to some extent to impair the activity of constables." [25] We may expect, therefore, to find actual conditions not so good as the law to the extent that public opinion fails to require or sustain their enforcement, and to the extent that hypersensitiveness or hysteria is ready to attack the police where absolutely overwhelming proof can not be furnished at the moment.

The construction of the law by the courts — itself both

[25] *Report, Roy. Com.*, p. 125 (somewhat abridged).

a result and a maker of opinion — is likewise an important factor in deciding what legislation will achieve. Wherever magistrates disagree as to the precise intention of the statute, a twilight zone is created, in consequence of which the scope of the law is indirectly narrowed; for official policy tends to restrict itself to acts that the courts will be sure to uphold.[26] Finally, the rules, the policy, even the tradition of the police department in applying statutes and judicial decisions and in endeavoring to meet, without outrunning, the demands of public opinion, tend now to stretch, now to restrict, the law as it stands on the statute books. For example, the Danish statute punishes any exhibition or act that disturbs order, offends the sense of shame, etc. The courts, it is now pointed out, might have deprived the section of all its force by requiring the production of a witness whose sense of shame was actually outraged. They have, however,— undoubtedly governed by public opinion — construed the provision to refer to conduct which would naturally give such offence,— and the policeman's evidence is sufficient. This section has therefore been effective. On the other hand, the courts have held that it is no offence for prostitutes to gather in small knots on the streets,— as a result of which the phenomenon has latterly become more prominent in Copenhagen.

[26] The importance of this factor from a practical point of view is made clear by the following considerations: "Solicitation *per se* is not an offence." (*Report, Roy. Com.*, p. 119). "In a prosecution under the Metropolitan Police Act there must be evidence sufficient to satisfy the magistrate that the woman is a prostitute. Next, there must be evidence as to the actions of the woman showing that she was loitering in a thoroughfare or public place for the purpose of prostitution or solicitation; and, lastly, there must be evidence that her action was to the annoyance of the inhabitants or passengers." *Ibid.*, p. 49.

Prostitution in Europe

It is our present task to ascertain what actually happens in abolitionist communities and to compare the results with the conditions described in previous chapters. The practical outcome of the English statutes, as interpreted by the courts and as demanded by public opinion, is reflected in the regulations promulgated for the guidance of constables by the Commissioner of the Metropolitan Police. In respect to brothels, the London constable is instructed to "note in his pocket-book and report any house apparently used as a brothel." [27] The constable takes no further step on his own initiative; arrests are made on direction of borough or other authorities, after complaint by neighbors or others interested.[28] Prostitutes on the street are to be dealt with discreetly —"not to be interfered with unnecessarily." The names of women acting like prostitutes are to be reported; women engaged in soliciting are to be warned before arrest; [29] annoyance of passers-by is to be prevented.[30] The police act on their own initiative only if the behavior of the woman is offensive, annoying, or scandalous. The unobtrusive prostitute is not molested. Keepers of licensed premises, i. e., liquor establishments, refreshment houses, etc., are to be reported if they permit prostitutes habitually to resort to their establishments.[31]

[27] *Duty Hints, Metropolitan Police*, p. 11.
[28] As a rule, the police observe a suspected disorderly house on the request of the borough authorities, to whom results are communicated; the aforesaid authorities act by warrant or otherwise. Social and other organizations occasionally instigate prosecutions.
[29] "Prostitutes cannot legally be taken into custody simply because they *are* prostitutes; to justify their apprehension they must commit some distinct act which is an offence against the law." *Report Roy. Com.*, p. 49 (quoting White Book of the Department, pp. 338–9).
[30] *Duty Hints*, pp. 48, 57.   [31] *Duty Hints*, pp. 35, 54.

Abolition and Order

The limitations thus placed on the constable are partly due to the size of the area covered. I have already had occasion to remark how certain situations change qualitatively whenever they undergo a radical quantitative expansion. Centralized supervision of the individual conduct of sixteen thousand policemen dealing with so delicate a matter as prostitution is difficult in the highest degree. When does the conduct of a woman stamp her as a prostitute in such wise that a magistrate will sustain the constable who apprehends her? When does her conduct overpass the limits of toleration? Shall the patrolman enter suspected disorderly houses for the purpose of satisfying himself as to their character? In small towns, where everything readily becomes notorious, it is a comparatively simple matter to check up the doings of the police; where the head is sound and the motives are pure — as is regularly the case abroad — more or less initiative may be safely entrusted to a constable who is thus easily supervised. But in London the magnitude of the task would expose the patrolman to grave danger of corruption and collusion. He might be corruptly induced to overlook cautious violations of the law, if it were made his duty to be the aggressor in taking action; or he might be tempted to levy blackmail, difficult as that would be under existing circumstances.[32] His initiative is therefore restricted to concrete and overt instances. Further steps depend on the action of higher authorities, — a machinery readily set in motion by protest or complaint. The department thus has the guarantee of both evidence and supervision, since the parties who lodge the

[32] Testimony of *Sir Edward Henry, Report, Roy. Com.*

Prostitution in Europe

complaint will see to it that proper steps follow. In a peculiar degree, therefore, it is true that in London conditions depend on the state of public opinion.

In consequence of the policy described above in respect to street-walking, somewhat spotty conditions characterize the metropolis. Women are distinctly abundant in the streets radiating from and in the vicinity of Trafalgar Square, Oxford Circus, Regent Circus, and the various railway stations. As a rule they conduct themselves unobtrusively, communicating furtively with passers-by, though, after midnight, they are at times more aggressive. Whenever the police are sustained by the aroused public opinion of a given locality, improvement ensues; for the inhabitants of a given neighborhood having protested become checks on the police assigned to the district; unless action is taken along the desired lines, suspicion is awakened and protests accumulate. In this way, the Strand, only a few years ago one of the scandals of London, has been rendered comparatively innocuous. Besides the transformation wrought in particular spots, an unmistakable general improvement is noticeable throughout London. This is a fact familiar to travelers returning to London after an interval of a few years; it was practically the unanimous testimony before the Royal Commission. On this point it is hardly necessary to do more than to quote the words of Mr. W. A. Coote: "I have known London for the past forty years, and my memory goes back to quite forty-seven years. I knew the Haymarket and Piccadilly very well forty-seven years ago and I say that London to-day, compared with what it was forty years ago, is an open-air cathedral. Everything has gone for the better." [33]   The laws remain the same, but popular demand has caused, or enabled, police and courts gradually to make more of them.   The increased activity of the police is evidenced by the greater frequency of arrests, 2,409 in 1901, 4,206 in 1905.   The courts have more than kept pace.   Of the smaller number arrested in 1901, 274 (11.4%) were discharged: of the larger number arrested in 1905, 252 (6.3%) were discharged.[34]   The high percentage of convictions testifies to the discrete manner in which the police discharge their duties.

How stands it with the brothel or disorderly house? [35] A brothel — it may be well to repeat — is a house in which prostitutes live, to which they bring or in which they receive their patrons.   It has been held, however, that no brothel exists where only one woman prostitutes herself for money.   The room to which the street-walker retires with her prey is not a brothel in the meaning of the law.   But wherever two or more women occupy premises for the purpose of carrying on prostitution, a brothel exists, no matter what the subterfuge employed,— be the quarters in question their living-rooms, a pretended manicure or massage establishment, or what not.   Such resorts nowadays lead a stealthy, uneasy, transient life in many sections of London, including the suburbs.   In the West End a few fashionable brothels are found, located where they are least likely to be noticed, and transacting

[33] *Report, Roy. Com.*, p. 93.
[34] *Ibid.*, Return 7, XII, XIII.
[35] The term "bordell," properly meaning a licensed, recognized, or tolerated house of prostitution, is not employed at all in Great Britain.

Prostitution in Europe

their business with a limited clientele procured through introduction. Much more frequent, but also much less stable, are the brothels of the Haymarket region, masking as massage rooms, baths, as schools for the teaching of foreign languages or elocution, or as rheumatism cures. The women conducting these places advertise in certain periodicals and even send "sandwich men" parading through Regent Street and Bond Street.[36] The inmates are, however, very careful not to attract the attention of others in the same house or in the neighborhood; hence the places are open only during usual business hours, though they make appointments elsewhere for other times.[37] The police are, of course, usually informed; but in accordance with their policy are content to preserve

[36] These brothels not infrequently occupy the upper floors of buildings in Regent Street and Bond Street, the floors below being occupied by fashionable shops.

[37] The following are all brothel advertisements clipped from a popular one-penny weekly:

Skilful Treatment for Muscular Ailments given daily. Hours 12:30 till 7.— Shepherd, Edgeware Road, Marble Arch, W. (entrance in Little Queen Street). Assistant wanted at once.

Care of hands and nails.— Miss ——, Court Chambers, Marylebone Rd., 2nd Floor (entrance in Seymour Place). Assisted by specialist from Paris. Hours 12 to 7. Three languages spoken. Assistant wanted.

Electrical treatment for all muscular ailments.— Apply Nurse, —— Warren Street, Tottenham Court Road (adjoining Warren Street Tube), 1st floor. Hours, 12 till 8.

Newly opened Establishment.— Miss ——, Nail Specialist, —— Shaftesbury Avenue, Piccadilly Circus, W.

Specific Treatment for Rheumatism by Madame ——, —— Manchester Street, Manchester Square, W.

A Trained Nurse
Has Special Oils for Muscular Ailments.— Apply —— Allsop

Abolition and Order

decorum until outside agencies move; whereupon the brothel is broken up, the inmates being either arrested or dispersed. Certain sections of London have been greatly improved by organization work of this type. For example, the Central South London Free Church Council has been beneficially active in South London. In 1909, this organization prosecuted 68 brothel-keepers; in 1910, 53; in 1911, 32; the reduction being due not to decreased vigor, but to better conditions.[38] The activities of the police in this direction are exhibited in the following table: [39]

Year	Taken into Custody			Discharged			Convicted, held to bail, or committed to Reform School		
	Males	Females	Total	Males	Females	Total	Males	Females	Total
1901 145		243	388	11	27	38	134	216	350
1902 142		271	413	16	25	41	126	245	371
1904 292		442	734	30	55	85	260	386	646
1905 269		431	700	29	40	69	240	390	630
1906 264		403	667	24	40	64	239	363	602
1907 187		305	492	14	27	41	173	278	451
1908 154		192	346	13	19	32	132	152	284[40]
1909 184		219	403	17	17	34	160	174	334[41]
1910 110		182	292	9	16	25	90	139	229[42]

A certain amount of repressive activity, evoked in the same fashion — viz., by outside protest or actual disorder — goes on in reference to assignation hotels, and other resorts apt to be frequented by prostitutes. The public drinking-house is the object of more severe measures, in furtherance of the policy of reducing the number

Place, Flat D (entrance floor) next Madame Tussaud's, Baker Street Sta.

French lady would receive a few paying guests in her well-appointed and newly-decorated house.— Apply Madame ——, Hugh

of taverns. A license is in danger of cancellation, whenever prostitutes are harbored.

English activity in respect to prostitution thus involves the suppression of brothels and the gradual improvement of street conditions. Too little is accurately known regarding the dimensions of the prostitute army to decide how this policy affects the number of women engaged. There can be no doubt, however, that it diminishes the attractiveness of the career on the financial side; for the women are practically forced to pick up their customers on the street under conditions very unfavorable to the canvass for trade, and in the long run diminished returns must check the recruiting process, on the professional side at any rate. If by reason of the furtive and shifting manner in which the trade must be plied, the volume of

St., Victoria (Two Minutes from Station). Side entrance. Assistant wanted.

Sciatica and Rheumatism.

Skilfully treated by nurse. Also care of the feet. —— Glasshouse Street, Regent Street; one minute Piccadilly Circus. Hours, 12 to 7. Saturday, 12 to 6.

French lessons and conversation
Given by
Madame ——, 1 Oxford Street, W.
Hours 1 to 9.

In a single number of this sheet there are 44 unmistakable advertisements of this kind. A few weeks later, the above advertisements had mostly disappeared, new ones taking their place.

[38] Report, July 31, 1911.

[39] Compiled from the *Reports of the Commissioner of Police:* Acton, *loc. cit.,* pp. 4, 6, give police returns for 1841, 1857 and 1868.

[40] In 29 cases charges were proved and order made without conviction.

[41] In 34 cases charges were proved and order made without conviction.

[42] In 37 cases charges were proved and order made without conviction.

business is slighter, then beyond any doubt the amount of disease disseminated and the amount of financial waste are both correspondingly diminished.

Our main interest at this moment is, however, comparative. London, Berlin, Paris, and Vienna are cosmopolitan cities. London does not regulate prostitution; all the others do. London has no morals police; all the others have. London watches prostitution through the ordinary uniformed force acting under strict instructions; the others employ plainclothes men with special powers. London possesses no arbitrary police process; all the others do. Does London suffer in the comparison in respect to public order and decency? Most assuredly not. The Haymarket may perhaps be no better than the Boulevards, Friederichstrasse, or Kärntnerstrasse; it is in any case no worse. Conditions have improved everywhere; but I suspect there has been more amelioration in London and that it is likely to travel further than anywhere on the Continent. The cities differ, of course, in regard to many important elements,— race, tradition, ideals; and these elements affect more or less the aspects of social order with which we are dealing. But in any event the evidence warrants us in concluding that, taking the actual situation as we find it, the English metropolis shows no sign that it lacks a police instrument that the others possess. To prove that such an instrument confers no comparative advantage is, of course, conclusive against it; but our previous examination strengthens the case for abolition to the extent that it disclosed substantial disadvantages on the side of regulation.

I am by no means disposed to imply that London has

exhausted the possibilities of wise action in reference to prostitution,— that its procedure leaves nothing to be desired. There would, for example, appear to be no good reason why a prostitute calling herself " Nurse Dora " should be privileged to advertise herself on bill-boards circulating up and down Regent Street and Bond Street.[43] But at this juncture I am not especially concerned to indicate the defects of any particular abolition town. The issue is for the moment between regulation and abolition and we are interested in ascertaining whether, as the matter now stands, abolition communities necessarily fare worse in respect to external order than regulation communities, and whether, in general, abolition promises better or worse results than regulation.

The London method, it is often urged, scatters prostitution, thus rendering it more difficult to deal with and more dangerous to the innocent poor. Neither assertion is, as compared with regulation on the Continent, actually or necessarily true. In so far as prostitution tends to be associated with crime, dispersion is sound policy; the police of set purpose break up nests of crime. Evil-doers — prostitutes among them — are most dangerous in gangs; dispersion strips them of power, cunning, and daring. There are, however, limits to dispersion, fixed by rental, character of the neighborhood, etc., in consequence of which birds of a feather still continue to flock together. Hence the scattering is continually interrupted by brief fortuitous settlement here and there, or by longer

[43] These women conduct brothels in the sense that there are several " nurses " or " assistants " on the premises during business hours; if the customer is not pleased, photographs of available girls are shown and almost any desired type is promised on appointment.

joint sojournings in buildings out of which decent people are gradually edged. This happens in London; but, unfortunately for the contrast set up by regulationists, it happens everywhere else as well. Prostitution is assuredly no more widely scattered in London than in any of the other cities compared with it; maps showing its incidence would abundantly sustain this assertion. Berlin is in this respect precisely like London; the Berlin prostitute lives anywhere, wellnigh everywhere, and, besides, frequently possesses a key to a room in an apartment building close to the scene of her nightly perambulations. In Paris and Vienna, the amount of bordelled prostitution being negligible, the numerous non-interned women live where they please; in Vienna, indeed, as I have pointed out, the police rules expressly forbid needless interference with their preferences as to domicile; in Paris, they congregate in the congenial environment of Montmartre and the Latin Quarter; but they are not excluded from fashionable thoroughfares such as the Avenue Victor Hugo, or the spokes of the wheel radiating from the Arc de Triomphe. Abolition does not suffer by comparison with regulation in this respect.

An interesting light is shed on the relation of street and bordell, discussed in a previous chapter, by the experience of London. Regent Street and Piccadilly are still notorious for the number of loose women frequenting them; but far less so than formerly when " at certain hours they became so crowded with undesirable persons as to make the use of the streets irksome to respectable persons." [44] In this same area over three-hundred dis-

[44] *Report, Royal Commission*, p. 124.

orderly houses have been closed in consequence of legal proceedings in the division of St. James, covering about three-quarters of a square mile. The tightening of police control may explain the improvement in street conditions; but the coincidence of improved streets and closed brothels shows clearly that suppression of brothels does not necessarily result in aggravation of street conditions; there is, as I have previously pointed out, every reason to believe just the reverse.

A word as to the effect of abolition on the character of the police. I have emphasized the admirable quality of the continental police, due in the first place, unless I err, to the secure tenure, the independence, integrity, and intelligence of the commanding officers; the weak spot — and that of varying seriousness — is the morals division, which, capable of proving anywhere a localized infection, has in some instances become an open sore. That abolition is solely responsible for the difference I do not affirm; but it is at least noticeable that the police of the British metropolis have passed practically unscathed through the most searching criticism,— the strongest witness in behalf of their general probity, humanity, and helpfulness having been borne by those who know most of their relations with prostitution. Exceptions were indeed found; a force approximating 17,000 men could hardly be entirely lacking in black sheep. For example, the Royal Commission verified thirteen complaints preferred by superior officers against constables,— one of consorting with prostitutes, twelve of relations with brothel-keepers,[45]— all severely dealt with; but, on the whole, they

[45] *Report, Royal Commission*, p. 100.

Abolition and Order

" had no hesitation in coming to the conclusion that the force discharge their duties (in respect to prostitution) with honesty, discretion, and efficiency." [46]

The charge most readily made relates to the corruption of constables by prostitutes in the street with a view to securing immunity from arrest. I have shown the practical difficulties in the way of controlling this matter in regulated towns where certain women have the right to promenade,— a right which can be corruptly extended to others, and no one be the wiser; for who but the policeman can judge whether a prostitute is entitled to the privilege of the streets? In abolition London the situation is so far different, that any exceptions raise at once a presumption of wrong-doing or negligence. Hence, whatever the policy pursued, be it lax or strict, uniformity is necessary. A decade or two ago, when public opinion was indifferent, aggressive solicitation went on, not because it was paid for, but because no one objected; nowadays, certain streets have been cleared and nowhere is solicitation actively obtrusive, because public opinion is articulate and the police, however inclined, would not dare to play favorites.[47] Sir Edward Henry, testifying before the Royal Commission, declared: " No complaint, oral or written, has been made to me during the three and a half years I have been Commis-

[46] *Ibid*, p. 101.
[47] Whether the police even now make full use of their power to clear the streets is a matter on which opinions differ. Certain witnesses before the Royal Commission indulged in criticism (*Report*, p. 81). The Commission ultimately came to a conclusion on the whole favorable to the police. In my own opinion, it is impossible to reach a single and simple verdict. London is better or worse according to the requirement of more or less localized public opinion, the general tendency being towards improvement.

sioner, charging the police with levying blackmail from women of the unfortunate class. I am satisfied that if any individual man were to take money from these women it would come to the knowledge of his comrades, who would look upon him as an unmitigated blackguard and that he could not remain in the force for long. I do not say that individual instances of taking money may not occur, but the whole force know that any proved misconduct of this sort would be severely dealt with. It is quite impossible that there should be any systematized blackmailing, because the variation in the beats is so great and in a street like Regent Street where, on either side there are parts of ten beats, it would not be of the slightest use to a woman to bribe the first constable she came to, because she would only go a few yards before she came to another beat. Therefore anything like a system of blackmailing is impracticable and certainly could not exist many days without being known to the authorities." [48]

To restate briefly the upshot of the foregoing discussion: as compared with cosmopolitan continental cities that regulate prostitution, London has lost nothing and actually gained something through its abolition policy. No community has as yet envisaged and attacked the entire problem involved in commercialized prostitution,— no community, I say, whether regulationist or abolitionist. On the whole, as we shall also see in the next chapter, abolitionist cities have been the more active in initiative, but the aggressive conscience of the world

[48] *Ibid.*, p. 129, slightly abridged. Sir Edward Henry's evidence is fully sustained by that of Mr. Coote, p. 83.

Abolition and Order

has too recently awakened to have as yet achieved a great deal. As to the two matters now concerning us — order in the streets and brothels — the lowest level reached in London nowhere falls as low as in the continental capitals where regulation is in vogue.

The police of the English metropolis is under the control of the Home Office of the National Government; in all other towns, the force is managed by the Watch Committee of the Town Council.[49] The latter are therefore, perhaps, a bit more sensitive to public opinion and depend more nearly on the tone of the municipal government. Fortunately in Great Britain this tone is nowadays high, the membership of the Watch Committee being scrutinized with especial care. This has not, however, always been the case. As recently as the nineties the Chairman of the Watch Committee and head of the licensing board in Liverpool was the attorney of the brewing interests, and brewers were largely represented on the committee itself. It was no accident, perhaps, that with these conditions the town possessed a protected vice district containing upwards of four hundred houses and that the public houses (saloons) systematically harbored prostitutes. A vigorous agitation, the machinery of which is still preserved and in motion, resulted in a complete rehabilitation of the local government. The liquor interest was excluded from the Watch Committee and neither in Liverpool nor elsewhere is it now regarded as fit to be represented thereon; the unholy alliance between prostitution and liquor has been largely

[49] The National Government is, however, not wholly without power even over provincial police forces. Mr. Fosdick will give details in the book previously referred to.

destroyed by the ruthless cancellation of licenses; in Liverpool the number has already been reduced from 2,500 to 1,700.[50] A determined and systematic effort has also been made to restore the streets to decency and to destroy brothels. For this work, in the provinces and Scotland, as in London, no special police machinery exists. Prostitution is handled by the regular force, uniformed or plain-clothes,— by men, that is, who deal with all other infractions of law. There is no morals division; nor is any effort made to list or catalogue the prostitute as such. The genial inspector of the Birmingham police, to whom I am beholden for an inner view of the police situation there, was conscious of no necessity for any special machinery. He did not know how many prostitutes there were in Birmingham,— no police officer had ever tried to find out. He could not tell, therefore, whether they were more or less numerous. Why should he? The law-abiding prostitute must be the concern of other agencies. The law-breakers among them he knew and watched precisely as he knew and watched law-breakers of other kinds. Walking the streets at midnight, he pointed out to me women who were thieves and pickpockets,— in whom he was interested for that reason and not simply because they were prostitutes; and he showed me their haunts,— precisely as the haunts of law-breakers, prostitutes and others, were pointed out to me in London. No extraordinary mechanism,— no

[50] In Glasgow the number of licensed premises has steadily declined from 1,819 in 1892 to 1,565 in 1911. *City of Glasgow Police, Criminal Returns,* 1911, p. 56. In Birmingham, the reduction has been relative, not absolute; there were 2,163 licensed establishments in 1881, ratio to population 1:188; 2,368 in 1911, ratio to population 1:354. (*Report of Police Establishment* 1911, p. 18.)

mechanism, I mean, not otherwise needed in dealing with urban crime,— was needed in either place for this purpose; and no lack of knowledge or power to cope with individuals or with emergencies was felt or betrayed; nor was the integrity of the force imperilled by its dealings with prostitution, for that integrity was safeguarded by the quality of the head officers, by the principles on which recruits were procured, and by the limitations erected by statute.

In these circumstances, the provincial like the London brothel leads a stealthy existence. Two or more women occupy a house or flat[51] for a brief period. The more prosperous occupy small houses on the edge of town; the word is passed through cab-drivers or from " friend " to " friend." In certain sections of Manchester the position of the window shades and of the front door is a signal to the initiated. In the side streets leading from Oxford Street, Manchester, many doors are significantly ajar up to the late hours of the night. Shortly conscious of being observed, the women fold their tents and steal elsewhere, repeating the performance. Not infrequently, neighbors complain and the town authorities apprehend the inmates, subjecting them to fine or imprisonment. Statistics convey some notion of the vigor of the policy, — none as to whether the evil decreases or increases. In Liverpool, for example, there were 162 prosecutions for brothel-keeping in 1902, with 147 convictions; 196 prosecutions with 116 convictions in 1910; in the nine years from 1902 to 1911, there were altogether 1,720 ar-

[51] In Birmingham and Manchester there are no "flats" in the London sense.

rests, 1,411 convictions.[52]   In Edinburgh, the number
of brothels known to the police shows a marked diminution,— from 45 in 1901 to 29 in 1911,— not unconnected
perhaps with increased severity on the part of the authorities who arrested nine women of the larger number
(45) in 1901, thirty-five women of the smaller number
(29) in 1911.[53]

Street conditions have undergone precisely the same
evolution previously described as generally taking place.
Time was — and that within recent memory — when
importuning on the main highways was wellnigh unrestrained.   Nowadays the prostitute walks more or less
swiftly by, indicating her object by a stealthy glance or
mumbled word.   Hoping for a nibble she retires into a
side street waiting to be approached by her supposed
quarry.[54]   If disappointed, she resumes her inoffensive
promenading.   The public houses are less and less used
for this purpose, because the publican fears the loss of his
license.   If an arrangement is perfected, the pair retire
to the woman's room or to an assignation hotel, though
the latter operate with great caution.   Parks, cabs, even
railway compartments are utilized.   Not infrequently a
journey to a suburb is urged; in Liverpool, a street-
walker suggested " Bootle," several miles distant, as the

---

[52] *Report of Police Establishment* 1910, p. 66 (Liverpool, 1911).
Similar information is contained in the corresponding reports of
other cities.

[53] For Edinburgh statistics I am indebted to the courtesy of the
chief constable, R. Ross, Esq. It will be noted that in 1911 the
number of women arrested exceeds the number of known brothels.
This is accounted for by the fact that the brothels contain several
women each.

[54] In the provincial cities as in London, women are more prominent in the Arcades than in the streets, as Arcades are private
property.

nearest place that was sure of being free from interruption or molestation.

The policy described keeps the brothel inconspicuous and relatively infrequent; it renders the streets fairly unobjectionable. Does it accomplish anything more? The officials are entirely candid on this point. The Birmingham inspector " does not believe that the amount of prostitution has been decreased through keeping it ' on the move ' or through punishment. It disappears here, to reappear there. Girls are easily found; but "— and I shall recur to the point —"they tempt less." A prominent and experienced member of the Watch Committee expressed similar views: " The present policy drives women from one cover to another; it prevents anything like a tropical growth." In Edinburgh the actual number of notorious prostitutes appears to have been reduced, for the police returns, 424 in 1901, had shrunk to 180 in 1911.[55] The Chief Constable of Liverpool inclines also " to think that the decline of the figures over nine years corresponds with a reduction in professional prostitution, but it seems quite possible that the reduction is due to the professional being ousted by the amateur." [56]

It seems beyond dispute that prostitution, like any other business enterprise, suffers when deprived of the advantage of position. What hinders, reduces. The actual number of customers that can be picked up by a street-walker compelled to forego all positive advances, or a woman living in a brothel the location and character

[55] Communicated by Chief Constable.
[56] *Report*, 1910, p. 67 (slightly abridged).

of which can only be allowed to leak out surreptitiously, is bound to be diminished; and the diminution of customers means the diminution of waste and disease. The inducement to join the professional ranks is thereby lessened.

It is not pretended that repression and punishment achieve anything with the hardened offender. The Chief Constable of Glasgow reporting to the corporation of the city, states: "The imposition of a fine does not prove a deterrent; any person may pay the fine and the woman continue her way of life." [57] The Chief Constable of Liverpool reports as " a typical, not exceptional " case that of a prostitute fifty years old, first convicted in 1884 and in 1910 sent to prison on her 156th conviction." [58] In Edinburgh, coincidently with the reduction in the number of notorious women, the number of arrests rose from 158 in 1901, to 773 in 1911,— it reached 1,020 in 1910. Did the increased frequency of arrests, due to the instructions issued to the police to act without warning lead to an exodus from the city? Not improbably; but it was futile for the reform of those who remained, for some of them were convicted as many as eight or ten times in a single year. During the first six months of 1911, 331 women under 23 years of age were sent to Glasgow prison; 220 of these were convicted of importuning; only 72 of the entire number were first offenders; among the others some had been previously convicted as many as 34, 50, or even 69 times.[59] Nor are hard-labor sentences more efficacious on the

[57] *Criminal Returns,* 1911, p. 6.
[58] *Report, loc. cit.,* p. 45.
[59] *The Shield,* Nov.-Dec., 1911, p. 78.

Abolition and Order

Continent in deterring women from continuing a dissolute life. Of those thus punished at Stockholm, between 1882 and 1884, 96.9% persisted in their evil courses after the expiration of their prison terms; between 1885 and 1889, 98.3%; between 1890 and 1894, 96.7%; 96.8% in the period 1895–1899; 96.7% in 1900–2. The small remnant did not necessarily do better; they may have left the city or escaped notice.[59a] In regulation, as in abolition communities, the system of fining and imprisoning offenders — be they prostitutes or not — is futile, expensive, and demoralizing.

Meanwhile, below the surface, lie the frightful evils out of which professional prostitution comes. An acrid controversy in Glasgow between the Inspector of the Parish and the Chief Constable throws a flood of light on a situation which neither regulation nor abolition touches. The former cites the volume of existing immorality, the frequent violation of children, the existence of ice-cream shops which are merely cloaks for indecency; the latter replies that prostitution is in itself no crime, that arrests can be made only where habitual prostitutes are guilty of importuning, that the difficulties of proof in case of immoral establishments are very serious, and that incidental prostitution and immorality lie outside the province of the police.[60] Thus even though regulation is condemned, it is necessary to remember that the serious problem remains. This must not be overlooked. Our immediate concern is however, once

[59a] *Reglementeringen i Stockholm*, pp. 91–92.
[60] The documents in the case are: *Memorandum on a Social Evil in Glasgow*, published by authority of the Parish Council, October, 1911; *Social Evil in Glasgow, Report by the Chief Constable*.

more, simply as to whether the provincial and Scottish towns lose anything through not possessing the regulatory apparatus found in continental towns of the same size. There can be but one opinion on this point: no single phenomenon can be cited tending to show that the situation would be bettered by regulation or that it suffers for the lack of it.

The comparison between regulation and abolition can, however, be most fairly made on the Continent, where the manner of living, the point of view, and the social traditions of regulation and abolition communities are more nearly alike. Moreover, the abolitionist cities that enter into the comparison have all had regulatory systems,— some of them quite recently. What have they lost through abolition? How do they bear comparison with those that still retain regulation?

The subject is by no means a simple one, in part at least because its discussion has been carried on in a spirit of acrimonious controversy. Complete and dispassionate accounts of conditions during and after regulation either in regulated or abolitionist communities have nowhere been prepared; the only reliable statistics in existence deal merely with certain phases of the evil, and leave unsettled the question as to whether other phases have become better or worse, after or in consequence of abolition. Moreover, all the cities involved have grown with amazing rapidity; they have become larger, richer, more luxurious, in some ways more frivolous. They compete with each other and even with much larger towns in brilliancy and seductiveness. This increased playfulness is certainly reflected in the increase of some forms of immorality without involving in any degree the issue between regulation and abolition.

Continental abolition has usually required two steps. In the first place, bordells were suppressed; after a brief interval, registration and medical inspection have been abandoned. Whatever has happened in consequence of abolition, the mere suppression of the bordell can have had little immediate or direct effect. The bordell was, as previously pointed out, moribund anyway; its legal extermination involved hardly a perceptible shock. At Zurich eighteen houses, containing fifty-seven women were forcibly closed, at Rotterdam four with twenty women, at Copenhagen three. On the face of the matter, it may, therefore, be affirmed that nowhere in Europe has the closing of bordells as the first step towards abolition involved unfavorable consequences.

This is not to say that the other forms of prostitution — the concealed brothel, the counterfeit employment,[61] the low drinking-shop, the dance hall, etc., have been lessened or mitigated by the abolition of the bordell. Whether any particular surreptitious form of bordell exists or not is not a question of abolition or regulation, but of the law, the manner of its enforcement, the condition of public opinion, the attitude of the courts, and the general feasibility of effective repression. Many of these forms were briefly characterized in the opening chapter. They are found everywhere,— in regulated cities, such as Hamburg and Budapest, where the bordell is officially favored; in Vienna, where, though officially

[61] I refer by this description to spurious cigar shops, manicure establishments, etc.

reprobated, it still continues to exist: in Munich and Berlin, where it is no longer tolerated; and just as well in abolition towns,— Copenhagen, Zurich, and Christiania, for example. I have no desire to understate the facts. Resorts serving the purpose of bordells are almost universally met with — with or without regular bordells. I have touched on the English brothels and the Berlin bars. In Amsterdam, one finds clubs or pretended "pensions," to which the visitor is conducted by a cab-driver or directed by an acquaintance or a hotel porter and in which he is entertained in whatever fashion he prefers. Along the Binnenrotte in Rotterdam and in the narrow out-of-the-way streets of old Zurich, cigar shops,[62] whose outfit consists mainly of empty boxes and bedizened females, unmistakably proclaim their purpose. The purchaser of one of the few cigars in stock, unless an object of suspicion, need only lay a coin of moderate size on the counter in payment; he will soon learn that there is no change in the drawer, but that there are other ways of squaring the account.[63]   If he prove obdurate, the drawer is somehow discovered to contain the necessary change; if he seems to be impressionable, his attention will be called to a photograph and the inner salon will be recommended. In many towns, too, " American bars " are found, most of them liquor establishments behind the counters of which prostitutes hand out liquor and encourage assignations. The proprietors escape

[62] This particular form of humbug is impossible in Austria-Hungary where the sale of tobacco is an imperial monopoly.
[63] There are between fifty and sixty of these shops in Zurich. At times a servant is saleswoman; the prostitute herself lolls in the rear room.

punishment because the assignations are fulfilled elsewhere than on his premises. Filthy establishments more flagrantly devoted to the same purposes exist in abolition Zurich as in regulation Bremen.[64]

Would these establishments revert to bordells, if the transformation were allowed or forced? Perhaps, to a limited extent. But the change would simply convert a few furtive and ill-patronized resorts into notorious and well-attended bordells, the rest remaining by preference what they now are. The net outcome would be bad, not good. Meanwhile Christiania proves that the forms in question do not result merely from suppression of the bordell, for the Animierkneipe with female service does not exist there and counterfeit employments are rare.

The weight of authority — lay and official — unquestionably favors the view here taken,— that the suppression of the bordell has operated in the public interest. True enough, a writer discussing the entire evolution of the problem, claims that the disappearance of the bordell in Zurich has been accompanied "by an increase of secret 'hole and corner' prostitution, beyond the scope of the law," [65] but no argument or evidence shows that abolition is in any wise responsible for the fact, if fact it be. It is assuredly not without significance as militating towards a directly opposite conclusion that prosecutions for pandering [65a] have in the long run decreased, not

[64] It is no uncommon error for regulationists to suppose that these abominations occur only or mainly in abolition towns. Such a mistake appears to be implied in the account of Zurich by Müller and Zürcher, *Zeitschrift*, XIV, p. 205.
[65] Weiss, *loc. cit.*, p. 125.
[65a] The word pandering is here used in a very broad sense, as

Prostitution in Europe

increased, although the suppression of bordells would, if general conditions actually deteriorated, necessarily lead to an increase in the activity of the pander. The bordells were closed in 1898: in 1895, 22; in 1896, 19; in 1897, 27 persons were convicted on the charge of pandering. During the next three years, 30, 33, and 25; during the last five years, 13, 23, 28, 26, and 22 respectively. The learned chief of the Zurich police declared to me that the bordell system "had earned practically universal disapprobation. No one would now again urge the introduction of tolerated houses, not even the un-prejudiced and liberally-disposed. Houses where a madame can hire out girls and acquire profits are not wanted by any one." An important official in Christiania urged that whether regulation is desirable or not, the destruction of the bordell was an advantage. The Amsterdam police favored their extirpation and after fifteen years' experience "are still opposed to them." The foregoing judgments are based on police grounds; assuredly the case against the bordell would be all the stronger, were indirect considerations also allowed to weigh.

Nowhere does the suppression of the bordell aggravate the domicile problem, which, as a matter of fact, settles itself in abolition towns, just as it does in regulation towns. The English, Swiss, Dutch, and Scandinavian prostitutes seek rooms in sections occupied by the poor, usually paying a considerably higher rental than is paid by decent folk. In some cases their character

a translation of "Kuppelei" which includes all forms of promoting prostitution.

Abolition and Order

is concealed and their business transacted elsewhere; in others, when neighbors or fellow-tenants are too poor or too careless to protest, the women utilize their own lodgings. The street-walkers of London tend to congregate in apartment houses or " mansions " from which respectable families are crowded out; in the provincial towns they occupy small houses. If renting of rooms to prostitutes is in itself made a crime, the law is broken, as at Berlin, and of course most regularly in case of the more clever and well-to-do; or the stupid and wretched are pushed into vagabondage rather than out of prostitution. Some interesting statistics on this point come from Zurich where, since 1897, the renting of a domicile to a prostitute constitutes a punishable offence. As the execution of the law has been more efficient, the percentage of homeless prostitutes, who sleep in public lodging-houses or elsewhere, now here, now there, betrays a tendency to increase. Police statistics, dealing with 361 prostitutes, in 1904, show 69.8% having a regular domicile, 30.2% without domicile; in 1908, of 399 women, the proportions were 52.6%, 47.4% respectively; in 1910, of 601 women, 62.2% and 37.8% respectively.[66] The domicile problem is indeed soluble only as the general problem of prostitution itself is solved; it is made neither better nor worse by abolition.

The preceding discussion makes clear that the bordell played but a slight part in the prostitution-economy of Norway, Denmark, Holland, and Switzerland at the time of its abolition. The step was of moral rather than of immediate practical importance. It indicated a change

66 Müller and Zürcher, in *Zeitschrift,* XIV, p. 198.

Prostitution in Europe

in the attitude of society, that might in time produce results; but there was no perceptible result at the moment.
How stands the situation in respect to order in the
streets? Was the abolition of control attended by increased prominence of prostitutes in the public highways
of continental towns or greater difficulty in keeping
track of them, where advisable to do so?

Of the abolition cities that I visited, prostitutes are
most prominent in the chief thoroughfares of Copenhagen, particularly in the vicinity of the Tivoli, a popular
amusement resort in the heart of the town, and on the
street corners and open squares near-by; they loiter alone
or in small groups, making no aggressive effort to attract attention; from time to time they retreat into the
cafés or variety shows abounding in the vicinity. The
main shopping street of Christiania — Karl Johans
Gade — appears to be free of promenading prostitutes
by day; at night, they are in distinct evidence there and
in amusement gardens close by; once more their demeanor
is quiet and unobtrusive. In the Hague the street prostitute is barely noticeable; an occasional woman is observable in the crowds that night and day push through
the busy little street on which most of the retail shops
are found; others can be hunted down in low cafés.
Rotterdam — a city of different type — presents a
slightly different aspect. In the earlier hours of the evening, women hasten to the skating-rink, dance halls and
cafés. When, at midnight, these resorts close, prostitutes appear for a while on the streets. The streets of
Amsterdam were, at the time of my visit, the cleanest I
had anywhere observed; the ordinance authorizing arrest

of the prostitute for promenading has been enforced with sufficient vigor and discretion to attain its object. Zurich is not substantially different from other abolition towns. As late as midnight only occasional and cautious street-walkers were to be observed; in reply to a question, an inquirer was informed by one of these that she would shortly leave for Geneva,— a regulation town,— " there is too little doing here." Women, of whose character their appearance leaves no doubt, survey the male passer-by and retreat into a side street to give him an opportunity to seek an interview; but unless intoxicated, they quietly await his approach.

The number of police arrests required in order to bring about the conditions above described does not seem excessively large. In Christiania, I was officially informed that " arrests for solicitation were few "; in Amsterdam (population 580,960) 370 arrests were made in 1910, 382, in 1911.[67] The situation in Copenhagen (population 462,161) is portrayed by the following statistics: for soliciting, offending against " the sense of shame," [68] and " vagabondage," 288 arrests were made in 1907, the year succeeding the repeal of regulation; in 1908, 344; in 1909, 432; in 1910, 414; in 1911, 353. The total, not large in any case, is due to the inclusion of vagabondage, to the growth of the city, and to a judicial decision to the effect that prostitutes congregating in the streets cannot be arrested or dispersed; for out of these casual gatherings occasional disturbances leading to subsequent arrests sometimes arise.

[67] Personally communicated by police head.
[68] I. e., Violation of Section 2 of the laws of 1906.

Prostitution in Europe

Have conditions in the towns above named been affected for the worse by the sudden and recent change from regulation to abolition? I did not find a single police officer who answered that question in the affirmative. The division chief at Copenhagen stated to me: " Regulation was entirely dispensed with in 1906; in the interval the police have learned how to procure all the information and to take all the steps for which at one time a morals police and regulation were supposed to be necessary." [69]   When the new law abrogating police control was proposed, objection was made on the ground that, in the absence of police power to confine prostitutes to specific localities, they would infest the whole city: " It has not happened; prostitution is more scattered and thus more readily handled, but it does not invade all sections.   The suppression of summary police punishments has done no harm; the ordinary courts with their usual processes have proved adequate to maintain order and decency.   Conditions are at least as good as under the old system; some streets have been entirely freed; the main streets are no worse; clandestine prostitution has not been aggravated; indeed up to now nothing has happened to cause us to regret,"— with which the grateful official " touched wood! " [70]   Elsewhere, I was informed

[69] The number of women enrolled had been as high as 700.
[70] For a detailed discussion of this point see a paper by E. M. Hoff, " *On the Effects of the Law of March* 30, 1906 " (Copenhagen, 1909).   Dr. Hoff, quoting an unfavorable utterance by Judge Cold respecting "the armies of loose women in the Vesterbro quarter," remarks: "If we should go out to the Vesterbro in the expectation of unpleasant experience in the way of public morals, we should be disappointed.   Vesterbro makes the impression of not having changed essentially since the passage of the law.   There is certainly no offence to be feared by anyone walking through the streets; of course loose women whose manner is not characterized by great

Abolition and Order

that the former partisans of regulation were "struck dumb."[71] If abolition were working badly, one would hear "I told you so" from its original opponents; there are, as a matter of fact, very few regulationists any longer in Copenhagen, though certain points to be shortly discussed are not yet clear. Officials of the same rank in Christiania stated: "Regulation will never be restored." The partisans of regulation have steadily diminished in number and volubility. An incident reported from Christiania, however, is interesting as showing that everything that has happened since abolition has not necessarily happened on account of abolition. In 1899 it was, for example, pointed out at a medical conference in Christiania that street conditions had become temporarily worse. The speaker attributed the fact to abolition; but the argument was presently refuted by the statement that the real reason for deterioration was the instruction to the police that "they had no right to interfere with soliciting unless it was done in a distinctly indecent manner." Stockholm has not yet abolished regulation, but the system has decayed so rapidly that bad results ought to be perceptible, if regulation was really of any consequence whatsoever. I have already called attention to the sudden drop in the new enrolments, from 119 in 1903 to 67 in 1904; the number of annual inspections fell from 20,849 in 1903 to 6,652 in

reserve may be noted, but the same was true formerly and had been true for years. In general, conditions can fairly be described as quiet." (p. 2, somewhat condensed.) I visited the quarter at different hours, day and night, and fully concur in Dr. Hoff's contention that prostitution is not more conspicuous than in similar neighborhoods elsewhere in Europe.
[71] Völlig stumm.

Prostitution in Europe

1911. The institution thus shrank two-thirds within a few years, " without any resultant disadvantages from the standpoint of public order; an activity that can be reduced 66 2-3% without a trace of inconvenience can hardly be regarded as necessary for the public welfare." [71a] In Holland the abolition movement spread from town to town,— an improbable course, had the absence of regulation done harm. The Chief of the Hague police assured me that he " cherished no regret on the score of abolishing regulation or bordells "; the division chief admitted that, although having been a regulationist during the regulation period, experience with the alternative system had made him a strong abolitionist; he would " advise all cities to abolish regulation and none to introduce it." No stronger expressions were anywhere used than by the Amsterdam Chief and his staff; they were outright abolitionists; they believed regulation inseparable from police corruption — an opinion echoed elsewhere as well; they found no greater difficulty in handling the problems — criminal or other — in consequence of abolition. In either case " incessant vigilance and effort " were required. It is true that the police officials of France and Germany give quite different accounts of what is to be observed in abolitionist communities; but these statements are usually based on prophecies made during the controversial period. The Swedish commission reports on hearsay that " the experience of countries which do not have special suppression of whole-time prostitution as such " is deplorable; but Professor Johansson notes in reply that " it would have been well to indicate the countries

[71a] *Reglementeringen i Stockholm*, pp. 132-3.

332

in question." [72]   Christiania alone is mentioned by name,
and as to that, candor requires them to add that " nothing
really importunate or offensive was observed in the conduct of the women." [73]

I have given above the verdicts of the police who
have lived under both systems, an experience entitled to
great weight.   There is every indication that the popular verdict coincides.   In the Canton of Zurich, a refer-
eudum, proposed in favor of returning to the abandoned
system, was defeated by a vote of 49,806 to 18,016.[74]
A newspaper comment on the result warns the " interests" in favor of regulation that " every proposition
emanating from them is hopeless.   If ever a revision of
the present statute is undertaken, the initiative will have
to come from disinterested jurists, physicians, and judges.
We hope there will be no such occasion." [75]

A comparison of the streets of abolition cities with
those of regulation cities sustains the conclusion to which
the preceding statements point.   Christiania is as decent as Stuttgart.   As between Zurich and Geneva, the
contrast is all in favor of Zurich, though it is twice as
large.   Even the sea-port towns constitute no exception.
Copenhagen and Rotterdam are at least as quiet as
Bremen and Hamburg; indeed it would be impossible to
find in the abolition sea-ports anything resembling the
street scenes enacted in the bordell quarters of regulated
ports.   The sailors' quarter of Rotterdam — the Schie-
damschedyk — is a cosmopolitan affair, with drinking and dance halls of variegated character.   Prosti-

[72] *Loc. cit.*, p. 46.   [74] Weiss, *loc. cit.*, p. 121.
[73] *Ibid*, p. 47.   [75] Weiss, *loc. cit.*, p. 123.

tutes and their customers come together in them; at times a woman standing in a door-way salutes a passer-by. But up to the small hours of the night, the streets were free of scandal.

Reference to the statutes previously described will show the reader that the police generally enjoy the right to proceed against the prostitute as a vagabond. This is the abolitionist counterpart of the regulationist provisions directed against women " without a definite domicile." The vagabondage proviso is largely used only in Copenhagen, where there exists great difference of opinion as to its value. Its prominence in the Danish law betrays the dread under which the lawmakers worked. It was feared that simple repeal of regulation might be interpreted to mean that the law had no objection to a woman's earning her living by prostitution;[76] the prostitute was therefore made expressly amenable to punishment as a vagabond, if proved to be without proper means of support. Most of the arrests in the statistics before given[77] are due rather to vagabondage than to solicitation — 217 out of 288, 241 out of 344, 251 out of 432, 243 out of 414, 200 out of 353. The provision operates in this way. The police having noticed a woman walking the streets (not soliciting) at all hours, presume her to be without legitimate occupation; she is warned; on a second warning her name and address are taken and a printed notice is sent, requiring her to obtain employment and to report the fact. Between 200 and 300 notices of this kind are annually sent; in 1909,

[76] Regulation, of course, expressly recognized her right to do this, if she were registered.
[77] Page 329.

216 women were once punished, 45 twice, 11 thrice on this charge.[78]

Serious objections are raised to this method of dealing with prostitution. It is criticized as an indirect method of making prostitution in itself a crime, and open as such to the objection that it bears on the woman alone, and on only the stupid woman at that. Justice would require that vagabondage be similarly treated, be the vagabond a man or a woman; but this statute undoubtedly involves discrimination in favor of the male vagabond. A quasi-regulatory system might undoubtedly be introduced beneath its cover by a reactionary official. The provision is at any rate a somewhat disingenuous subterfuge, for, strictly speaking, the vagrant is homeless; but the prostitute may be treated as a vagabond, despite the fact that she possesses a home.

From a practical point of view, there is the further objection that the statute is so easily evaded as to make its application uncertain and inequitable. The street-walker, attacked as a vagrant without means of support, claims to be a servant, earning a minimum sum,— say twelve crowns monthly; she escapes punishment by pointing to the old woman for whom she works, though the correct relationship is just the reverse, for the older woman is the servant of the prostitute; or the accused vagrant becomes a cigar-vender, a "laundress," a "friseuse," thus increasing the number of counterfeit employments. Like regulation, the vagrancy provision results in harrying the dull unfortunates, while leaving the

[78] The penalty is the workhouse for 12 days, 18 days, etc., up to 90 days.

Prostitution in Europe

more pretentious and the more clever quite unscathed.

Of the other results feared in connection with abolition, none have materialized to a perceptible extent. It was urged, for example, that when bordells were dismantled, men would annoy respectable women on the streets. It is indeed one of the queer features of all police dealings with prostitution, that, whereas solicitation by a prostitute is an offence, accosting by men is, unless outrageously flagrant, quite overlooked. This is generally true in both abolition and in regulation countries; but curiously enough, the evil is worse in regulated Germany than anywhere else. In Swiss, Dutch and English towns — all abolition — the offence is exceptional; in Berlin, many men habitually turn in order to observe women, and at night do not hesitate to venture a word by way of experiment. The annoyance of decent women has, therefore, not followed as a result of abolition and is commonest in certain regulation countries,— not, however, in my opinion, as a consequence of regulation.

It was feared that under abolition the percentage of pimps or souteneurs would rise; there is, however, no confirmatory evidence. Even bordell women frequently support pimps; the low grade prostitute everywhere has her pimp, regardless of regulation or abolition, and everywhere protects him loyally, as the few successful prosecutions show. In something over a year, only 39 men were arrested as pimps in Rotterdam, 30 of whom were sentenced to hard labor in a tramp-colony for terms running from three months to three years.[79] The

[79] Communicated by police authorities.

bully is indeed a parasite unaffected by the existence of either regulation or abolition as such.

The situation as regards houses of assignation is everywhere on the Continent in such confusion that no definite statement is possible. I have pointed out the fact that these resorts are unopposed in Paris; are harried from time to time in Germany, chiefly on the score of furnishing facilities to clandestine prostitutes; are tolerated in Budapest, on condition of submitting to certain rules,— with the result that both regular and irregular resorts exist there. Abolition towns are in theory hostile to *rendezvous* houses; but it can not be said that their prosecution has yet accomplished much more than the enforcement of greater caution and quiet — no slight gain, to be sure,— in the conduct of the business. The actual reduction in their number is, as far as one can judge, nominal.

Regulationist police are honestly afraid that abolition renders it difficult or impossible to keep track of prostitution. I have pointed out what seems to me the real inwardness of regulation,— that it furnishes the police with a method of keeping in touch with criminal and criminally-inclined prostitutes and their associates. The registered prostitute is tethered to the police; once or twice a week she is pulled back; she can not get far away without being noticed; if she does, her disappearance is soon known and efforts at least are made to trace her. Abolition is said to do away with all this and to leave the police helpless.

But the case is not so desperate after all. The continental police have methods of keeping up with other people,— reputable and criminal alike; and if the machinery which keeps up with the reputable will not answer for the prostitute, assuredly the machinery which is with such difficulty eluded by law-breakers will. For example, life and property are probably equally secure in Hamburg, Rotterdam, and Birmingham. Hamburg has a well organized regulatory system; Rotterdam is abolitionist, but catalogues prostitutes; Birmingham is abolitionist and ignores the prostitute until she becomes disorderly or criminal, whereupon, like other disorderly or criminal people, she suffers as such. " As far as crime is concerned," a prominent London police official remarked to me, " crime committed by a prostitute is not different from other crime; it is handled just as other crime is handled and no weakness has been felt in consequence of this procedure." In this, as in all the other points considered, if abolition has done no harm, regulation could at best have done little or no good. Nor does it follow that thoroughgoing abolition is at all inconsistent with just as complete knowledge of local prostitution as is possessed by regulationist police, should such information be desired. The English police, as I have said, take no interest in the matter until the law is violated,— of course, knowing and observing women given to transgression, precisely as they know and observe other suspects. Influenced doubtless by continental tradition, the police of abolition Rotterdam catalogue women of suspected virtue; they possess a list of 1,465, eight hundred of whom are professional and avowed prostitutes. The police of abolition Zurich know 400 persons who rent rooms for prostitution though the evi-

Abolition and Order

dence falls short of technical completeness; in Christiania some 500 prostitutes are known to the authorities; the Amsterdam Bureau is preparing a list for all Holland; after four years of work it contains some 7,000 names; similar lists of pimps, traffickers, etc., with photographs where possible, are found there just as in regulationist Dresden or Vienna. The houses in which the prostitutes of Amsterdam live have also been studied. At first two, afterwards four, men were assigned to the task with the result that increasingly complete information has been procured. In 1908, 292 houses with 548 girls were located; in 1909, 366 houses with 656 girls; in 1910, 510 houses with 854 girls; in 1911, 597 houses with 968 girls.[80] Copenhagen, fearful of a too sudden plunge into abolition manages through its " warnings " to reach a similar result; some 300 to 400 women are thus kept under observation,— though, as happens under regulation, the women do not report as systematically as the law contemplates, some evading, some leaving, some being in prison.[81] It is clear, therefore, that abolition is consistent with as complete knowledge of the local situation as the authorities think it worth while to procure; in Holland, indeed, there has been more activity along this line since abolition than previously.

For the sake of completeness, it is perhaps worth while to insert another word before closing, as to the bearing of abolition on other forms of prostitution than those I

[80] The police heads are careful to affirm that these figures indicate not an increase of prostitution, but increased knowledge of its whereabouts.

[81] For the facts comprised in the foregoing account, I am indebted to the courtesy of many officials in Holland, Denmark, and Norway.

Prostitution in Europe

have considered at some length,— the dance hall, the café, and similar establishments that furnish the prostitute an advantageous opening. Neither regulation nor abolition as such involves any particular policy in reference to these resorts. On the Continent little has been done to insure their decent conduct or to interrupt their connection with the exploitation of vice. In Great Britain, the liquor and amusement traffic have been more effectually supervised and beyond question with good results, as far as the matter has yet gone. But effective management of the difficulties here touched on takes us far beyond the immediate subject of our present inquiry. For vicious liquor and amusement resorts are not bad because prostitutes fasten upon them; prostitutes fasten upon them because they are bad. They are problems, therefore, to be dealt with quite irrespective of prostitution, though prostitution is indeed deprived of a foothold and an incentive when they are thus dealt with.

That abolition favors police honesty is the unanimous testimony of officials who have experimented with both systems. I was informed at Zurich that the bordell system associated with regulation had resulted in corruption that "for so small a town had reached enormous proportions." An official report of the year 1892 declared that proof of punishable pandering was rarely possible because "before the investigation ordered could be accomplished, the accused had received notice of their peril through some secret channel or other." [82] Again, in Copenhagen, I learned that, as elsewhere, at the time

[82] Quoted in *Die Prostitutionsfrage in der Schweiz, loc. cit.,* p. 37.

when police and prostitute were closely related, corruption prevailed; a certain inspector even owned an interest in a house of prostitution and committed suicide on exposure. The Dutch police are outspoken to similar purpose. As I pointed out in dealing with Germany, general corruption is nowhere alleged and the integrity of the head officials is never impugned; but it is believed that, wherever the partial regulatory policy is in operation, that is, wherever one rule is applied to some women, another to others, a condition is created favorable to more or less demoralization.

It is, however, obvious that, while abolition at once places all prostitutes on the same footing before the law, it does not necessarily follow that a morals police is superfluous. The morals police is imperilled if it is in a position to award favors; under abolition, this peril disappears. Now that this particular force is no longer exposed to any peculiar danger, is it not worth retaining in the interest of specialization? European experience does not warrant an affirmative answer. Regulation Rome deals with its problems without morals police. Certain towns of abolition Holland tend to create a morals division to observe prostitution; a few men are detailed for the purpose at the Hague; two inspectors, one social worker and twelve patrolmen at Rotterdam.[83] Copenhagen retains a morals police. The English cities are, of course, without any such division. It would appear that the scope of a morals police in abolition cities is at best narrow. Certain it is that no European city relies on the existence of the morals police to maintain

[83] This force also has certain other dutites.

the integrity of the main body of the force. That integrity is undoubted, but it is due, as I have already pointed out, first and foremost to the character and tenure of the upper officials, to the way in which patrolmen are chosen and trained, and to the sort of relation that exists between the police department and the other government departments.

CHAPTER X

In the preceding chapter I remarked that though abolition may be accompanied by a *laissez-faire* policy, this is not necessarily the case. The situation in respect to venereal disease best illustrates this statement. We shall see that the public in England is well-nigh entirely indifferent on the subject; almost total *laissez-faire* prevails there. Abolition Scandinavia has, on the other hand, displayed great vigor and originality in grappling with the problem of disease. Abolition includes, therefore, the countries least active and most active in this respect, — both extremes.

The Norwegians were in this matter first in the field with a scheme, the essential points of which can be most clearly stated by means of a contrast with regulation.

Prostitution in Europe

Regulation endeavors to protect the public health by safe-guarding through police agencies the health of registered prostitutes,— these prostitutes being periodically examined by police surgeons and forcibly treated when found diseased; the distinctive features of sanitary regulation are, therefore, its limitation to professional inscribed prostitutes, its management by the police, and the prison-like nature of the cure. In contradistinction to this procedure, the unsatisfactory nature and outcome of which we have discussed, the Scandinavian experiment, generally speaking, aims to reach all those suffering with venereal disease, men and women alike; and it seeks to accomplish this end by transferring the function from the police to the health department, by the provision of free treatment, and by endeavoring to enlist the patient's aid in ascertaining the source of infection, and in the isolation and cure of disease. Separation from the police is intended to allay the patient's dread of becoming involved with the criminal authority, and, as nearly as may be, to establish the feeling that venereal disease is after all a disease and not a crime,— an evil that, aside from all else, requires consideration on its own account. The voluntary nature of submission to treatment is intended still further to deepen the impression that the entire matter is left to the patient's intelligence and self-interest — precisely as though he were otherwise afflicted; free treatment is designed to strengthen the inducement and to dispose of the competition of quacks.

The Norwegian law under which this system has been organized dates from 1860; by its terms local health

344

Abolition and Disease

boards with very extensive powers in reference to epidemic and contagious diseases were organized; and these boards were left free to determine what precautions should be taken and to require reports.

In order to assist the health — not the police — authorities in controlling the diseases in question, all physicians are required to report daily — usually without names [1] — their venereal patients, to furnish the patient with a copy of the laws relating to the communication of venereal disease [2] and to require the patient to sign a statement acknowledging the fact that he (or she) has been thus explicitly warned.[3] The physician also

[1] Names are given when the physician feels that the patient is likely to spread infection, or when the patient is sent into a hospital.

[2] A copy of the following slip is given to the patient:

Attention is called to the following sections of the Penal Code:

Sec. 155. Whoever, with knowledge or conjecture that he is suffering from a contagious sex disease, infects or exposes to infection another person, by means of sexual intercourse or immoral contact, shall be punished with imprisonment for not more than three years.

The same punishment is provided for those who connive at enabling any person who is known or suspected to be afflicted with a contagious sex disease, to infect in the above manner or expose to infection, another person.

If the person infected, or exposed to infection, be married to the guilty person, public prosecution shall take place only on application by the injured party.

Sec. 358. Imprisonment for six months or less is the punishment for anyone who, without calling attention to the danger of infection,

1. Causes a child to be nursed, knowing or suspecting the child to be afflicted with contagious syphilitic disease, or engages anyone to nurse such child, or

2. Knowing or suspecting that he (or she) is suffering from contagious syphilitic disease, enters the household of another as servant, or remains in such service, or receives a strange child to nurse it, or aids in bringing about such conditions.

The same punishment is provided for those who engage or, having engaged, retain, any person known or suspected to suffer from contagious syphilitic disease, as nurse for a child, or who aids in bringing about such engagement or retention in service.

[3] I herewith acknowledge, that Dr. —— has called my attention to

345

endeavors to ascertain the source of the infection and the person inculpated is reported to the Health Office. This latter individual on calling by invitation [4] is informed of the nature of the charge — the name of the accuser being withheld — and is invited to submit to examination at a hospital or by a municipal physician. No compulsion is applied; the advantages of knowing the truth and the offer of free and skilful treatment in complete privacy form the entire inducement. If disease is thus proved to exist, treatment can be compelled, to the extent of forcibly confining the infected person in a hospital. But reliable persons receive ambulatory treatment at the hands of municipal physicians,— men, at the office of the physician, women at the Board of Health office where a woman physician is on duty. The police are invoked only if an individual having been " denounced " neglects or refuses to comply with the summons of the Health Department. Persons who, having knowledge of their infectious condition, communicate disease, are punished with imprisonment for not exceeding three years.

The Danish law dealing with the subject represents a

the following points:
1. That I am suffering from *Syphilis*.
2. That my disease is contagious for at least .. years.
3. That I am punishable, if I in any way expose others to infection.
Copies of Penal Code, Sections 155 and 358 received.
                    Date.
                              Signature.

[4] The invitation is as follows:

                    Christiania Health Board,
                        Second Health Inspector.
You are respectfully requested to report at the office at No. 55 Akers Street, third floor, ... as it is desired to talk to you.
                    Christiania, the .... 19....

Abolition and Disease

gradual evolution greatly hastened in its final stages by the Norwegian example.[5]   The proffer of free treatment dates back to 1788; a law of 1874 sought to impose an obligation to take advantage of this opportunity; in the law of March 30, 1906, fifteen of the eighteen paragraphs which compose the statute deal with the problem of venereal infection.[6]   The main provisions are the following:[7]   It is made a punishable offence to communicate venereal infection even as between husband and wife; any person who in ignorance of his or her condition infects another is liable for the medical charges and damages; venereally infected persons may, regardless of their ability to pay, receive free treatment from the municipality; they are in duty bound to submit to such free treatment if they are themselves unable to employ a physician; if the manner of living of the patient is such as to endanger others, or if the patient does not observe directions, or is a pauper in receipt of aid, he or she may be forcibly interned,— *the decision to rest with the police officials*[8] ; patients can be required to continue under medical observation even after the conclusion of their regular treatment; every physician is obligated to

[5] Hoff, *loc. cit.*, p. 5.
[6] For the text of the statute, translated into English, see Appendix.
[7] It should be mentioned that in Germany too a start has been made in this direction.
Section 223 of the German Penal Code can be invoked against any person "injuring the health of another;" the penalty is imprisonment up to three years or fine up to 1,000 marks. There is considerable agitation in favor of provisions explicitly aimed at venereal disease. See, e. g., M. Homburger, *Die strafrechtliche Bedeutung der Geschlechtskrankheiten, Zeitschrift* XI, pp. 28, 63, and 205.
[8] This is an important variation from the Norwegian prototype and indicates the compromise spirit that here and there appears in the Danish law.

347

hand venereal patients a printed warning against marriage and against sexual intercourse, and to explain the legal liabilities incurred through violation of this injunction; every physician must report the instances in which such action has been taken by him [9] ; patients are free to indicate the supposed source of their infection, though not obliged to do so, and the physician may in his discretion report such alleged source to the police, who may or may not take action thereon; a child, suffering with syphilis may not be nursed by any one other than its own mother; nor may a syphilitic wet nurse continue the practice of her vocation. A woman arrested for any offence connected with prostitution or on the charge of infecting another may with her consent be medically examined through the police; in case of refusal to submit, the courts shall have the power to order the same; compulsory examination must be carried out by paid municipal physicians of the same sex as the accused; these same physicians are obligated to examine all applicants and to treat all venereal patients without either demanding or accepting a fee; in Copenhagen municipal clinics must be maintained by the department of health in different parts of the city; the patient can be required to return for treatment at appointed times and if sent to the hospital may be compelled to remain until discharged by the physician. Should the patient fail to obey instructions, the case must be reported by the attending physician to the City physician, who is authorized to take action.[10]

[9] The law does not require that the name of the patient be reported, but it must be correctly given to the physician.

[10] Slips containing instructions as to the nature of the disease, the

Abolition and Order

The municipal clinics, maintained for the purposes above stated, seven in number, are prominently announced on every advertising obelisk. As indicating the direct way in which the subject is handled, I reproduce on page 350 the bulletin.[11]

At Rome, side by side with the ineffective municipal regulatory system previously described, the royal government of Italy has, by a law approved August 1, 1907, instituted a dispensary system, in many respects closely following the Danish type. The measure provides for "gratuitous public prophylaxis of gonorrhœa, soft chancre, and syphilis."[12] The dispensaries are to be organized by the communes acting in coöperation with the ministry of the Interior, or in default of such arrangement, by the Interior department itself; the expense is to be borne by the commune assisted by governmental aid; physicians shall be appointed by the government; "they shall treat without any distinction all sufferers from venereal diseases who apply to the dispensaries. The cure is gratuitous for all alike."[13] Provision is further made for hospital facilities. Supplementary sections endeavor to bring professional prostitutes within the scope of the act.

Between the Italian and the Scandinavian legislation above summarized there is, however, an important distinction. The Italian scheme is wholly and unconditionally voluntary and hygienic; it lacks altogether com-

patient's proper conduct while under treatment and the penalties to which misconduct may lead are also, as in Norway, handed to him or her.

[11] Its dimensions are 17"x26".
[12] *Sanitary Laws,* revised text, Section III, Articles 136–156.
[13] *Ibid.,* Article 144.

AT THE FOLLOWING PLACES AND FROM THE FOLLOWING PHYSICIANS, ALL PERSONS SUFFERING FROM VE-NEREAL DISEASE, REGARDLESS OF ABILITY TO PAY, HAVE THE RIGHT TO DEMAND FREE TREATMENT WITHIN THE HOURS INDICATED:

CONSULTATIONS FOR MEN

PLACE	NAME OF PHYSICIAN	MON. Day	MON. Even.	TUES. Day	TUES. Even.	WED. Day	WED. Even.	THUR. Day	THUR. Even.	FRI. Day	FRI. Even.	SAT. Day	SAT. Even.
Rudolph Berghs Hospital	Ravn	12½-1½				12½-1½		12½-1½	6-7	12½-1½			
Rudolph Berghs Hospital	Jersild	9½-10½				9½-10½		9½-10½		9½-10½			
Isted Street 30	Meincke	3-4	6-7	3-4	6-7			3-4			6-7	3-4	
Griffenfeldt Street 8	Einar Petersen	2-3				2-3		2-3			6-7		
Griffenfeldt Street 8	H. Levy		6-7	10-11	6-7	10-11				10-11			
Osterbro Street 56 D	H. Sorensen			9½-10½		9½-10½		9½-10½				9½-10½	
Osterbro Street 56 D	C. E. Jensen	3-4			6-7	3-4	6-7		6-7	3-4			
Torve Street 12	H. Bonnesen		6-7	8½-9½		8½-9½				8½-9½			
Torve Street 12	P. Haslund			3-4	6-7			3-4	6-7			3-4	
St. Kongens Street 46	Goldschmidt			11-12	6-7			11-12		11-12		11-12	7-8

CONSULTATIONS FOR WOMEN

PLACE	NAME OF PHYSICIAN	MON. Day	MON. Even.	TUES. Day	TUES. Even.	WED. Day	WED. Even.	THUR. Day	THUR. Even.	FRI. Day	FRI. Even.	SAT. Day	SAT. Even.
Rudolph Berghs Hospital	Ravn		6-7	9½-10½						12½-1½	6-7		
Rudolph Berghs Hospital	Jersild												
Isted Street 30	Miss Hamburger	10-11		10-11				10-11					6-7
Griffenfeldt Street 8	Einar Petersen									2-3		10-11	
Griffenfeldt Street 8	H. Levy				6-7		6-7						
Osterbro Street 56 D	H. Sorensen					9½-10½							
Osterbro Street 56 D	C. E. Jensen				6-7		6-7				6-7	3-4	
Torve Street 12	H. Bonnesen	3-4				8½-9½						8½-9½	
Torve Street 12	P. Haslund				6-7						6-7		
St. Kongens Street 46	Goldschmidt									11-12	6-7		
Venders Street 8	Miss N. Nielsen		6-7			10-11		10-11	6-7	10-11			

Health Board of Copenhagen, April 1, 1912.

Abolition and Disease

pulsory features, addressing itself unreservedly to health, without regard to either order or morals. A ministerial circular, interpreting its scope and purpose declares: " Any construction of the law aiming to ascertain the presence of disease is unlawful and in opposition to its purport, because the police spirit leads to the concealment of disease and avoidance of cure. Compulsory action is offensive to the liberty and dignity of human personality. The prophylaxis of venereal disease is to be kept entirely distinct from the protection of morals and the measures of the police. The two services differ in object,— the one having a hygienic end, the other aiming to protect public order. Confusion is dangerous and constitutes an abuse." [14]

As contrasted with this thoroughgoing acceptance of the voluntary point of view, the Danish policy retains certain vestiges of police complicity. It includes, for example, the right of compulsory examination in case of women arrested for offences indicative of professional prostitution [15] ; it continues to relate the police to venereal disease, through the compulsory proviso above cited and through the provisions encouraging the disclosure of the supposed source of the infection.[16]

As to the wisdom of the above mentioned provisions

[14] Ministry of the Interior, Direction-General of Public Health. Telegraphic Circular to the Prefects of the Kingdom: " The Prophylaxis of Venereal Diseases." (Abridged.)

[15] If the woman objects, examination can be made only if ordered by the court. As a matter of fact, objection is rare, as the courts would not hesitate to grant the necessary authority.

[16] This provision was in a somewhat different form included in the *Regulatory Statute of 1866*, where it was provided that a registered prostitute could be punished if she knowingly communicated infection; but punishments were rare, since the girl could always shield herself behind the fact that the police surgeons had

Prostitution in Europe

grave doubt exists. They are unquestionably in conflict with the spirit animating the statute as a whole. Dr. Santoliquido, the author and administrator of the unqualified Italian scheme, is strongly of the opinion that the slightest taint of police complicity or the slightest suggestion of publicity seriously impedes the utilization of the facilities offered.[17] The Danish lawmakers were evidently afraid to be thoroughgoing. On the one hand they were entirely clear that regulation failed, not only because it reached no men and relatively few women, but because the association of disease with crime tended to drive disease into hiding. They saw that, to entice it out, to ensure more general, more skillful, more thorough treatment, the interest and the intelligence of the patients had to be appealed to; they must be taught to be cured for their own sakes and that of others; and in order that every obstacle thereto might be removed, treatment offered in a scientific spirit must be made free and accessible. They feared, however, to leave the matter at this point; they felt that some provision had to be made for backsliders; and to keep these under treatment, even against their own inclination, the intervention of the police was made possible. Undoubtedly the individuals immediately concerned may thus gain,— for they may be helped. But the danger is that unfortunate indirect effects may more than outweigh the direct favorable effects. The vestige of the police spirit may hinder the very transformation in the attitude of those afflicted

pronounced her well — an interesting illustration of the way in which the medical examination may defeat its own object.

[17] His views are stated in his *Report to the Tenth International Congress of Hygiene and Demography*, held at Paris, 1900.

that the legislation hoped to bring about. Thus incidental compulsion may tend to tear down what the law as a whole endeavors to build up.[18]

As opposed then to the Italian policy of leaving the matter wholly to individuals and endeavoring to educate them to take advantage of abundant facilities, the Danish plan leaves the matter to individuals, if the individual is willing to act intelligently; but it endeavors to coerce the rest. There is, however, some doubt as to whether the second part of the Danish arrangement does not tend to defeat the first. Even under police regulation we observed that most was achieved where force was most completely dissembled; and, wherever, as at Paris, police regulation and voluntary hospital facilities are both provided, the latter are far more effective than the former. Moreover, the remnant of police compulsion is always in danger of relapsing into regulation, applicable mainly, perhaps altogether, to women,— a policy to which we have discovered insurmountable objections.

From the standpoint of the theory of the law, then,— that abundant facilities for treatment coupled with an unqualified appeal to the intelligence and self-interest of the patient is likely to reach, on the whole, the largest number of the afflicted — grave question may also be raised regarding denunciation of the source of a par-

---

[18] Dr. Hoff points out (*loc. cit.*, p. 8) that similar police assistance may also be procured by the health authorities in dealing with other contagious or infectious maladies. Practically, however, it would seem that the cases are not entirely analogous, since one of the main difficulties in getting control of venereal disease lies in the police association with the subject which has to be effaced. Moreover, the repugnance to publicity, and the sense of shame attending venereal infection are also factors to be reckoned with.

ticular venereal infection. On its face, the transaction
appears reasonable enough: a sufferer, after interrogation by his physician or of his own motion, may report
his belief that he was contaminated by this woman or
that.[19] The information communicated by the doctor
to the police is held in strict confidence, and the person
involved may be requested to call at police headquarters;
where, being informed of the nature of the accusation,
it is suggested that he (or she) consult a physician,—
a municipal physician or a physician of the individual's
own choosing; should he (or she) be reported as ill,
treatment may be compelled, if the individual declines
otherwise to submit.[20]

On its face, I say, this looks like a not unreasonable
method of attacking infection at its source in the case
of persons who lack the conscience or the intelligence
to act of their own accord; for clearly the foci thus
reached might, if left alone, have continued, ignorantly
or malevolently, to breed further contamination. Denunciation aims to bring these concealed sources to light;
offers them treatment, if they are intelligent enough to
take advantage of such opportunity; and adds the state's
right and power to compel a proper course of action, if,
for any reason whatsoever, they are differently minded.

[19] I take the case of an infected man; the same process applies
to an infected woman who is free to denounce the man responsible for her condition.
[20] The action of the police is based on Section 181 of the Penal
Code reading as follows:
Sec. 181. When anyone knowing or suspecting himself to be infected with venereal contagion, has intercourse with another person, punishment by imprisonment shall be imposed, or, under aggravating circumstances, detention at hard labor in the House of
Correction.

Abolition and Disease

As a matter of fact, the thing is by no means so simple. In the first place, with the best intention, the patient may be mistaken as to the source of his or her infection. Prostitution is promiscuous on both sides. The women notoriously consort in quick succession with many men; men often consort with different women. The periods of incubation are more or less indefinite and variable, so that a mere reckoning back to a particular act of intercourse is not conclusive. In one set of cases, carefully studied from this standpoint,[21] over half of those questioned were unable to throw any light on the subject.

The very difficulty in question opens the way to error and abuse. Despite the confidential fashion in which the subject is handled, the humiliation involved in a mistaken or false accusation is no trifle. The same principle holds here as in respect to arrest for alleged solicitations — a single error is worse than a hundred omissions. It is a totally different thing from a mistaken allegation that some other infectious disease exists in a given house or person,— diphtheria, for example, or scarlet fever. The manner in which venereal disease is usually contracted, the implications attending its presence, set it off in a class by itself, and open the door to abuses for which other contagious diseases give no opportunity. A procedure that might, therefore, be safely employed in reference to scarlet fever, if feasible

[21] Oppenheim and Neugebauer (*Zeitschrift* XII, p. 314) give the results of an endeavor to locate the sources of 2,472 infections; 1,365 of those afflicted were unable or refused to give any helpful information. Some patients desire to screen their partners; some are plainly unreliable; others have offended so frequently that their answers are mere guesses. See *Ibid.*, p. 306.

or necessary, may be totally inapplicable to syphilis. The experience of Copenhagen has quite fully justified these doubts. Denunciation is an invitation to blackmail; it can be and has been employed by men simply to rid themselves of women of whom they have tired; for, while in theory equally applicable to both sexes, under existing conditions women have most to fear from it. For this reason, physicians do not regularly report to the police the alleged sources of infection; nor do the police always act even on such denunciations as reach them. But despite the caution with which the police act, it happens not infrequently that denounced women prove on examination to be free of infection. Women wishing to be revenged upon former " friends " or lovers do not hesitate to employ the same device; and not infrequently with a similar result. The following table shows the results of the examinations made at the instance of the Copenhagen police during a series of years: [22]

Year	No. Examined	Men	Women	No. Men ill	No. Women ill	No. persons reported for not continuing treatment		No. of these reached
						Men	Women	
1907	410	22	388	21	172	154	37	68
1908	609	61	548	54	195	218	60	89
1909	739	36	703	28	226	238	95	112
1910	822	25	797	14	155	336	130	141
1911	780	40	740	24	160	364	117	133

The figures above given by no means represent all the accusations filed with the police. They are those

[22] Compiled from *Police Reports*. Slight discrepancies in the totals are due to the occasional appearance of the same person more than once.

Abolition and Disease

only that the department felt justified in following up.
As the police cannot permit themselves to be made an
indiscriminate instrument of private oppression or venge-
ance, they use their own discretion as to whether they
will act on a given " denunciation." Necessarily therefore their action is so uncertain as to be quite ineffective;
with anything less than the most complete integrity it
might readily be something worse than uncertain. The
officials are therefore in serious doubt as to whether denunciation is workable even under the comparatively simple conditions of the Norwegian and Danish capitals; of a
commission of nine persons recently appointed to consider the question in Copenhagen, five members favored
repeal; four favored retention, not on the ground of its
general value, but as a means of reaching utterly reckless
or insane individuals who go so far as to boast of their
success in disseminating disease.[23]

But perhaps a more serious objection to denunciation
from the purely sanitary standpoint lies here;— that it
continues the hurtful association of venereal disease with
the police. It works in this respect like the reporting of
patients who break off treatment without authorization.
A certain number can, of course, be laid hold of. Of
1,749 cases recorded in the table given, 543 were
compelled or induced to resume treatment. This is, of
course, so much to the good; but suppose it impedes
the wider acceptance and operation of the voluntary
principle, on which, in the long run, the success of the
dispensary system depends? The large number of dis-

[23] A case was reported of a man who kept a list of those he supposed himself to have infected.

Prostitution in Europe

appearances above noted suggests the repellent outcome
of this traditional association, which must be completely uprooted, if persons ill of venereal disease are
to seek treatment as readily as those ill of measles or
mumps.[24]

The final columns of the table given on page 356 deserve comment on another score. During five years,
1,749 persons discontinued treatment for venereal disease
before they were dismissed by their physicians: of them,
1,310 were men, 439 were women. It would appear,
therefore, that men may be less intelligent and conscientious than women in the pursuit of regular and
voluntary treatment. Either sex may, of course, be
the means of indefinitely spreading infection,— women
by infecting a series of men, men by infecting a series
of women. If compulsory medical examination and
treatment (i. e. regulation) are therefore to be applied
to only one sex, they ought, in the light of the Copenhagen figures, to be applied to men rather than to
women,— for of the two sexes, compulsion, if desirable,
would be best applied to the sex that makes the less use
of voluntary opportunity.

The problematical points above discussed do not, however, touch the heart of the subject. At bottom, the issue between regulation and abolition turns upon this question: are the ravages of venereal disease more likely
to be mitigated by the medical examination and compul-

[24] A counter advantage ought also to be mentioned. The fear of
a possible denunciation probably induces some who find themselves
diseased to submit to treatment. And a counter disadvantage:
women are much more often denounced than men,— a survival of
the unfairness of regulation.

Abolition and Disease

sory treatment of registered prostitutes, assuming such examination and treatment to be as intelligent as they can be made, or by the provision of free, abundant and confidential opportunities for all sufferers, assuming that the dispensaries are as well conducted as they can possibly be? In behalf of patient and thorough experimentation along the latter line, the failure of regulation is of course the first and perhaps most powerful argument. The Italian sanitarians lean largely on another,— that compulsion can in no event be defended, since it involves an infraction of personal liberty. In my judgment, it is a pity to raise a metaphysical issue of this kind. Could it be once proved that compulsion succeeds, society would probably not permit itself to be balked by abstract principles of personal liberty; a not dissimilar argument by anti-vaccinationists has been peremptorily overruled by most civilized states. No individual's liberty can be made to include the privilege of spreading contagion, if a demonstrated method of checking the process is known. In this volume, I have throughout endeavored to meet regulation on its own ground. A verdict unfavorable to regulation has been found in the first instance, not because it violates personal liberty, but because it fails; because it is at least useless in respect to order, and worse than useless in respect to venereal disease. In the same way, the voluntary system is recommended, not because it is consonant with modern theories of individuality, but because it may prove the most effective way of throwing light upon the dark corners in which disease huddles and multiplies.

Experience affords as yet no conclusive proof of the

superiority of the voluntary system. Its introduction
is too recent and too limited to have as yet affected the
general situation. Moreover, the system can not be
judged until communities have been educated to take advantage of it, or — what comes to the same thing — until
it becomes evident that it is impossible to educate the
afflicted to take advantage of it. Time is a most important factor in this matter. The ancient police association must altogether die out; even the feeling of
personal humiliation about contamination must be taught
to subordinate itself to a realization of the duty of submitting to competent treatment. It is not surprising to
find that the women formerly registered in Copenhagen
used their freedom in the first instance to stay away;
the more intelligent consulted private physicians, but the
others simply ignored their condition. This experience
does not prove either the wisdom or necessity of regulation; it proves only the baneful effect of associating
hygiene with the police and the necessity of patience until
the former association is dissolved and an entirely new
association created.

How far results may be claimed for the voluntary system, I shall consider in a moment. But certainly the way
the system operates creates a presumption thus far in
its favor. Notwithstanding the partial retention of the
police connection, the dispensaries of Copenhagen are
already treating more women than formerly were reached
by regulation; in the year 1910, of all cases reported to
the Health Office, 40% had taken advantage of the dispensaries. The following tables exhibit the attendance

Abolition and Disease

of new patients at the free dispensaries during the years 1910 and 1911 : [25]

Year	Men	Women	Children	Sent into Hospital	Reported for failure to keep up Treatment
1910	3,991	1,090	78	750	238
1911	3,748	1,165	72	644	277

Moreover, the attitude of the prostitutes themselves is perceptibly changing. I mentioned above that at the outset they refused to attend the dispensaries. I was, however, reliably informed that this is no longer the case to anything like the same extent. Women who formerly endeavored to " evade the whole thing " describe themselves now as only " too glad to come." M. Augagneur submitted to the French Extra-Parliamentary Commission a comparative table strongly confirmatory of the Danish experience. The record in question runs from 1876 to 1903; it shows the number of women — registered and non-registered prostitutes respectively — who were treated for venereal disease at the Hospice de l'Antiquaille: in 1876, 835 registered prostitutes, 281 non-registered. Thereafter, the former steadily declined with the inevitable disintegration of the regulatory system; the latter tended to rise. In the final year (1903) the registered prostitutes compulsorily treated numbered only 180; the clandestines voluntarily treated had increased to 327,— i. e., the number receiving voluntary treatment was almost twice as large as the number re-

[25] These figures may be found in the Health Reports of Copenhagen. For the form in which they appear above I am indebted to the courtesy of Inspector Schepelern-Larsen.

ceiving compulsory treatment, despite the continuance of the police association.[26]

The attitude of the medical profession is an interesting indication of the way in which the new law has worked. At the outset, nine-tenths of the Copenhagen doctors were regulationists; even those favorable to abolition were fearful of sudden abolition. Nowadays the medical professions of both Christiania and Copenhagen are described as practically unanimous against regulation. Dr. Hoff in his vigorous pamphlet above quoted declares that the Danish law may indeed be modified as to details; but its main outlines are secure. And this, despite the fact that the free dispensary has practically effaced the specialists in venereal diseases,— an incidental result philosophically accepted by those whom it has affected.[27]

A word as to one other peculiarity of the Scandinavian laws,— viz. the notification of venereal disease. In Christiania, physicians are required to report daily to the Health Department, without names, new patients suffering with any venereal disease.[28] The Danish law is similar; while other contagious diseases are notifiable with names, venereal diseases are notified without names as a rule. The policeman on the beat collects the notices as he makes his rounds. A circular, dated July 1, 1912, institutes a similar form of notification in Sweden. It is stated that all cases of contagious sexual disease must be reported by the attending physician in franked en-

[26] Annexes, *loc. cit.*, p. 263.
[27] Some of these were partly compensated by being made dispensary physicians.
[28] Originally the physicians made a monthly report.

Abolition and Disease

velops to the " official physician of the province or the board of health, with the name of the disease, the age and sex of the patient, but without name and address." Notification answers in general a statistical purpose; but in Denmark, a patient who interrupts treatment may be reported by name and find himself forced to continue treatment or to fly. It is impossible to discover that notification itself has had any bad effects whatsoever. It appears rather to have assisted in making the sufferer realize his danger to others,— precisely as the notification of other diseases has resulted in increased conscientiousness. The fear one observes among English abolitionists, that notification may prove an indirect method of reinstating regulation of one sex is baseless, in so far as Denmark and Norway are concerned.

Of the other abolition countries,— Great Britain, Switzerland and Holland, none has as yet taken the disease problem seriously. *Laissez-faire* — an unreasoning, prejudiced *laissez-faire*, at that — still prevails.

In England, the public authorities concerned with the prevention and treatment of disease have thus far made " no organized effort to diminish the prevalence of venereal disease," nor would the desirability of their interesting themselves in the matter " be accepted as indisputable." [29] The hospital provisions for venereal diseases are utterly inadequate. Indoor accommodation in the large voluntary hospitals of London there is practically none,— and this even in teaching hospitals. It is held that " it is unreasonable to expect subscribers to spend

[29] R. W. Johnstone, *Report on Venereal Diseases* (Local Government Board, London, 1913) p. 1.

363

their money on rescuing persons from the consequences of their sins." [30]   The Inspector for the Local Government Board reports that "no beds or wards were reserved for infective venereal cases in any of 30 general hospitals visited in London and the provinces.   In one of the London hospitals, a rule precluded the treatment of unmarried women suffering from venereal disease, though no such rule existed with regard to unmarried men." [31]   A more liberal policy characterizes the out-patient departments, though their organization and equipment are both defective.   The poor law infirmaries and workhouses are apt to be better equipped; and it is interesting to note in passing that the administrators of these institutions when asked for their "opinion regarding the advisability of endowing the guardians with the powers of compulsory detention (of those seeking treatment for venereal complaints) were practically unanimous in declaring that it would deter patients from coming."   A few special hospitals called lock-hospitals (the name is etymologically obscure, but has nothing to do with "lock-up") are also devoted to the care of venereal patients.   Of these, recent writers state: The lock-hospitals are pathetically meager, containing "in London 136 beds for females, 27 for males; elsewhere about 70, making perhaps 250 in the United Kingdom." [32] Out-patient services are also found in connection with the lock-hospital.   English conditions in this respect

[30] *Ibid,* p. 20.
[31] *Ditto* (all slightly abridged).
[32] White and Melville, *Venereal Disease, its Present and Future.* Paper read at Annual Congress of Royal Institute of Public Health, held at Dublin, August, 1911, p. 15.

therefore deserve the severe language of Sidney and Beatrice Webb: " The man or woman suffering from gonorrhœa or syphilis, even if the innocent victim of another's guilt, is refused admission to the voluntary hospital; deterred, and as often as possible, hustled out of the workhouse; and wholly unprovided for by the local health authority." [33]   Moreover, the method of conducting the only available resort — the lock-hospital — is more or less repellent.   The patient is made to feel that his cure ought also to be a penance.   The head nurse opens and reads all letters sent or received, a measure that marks off the venereal from any other patient.   The sanitary spirit is as yet quite undeveloped: " I don't believe in making it safe "— remarked the secretary of a lock-hospital to me, just as we entered the children's ward, where thirty to forty innocent victims were under his care, the moral and medical aspects of the problem as yet hindering each other in his mind!

The abolition cities on the Continent are in respect to hospital facilities much better off, for dermatological clinics, including beds for venereal diseases, form part of the general hospitals in large cities.

I have now briefly described conditions as to the laws and hospital provisions relating to venereal disease in various abolition countries.   The issue between abolition and regulation ought in theory to be determinable by an inspection of statistical results, contrasting the results in regulation and abolition countries respectively.   Is this the case?

[33] *The Prevention of Destitution* (London, 1912) p. 33.   See also notes, pp. 43, 44.

Prostitution in Europe

There are many reasons why a summary method of settling the question by results is inapplicable. In the first place, available data are neither sufficiently reliable nor sufficiently complete.[34] Recent improvements in diagnostic art show the existence of venereal disease where mere clinical examination — up to recently the sole reliance of the physician — is incapable of discerning it; in some cases, the same improvements now result in a negative diagnosis where superficial appearance might formerly have led to a positive opinion. Hence one serious defect of even conscientiously compiled figures. But there is another serious source of error. Such general statistics as exist are in an extraordinary degree fractional and unscientific. Only in certain small sections of Scandinavia has a more or less accurate system of reporting been in vogue for even a relatively short period. Elsewhere our inferences must be based on hospital and insurance reports or rough personal estimates. In these conditions, so narrow a question as the issue between regulation and abolition does not lend itself to statistical determination.[35]

[34] Such data as exist can be found in various treatises on venereal disease; e. g., in Blaschko, *Hygiene der Prostitution.* Summarized statements are given by White and Melville, *loc. cit.,* etc.

[35] Blaschko's summary of the defects of the statistical procedure is well worth reproducing. Three methods have been employed:

(1) Comparison of amount of disease found among inscribed prostitutes with that found among non-inscribed prostitutes. The latter is higher, but that is due less to lack of medical control than to the lower age.

(2) Inquiry as to source of infection. Not significant since we know nothing of the ratio of the two groups (registered and non-registered) to the number of their customers respectively.

(3) a. Comparison of the incidence of venereal disease in places with and without regulation.
b. Comparison before and after abolition.
c. Comparison of places where regulation has been strict with

Abolition and Disease

Statistics and opinion, however, both concur in an indirect contribution to the problem. Venereal disease is shown by both to be so widely prevalent in regulated cities that one marvels whether the situation could really be any worse under even the most radical *laissez-faire* abolition. It is a truism that physicians eager to equip themselves as specialists in venereal disease resort to the crowded clinics of Paris, Vienna, and Berlin, all regulated towns, because there disease is found in greatest abundance and richest variety,— a strange comment on the alleged efficacy of regulation! On the basis of all available sources of information, Blaschko calculates that of the clerks and merchants in Berlin between 18 and 28 years of age, 45% have had syphilis, 120% have had gonorrhœa; 77% have had syphilis, 200% have had gonorrhœa in Breslau.[36] Similar inquiry among students shows according to the same investigator, that " in the course of his four years at the University, every student is venereally infected at least once,— a statement that no one familiar with the facts will be inclined to question."[37] Pinkus declares that in Germany one man in every five has had syphilis,[38] and that gonorrhœa averages more than one attack per man.[39]

An attempt was made by the Prussian Government to take a census of the amount of venereal disease among

places where it has fluctuated. These ignore other factors that greatly influence the phenomenon in question. (Art. *Die Prostitution*, pp. 1243–44, abridged).

[36] *Hygiene der Prostitution, loc. cit.*, p. 31. If the incidence of gonorrhœa is placed at 200%, the average is two attacks.

[37] *Ibid.*, p. 32.

[38] *Verhütung der Geschlechtskrankheiten*, p. 7.

[39] *Ibid.*, p. 21.

Prostitution in Europe

men in the Kingdom on April 30, 1900. It developed —
as far as the returns showed — that in general on that
day 28 men out of every 10,000 were infected; in Berlin,
however, the average was 142 per 10,000; in cities of
over 100,000 inhabitants, 100 per 10,000; in the cities
of over 30,000 inhabitants, 58 per 10,000; in cities under 30,000 inhabitants, 45 per 10,000. The results may
be represented thus:

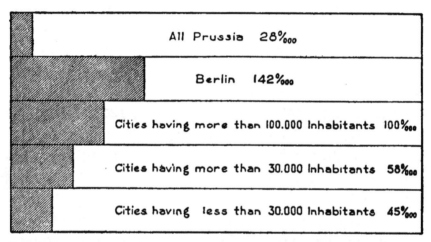

FIGURE I.— Venereal disease among males in the population of Prussia, April 30, 1900.

The inference to be drawn from Figure I is obvious:
the amount of venereal disease is in direct relation to
the size of the town. The figures given cannot accurately represent the actual totals; but they may nevertheless give a fairly reliable indication of relative conditions. The steady decrease with the size of the city
appears to suggest the main, perhaps the sole important
concrete factor, viz., the size of the city; a factor upon
which we shall stumble again in another connection.

368

Abolition and Disease

A similar inquiry was also made in Sweden, with a view to determining how many persons were under treatment for infectious venereal disease January 31, 1905. A questionnaire was sent to 1,264 physicians, of whom 1,181 replied.[40]   The Swedish and Prussian figures are set side by side in the following table:[41]

SWEDEN (JAN 31, 1905)			PRUSSIA (APR. 30, 1900)		
	Soft			Soft	
Syph.	chancre	Gon.	Syph.	chancre	Gon.
Stockholm (pop. 317,964) ....23.	1.2	31.2	Berlin 23.6	5.8	53.2
Göteborg (pop. 138,030) 15.6	1.4	18.9	Seventeen cities of more than 100,000 inhab..17.8	3.5	32.6
Malmö (pop.) 70,797) 14.4	3.1	28.6	Forty-two cities 30–100,000 ...10.8	1.9	19.6
Norrköping (pop. 44,378).11.3	0.3	16.8	Whole King-dom 5.1	1.1	9.9
Whole Kingdom. 3.6	0.3	5.4			

A more definite impression is obtainable regarding the incidence of venereal disease in European armies: do the curves thus arrived at throw any light on the issue between regulation and abolition?   The subjoined graph (Fig. II) embodies the official statistics of the war offices of Europe from 1881 to 1905.

At first sight, the graph might be interpreted as a conclusive argument in behalf of regulation.   But careful consideration entirely changes its significance.   In the first place, the earlier or more unfavorable English statistics are stated to be altogether unreliable.   It is indeed on the face of the matter impossible to credit anything like the precipitous decline depicted.   More-

[40] To the Prussian blank it is stated only 63.45% of the physicians applied to responded. *Report, Swedish Com.,* Vol. III, p. 1.
[41] *Ibid., pp.* 15–10.

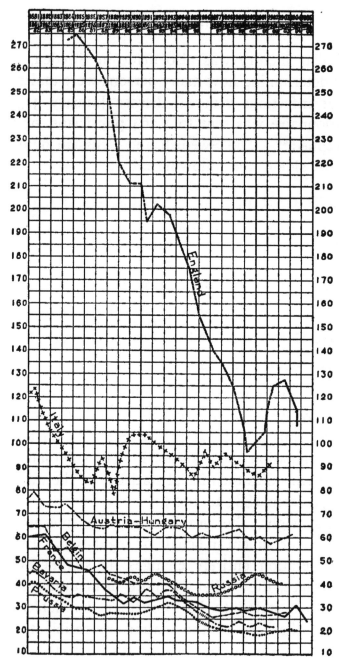

FIGURE II.—Venereal disease in European armies.

370

Abolition and Disease

over, the implied comparison is itself unfair. A continental army includes the youth of the entire nation,— all those between certain ages,— city and country boys alike; the good elements dilute the showing that would be made by the bad. The English army, on the other hand, is a volunteer force, largely recruited from among the adventurous and the derelict,— precisely those among whom an inordinately large proportion of venereal disease would naturally occur. The continental curves may represent the condition of the total male population of the ages in question; the English curve speaks for only a single section and the two cannot be directly compared. Moreover, the very magnitude of the discrepancy is fatal to its explanation by regulation. The marked variations between the armies of regulated countries,—Italy, Austria, and Prussia, indicate clearly the existence of other factors. Finally, there is observable a general movement downwards coinciding with the breakup of regulation on the Continent. If regulation exerts a perceptible effect, its narrowing scope ought to be attended by a gradual rise in the curves, instead of the reverse.

To whatever the general differences in the curves be due, there is nothing in them to suggest that regulation plays any rôle whatsoever. Closer consideration of separate curves will establish this proposition beyond dispute. The English Contagious Diseases Acts, under which medical inspection of prostitutes was instituted, were repealed in 1886,[42] the very year in which the graph records the highest incidence of venereal disease in the army. Repeal was followed, not by a rise, but by a fall

[42] The laws were suspended in 1884.

that, except for the interlude created by the Boer War, has continued almost uninterruptedly from that day to this. Regulation was at its height in England from 1870 to 1882. In the former year, of 38,408 recruits inspected, 15.78 per thousand were rejected on the score of syphilis; the number of recruits increased during the period in question to 45,423, of whom in the last year of effective regulation 10.72 per thousand were rejected for the same reason. Is this improvement attributable to regulation? Clearly not; for the rate of rejection has declined since abolition more rapidly than at any other time: in 1886, 77,991 were examined and 8.18 rejected per thousand; in 1897, 59,986 were examined and 3.47 rejected per thousand.[43]

[43] The complete statistics taken from the *Army Medical Reports* are as follows:

Report for the Year	Total number of Recruits Inspected	Recruits rejected For Syphilis	
		Number	Per 1,000
SLIGHT REGULATION			
1866	20,410	338	16.56
1867	26,646	440	16.51
1868	23,543	303	12.88
1869	17,749	291	16.40
REGULATION AT ITS HEIGHT			
1870	38,408	606	15.78
1871	36,212	593	16.38
1872	28,390	445	15.67
1873	24,895	411	16.51
1874	30,557	481	15.74
1875	25,878	327	12.63
1876	41,809	634	15.16
1877	43,803	680	15.52
1878	43,867	665	15.16
1879	42,668	573	13.43
1880	46,108	538	11.67
1881	47,444	593	12.50
1882	45,423	487	10.72
REGULATION SUSPENDED			
1883	59,436	583	9.81
1884	66,882	707	10.57
1885	72,249	706	9.77

Abolition and Disease

The annual admission of enlisted men to hospitals for venereal diseases tells the same story. In 1886 — the year of the repeal, this reached the startling total of 267.1 to the thousand; by 1900, the figure had fallen to 93.2; it rose to 125 in 1903, and fell thereafter steadily to 66 in 1909.[44]

The curve (page 374) [45] shows admissions, per thousand of strength, for syphilis (primary and secondary) in the army at home and in India for the years 1880–1908.

Report for the Year	Total number of Recruits Inspected	Recruits rejected For Syphilis	
		Number	Per 1,000
	ABOLITION		
1886	74,991	613	8.18
1887	60,976	494	8.10
1888	49,172	382	7.77
1889	53,904	358	6.64
1890	55,367	351	6.34
1891	61,322	300	4.9
1892	68,761	318	4.62
1893	64,110	314	4.90
1894	61,985	315	5.09
1895	55,698	194	3.48
1896	54,574	202	3.71
1897	59,986	208	3.47
1898	66,502	258	3.88
1899	68,087	182	2.67
1900	84,402	188	2.22
1901	76,750	177	2.31
1902	87,609	238	2.72
1903	69,533	211	3.03
1904	70,346	178	2.53
1905	66,703	156	2.34
1906	62,371	170	2.73
1907	59,393	107	1.80
1908	61,278	113	1.84
1909	50,208	89	1.77
1910	45,671	71	1.55
1911	48,178	89	1.85

From the foregoing table one must not infer that syphilis in the general population of Great Britain is rapidly decreasing, for it is impossible to say whether the recruits are fairly representative. See Johnstone, *loc. cit.,* p. 8.

[44] Complete figures are as follows: See page 375.
[45] For this drawing and the next I am indebted to Col. Melville.

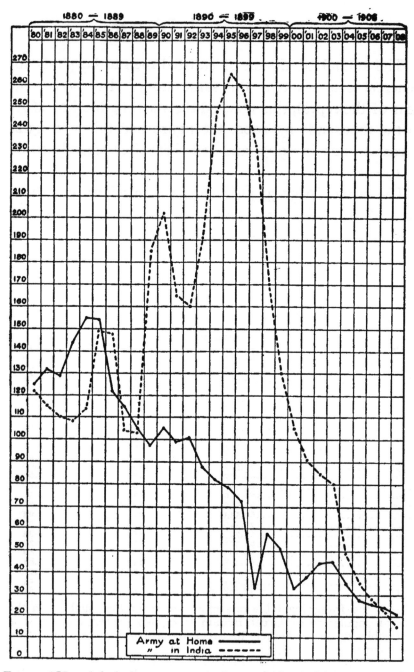

FIGURE III.— Admissions per 1,000 for syphilis, British army, 1880–1908.

374

Abolition and Disease

Finally, a comparison made between regulated and non-regulated military stations before and during regulation and after abolition exhibits capricious variations indicating clearly the negative outcome of regulation: (See Fig. IV, p. 376.)

Col. Melville's analysis is as follows: " The most obvious fact. is the parallelism of the curves. Though the curve for unprotected stations is on the whole higher, they follow the same general trend. They both fall at first, and from 1875, they both rise steadily. Regulation did not keep disease down between 1876 and 1882; its increase in unprotected stations was proportionately somewhat less than in the protected. The marked increase in the protected stations after relaxation of the rules in 1882 only continues the rise originating six years previously. Total repeal in 1886 is followed by a very marked fall in both curves, which, however, had

Statistics of the British Army. Admission to Hospital for Venereal Disease. Ratio per 1,000 of Strength.

Year	Home Army	Year	Home Army
1882	246.0	1896	158.3
1883	260.0	1897	139.7
1884	270.7	1898	132.7
1885	275.7	1899	122.4
1886	267.1	1900	93.2
1887	252.9	1901	105.4
1888	224.5	1902	122.7
1889	212.1	1903	125.0
1890	212.4	1904	107.6
1891	197.4	1905	90.5
1892	201.2	1906	82.0
1893	194.6	1907	71.9
1894	182.4	1908	68.4
1895	173.5	1909	66.0

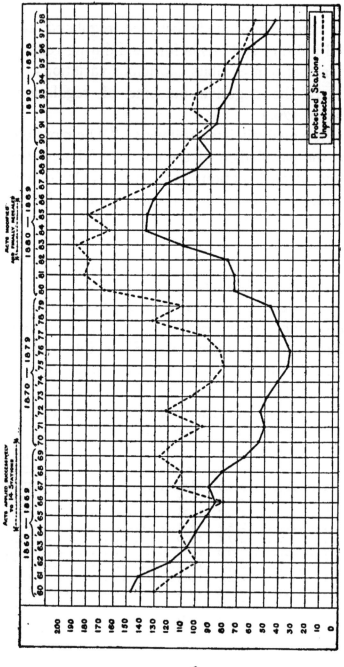

FIGURE IV.—Comparison of 14 protected with 14 unprotected stations in respect to admissions with primary venereal sores.

Abolition and Disease

begun in 1883 in the unprotected, and in 1884 in the protected, stations." [46]

German army statistics, intensively studied, yield a similarly negative result as to benefits of regulation in respect to the incidence of venereal disease. Recurring to Figure II (p. 370) we observe that the extent of infection decreased continuously from 1881 (as in all other armies except the Italian, where irregularities are considerable) up to 1900, despite the fact that, as has been shown, methods of medical examination were so crude that they probably caused more disease than they isolated. The Dutch curve has also consistently dropped,— most of all so, since abolition. [47] In Stockholm, the statistics exhibit the same decline, coincidentally with the gradual weakening of regulation. [47a]

Closer inspection of the Prussian statistics brings to light the one significant factor that we have already remarked in a previous correction, viz., the size of the community involved. It appears that during a series of years the percentage of venereally infected recruits is practically constant at 7.7%, despite the ups and downs of regulation meanwhile; but infection in different army corps shows wide discrepancies, varying from four per cent. in the XI, XIII, and XIV army corps to 20.7 per cent. in

[46] From C. H. Melville, " *The History and Epidemiology of Syphilis in the more Important Armies*," in *A System of Syphilis* by D'Arcy Power and J. K. Murphy (London, 1910) Vol. VI, pp. 96–98 (abridged).

[47] This is not included in Figure I. It is shown, however, on " Kurventafel A " along with all other foreign and American armies and navies in Josef Urbach's *Die Geschlechtskrankheiten und ihre Verhütung im k. und k. Heere*, etc. (Wien und Leipzig, 1912) p. 13.

[47a] *Reglementeringen i Stockholm*, pp. 130–2.

the III, which is stationed in and about Berlin. The same relation holds as to recruits. In the years 1903-5, 41.3 of the Berlin recruits were venereally infected; 30 per cent. of the recruits from Hamburg and Altona,— yet these are the most effectively regulated towns in the German Empire. I do not mean to imply that the amount of infection is to be accounted for by the existence of regulation, but rather that it is clear that regulation does not lessen it. The really important factor is the size of the town. For throughout the period just mentioned (1903-5) the extent of infection among recruits dwindled with the size of the places from which they were drawn; regulation had nothing whatever to do with it. Berlin, as I have said, showed an infection of 41.3 per cent.; towns of more than 100,000 inhabitants 15.8 per cent.; towns between 50,000 and 100,000, 10.2 per cent.; those between 25,000 and 50,000, 8 per cent.; smaller towns and the country districts, 4.4 per cent. The size of the garrison has a similar effect. A small garrison (less than 400) shows venereal infection of 11.9 per cent. in 1905-6; a garrison between 1,000 and 3,000, 16.9 per cent.; a garrison between 5,000 and 10,-000, 19.8 per cent.; garrisons of over 10,000, 26.6 per cent. Regulation can have had no influence whatever on these figures; and this is all the more certain in view of the fact, that though regulation has tended to disintegrate in the last two decades, the percentage of infection, everywhere a matter of the size of the place or the garrison, has in this period, everywhere in absolute amount markedly decreased: in the smallest garrisons, from 33.2 per cent. in 1885 to 11.9 per cent. in 1905; in the largest,

Abolition and Disease

from 36.8 per cent. in the former year to 26.6 in the latter.[48]

Evidence more direct, though of limited range in point of time, is contributed by various towns that have adopted the abolition policy. Of these, Christiania is by far the most satisfactory. It has the longest record and the most satisfactory statistics; for venereal diseases have been notifiable since 1876, though the form of notification has undergone some modification. If diagnostic means have not been too defective in the past, a stretch of something like 20 years is represented by the abolition experience of the Norwegian capital, which has increased in population during the period in question from something below 80,000 to almost a quarter of a million.

The official table (see p. 380) gives the local situation from 1876 to 1911, inclusive.[49]

In the period covered by these statistics, the population of Christiania has trebled; we might, therefore, expect a marked rise in the presence of venereal disease. As a matter of fact, the incidence of syphilis was never again so high as in the first year; with certain fluctuations,

[48] The main authority consulted in the above discussion is : Otto von Schjerning, *Sanitätsstatistische Betrachtungen über Volk und Heer* (Berlin, 1910) pp. 59–67. A general discussion of conditions in European Armies is given by Col. Melville, *loc. cit.*, pp. 58–72. Urbach's book, above referred to, gives the most recent and complete account of the Austrian-Hungarian army and navy with frequent references to other nations. None of these authorities are particularly interested in the question of regulation versus abolition, so that the facts are stated by them without reference to their bearing on this controversy. M. Augagneur (*loc. cit.*) discusses army statistics with close reference to our topic.

[49] Dr. Yngvar Ustvedt, Sundhetsinspector, *Beretning om de veneriske sygdomme i Kristiania*, 1911 (1912) pp. 6, 7.

Year	Gonorrhea			Soft Chancre			Acquired Syphilis			Congenital Syphilis			Total	Population	Reported total as percentage of population	Reported cases of syphilis as percentage of population
	Men	Women	Both	Men	Women	Both	Men	Women	Both	Men	Women	Both				
1876			593			419							1012	79 022	1.28	0.53
1877			909			134			297			33	1373	106 781	1.28	0.31
1878			1040			166			311			31	1548	112 977	1.37	0.30
1879	951	176	1127	200	114	314	211	154	365	21	15	36	1842	116 801	1.53	0.34
1880	1208	219	1427	265	99	364	263	156	424	21	22	43	2258	119 407	1.89	0.39
1881	1277	199	1468	353	78	431	302	151	453	33	39	72	2424	122 036	1.99	0.43
1882	1140	146	1286	530	127	707	308	188	496	21	23	44	2638	122 424	2.07	0.44
1883	1100	186	1286	257	49	306	175	111	286	21	15	36	1924	124 155	1.55	0.26
1884	1118	142	1260	203	57	265	172	126	298	17	22	39	1862	128 300	1.45	0.27
1885	997	186	1183	175	32	207	148	123	271	33	29	62	1723	130 790	1.32	0.25
1886	1095	99	1194	292	65	357	163	101	264	25	14	39	1854	134 036	1.39	0.23
1887	829	106	935	308	87	443	175	97	272	21	23	44	1694	135 615	1.18	0.23
1888	509	66	575	71	16	87	103	109	212	18	14	32	906	138 319	0.66	0.18
1889	585	85	670	73	8	81	187	107	294	10	22	32	1077	143 347	0.75	0.23
1890	679	60	739	213	25	238	330	178	508	16	13	29	1514	151 130	1.00	0.26
1891	759	42	801	180	15	195	303	170	473	10	10	20	1489	156 535	0.95	0.31
1892	935	90	1025	192	13	205	355	208	563	9	18	27	1820	161 151	1.13	0.37
1893	1069	97	1166	260	23	283	278	229	507	12	15	27	1983	167 588	1.18	0.32
1894	1283	121	1404	281	29	310	353	193	546	25	17	42	2302	174 717	1.32	0.34
1895	1482	126	1608	357	34	421	518	206	724	26	14	40	2793	182 856	1.52	0.42
1896	1471	149	1620	393	49	442	498	235	733	32	28	60	2865	192 554	1.48	0.41
1897	2031	173	2204	447	46	543	450	233	683	25	25	50	3480	203 337	1.69	0.36
1898	2125	207	2332	433	51	484	565	259	824	25	27	52	3692	221 255	1.67	0.40
1899	1966	191	2156	491	44	535	543	221	764	35	34	69	3525	226 423	1.56	0.37
1900	1871	170	2041	507	48	550	457	195	652	28	26	54	3297	228 929	1.44	0.31
1901	1684	174	1858	292	32	324	432	208	640	23	17	40	2962	224 909	1.27	0.30
1902	1576	159	1735	418	87	455	368	196	564	20	28	48	2902	225 709	1.24	0.27
1903	1570	183	1753	401	89	440	481	188	614	24	20	44	2851	223 649	1.27	0.29
1904	1392	139	1531	347	20	367	355	154	509	26	34	60	2467	222 878	1.11	0.26
1905	1384	139	1523	278	16	294	340	128	468	21	26	50	2385	228 774	1.08	0.23
1906	1108	132	1240	169	14	188	302	129	431	19	16	35	1889	229 894	0.82	0.21
1907	903	112	1015	188	10	143	251	123	374	10	25	35	1567	231 687	0.68	0.18
1908	1055	107	1162	198	21	219	278	184	412	24	26	50	1843	235 674	0.78	0.20
1909	1149	101	1250	172	19	191	315	142	457	31	27	58	1956	239 511	0.82	0.22
1910	1261	98	1359	206	14	220	332	141	473	27	13	40	2092	244 086	0.86	0.21
1911	1373	94	1467	827	27	354	856	168	519	19	17	36	2876	247 488	0.96	0.22

it fell, despite the marked increase in population, from .53 per cent. in 1876 to .22 per cent. in 1911. The decline in all three diseases taken together, though not quite so striking, is sufficiently noteworthy in the face of general conditions that might account for a rise: 1.28 per cent. in 1876, .96 per cent. in 1911. Abolition took place in 1887. During some of the following years a rise is observable, explicable in several ways: (1) It was the purpose of the law to induce disease, hitherto hidden, to come out into the open. The breaking of the police association, the prominence given to the free dispensary, ought to have brought out cases that under the old order were handled secretly and thus escaped reporting; a rise in the number recorded might mean not more fresh cases, but merely more cases under proper treatment. (2) Coincidently with the introduction of the new law, these diseases had to be reported daily, instead of monthly, and greater accuracy in this respect might account for a rise indicating not more disease, but more complete statistics.

The experience of Copenhagen is unfortunately too brief to be of commanding importance; a proper system of notification was introduced for the first time in July 1912. Available statistics, obviously very incomplete, make the following showing:[50]

Years	Gonorrhœa	Soft Chancre	Acquired Syphilis	Syphilis	Congenital Syphilis	Total
1907	5,684	728	1,869	39	63	8,383
1908	6,320	1,164	2,349	63	61	9,957
1909	6,029	1,034	2,108	57	52	9,280
1910	6,076	848	2,330	39	85	9,378
1911	6,500	692	2,543	66	87	9,888

[50] They are taken from the report mentioned in the next note.

Prostitution in Europe

During five years there has been on the face of the figures a rise of 18 per cent. in the total number of cases reported. Does this indicate wider contamination as a result of abolition? Let us consider. During the same period the population increased from 426,540 to 462,161, i. e. 8 per cent.), so that to some extent at least the apparent increase is relative, not absolute. Moreover, the entire tendency, here as in Christiania, has been to lay hold of as many infected persons as possible; in other words, unless more cases were brought to light for some years to come, the dispensary policy would be a failure. Indeed, in the early years, the dispensary physicians were paid per patient, in order to enlist their active coöperation in ferreting out foci of infection.

Graphic representation shows that abolition has done no harm, even though the most unfavorable interpretation be placed upon the figures. The rapid decline immediately prior to repeal would appear to indicate that abolition took place when Copenhagen was, in respect to venereal disease, in the trough of the wave. Free dispensaries brought some hidden cases to light; hence, a brief rise,— a reaction from which is already in progress, partly explicable, perhaps, by the extinction of some active foci through treatment.

The curves (pp. 383, 384, 385) show the course of venereal diseases in Copenhagen on the basis of the Reports of the Health Department.[51]

In relation to population, the following table shows the incidence of venereal disease per 10,000 inhabitants

[51] *Aarsberetning angaaende Sundhedstilstandet i København* for 1910. (Copenhagen, 1911) p. 36. The figures for 1911 above given were contributed by Stadslæge Dr. E. M. Hoff.

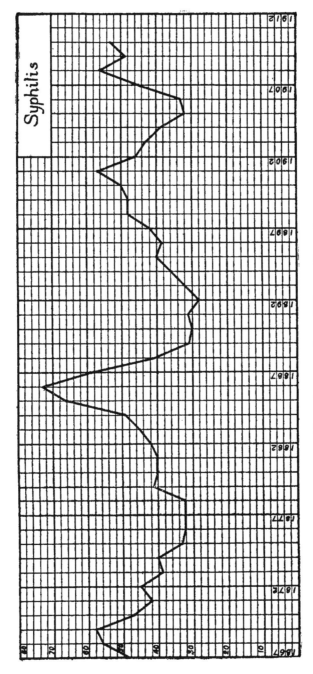

FIGURE V.—Course of syphilis at Copenhagen.

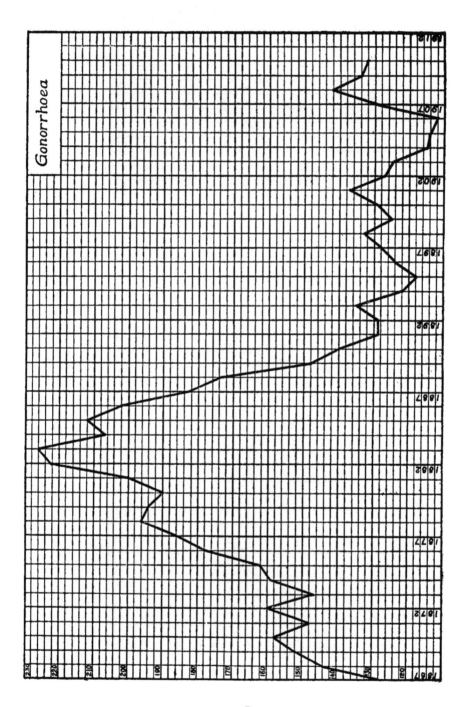

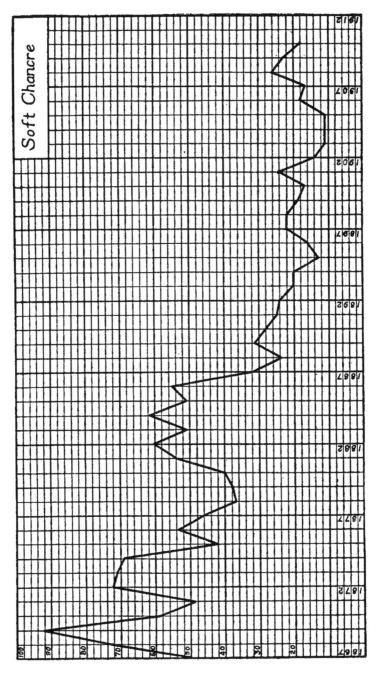

FIGURE VII.— Course of soft chancre at Copenhagen.

Prostitution in Europe

since 1867. Needless to repeat, only the statistics of more recent years are of any genuine consequence:[52]

Year	Gonorrhœa	Soft chancre	Syphilis	Year	Gonorrhœa	Soft chancre	Syphilis	Year	Gonorrhœa	Soft chancre	Syphilis
1867..	28	50	49	1882..	222	60	42	1897..	128	22	42
1868..	144	73	56	1883..	226	51	45	1898..	133	22	48
1869..	152	92	58	1884..	207	61	49	1899..	125	19	48
1870..	158	59	47	1885..	212	51	66	1900..	129	17	50
1871..	148	49	42	1886..	202	55	73	1901..	137	24	57
1872..	160	72	45	1887..	183	32	59	1902..	127	14	46
1873..	147	71	39	1888..	174	24	41	1903..	125	11	43
1874..	159	69	40	1889..	148	31	31	1904..	115	11	39
1875..	162	42	33	1890..	140	28	30	1905..	114	11	32
1876..	178	53	32	1891..	129	25	31	1906..	112	18	33
1877..	186	46	32	1892..	129	24	28	1907..	129	17	45
1878..	196	37	32	1893..	135	20	32	1908..	142	26	56
1879..	194	38	41	1894..	122	20	36	1909..	134	23	49
1880..	190	40	40	1895..	118	13	40	1910..	132	18	53
1881..	200	54	40	1896..	124	16	39	1911..	140	15	58

Dr. Rudolf Krefting, of Christiania, has plotted out two highly interesting curves by way of depicting and comparing the course of events in Copenhagen and Christiania in respect to syphilis.[53] (See Fig. VIII, p. 387.)

Despite considerable variations, the dotted line shows, as we have already observed, that there was relatively to population less syphilis in Christiania in 1910 than in 1890; that, though the amount of disease treated in abolition Christiania was in the years immediately succeeding repeal greater than the amount reported in Copenhagen, conditions rapidly improved, so that the situation is now well in hand. The maximum was reached almost twenty years ago (1895). The Copenhagen curve

[52] *Ibid.*, p. 37.
[53] From "Om luesoverfrelse," (*Tidsskrift for den Norske laege-forening.* Nr. 5 og 6, 1912).

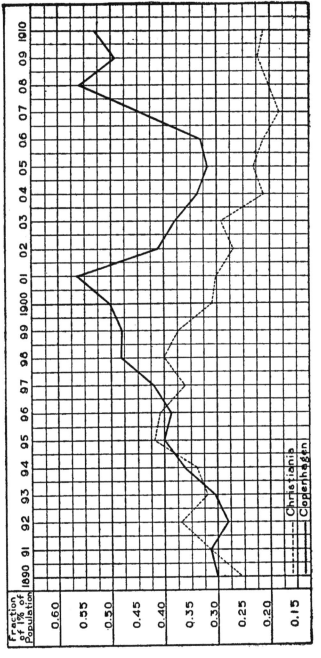

FIGURE VIII.—Copenhagen and Christiania compared in respect to syphilis.

Prostitution in Europe

continues to rise until 1901, when it falls unaccountably, rises on repeal of regulation and shows a declining tendency as the new system gets to working more smoothly. In any event, Copenhagen with control and with an imperfect system of notification actually shows almost uninterruptedly more syphilis than Christiania without control and with a much more thorough system of notification.[54] That abolition alone is to be credited with the decline or with the difference between the two cities cannot be maintained; for similar declines — less credible, perhaps, inasmuch as the data are less reliable — are observable under regulation also. A very marked instance I have just noted, viz., the decline in reported cases of syphilis at Copenhagen between 1901 and 1905, — while regulation was still in vogue. That abolition with the dispensary system treats more disease than regulation is beyond all question; that it treats enough more to affect sensibly the disease curves one may believe, but may not yet hold to be scientifically demonstrated. But this is not essential, for unless the evidence is clearly in its favor, regulation falls to the ground. As to this, there is no question whatsoever. The medical profession, the health authorities, the police of both Christiania and Copenhagen are wellnigh unanimous in their conviction on the basis of experience and statistics that abolition has done no harm; and if abolition has done no harm, assuredly regulation can have done no good.[55]

[54] The above comparison is partly based on Dr. Krefting's dissertation above cited, and on a manuscript essay in French, unpublished as yet at the time of my visit to Christiania, which Dr. Krefting courteously placed at my disposal.
[55] I have throughout this volume refrained from attaching much

388

Abolition and Disease

A single bit of evidence may also be gleaned from the experience of Zurich. The records of the Policlinic (out-patient department or dispensary) and the cantonal hospital are available since 1894. Bordells were forbidden in 1897. The population of the city was at that time 140,000; by 1911, it had risen to 195,600. Yet the total number of cases treated at the dispensary fell from 483 in the former year to 392 in the latter. The number of venereal patients admitted to the cantonal hospital, 114 in 1897, has now risen to 251, but the ratio

importance to mere opinions as to the results of experience with either of the policies in question. It is indeed amazing to observe what definite convictions are based on brief or one-sided experience or on hearsay evidence, and this is true of abolitionists and regulationists alike. Though opinion is thus of little weight, a change of opinion forced by the failure of prophesied ill results to materialize may be not without significance; and of such change there is abundant evidence in both Christiania and Copenhagen. In the former, as late as 1898, a discussion in the Norwegian Medical Society (reported in *Prostitution i Kristiania*, 1899) showed the existence of regulationists in the medical profession. Their views were vigorously combated by City Physician Bentzen and others who proved that regulated Norwegian towns were liable to precisely the same fluctuations that followed abolition at Christiania (pp. 36–38). By the time of my visit (fourteen years later) the voice of the regulationists — so I was everywhere assured — had practically become silent — a change of attitude hardly open to misconstruction. In Copenhagen the issue is more recent and more controversial; but the trend of opinion appears to be in the same direction. I was assured that it would be practically impossible to find a physician who desired a return to the old system; Professor Ehlers, a distinguished specialist, declared, "There is absolutely no professional sentiment any longer in favor of regulation; the situation is probably better and most certainly no worse"; another physician stated: "Nothing has been lost, even if it is not yet easy to prove what has been gained"; Dr. Hoff, the Health Officer, assured me that regulation sentiment had entirely died out among the medical profession. But the best proof is after all the steady encroachment of abolition: Copenhagen would not have imitated Christiania had abolition aggravated conditions there; now Stockholm is about to follow suit: does not this indicate a growing and spreading disbelief in the efficacy of regulation and a growing confidence in the advantages of abolition?

to population has decreased. These facts are indicated on Figures IX and X.

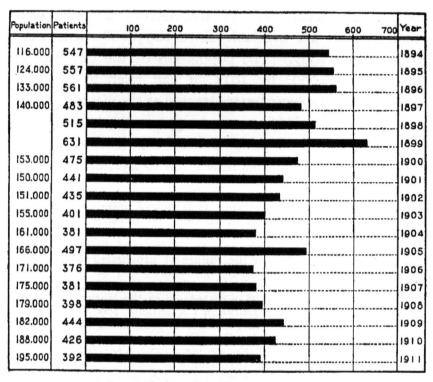

Population	Patients	100	200	300	400	500	600	700	Year
116.000	547								1894
124.000	557								1895
133.000	561								1896
140.000	483								1897
	515								1898
	631								1899
153.000	475								1900
150.000	441								1901
151.000	435								1902
155.000	401								1903
161.000	381								1904
166.000	497								1905
171.000	376								1906
175.000	381								1907
179.000	398								1908
182.000	444								1909
188.000	426								1910
195.000	392								1911

FIGURE IX.—Venereal diseases, Zürich Policlinic.

Let us now bring together the results of the two chapters in which we have discussed this problem. In the first place, let me remind the reader of the absurdity of supposing that regulation means that the authorities are alive to the problem of venereal disease and that abolition means that they close their eyes to it. Regulation means simply that the police deal with a very small portion of venereal disease; on the Continent, at least, abolition means that the health authorities are energetically attempting to reach more and more of it.

Abolition and Disease

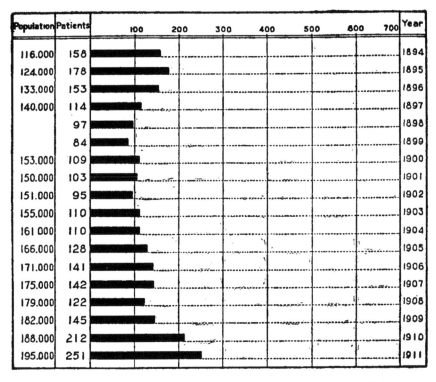

Population	Patients	100	200	300	400	500	600	700	Year
116.000	158								1894
124.000	178								1895
133.000	153								1896
140.000	114								1897
	97								1898
	84								1899
153.000	109								1900
150.000	103								1901
151.000	95								1902
155.000	110								1903
161 000	110								1904
166.000	128								1905
171.000	141								1906
175.000	142								1907
179.000	122								1908
182.000	145								1909
188.000	212								1910
195.000	251								1911

FIGURE X.— Venereal diseases, Canton hospital, Zurich.

In the second place, we must emphasize the fact that venereal disease is inevitably attendant upon sexual promiscuity. Venereal disease is an evil in itself and deserves to be combated with all the resources and facilities known to science and to sanitation; but so long as prostitution exists, venereal disease will remain serious and widespread; we have discovered absolutely no reason — statistical or other — to believe that regulation at all reduces its ravages; there is, however, good reason to believe that the bordell and the medical examination contribute to its aggravation by increasing miscellaneous commerce and by decreasing resistance.

391

On the other hand, there is no ground — statistical or other — for believing that abolition increases disease; there is excellent reason for believing that abolition, plus a deliberately planned and organized dispensary system, has already proved a mitigating factor and is capable of much greater usefulness than has yet been anywhere realized.

This summary still leaves on our hands the problem of understanding the fluctuations of venereal infection. But in this respect, venereal disease is one with other infections and contagions. All alike are subject to unaccountable ups and downs. We know as yet practically nothing of the factors which determine the rise and fall of infectious disease curves, or the outbreak and the subsidence of epidemics. Apart from any prophylactic measures yet known to science, such scourges as syphilis and gonorrhœa wax and wane. Throughout the world, there is some evidence to suggest that aside from temporary disturbances due to war,[56] they have been for a decade or two in the declining stage; whether this is temporary or permanent we have absolutely no means of telling; experience suggests the former, but time alone will tell.

I would not, however, convey the notion that all fluctuations are mysterious and spontaneous and that therefore nothing can be accomplished by intelligent action. The army curves are an argument against any such fatalistic view. With increased keenness of military competition, every factor conducive to efficiency has to be reckoned

[56] E. g., the Boer War, which undoubtedly accounts for the rise in the English army curve 1900–1903. See Figure II, p. 370.

with; the outcome of war would, it is felt, depend not only on battleship tonnage and the paper strength of the army, but on the health of the crew and of the enlisted men; their physical vigor is at least as important as smokeless powder and a powerful rifle. Almost simultaneously, therefore, the war authorities of Europe have undertaken to compete with the tavern and the wanton. Games are cultivated, places of recreation provided, the spirit of emulation has been aroused; and instruction is given,— the enlisted man is taught that continence is possible and wholesome; he is urged, if he has indulged himself, to employ prophylactic measures; [57] in the highly probable event of their failure, he is to have prompt recourse to the surgeon. A successful effort to bring about more sparing use of alcohol has perhaps done more than anything else to make these devices and suggestions fruitful.

The indisputable improvement that intelligent endeavor has thus effected in all European armies is a strong argument in behalf of applying a similar policy to the general population. I have said that venereal disease is an evil in itself,— a serious drain on the efficiency of the body politic. That nation which first succeeds in reducing it will have scored heavily on its competitors. The German Society for combating venereal disease [58]

[57] In Germany, slot-machines were at one time set up in barracks and on board warships from which for a small coin protective remedies could be procured, but popular objection has forced their removal on the ground that their presence suggested debauch and deceived soldiers and sailors. But the remedies are still easily procurable; of their value, there is grave doubt. See Melville, *loc. cit.*, pp. 91-95; von Schjerning, *loc. cit.*, pp. 66, 67.

[58] The Society was founded by Dr. Blaschko, and publishes the valuable journal which I have freely cited.

Prostitution in Europe

is the most vigorous organ in Europe engaged in the cultivation and dissemination of this point of view. Waiving consideration of other aspects of the problem of prostitution, for the time being, it urges that the same methods be employed in the contest with venereal disease that are invoked against other scourges: medical research for the means of prevention, isolation and cure; enlightenment of all those afflicted or liable to affliction in order that the willing intelligence of the patient may coöperate with the rational intent of the community. Thus tuberculosis, measles, small-pox, cholera and other pests have been attacked with some measure of success. Venereal disease offers indeed peculiar difficulties, but they are difficulties that only strengthen the argument for intelligence and resource broadly utilized. If this be true, the situation described does not call for regulation, tending, as it does, to concentrate its fire upon a few foci, and to cover up other sources of infection so that they fester in darkness, but rather for the more liberal and enlightened policy, which, if not identical with abolition, follows naturally in its wake.

CHAPTER XI

THE OUTCOME OF EUROPEAN EXPERIENCE

IF the preceding pages may be assumed to have exhibited the present condition of prostitution in Europe, the reader need not be long detained for the purpose of summarizing the main inferences to be drawn from them. It must be clear that prostitution is far more widespread than superficial appearances indicate; that its roots strike deep, socially and individually; that police regulation has proved unnecessary, in so far as the keeping of order is concerned, and positively harmful in its bearing on the problem of venereal disease. Further elaboration of these points would involve needless iteration. But we may well ask whether European experience suggests any broader reflections with which this study may appropriately be brought to a close.

Whatever one may hold as to ultimate dealings with the subject, it is clear that prostitution is at any rate a modifiable phenomenon. For example, no matter what conditions exist at this very moment, they are capable of aggravation. If bordells are established and allowed a free hand in procuring inmates and business, if a community ceases to be concerned as to the condition of the streets, as to the conduct of the liquor and amusement traffic; there is no doubt that under these circumstances the number of prostitutes and the volume of business

transacted by them would at once increase, and in consequence, also the amount of waste and disease traceable
thereto.

The converse of the proposition is equally true. If
prostitution and its evils can by social arrangements be
increased, they can also by social arrangements be lessened. If unhampered exploitation and prominence make
matters worse, then interference with exploitation and
prominence makes matters better. I am not suggest-
ing that such interference has unlimited possibilities.
Making every allowance, however, I believe that the student of prostitution in Europe is warranted in declaring
that, with the suppression of bordells and of the white
slave traffic, and the maintenance of improved external
order, a substantial amount of good has been accomplished, even if new problems have simultaneously developed in consequence of the growth of cities and the ac-
cumulation of wealth; further, it may safely be maintained that these efforts have not yet reached their limit.

What are we fairly justified in expecting from directly repressive action on the part of the community?
Prostitution is, as I endeavored to show in the chapters
on demand and supply, a phenomenon arising out of the
complicated interaction of personal factors and social
conditions. Looked at from this point of view, the attempt to stamp it out completely by summary, even though
persistent, action, cannot be hopefully regarded. The instrument which a municipality must use to that end is the
police. Now the police is an instrument which, serving,
as it does, many useful purposes, must be preserved as
nearly intact as may be. We have seen that contact with

The Outcome of European Experience

prostitution threatens its integrity and efficiency. On the police, therefore, no more can be laid than it is capable of bearing. Just what this load is must be separately determined for every community and, in large cities, for different parts of the same community. Where the general level of administration and discipline is high, more can be safely demanded than in communities in which the level is lower; where public sentiment is active and definite, the burden may be further increased; where local organizations observe, complain and follow-up, the danger of a police breakdown is still further diminished.

It is evident, however, that, even amidst favorable general conditions, the very nature of the instrument employed involves, under the complicated conditions of modern life, limitations against which one soon runs. Police repression can be directed mainly against professional prostitution and its exploiters. Unquestionably it has a valuable function to discharge in removing stimulation and reducing suggestion, as also in minimizing opportunities for demoralization. But in so far as the prostitute herself is personally concerned, repression becomes operative only after the woman has been wrecked. It penalizes an accomplished fact. Powerless to crush this fact out of existence, powerless for the most part to transform the fact, sheer repression might still hope to deter the beginner by its forbidding prospect; but unfortunately, the beginner is less affected by the penalties awaiting her, because she never believes, at the start, that she is destined to end in the mire. If, therefore, prostitutes are manufactured by unschooled human nature and imperfect social institutions, they cannot in the mass

Prostitution in Europe

be stamped out by brute force; they must be prevented rather than suppressed,— prevented, too, on both sides, in the sense that the sources of supply must be closed and the demand diverted into other channels.

Moreover, repression, in order to realize its full possibilities, requires an abundance of institutional facilities such as now nowhere exist.   I have repeatedly adverted to the utter futility of the fines and short term sentences hitherto generally imposed.   Repression, successful up to the limits of its inherent possibilities, must involve the endeavor to wean the professional prostitute from one way of living and to equip her for another.   Reformatories, labor-colonies, hospitals and similar institutions have, therefore, to be made adequate to the load which an aggressive policy places upon them.   At this moment no city sustains even what it now requires.

It is a further limitation of the repressive policy, as ordinarily conceived, that it operates almost altogether upon the woman.   We are reminded of the dual nature of prostitution.   It involves two partners.   Imagine every brothel closed, every street-walker incarcerated.   To the extent that stimulation and suggestion have by these measures been reduced, demand has suffered a check. But a strong demand still remains, unaffected by repressive measures directed merely against dissolute women.   Certain stimuli have been removed; otherwise appetite is left where it was.   Its gratification is impeded, — made more difficult and more expensive.   But these are not insuperable obstacles in the presence of that volume of supply which, if inoffensive, is hardly reached by repressive police measures.   Indeed, part of what was offensive is changed in form rather than entirely driven from the market.

Repression encounters difficulty at still another point. Prostitution is all too frequently a parasitic phenomenon that attaches itself to other phenomena, sometimes innocuous, sometimes necessary, sometimes part and parcel of national life or social tradition. Street-walking and the bordell are not thus intertwined with other activities; they represent prostitution in its barest, simplest, most undisguised form, and as such may be, with comparative ease, successfully attacked by police methods. But when prostitution insinuates itself into the ordinary life of the community, subtly, inoffensively, imperceptibly taking advantage of the forms in which business is transacted, social life carried on, or recreation enjoyed,— then the difficulties in the way of effective action are more serious. The cruder forms of prostitution are easily reached; — easily, I say, because, even though the task has been nowhere achieved, there is, in the nature of the case, no reason why a well-governed community should fail to achieve it; but the subtler forms present problems so different in kind that in dealing with them agencies and influences of a totally different character must be employed.

I do not mean that repression will have accomplished little. On the contrary, important good is achieved at the moment and still more in the long run. But prostitution as a formidable problem will still remain. Repression is, on the whole, what physicians call symptomatic treatment; it may achieve something more than alleviate the ravages, but it does not cure the disease.

Prostitution in Europe

It does not necessarily decrease the thing in the same ratio in which it alters appearances.

What would conceivably happen in a city like London if the police, spurred and controlled by an active popular impulse, accomplished all that could be humanly expected? Street-walking of a provocative character would disappear; the advertised brothel would cease to exist; the public house (saloon) would strictly enforce the law against the harboring of prostitutes; the obvious forms of spurious employment would be dispersed,— rendered more circumspect and much less readily accessible; prostitutes would disappear from the lobby and promenade of the variety theaters, etc. The pimp, the exploiter, the third-party interest would be severely checked and, with that, the tropical growth due to them. We may also assume that a vigorous and adequate hygienic policy would lessen the volume of disease, and effect quicker and completer cures. In a word, prostitution as an offensive and aggressive activity would be more or less done for; and the loss through disease would be minimized.

What would be gained? The inducement to enter the life or to persist in it would be lessened; the total volume of business and the volume transacted by any one woman would be decreased; the financial waste would be less; the amount of disease disseminated would be less; the demoralization of the woman would often be less complete, less overwhelming, less irretrievable: surely, very important gains.

Well drawn, well codified, well executed laws could accomplish this. Any civilized society utilizing the resources and instrumentalities that every such society has

within its reach, can, if really so minded, ultimately reduce prostitution and its ravages so far by direct action.

It is well worth doing; it is, humanly speaking, a possible undertaking, even though, I repeat, nowhere as yet
by any means accomplished. Let us not, however, deceive
ourselves into thinking that such a direct frontal attack
absolves us from effort in other and different directions.
Further achievement depends upon alterations in the constitution of society and its component parts. In so far
as prostitution is the outcome of ignorance, laws and
police are powerless; only knowledge will aid. In so far
as prostitution is the outcome of mental or moral defect, laws and police are powerless; only the intelligent guardianship of the state will avail. In so far
as prostitution is the outcome of natural impulses denied
a legitimate expression, only a rationalized social life
will really forestall it. In so far as prostitution is
due to alcohol, to illegitimacy, to broken homes, to bad
homes, to low wages, to wretched industrial conditions —
to any or all of the particular phenomena respecting
which the modern conscience is becoming sensitive,—
only a transformation wrought by education, religion,
science, sanitation, enlightened and far-reaching statesmanship can effect a cure. Our attitude towards prostitution, in so far as these factors are concerned, cannot embody itself in a special remedial or repressive policy, for in this sense it must be dealt with as part of
the larger social problems with which it is inextricably
entangled. Civilization has stripped for a life-and-death
wrestle with tuberculosis, alcohol and other plagues. It
is on the verge of a similar struggle with the crasser

forms of commercialized vice. Sooner or later, it
fling down the gauntlet to the whole horrible thing.
will be the real contest,— a contest that will tax the
courage, the self-denial, the faith, the resources of humanity to their uttermost.

Appendices

APPENDIX I

PARIS REGULATIONS [1]

Duties and Prohibitions Imposed on Public Prostitutes.

Public prostitutes are required to report at the Health Dispensary for medical examination at least once a fortnight at dates that will be fixed for each case.

They are ordered to show their sanitary cards whenever requested to do so by police officers or agents.

They may not walk about in public streets before the street lanterns have been lighted, nor, in any season of the year, before seven o'clock in the evening; nor may they remain in the streets after midnight.

There must be nothing about their deportment or their attire that attracts attention in an offensive manner.

They are expressly forbidden to speak to minors or to men accompanied by women or children, or to entice anyone in a loud voice or with persistence.

They are forbidden to loiter in the streets, to gather in groups, to walk about in groups, to pass the same points too frequently, as they go up and down, and to have their "pimps" walk with them or behind them.

They are not permitted to be in the vicinity of churches (Catholic or Protestant), schools and lycées, covered arcades, boulevards, the Champs-Élysées, the railway stations and their approaches, and the public parks.

They are not permitted to live in houses in which there are boarding-schools or day-schools.

[1] Translation of the most recent Règlement dated October, 1878.

They are likewise not permitted to share their lodgings with a lover or with another prostitute.

They must never solicit from their windows.

Any woman violating the above instructions, or resisting officers of public authority, or giving wrong information as to her address or name, incurs the risk of certain penalties, the severity of which is in accordance with the seriousness of the offence.

IMPORTANT NOTICE.— The card issued to prostitutes at the time of their enrolment is not to be regarded as an authorization, and must in no way be taken as an encouragement to vice, or as an obstacle to decent employment.

The card enables the administration to determine whether the public prostitutes — in their own interest as well as in the interest of the public health — are reporting regularly for the medical examinations which are provided for them as long as they continue practising prostitution.

A woman may at any time be stricken from the list and have her card recalled, if it be shown that she no longer draws her means of subsistence from prostitution.

Furthermore, the necessary confirmation of the above fact will be sought with reserve and discretion.

INSTRUCTIONS GOVERNING THE VARIOUS OPERATIONS OF THE MORALS SERVICE.

CLANDESTINE PROSTITUTION

§ 1. *Searches and scrutinies carried on in private houses in furnished-room houses, and in cafés and saloons.*

The inspectors of the active morals service, when informed that a certain private house or furnished-room house is being secretly used as a resort for prostitution, will immediately report such information to their Officier de paix, who will draw up a statement for the Chief of Municipal Police.

The Chief of Municipal Police will cause exact and precise data to be gathered, which will be reported to the Préfet de Police by the Chief of the 1st Division, who, if that be desirable, will advise the Préfet to issue a search-warrant.

This warrant, issued in accordance with article 10 of the Law of July 22, 1791, and having effect at any hour of the day or night, in cases of public notoriety, shall then be transmitted to the Chief of Municipal Police, together with a note giving the necessary directions to assist in carrying it out.

The inspectors ordered to the search will report to the Commissaire of police of the quarter, to advise him of their mission, so that he may be in readiness to furnish aid when aid shall be required.

The authorization to live in furnished rooms, granted to prostitutes who, by reason of their age or their infirmities, cannot secure places in brothels, and cannot afford to live in quarters of their own, has no other purpose than to enable them to find a home. Such authorization does not exempt them from the consequences of the offence of practising prostitution in the furnished rooms inhabited by them.

It would be proper, therefore, to arrest women, if, in the course of search made in execution of such a warrant, they should be found in the company of men enticed by them, which fact would furthermore constitute a charge against the keeper of the house, being an infraction on his part of article 5 of the Ordinance of November 6, 1778. But such arrests should not be made if the women are found with men with whom they regularly share those lodgings, being the concubines of such men, a fact which it

Prostitution in Europe

would be easy to establish by referring to the list on the police register.

As for cafés, saloons, or other places where liquor is sold, and in which clandestine prostitution is encouraged, the Commissaires of police may enter such places, without a warrant, up to the closing hour, or even later, if such establishment should remain open in violation of the police ordinances.

They may go through public meeting places, if necessary, in order to ascertain infractions of article 14 of the Ordinance of November 8, 1780.

Inspectors who, in the course of their watches, may observe conditions constituting violations of the above nature, will inform the Commissaire of police of the quarter.[1]

§ 2. *Girls not under supervision.*

Inspectors must proceed with the greatest caution in the cases of girls not under supervision, whom they may meet in the public streets, and must not arrest them except after a surveillance resulting in the observation of a number of distinct acts of soliciting.

In a public place commonly known to be a resort for prostitution, it is proper to arrest a girl not under supervision, when there is evidence of the actual act, or an admission on the part of the girl or of the man found with her, that the girl has solicited him to the act of debauchery.

[1] The Cour de Cassation has rendered several decisions (June 30, 1838; July 14, 1838; March 30, 1839) to the effect that the procès-verbaux and reports of the inspectors of police are not in themselves sufficient, in the absence of additional proof, to establish the fact that the infractions have occurred. The same is true of a procès-verbal drawn up by a Commissaire of police, from the report of an inspector of police, unless the former has verified the facts himself.

But these legal decisions do not deprive police officers of the right to ascertain infractions; however, their reports must be confirmed either by the admission of the delinquents that the facts are as stated, or by such methods as the tribunal may consider it proper to order.

408

Appendices

Whatever may be the circumstances under which they have been arrested, girls not under supervision must, in accordance with the procedure outlined in the circular of March 24, 1837, be transferred as promptly as possible to the Bureau of the Commissaire of police of the quarter in which the arrest has taken place, and they must there be interrogated without delay.

Inspectors will always adopt an attitude towards such women, that will be in accordance with the dignity of the administration, except when legally confirming insults or assaults made on them by such women. They will absolutely refrain from in any way encouraging the women to solicit them.

When handing over a girl not under supervision, to the discretion of a Commissaire of police, inspectors will place in the hands of such official, unless he is in receipt of a complete declaration from them, a detailed report of the acts of which the girl is accused.

After having handed over a girl not under supervision, to the discretion of a Commissaire of police, or after having aided a Commissaire of police, while executing a warrant, in a public place, in making the arrest of a girl not under supervision, inspectors will at once ascertain whether such girl is really domiciled at the address given by her, and whether she is known by the persons whose servant or employee she states she has been.

They will carefully gather information as to her behavior and means of subsistence, and will report all facts thus obtained, in a special report to the Chief of Municipal Police, who will transmit the report to the Chief of the 1st Division.

Inspectors should never lose sight of the fact that the object of searches and scrutinies executed in pursuance of a warrant is to get at women or girls who are engaged in public prostitution, and not at those whose sole offence is an act of private debauchery, which, reprehensible though it may be, should not expose the woman committing such acts to the consequences that should be borne only by real prostitutes.

For instance, the mere fact that a woman is found in a furnished-room house, or in a public place, in the very act of debauchery, is not sufficient evidence to show that the woman is guilty of prostitution, if she has regular relations of this nature with the man found with her, and if no act of soliciting to paid debauchery is set forth. It is expressly recommended, that when women are found sleeping alone, even in places that have a bad reputation, no steps be taken to arrest them, unless the circumstances are such as to convince the Commissaire of police that such women have been engaged in an act of prostitution. The Commissaires of police will carefully, and without delay, investigate the circumstances causing the arrest of girls not under supervision; after having heard the arrested person, they will decide whether the arrest is to hold good. Should they consider it desirable to take immediate steps to ascertain certain facts, they may have a telegram sent for that purpose to the Chief of Municipal Police, by the Officier de paix of the arrondissement.

They will draw up a procès-verbal of the interrogation through which they have put the persons arrested. They are expressly forbidden to make use of printed blanks in conducting this interrogation.

II

TOLERATED PROSTITUTION.

§ 1. *Brothels.*

Inspectors must keep tolerated brothels under daily surveillance, in order that they may be certain that no infrac-

Appendices

tions of public order and decency take place there, and that the women keeping such houses comply rigorously with the special requirements made of them, as well as with the general regulations for public order, notably with those concerning the apparel and the number of girls permitted to go out, and the hours of leaving and returning.

As far as departures and returns are concerned, which take place by stealth after the closing hour, such acts do not constitute a punishable infraction except in so far as they may be the cause of noises of a nature to disturb the public peace.

Inspectors will hand in without delay, in the form of a special report, an account of any serious or extraordinary occurrence taking place in such houses, and will repeatedly warn the mistresses of such houses that the latter must immediately report any such event to the Commissaire of police of their quarter, unless they have an opportunity, within the proper hours, to notify the administrative Bureau of the Officier de paix assigned to the morals service.

Inspectors will strictly enforce the prohibition, issued to mistresses of houses, forbidding them to grant admission to students of the lycées, or of civil and military schools, when in uniform, or to any young men under eighteen years of age, and will report any infractions of this rule.

§ 2. *Enrolled Women.*

Inspectors will see to it that all the provisions of the decree of September 1, 1842 are carried out.

They will require individual prostitutes, not connected with brothels, when met with in inspections of furnished-room houses or other places, or in the course of the inspectors' street duty, to show their cards, in order that the inspectors may know whether the prostitutes are prompt in reporting for medical examination, and in order that those who have missed examinations, a list of whom is given out

411

twice a month by the administrative bureau, may be traced and called to account. When a girl makes a statement in explanation of her not having the card, which the inspector has reason to believe is untrue, he may accompany her to her home.

Inspectors who are ordered to bring an enrolled woman to the administrative office, and who do not find such woman at her home, will do no more than report that fact. They will leave no word as to the object of their call, in order that the woman wanted may not be tempted to conceal her whereabouts.

§ 3. *Disappearances of girls.*

The search for girls who have disappeared must be carried on with the greatest possible discretion.

In the cases of girls who have returned to their families, or who have taken up honest work, or who appear to be no longer deriving their means of livelihood from public prostitution, inspectors will merely report the present circumstances of the girls, in a special report.

Of the girls who have disappeared, only such are to be brought to the administrative Bureau, as have been found in brothels, or in the homes of other prostitutes, or in furnished-room houses or private houses, when none of the circumstances given above as exempting them from arrest under this head, is applicable to them.

III

TRANSFER OF ARRESTED WOMEN TO THE PRÉFECTURE.

Prostitutes arrested by inspectors in Paris or in the suburbs, who cannot immediately be taken to the Préfecture de Police, will be kept at the station-houses, from which they will be sent to the Dépôt.

Appendices

(On Sodomy, here omitted.)

v

ADMINISTRATIVE SERVICE.

Before any other action is taken, the Interrogating Commissaire, Head of the Morals Bureau, should examine all documents relating to the arrest of girls not under supervision, in order to determine in what cases there is good reason for postponing the physical examination.

The interrogation of girls not under supervision is conducted by the Interrogating Commissaire himself; he reads to the girl the declaration made by her, and has her sign the procès-verbal of the interrogation; if necessary, he interrogates the officers.

Whenever it may be necessary to enroll a girl not under supervision, who is of age and who refuses to submit to the sanitary and administrative requirements, or, whenever it may be necessary to enroll a girl who *is not of age,* the case will be decided by a commission consisting of the Préfet or his representative, the Chief of the 1st Division, and the Interrogating Commissaire, instead of, as heretofore, ending with a written statement of the facts. This commission will interrogate the woman arrested as well as the officers.

It is important to bear in mind that prostitutes, at the time they are enrolled, receive a printed notice informing them that on their application their names may be removed from the surveillance lists, when some verification has been made of the fact that they have ceased practising prostitution. This verification should be made with discretion and reserve.

Prostitution in Europe

In the matter of disciplinary punishments imposed on enrolled women, the procedure will continue to be as heretofore, that is, punishments will be assigned by the Préfet,
on the motion of the Interrogating Commissaire, approved
by the Head of the 1st Division. However, in any case
of appeal by an enrolled woman from the punishment imposed upon her, such appeal shall be referred immediately
to a commission consisting of the Préfet de Police, or his
representative, and two Commissaires of Police of the City
of Paris, chosen by rotation from the list of such officials.

Decisions of this commission will be made after hearing
the arrested person as well as the officers, if that be necessary.

When the commission is not presided over by the Préfet
in person, its decisions must be ratified by him.

To make certain the permanence of the service, the sub-
Chief of the 3rd section of the 2nd bureau will bear the
title of *supplementary* Interrogating Commissaire, but his
services will not be called on except when the titular interrogating commissaire is prevented from being present.

VI

MEDICAL SERVICE.

Although no cases have as yet arisen in which it has
been necessary to use force in making the physical examination, the medical service is recommended to refrain
from taking such steps in any case in which they may meet
with resistance.

Such an occurrence should at once be brought to the
attention of the Préfet.

APPENDIX II

BERLIN REGULATIONS [1]

In the Police District of Berlin, a person of female sex who has been assigned, because of her practising immorality as a trade, to the surveillance of the Health Police, is subject to the following restrictions:

1. She must submit to medical examination as to her condition of health, in accordance with directions given her.

2. She must appear promptly, at the time set for her, for medical examination, and furthermore, as soon as she observes any indication of illness in her genitals, or in her inguinal glands, she must report at once to the Chief of the Morals Police and state her trouble.

3. Medical examinations ordered by the morals police, to take place in her own home, must be permitted without resistance.

4. When found afflicted with a venereal or skin disease, or with any contagious disease, she is obliged to submit to being committed to such hospital as may be designated by the authorities and to comply with the requirements of the treatment until she is cured. Furthermore she must punctually discharge the duties imposed upon her by the morals police in any home treatment ordered by that body, or in any treatment supplementary to hospital care.

If found infested with vermin, she must submit to the treatment as officially outlined.

[1] Translation of the most recent regulations, dated Dec. 7, 1911.

Prostitution in Europe

In the hospital she must comply with the orders of physicians and officials, as well as with the rules of the house; in case an absence has been allowed, she must report promptly on the expiration of the term granted.

5. She is not permitted to lounge about, in an offensive manner, in the streets or squares of the city, to entice men to lechery by addressing them, or to appear in the company of a person known by her to be under the surveillance of the morals police, or known to her as a pimp.

She is not permitted to stand or sit in doorways or entrance-gates.

She must comply absolutely with the instructions of the criminal officers who display the proper badges, which instructions are given for the maintenance of public order and public decency. This does not touch upon the rights of uniformed officers of supervision.

6. Except for very urgent reasons, she must not enter the following streets or places:

Lustgarten, Tiergarten, including Königsplatz, Friedrichshain, Humboldthain, Victoriapark, Unter den Linden, Friedrichstrasse, Belle-Alliance-Platz, Wilhelmstrasse, Potsdamerstrasse, Bülowstrasse from Zietenstrasse to Yorckstrasse, Linkstrasse, Lützowstrasse, Potsdamerplatz, etc.

7. She is not permitted to loiter in the vicinity of churches, schools, higher institutions of learning, buildings of the Royal Government or other public buildings, especially military barracks. She must not visit theaters, circuses, or exhibitions, or the concert gardens connected with them, the Zoological Gardens, the Museums, the railway stations (unless it be to purchase a ticket for railway passage), or, finally, any places that may be named in later orders of the police authorities.

8. In public meeting places she must not attract undue attention to herself.

Appendices

9. She may not enter into any manner of relation with male or female persons under 21 years of age, and, particularly, must not engage such persons as servants.

10. She must guard carefully against permitting the fact of her living in a certain house from becoming the occasion of any offence or disturbance, either in the house itself or in the immediate vicinity. Failing to prevent such offence, and having once been warned without effect, she must leave the house within the time indicated by the morals police when issuing the order of removal to her.

11. At any hour of the day or night, she must grant immediate admission to the police officer who calls in order to inspect her dwelling, or procure such admission for him, and give as much information as she may possess concerning persons found in her rooms.

12. If she is found in any resort known to the police as a place where prostitutes congregate, and if complaints have been made concerning irregularities at that place, she may be ordered by the morals police to refrain from entering such place.

13. She must not appear at the windows of her own dwelling, or of any other dwelling, in any manner that may give offence.

14. When asked, she must truthfully give the address of her home. She must personally report every change of address, at the registry of the morals police, not later than the next prescribed medical examination. In written petitions to the morals police, her present address must always be given in full.

15. She must not have her abode in the vicinity of churches, schools, or higher institutions of learning, buildings of the Royal Government, or other public buildings, especially military barracks, nor must she have her abode

on the streets and squares to which access is denied her in Paragraph 6 of these regulations. As soon as her occupation of such dwelling as may be prohibited by this paragraph (15) is discovered, it is her duty to give up such dwelling, on the order of the morals police, within the period indicated by that authority.

16. She is not permitted to grant a lodging to her pimp in her own dwelling.

17. She must keep her control-book, and the identification card issued to her at dismissal, in intact condition, until they are handed over to the proper person; she must not leave either the identification card or the control-book in the keeping of other prostitutes or of any other persons not having any right to receive such documents.

18. When in the offices of the morals police, she must conduct herself quietly and decently, and comply absolutely with the instructions of the supervising staff and the physicians.

19. In accordance with § 361 sec. 6 and § 362 of the Penal Code for the German Empire, infractions of these rules are punished by imprisonment for not more than 6 weeks; the sentence may also provide that the condemned, after paying this penalty, is to be handed over to the State Police Department (Landespolizeibehörde), which body will have the discretion of committing the discharged prisoner to a workhouse, or a protectory, or house of correction, or other asylum, or of assigning her to labor of public utility, for a period not exceeding 2 years.

When proof is furnished of an honorable moral deportment and of the exercise of a respectable calling, as well as in cases of marriage, surveillance by the morals police will be discontinued on application.

All persons of female sex who are under the surveillance of the Berlin Morals Police, are subject to the above reg-

Appendices

ulations, even though they may actually reside in one of the following districts:

Treptow, Reinickendorf, Tegel, Weissensee, Pankow, Tempelhof, Britz, Friedenau, Schmargendorf.

Persons of female sex living in Charlottenburg, Schöneberg, Wilmersdorf, Rixdorf, Lichtenberg, Friedrichsberg, Stralau, or Boxhagen-Rummelsburg, but subject to the morals police, not of those localities, but of Berlin, are likewise required to observe these regulations. They must particularly report at the Berlin Morals Police Office, on the days and at the hours set for them, until such time as they may be assigned to surveillance by the morals police of their own community, and made subject to medical examinations in such community.

These regulations go into effect on February 1, 1912.

(A printed circular as to the nature of various venereal diseases, and the precautions to be observed, is also given to every inscribed woman.)

APPENDIX III

HAMBURG REGULATIONS. (*a*) [1]

PRECAUTIONS AGAINST INFECTION WITH VENEREAL DISEASE.

(Directions to inscribed women; omitted here.)

II

INFORMATION AS TO THE MANNER OF FILING CERTAIN COM-
PLAINTS AND AS TO HOUSES OF REFUGE.

Should a keeper of furnished rooms attempt to prevent
the departure of a controlled girl, or retain possession of her
effects, or make any claim for payments of whatever nature (such as repayment of money advanced, or for articles of clothing furnished by him), the girl, if not in a
position to file complaint at the office of the morals police,
should, on the occasion of her next medical examination,
apply to the officers of the morals police, so that an investigation may be made.

The officers are also ready to give the girls information
concerning Houses of Refuge where they may obtain shelter pending their return to a decent mode of life.

III

POLICE REGULATIONS FOR WOMEN UNDER STRINGENT SUPER-
VISION OF THE MORALS POLICE.

§ 1. After being assigned to stringent police supervision,
women so assigned will submit at once to examination by

[1] Translation of most recent regulations, dated September 1, 1909.

the head Police Physician or his representative, and, thereafter, to regular examination, twice a week, by the Medical Inspector appointed by the Police Department, at the place ordered by the Police Department, and at the time set by the Police Department. If, in the judgment of the Police Department, additional examinations are also necessary, the women will submit to them also, and will report promptly at the time and place indicated for that purpose.

§ 2. They must immediately report to the Police Department any symptoms of disease which they may have observed on their persons. Such immediate report may be omitted only when the regular examination of the medical inspector is to take place later in the day on which the symptom has been observed.

§ 3. At all examinations they must present themselves in clean clothing and in a condition of sobriety and bodily cleanliness.

§ 4. They must unhesitatingly comply with the instructions of the medical examiners.

§ 5. If the physician orders hospital treatment, they are obliged to submit to being transferred to such hospital as may be appointed by the authorities. There they must remain until the physician orders their discharge. During their detention at the hospital they must comply with the instructions of the physicians and officers of the institution, as well as the directions of the nursing staff, conduct themselves in an orderly and modest manner and observe the rules of order. It is forbidden to bring flowers, books, foodstuffs, beverages, or tobacco, to the hospital, without the permission of the physician, or to receive or utilize such articles at the hospital without such permission. It is strictly forbidden to make use of any apparatus, instrument, bandage, chemical, or medicament, on one's own authority. Temporary absence from the hospital is only

Prostitution in Europe

permitted with the approval of medical and police authority.

§ 6. Within 24 hours they must personally report any engagement of, or change of residence, at the office of the morals police (City Hall, 3d Story, Room 129), between the hours of 9 A. M. and 2 P. M., in addition to discharging any formalities as to reports of residence that may be required of all the members of the population. When about to leave Hamburg, permanently or temporarily, they must likewise personally report their departure at the same office, before 11 A. M. Within 24 hours after returning to Hamburg, they must personally report that fact at the office of the morals police.

§ 7. They must immediately grant admission to the police officer who calls in order to inspect their dwellings.

§ 8. They must comply at once and without fail with all instructions of the police issued to them for the preservation of peace and order, as well as for the administrative purposes of the morals police, without thereby forfeiting their right to lodge a subsequent protest.

§ 9. They must likewise comply with any commands or prohibitions of the police, other than those enumerated in these regulations, but issued in the interests of the administration of the morals police.

§ 10. They are not permitted:

1. To live or spend the night in any houses other than those approved of by the morals police for the use of such women, to consort with men in other than the approved houses, or to wander about homeless, as vagrants,

2. To have minors in their homes, take in other persons as boarders, or keep female servants under 25 years of age,

3. To grant access to their dwellings, not to mention

the granting of sexual intercourse, to persons who are minors,

4. To appear visibly at the window or front door of the house they live in or of any other house, or to attempt to attract men by tapping, knocking, calling, or in any other manner,

5. To accost men in the street or in other places accessible to the general public, to entice them, either by means of beckoning or of other gestures, or to molest them in any manner,

6. To appear in public in any manner that may offend decency, or to appear in striking apparel,

7. To spend the hours between 11 P. M. and 6 A. M. in any other place than in their homes,

8. To frequent the following streets and places: Alter Jungfernstieg, Neuer Jungfernstieg, Alsterdamm, Neuerwall, Alterwall, Reesendamm, Rathausmarkt, Burstah, Adolphsplatz, Grosse, Johannisstrasse, Mönckebergstrasse, Steindamm, Reeperbahn, Spielbudenplatz, Dammthorstrasse, Harvestehuderweg, An der schönen Aussicht, Schwanenwik, An der Alster, and the Wallanlagen,

9. To visit the following institutions, theaters, and grounds, or the parts thereof indicated: Stadttheater, Thaliatheater, Deutsches Schauspielhaus, Hansatheater, the box seats and orchestra stalls of the Carl Schultze Theater and of the Hamburger Operettentheater, seats on the first level of the Neues Operettentheater, the Museums, the Zoological and Botanical Gardens, the Velodrom, any seats or stands at the Races except second balcony or standing room, boxes, balcony and stalls at the circuses, functions under the auspices

of the Allgemeiner Alster Club, particularly regattas, public music halls and public dance halls
(except those at No. 25 Neustädterstrasse and
No. 10 Mohlenhofstrasse),

10. To enter any saloons, restaurants, cafés, concert
halls and music halls in the City of Hamburg or
in the following suburbs, united with the City by
the Law of June 22, 1894: St. Pauli, Eimsbüttel,
Roterbaum, etc.

11. To ride in open carriages,

12. To make use of any apartments in the bath-houses
of this city, other than those reserved for the use
of individual bathers, and especially, to make use
of the swimming-pools of such establishments,

13. To employ, or permit others to practise for them,
any device or process calculated to deceive the
medical inspectors,

14. To support a pimp or visit the dwellings of such, or
to receive pimps in their own homes.

§ 11. Any woman under supervision, who offers reasonable assurance that she has completely abandoned vice
as a livelihood, and is engaged in the pursuit of a legitimate
calling, may be provisionally liberated, either wholly or in
part, from the necessity of observing the regulations of the
morals police, and, in case her conduct within a certain
period, the length of which is to be designated for each
special case, offers no reason to suppose that she will continue her practice of the vicious trade, the surveillance to
which she is subject will be finally discontinued.

§ 12. In accordance with § 361 sec. 6 and § 362 of the
Penal Code, infractions of these regulations are punished
by imprisonment for not more than 6 weeks and commission to the State Police Department (Landespolizeibehörde),
for detention in a workhouse for not more than 2 years.

Appendices

HAMBURG REGULATIONS. (*b*)

POLICE REGULATIONS FOR WOMEN UNDER LIMITED SUPERVISION OF THE MORALS POLICE.

§ 1. After being assigned to limited police supervision, women so assigned will submit at once to examination by the head Police Physician or his representative, and then to the regular medical examinations that will be set by the Police Department.

§ 2. They must immediately report to the Police Department any symptom of disease which they may have observed on their persons. Such immediate report may be omitted only when the regular examination by the medical inspector is to take place later in the day on which the symptom has been observed.

§ 3. At all examinations they must present themselves in clean clothing and in a condition of sobriety and bodily cleanliness.

§ 4. They must unhesitatingly comply with the instructions of the medical examiners.

§ 5. If the physician orders hospital treatment, they are obliged to submit to being transferred to such hospital as may be appointed by the authorities. There they must remain until the physician orders their discharge. During their detention at the hospital they must comply with the instructions of the physicians and officers of the institution, as well as with the directions of the nursing staff, conduct themselves in an orderly and modest manner and observe the rules of order. It is forbidden to bring flowers, books, foodstuffs, beverages, or tobacco, to the hospital, without the permission of the physician, or to receive or utilize such articles at the hospital, without such permission. It is strictly forbidden to make use of any apparatus, instrument, bandage, chemical, or medicament, on one's own authority. Temporary absence from the hospital is only permitted with the approval of medical and police authority.

§ 6. Within 24 hours they must personally report any engagement of or change of residence at the office of the morals police (City Hall, 3d Story, Room 128), between the hours of 9 A. M. and 8 P. M., in addition to discharging any formalities as to reports of residence that may be required of all the members of the population. When about to leave Hamburg, permanently or temporarily, they must likewise personally report their departure at the same office, before 11 A. M. Within 24 hours after returning to Hamburg they must personally report that fact at the office of the morals police.

§ 7. They must immediately grant admission to the police officer who calls in order to inspect their dwellings.

§ 8. They must comply at once and without fail with all instructions of the police issued to them for the preservation of peace and order, as well as for the administrative purposes of the morals police, without thereby forfeiting their right to lodge a subsequent protest.

§ 9. They must likewise comply with any commands or prohibitions of the police, other than those enumerated in these regulations, but issued in the interests of the administration of the morals police.

§ 10. They are not permitted:

1. To live in a house which the police authorities have declared to be unsuitable for them, to spend the night with men or consort with men in any other house than their own dwelling, or to wander about homeless, as vagrants,

2. To take in another person as a boarder, to have

426

Appendices

any minor children (their own or those of others) in their rooms, or to keep a female servant who is under 25 years of age,

3. To grant access to their dwellings, not to mention the granting of sexual intercourse, to persons who are minors,

4. To appear visibly at the window or front door of the house they live in or of any other house, or to attempt to attract men by tapping, knocking, calling, or in any other manner,

5. To accost men in the streets or in other places accessible to the general public, to entice them, either by means of beckoning or of other gestures, or to molest them in any manner,

6. To appear in public in any manner that may offend decency, or to appear in striking apparel,

7. To spend the hours between 11 P. M. and 6 A. M. in any other place than in their homes,

8. To frequent the following streets and places: Alter Jungfernstieg, Neuer Jungfernstieg, Alsterdamm, etc.,

9. To visit the following theaters, institutions, and grounds, or the parts thereof indicated: Stadttheater, Thaliatheater, Deutsches Schauspielhaus, Hansatheater, the box seats and orchestra stalls of the Carl Schultze Theater, seats on the first level of the Neues Operettentheater, the Museums, the Zoological and Botanical Gardens, the Velodrom, any seats or stands at the Races except second balcony and standing room, boxes, balcony and stalls at the Circuses, functions under the auspices of the Allgemeiner Alster Club, particularly regattas, public concert halls and public dance halls (except the Elbhalle and those at No.

25 Neustädterstrasse and No. 10 Mohlenhofstrasse),

10. To enter any saloons, restaurants, cafés, concert
    halls, and music halls in the City of Hamburg or
    in the following suburbs, united with the City by
    the Law of June 22, 1894: St. Pauli, Eimsbüttel,
    etc.,

11. To ride in open carriages,

12. To make use of any apartments in the bath-houses
    of this city, other than those reserved for the use
    of individual bathers, and especially, to make use
    of the swimming-pools of such establishments,

13. To employ, or permit others to practise for them,
    any device or process calculated to deceive the
    medical inspectors,

14. To support a pimp or visit the dwellings of such, or
    to receive pimps in their own homes.

§ 11. Any woman under limited supervision, who offers
reasonable assurance that she has completely abandoned
vice as a livelihood, and is engaged in the pursuit of a
legitimate calling, may be released from the supervision to
which she is subjected.

§ 12. In accordance with § 361 sec. 6 and § 362 of the
Penal Code, infractions of these regulations are punished
by imprisonment for not more than 6 weeks and commission to the State Police Department (Landespolizeibehörde),
for detention in a workhouse for not more than 2 years.

APPENDIX IV

VIENNA REGULATIONS.[1]

The following police regulations for the supervision of prostitution are issued in accordance with § 22 of the Ordinance of the Imperial Government of Lower Austria, dated February 9, 1851, L. G. u. Reg. Bl. No. 39,[2] on the Jurisdiction of Police Departments; and with reference to § 5 of the Law of May 24, 1885, R. G. Bl. No. 89.[3]

I. THE SUPERVISING AUTHORITY.

§ 1. The supervision of female persons who make a business of selling their bodies for vicious purposes, is incumbent on the District Police Commissariats[4] and on the Division for Morals Police Affairs of the Department of Police.

II. ASSIGNMENT TO SUPERVISION.

§ 2. In accordance with the provisions of this edict, assignments to supervision may be made either by the Department of Police or by the Police Commissariats. But no such assignments may be made without the previous declaration, on the part of the prostitutes, that they wish to be put under supervision.

[1] Translation of most recent regulations, dated June 1, 1911.
[2] *Landes-Gesetz und Regierungs-Blatt,* No. 39.
[3] *Reichs-Gesetz-Blatt,* No. 89.
[4] *Bezirks-Polizeikommissariaten.*

Prostitution in Europe

§ 3. Women must not be assigned to supervision if they are:

    (a)   girls under 18 years of age,
    (b)   virgins,
    (c)   pregnant,
    (d)   married and not legally divorced,
    (e)   afflicted with contagious diseases.

Prostitutes with venereal diseases must be committed to hospital treatment before their assignment to supervision.

§ 4. Women about to be assigned to supervision must prove their identity, and, particularly, their legal domicile, by presenting the proper documents. If necessary, a delay may be granted within which such papers are to be procured. This delay does not postpone the assignment to supervision.

They must be thoroughly interrogated on their circumstances and on the reasons which have caused them to enter prostitution. In this interrogation, which is to be conducted with due consideration for the peculiarities of each case, particular effort must be made to determine whether the women are aware of the significance of their step.

Finally, they are to be subjected to an official medical examination.

§ 5. Minors may be assigned to supervision only by the Department of Police, and by that Department only when complete moral indifference, without any hope of betterment, has been unmistakably ascertained.

In all cases in which there is even the remotest possibility of improvement, the assignment to supervision is to be postponed until such time when the attempts at reform may be regarded as finally ineffective. But every opportunity must always be offered to the legally constituted guardians of minors, to use the influence for good imposed on them by their position as guardians. With this object in view, such legal guardians are to be invited to the office, but every precaution must be taken to guard their reputations. If they reside outside of Vienna, the necessary negotiations should, under ordinary circumstances, be carried on directly with them, and not through the intermediation of the police authorities of their homes.

In order that the minor may be enabled, if possible, to return to a decent mode of life, constant communication must be maintained, in every case, with the Surrogate's Office, and, wherever it is feasible, with the charitable organizations active at the time.

§ 6. No kind of certification of assignment to supervision is to be given to the prostitute; yet, she is to be subjected to verbal instruction on the essential contents of the police regulations.

§ 7. In the case of every prostitute, her possible previous sentences and venereal diseases are to be ascertained, either from the records of the Vienna offices, or through correspondence with the authorities in such localities as may previously have assigned her to supervision.

§ 8. Prostitutes of foreign domicile whose coming to Vienna was merely for the purpose of being assigned to supervision here, are to be deported from the city, in application of the Law of July 27, 1871, R. G. Bl. No. 88.

III.   DWELLINGS OF PROSTITUTES.

(a) *Prostitutes who practise prostitution in their own homes.*

§ 9. Such prostitutes as practise prostitution as a trade in their own homes are obliged, in their choice of abode, to obtain the approval of the proper Police Commissariat. In granting this approval it must be borne in mind that such dwellings must be as distant as possible from the main lines of traffic, and not in the vicinity of schools, churches, or other public buildings, and not in any other places where their presence might give offence.

§ 10. Such prostitutes are not permitted to live with persons in whose households there are minors under the age of 18.

§ 11. Not more than three prostitutes who are under supervision may live with the same mistress of furnished rooms.

Such lodgings as may exist when this edict goes into effect, which do not fulfill the above requirements, are either to be gradually ordered vacated by prostitutes, at such opportunities as may offer, or the number of prostitutes is to be reduced to the prescribed limit.

§ 12. In the choice of their dwellings, as much liberty as is feasible is to be allowed such prostitutes as have homes of their own which they do not share with other prostitutes.

§ 13. There is to be no relation between the prostitutes and the mistress of their rooms other than that of tenant and landlady. No other influence must be exerted by the landlady over the prostitutes; particularly, the landlady must have no share or percentage in the proceeds of the vicious trade, nor must she hinder the prostitutes from moving out of the house, nor must she serve alcoholic beverages to the prostitutes or their customers.

Prostitutes are not permitted to live with landladies who violate the above regulation, provided that the nature of the offence has been explained to the offender, without effect.

§ 14. The Police Department is furthermore privileged at any time to forbid a prostitute to live in a certain house, or with a certain landlady, without assigning a reason for such prohibition.

Appendices

§ 15. Dwellings of prostitutes must be kept under constant thorough surveillance. Admission to such dwellings must be granted at any time to the officials sent for the purpose of inspection of the dwellings.

(b) *Prostitutes living in brothels.*

§ 16. The establishment of brothels, that is, of lodgings in which prostitution is practised as a business, and in which the mistress of the house figures as the entrepreneur or manager of the business, is to be prohibited.

Brothels already in existence are to be inspected regularly, without the previous knowledge of the inmates, both by the Commissariats and by the Police Department, by the former at least once every three months, and by the latter at least once every half-year. The inspections will be conducted by an officer of the reporting staff and an official physician.

The inspection is to include a scrutiny of all the rooms, an examination of the list which the mistress is required to keep (giving the name, personal data, day of admission, and day of departure, of each prostitute), a medical examination of the prostitutes to determine the existence of any physical abuses or maltreatments, and an inquiry into the manner in which all the remaining orders issued for the management of the brothel have been complied with.

At these inspections, furthermore, prostitutes must have an opportunity to make any complaints of whatsoever nature, without pressure from anyone, and it must be determined whether any difficulties are being put in the way of their leaving the house.

§ 17. The Commission of the Police Department may, as a result of the inspection, adopt such measures as appear to it to be for the best interests of the public, from the standpoint of hygiene or from that of the Morals Police Service.

Prostitution in Europe

Should the Commissariat consider such measures desirable, it must apply for the approval of the Police Department, simultaneously submitting the record of the inspection to the Department.

§ 18. The employment in brothels of servants who are minors is not to be permitted.

§ 19. The Police Department may at any time order the closing of a brothel; particularly, when there have been infractions of the provisions of §§ 17 and 18, or even of § 13, the provisions of which are intended to be applied to brothels also.

(c) *Prostitutes who practise prostitution outside of their homes.*

§ 20. Prostitutes who practise prostitution outside of their homes are not as a rule limited to any locality in the choice of their dwellings. But even they may be forbidden to live in a certain house, when definite acts of theirs have been the occasion of complaints that have been shown to be well-founded.

IV. NATURE OF THE SUPERVISION.

§ 21. A prostitute subject to supervision is required to report twice a week, at times set for her, for official medical examination.

§ 22. A prostitute found, when being officially examined, to be afflicted with a venereal disease, is required to report for treatment not later than 6 P. M. on the same day, at the hospital to which she is referred by the Commissariat of the district in which she lives, under pain of compulsory transfer, should she neglect so to report. For this purpose, she must apply to the Commissariat of her district, for a certificate of commitment.

§ 23. A prostitute received at the hospital must remain

Appendices

there until her discharge is ordered by the physician treating her, and while there, must comply with all instructions.

§ 24. A prostitute discharged from the hospital must comply with the requirements of any additional outside treatment or observation of her condition, by presenting herself for examination at such intervals as may be set by the Sick Division.

In order that diagnosis, hospital treatment, and instructions for supplementary outside treatment may be entered on the sick card, the latter should be enclosed with the certificate of commitment that is sent to the office of the hospital when a prostitute is committed to such hospital. This card remains at the hospital until the prostitute is discharged or until the conclusion of any supplementary outside treatment or observation that may be ordered. The Police Department must be reminded that the card is still at the hospital, by means of a note to that effect, written on the sheet that carries the notification of dismissal to the Police Department.

Should the necessity of a new commitment of the prostitute to the hospital arise between the time of discharge and the termination of the outside treatment, effort should be made to have her committed to the hospital that is still in possession of her sick card, or to induce the former hospital to send the card to the hospital in which the prostitute has been received.

§ 25. A prostitute under supervision must give notice within 24 hours of every change of address, to the Commissariat of her former district as well as to that of her new district.

The control-sheet is at once to be sent to the proper (new) Commissariat through the Police Department.

§ 26. For reasons connected with the administration of the morals police, a prostitute under supervision is not permitted to stroll through the streets in the company of other prostitutes or of pimps, or to grant shelter to pimps in her home.

In other respects the prostitute is, in principle, to be bound only to comply with those general regulations for public morality and decency that are applicable to all persons.

§ 27. In the interests of public order and public decency, and on application of the Police Commissariat, orders may be issued for the purpose of abating a nuisance due to the behavior of prostitutes inhabiting a certain house or street in large numbers.

But the scope of these orders must not exceed what is absolutely required by the actual local conditions.

V.   OFFICIAL MEDICAL EXAMINATION OF PROSTITUTES.

§ 28. The official medical examination must include all portions of the body, and involve, if necessary, a use of all the scientific apparatus which has been developed by the progress of medical knowledge, and which is at the disposal of the official physician. The use of the metroscope is particularly recommended.

In addition to making the examination, the physician should also, in each case, inform the women of its purpose, as well as of the nature of the first indications of contagious diseases, and of the danger involved in such diseases, and of the means of preventing infection by observing the proper hygienic precautions.

§ 29. If the official physician finds the prostitute to be infected with a venereal disease, he must without delay send a medical certificate to that effect to the Police Commissariat having jurisdiction in this case. He must warn the prostitute as to the obligations imposed upon her by §§ 22 and 23, and order her to stop having sexual intercourse, simul-

Appendices

taneously calling her attention to § 5, item 3, of the Law of May 24, 1885, R. G. Bl. No. 89.

§ 30. The physician must enter the name of any prostitute whom he commits to the hospital in the list of inspections which he is required to keep.

The final hospital diagnosis, which is transmitted to the Police Commissariat after the dismissal of the prostitute from the hospital, must be sent to the physician for entry on his inspection list.

§ 31. Prostitutes who fail to appear for official medical examination, even though such failure occur only once, must immediately be reported to the Police Commissariat, which, unless adequate reasons for the omission are advanced, will at once cause the arraignment of such prostitutes. Such arraignment does not preclude the instituting of penal proceedings against the prostitutes.

Likewise, those prostitutes that do not appear at their official medical examination at the time set, are to be reported to the Police Commissariat in order that penal proceedings may be instituted.

VI. DEPARTURE FROM SUPERVISION.

§ 32. A prostitute desiring to retire from supervision must make personal declaration of such desire to the Commissariat and undergo an official medical examination. If she is found, at this examination, to be afflicted with a venereal disease, she is to be committed to a hospital and her declaration of departure is not to be noted until she has been dismissed from the hospital.

§ 33. A prostitute under supervision who evades supervision without a previous notification of her desire to be dropped from the list, is to be prosecuted at once, unless she is in a position to show that she has led a decent life since ceasing to comply with the supervision.

§ 34. The Police Department must at once be notified of names dropped from supervision; the women's control-sheets must accompany such notification.

§ 35. Any further surveillance that may be necessary after dropping a prostitute from the lists, must be conducted in accordance with the principles governing the supervision of prostitutes not under control.

VII. SURVEILLLANCE OF PROSTITUTES NOT UNDER SUPER-
VISION.

§ 36. It is incumbent on the Police Commissariats, as well as directly on the Office for Morals Police Affairs, to determine what persons are carrying on prostitution in a commercial manner, without having declared their entrance under supervision.

§ 37. The Imperial Safety Guard, as well as such Imperial Police agents as are not specifically entrusted with surveillance over prostitution, may take steps against women practising prostitution, only when the facts have been established beyond any possibility of doubt, or when there are special reasons for interference, as, for example, § 516 of the Penal Code, § 1 of the Law of May 24, 1885, R. G. Bl. No. 89, or § 11 of the Imperial Ordinance of April 20, 1854, R. G. Bl. No. 96.

§ 38. Only such police officers as are specifically entrusted with the surveillance over prostitution may accost or detain persons merely on suspicion of their practising immorality as a trade, and then only after having repeatedly, in the course of observations held on a number of different days, gathered material of a nature to justify such action.

Other police officers, when merely suspecting the practice of commercial prostitution, will limit themselves to a report of their observations.

Appendices

§ 39. Special attention is to be paid to the lower class of saloons.

Every legal means must be used in prosecuting the owners of such places as may arouse suspicion by the employment therein of female persons for other tasks than those connected with the sale of liquor. In cases that are clear, the Labor Department must be informed of the facts. Owners of such places must be denied all concessions within the gift of the police, such as the license to keep open after the regular closing hour, or to provide musical entertainment. If they already hold such concessions, the latter are to be canceled.

§ 40. Persons practising prostitution commercially under the cloak of some regular calling are to be kept under the necessary surveillance.

§ 41. Investigation must be made of all complaints against persons suspected of procuring, or of practising prostitution commercially, as well as of all questionable advertisements in the daily press.

§ 42. In each case the investigation must be made with due regard for the reputation of the person suspected, and with a discretion that should be all the greater when the foundation for a penal case is weak.

VIII.   TREATMENT OF COMPLAINTS.

§ 43. Complaints made as to any offensive conduct on the part of prostitutes in the streets or in certain houses must be carefully investigated, and measures must be taken for the abatement of such nuisances.

IX.   PENALTIES.

(a) *For prostitutes under supervision.*

§ 44. The punishment of prostitutes under supervision, for violations of the Police Ordinances governing the surveillance over prostitution, is imposed by the Police Commissariats in accordance with § 5, item 2, of the Law of May 24, 1885, R. G. Bl. No. 89, and with Ministerial Ordinance of September 30, 1857, R. G. Bl. No. 198.

The penalty is detention for a period of from 6 hours to 8 days, depending on a very specific examination of the various circumstances constituting the offence.

§ 45. In the case of insignificant irregularities, particularly in the case of a first offence, prosecution may be omitted after the prostitute has been properly reprimanded.

§ 46. Legal proceedings in accordance with § 5, item 2, of the Law of May 24, 1885, R. G. Bl. No. 89, must not be instituted except when the offence provided for in that section is committed by a prostitute who has been punished several times by the police for a similar offence, in other words, when it is evident, both that the case is one of persistent disregard of police regulations, and that the severity of the penalty imposed by the police is not commensurate with the seriousness of the case. Under these circumstances the imposing of detention for more than eight days, or even commitment to a workhouse or house of correction, is permissible.

Whenever complaints are to be filed with the courts, the exact nature of the offence must be stated, and reasons must be advanced for asking the aid of the courts.

(b) *For prostitutes not under supervision.*
§ 47. Cases against prostitutes not under supervision may be tried either by the Police Commissariats or by the Police Department directly.

In connection with every trial, a résumé of the decisions made in each case must be drawn up.

§ 48. No punishment should be imposed on women accused for the first time of, or arrested for the first time for,

Appendices

commercial prostitution, especially when they are still young, even though the facts be beyond doubt, unless such punishment may be required, as a repressive measure, by the manifest depravity of the case.

In all cases in which it may seem not unreasonable to assume that the woman accused has been led into prostitution by circumstances of a temporary and accidental nature only, and that consequently her return to a respectable mode of life might be rendered more difficult by the stigma of a police penalty, no other action must be taken than the applying of such of the charitable provisions of § 5, as are applicable to the particular case.

Such charitable provisions must also be carried out, in the case of a prostitute not under supervision, when she is a minor, against whom a penal action has been instituted.

§ 49. No woman accused of the practice of commercial prostitution may be subjected to the official medical examination until the offence is finally proved.

§ 50. A prostitute found to be afflicted with a venereal disease at the official medical examination, must immediately be taken to the hospital. As a preliminary she must be informed of the rules provided for prostitutes under supervision, in §§ 23 and 24, which rules, under these circumstances, are applicable also to prostitutes not under supervision.

Punishments for infractions of these obligations are to be imposed in accordance with § 5, item 2, of the Law of May 24, 1885, R. G. Bl. No. 89, and in accordance with Ministerial Ordinance of September 30, 1857, R. G. Bl. No. 198.

§ 51. Penalties imposed by the police on persons convicted of the practice of commercial prostitution, must conform to § 5, section 1, or, in the case of persons previously punished for similar offences, to § 5, item 1, of the Law of

Prostitution in Europe

May 24, 1885, R. G. Bl. No. 89, and to the Ministerial Ordinance of September 30, 1857, R. G. Bl. No. 198.

The provisions of § 46 or of § 44 determine whether proceedings are to be instituted, in accordance with § 5, item 1, of the above law, and also, what is to be the severity of the punishment; yet, in assigning a penalty, the principle must be borne in mind that a prostitute not under supervision is to be treated with greater severity than one who is under supervision.

§ 52. When the police impose a penalty on a prostitute not under supervision, the facts of the case, and, particularly, the amenability of the accused, must be so formulated as to leave no misunderstanding in the mind of the latter, as to the offence imputed to her.

X. JURISDICTION.

(a) *Jurisdiction of the Police Department.*

§ 53. The following business is within the jurisdiction of the Office for Morals Police Affairs:

1. The functions conferred on this office in its capacity as headquarters for the surveillance of the white slave traffic, in accordance with the edict of the Department of Police, dated August 12, 1905.

2. All records of general nature concerning prostitutes under supervision, concerning the houses mentioned in §§ 9 and 16, and the mistresses of such houses, concerning prostitutes not under supervision, concerning pimps, and concerning procuring.

3. The instituting of proceedings to determine whether minors, or prostitutes who ply their trade outside of their homes, are to be placed under supervision.

4. Orders to evacuate streets or houses inhabited by prostitutes.

5. Management of such prostitutes not under super-

vision as may be traced by the officers assigned to the office.

6. Complete control over such trials as may, by reason of their importance, be assigned to the office by the President.

7. Keeping on file the complaints lodged with the Police Department, as well as with the Police Commissariats, as to the behavior of the prostitutes.

8. Supervision of the Commissariats with the object of maintaining a uniform application of the prostitution regulations.

9. Inspection of the punishment and fine books kept by the Commissariats.

10. Examination of the appeals made against the judgments of the Commissariats.

11. Consultations at regular intervals with the officials assigned to report on prostitution.

12. Collecting of material having reference to the regulation of prostitution, and advancing of proposals thereon.

(b) *Jurisdiction of the Police Commissariats.*

§ 54. The application of the prostitution regulations, in all matters in which § 53 does not stipulate the exclusive jurisdiction of the Police Department, is incumbent on the Police Commissariats.

The Commissariats must keep records on the following matters:

1. Prostitutes, in their district, under supervision,

2. Dwellings of prostitutes under supervision, who practise prostitution in such dwellings.

3. Mistresses or keepers of such dwellings.

Furthermore, the Police Commissariats must transmit the following material to the Police Department:

(a) Weekly reports of changes occurring in their **own** districts, in the number of prostitutes,

(b) Complaints as to the behavior of the prostitutes,

(c) Accusations of procuring,

(d) The documents provided for in § 47,

(e) After disposing of the cases, the reports of failure to appear for medical examination,

(f) The punishment-books (every month),

(g) The records taken in the inspections of brothels.

Finally, the Commissariats must report any changes in the number of houses mentioned in §§ 9 and 16, as well as in the mistresses of such houses, and they must also report all cases of failure to assign a prostitute to supervision in spite of the fact that the necessary preliminary condition provided in § 2 has been realized.

APPENDIX V

DANISH LAW FOR RESISTING PUBLIC IMMORALITY AND VENEREAL INFECTION, CONFIRMED BY HIS MAJESTY KING FREDERICK VIII ON MARCH 30, 1906.

§ 1. Police supervision of commercial immorality is hereby abolished. Police action against persons practising such trade is legitimate when it accords with the conditions, and proceeds in the manner, provided in the legislation on vagrancy (Lovgivningen om Løsgængeri). Yet, the order mentioned in the Law of March 3, 1860, § 2, must not be given unless warning has been previously issued.

§ 2. Anyone who incites or entices to immorality, in such manner, or who displays an immoral mode of life, to such a degree, as to offend the sense of decency, or to become a public nuisance, or to disturb those living in the vicinity, shall be punished by imprisonment, or, under aggravating circumstances, or for a repetition of the offence, by commitment to the penitentiary. If there are extenuating circumstances, the punishment may be commuted to a fine.

The same punishment is provided for any woman who practises immorality as a trade, provided that a male person, or a minor over two years of age, lives in the same dwelling with her, or that she receives visits for immoral purposes from male persons under eighteen years of age.

Any person not previously warned or punished for one of the above offences, may, instead of being punished, be simply warned, by the Police Department; but no warning may be issued if the accused demands sentence by law.

445

Prostitution in Europe

§ 3. The keeping of brothels is prohibited. Anyone violating this prohibition is punished by imprisonment in a house of correction or at hard labor, or by imprisonment on common prison diet. The same punishment is imposed on anyone guilty of procuring. Such persons as may, with the object of pecuniary profit, grant admission to their dwellings, to persons of different sex, in order that vicious practices may there take place, or such as let rooms, not for the purpose of prolonged habitation, but in order to provide an opportunity for immoral practices, or such as admit to their houses female persons under the age of eighteen, who are seeking gain by immoral practices, shall be punished by detention in prison or at hard labor. In the case of a repeated offence, the punishment may be increased to commission to a penitentiary for a period not exceeding two years.

It is forbidden to offer for sale, or to send out circulars concerning, or to exhibit a signboard concerning, any device calculated to prevent the consequences of cohabitation, to the general public, or to individuals not personally known to the seller, or to persons not distinctly specified. Violation of this prohibition is treated and punished in accordance with the rules governing violations of police regulations.

§ 4. The same punishment as that provided in § 181 of the General Civil Penal Code, shall be imposed on any person who, under the circumstances described in the paragraph cited, has carnal intercourse with the person to whom he or she is married, provided, that the latter has thereby contracted an infection, and makes a charge to that effect within one year after acquiring knowledge as to the contraction of the disease.

Anyone guilty of the offence described in § 181 of the General Civil Penal Code, or of the offence described above, must, when the other person, without having previously been informed of the danger of infection, becomes infected, not only indemnify the infected person for the expenses involved in the curative treatment, but must also pay damages to cover the sufferings and losses due to the disease.

§ 5. Persons afflicted with venereal diseases have the right, regardless of whether they are able or not able to defray the expenses of their cure, to demand treatment of such diseases at the public expense. Likewise, such persons are obliged to submit to such public treatment unless they can show that they have already engaged proper medical attention. If such persons are not situated in surroundings of a nature to furnish reasonable assurance that the disease will not be transmitted to other persons, unless such patients are removed, or, if the patients do not comply with orders given to prevent the infection of others, they may be committed to a hospital for treatment. When such steps become necessary, the district judges (in Copenhagen, the Director of Police) shall, with the approval of the Minister of Justices, issue the appropriate orders, and compliance with the obligation thus imposed may be forced by fines, imposed by the authorities cited, and, when such fines are of no avail, by arraignment by the police.

Those permanently in receipt of poor relief, who are found to be afflicted with venereal diseases, are to be committed to a hospital for treatment.

§ 6. Whenever, in the course of the treatment of a disease, or at the termination of such treatment, it is considered necessary, in view of the danger of infection, to keep the patient under constant supervision, he must be ordered by the physician, to present himself to the latter at certain fixed times, or, in lieu of such action, to furnish documentary evidence that another authorized physician has undertaken to treat him. Blanks to be used in issuing such orders may be obtained from the proper City or District Physician.

If the patient violates this order, or if the physician does not desire to treat him any longer, and if, on request to furnish evidence that his treatment has been undertaken by another physician, he neglects to do so, notification of this fact must be sent to the proper Public or Examining Physician, who will then order such patient to report at the Consultation Office, in accordance with the provisions of § 13 below.

§ 7. It is incumbent on every physician who examines or treats a patient for a venereal disease, to call the attention of the latter to the contagious character of the disease, and to the legal consequences of infecting other persons, or exposing them to infection, with the disease, and, particularly, to warn the patient against contracting marriage, while the danger of infection is still present. Blanks for issuing these admonitions may be obtained from the proper City or District Physician.

§ 8. In his weekly reports to the proper City or District Physician, every physician must distinctly state that he has carried out the provisions of the above paragraph, as well as indicate the number of persons to whom he has issued the orders described in § 6.

Violation of the provisions of §§ 6 and 7, and of the first section of this paragraph, shall be punished by fines not exceeding 200 kroner. Any one in these circumstances, who gives a wrong name, business, or address, to the physician treating him, shall be punished in accordance with § 155 of the Penal Code.

§ 9. An infant afflicted with syphilis may not be given to be nursed, to any woman except the mother of the child. Nor may any nurse who knows or thinks she is infected with this disease, accept the child of any other woman to

448

nurse. Violations of these prohibitions shall be punished by imposing the penalty provided in § 181 of the General Civil Penal Code, which also provides that any one convicted of such offence, shall, if the disease be transmitted, not only be obliged to indemnify the person so infected, for the costs of treatment, but shall also have to pay damages for sufferings and losses due to the disease. The same liability for damages shall be incumbent on such person as hands over a child whom he knows or has reason to know to be infected with a venereal disease, to the care of other persons, or who puts out such child to nurse, without having previously informed the foster-parents, or the nurse, of the fact that the child is afflicted, or suspected of being afflicted, with syphilis, and of the danger of infection involved in relations of this nature with such child. To put out such child to nurse is forbidden under any circumstances that would expose other children to infection; violation of this prohibition is punished by applying the provisions of item 2 of the first section of this paragraph.

These provisions are applicable also to such public authorities as put out children to nurse, or assign them to the care of foster-parents.

A child is considered to be suspicious, from the standpoint of syphilis, even though no indications of the disease have put in their appearance, in case either of the parents has contracted syphilis within the past seven years, and three months have not yet elapsed since the birth of the child.

§ 10. Any one accused of one of the offences provided for in § 1, § 2, § 4, or § 9, item 2, or in § 181 of the General Civil Penal Code, may, by his express consent, be subjected, under the auspices of the police, to a medical examination. In case of a refusal to be examined, the court may deliver a verdict, provided the accusation be considered well-founded, ordering the examination to be made without the consent of the accused.

§ 11. The medical examinations provided in § 10 will be held at the place indicated by the police, by the proper City or District Physician, or by a special Examining Physician appointed for the purpose. Compulsory examinations must be conducted, unless this right is expressly waived by the person to be examined, by a physician of the same sex as the latter, provided such can be found in the town itself or within such distance from it as to cause no considerable delay, and provided such physician is willing to conduct examinations of this nature.— Physicians discharging such duties shall either receive an annual salary, to be fixed by the local administration and approved by the Minister of Justice, or, if no such salary shall have been so fixed and approved, they shall be paid for each examination, as follows: For examinations of individuals to be conducted at the same place and time, 4 kroner for the examination of the first such individual, and 1 krone for each individual examined immediately thereafter; in addition they may be reimbursed for any outlay made for their transportation. In towns, such payments are to be made from the town treasury; in the country, from the provincial appropriations fund; and on the Island of Bornholm, from the provincial fund available for both town and country. For drawing up a certificate to indicate whether or not the person examined has been found to be afflicted with a venereal disease, no special payment shall be made to the physician.

§ 12. Likewise, but at times other than those set for the above examinations, Public or Examining Physicians shall examine, and, if it be necessary and feasible, without commitment to a hospital, shall treat any person who applies

Appendices

to them or is referred to them because of venereal infection. No payment may be required or accepted from the patient for such services. Payment shall be made out of the public funds in accordance with the rules followed heretofore.

In Copenhagen there must always be on hand a sufficient number of examining physicians, who are assigned to a daily schedule of attendance at offices in various parts of the city, at times set by the Health Board.

§ 13. Whenever the Public or Examining Physician considers it necessary, in view of the danger of contagion, to order patients to report to him at times to be definitely set by the physician, the latter shall so order, making use of the blanks officially provided for the purpose.

Compliance with this order may be forced by the imposing of fines, by the District Judge (in Copenhagen, by the Director of Police), with the approval of the Minister of Justice, and, should this fail to produce the desired effect, by arraignment by the police.

§ 14. Those committed to a hospital for treatment of venereal diseases at the public expense, shall not leave the hospital until they are discharged by the hospital physician. Violation of this provision is punished by imprisonment on common prison diet for not more than twenty days, or by ordinary imprisonment for not more than one month.

§ 15. The police may prohibit hotel-keepers, inn-keepers, and saloon-keepers from granting shelter, in their establishments, to female persons who have been sentenced for violating § 2 of this law, or from employing such female persons to entertain or serve the guests in such establishments.

Violations of this prohibition shall be punished by fines not exceeding 100 kroner, imprisonment on common prison diet for not more than two months, or imprisonment at

hard labor for not more than three months. If the offender
has not been previously sentenced or warned for the same
offence, a warning by the Police Department may take the
place of a sentence. But no warning shall be issued if the
accused demands sentence by law.

§ 16. In administering the provisions of this law for
imprisonment or penitentiary commitment, the rules set
by Chapter II of the General Civil Penal Code, as well
as by the Provisional Law of April 1, 1905, shall be followed. Trials for violations treated in § 2, § 6, section 2,
§ 7, § 8, section 1, § 9, § 14, and § 15, shall be conducted
as regular public police trials, but behind closed doors.
Fines imposed as a result of these public trials, are
added to the police fund; in Copenhagen, to the city
treasury.

§ 17. By the term " venereal diseases," as used in this
law, are meant the diseases known to medical science as
syphilis, gonorrhœa, and *ulcus venereum.*

§ 18. This law goes into effect six months after it has
been printed in the Law Journal; but the enrolment of immoral women, which has been carried on heretofore in
accordance with the Law of April 10, 1874, shall cease at
once. Simultaneously §§ 180 and 182 of the Penal Code,
and the Law of April 10, 1874, on Measures to Resist the
Spread of Venereal Infection, the Law of March 1, 1895, on
Changes and Additions in the above Law, the Law of April
11, 1901, on Additions to the two preceding laws, and the
Laws of February 11, 1863, § 8, final item, and of February 4, 1874, § 2, section c, together with all rules, regulations, and orders based thereon, are hereby abolished, as
such rules, regulations, and orders can no longer be enforced on the basis of the laws in operation before the going into effect of the Law of April 10, 1874.

INDEX

Index

Index

Pimps, 32–33, 95–97, 336.
Pinkus, F., 81, 83, 230, 234, 238, 244, 251, 257.
Police, 397, 399.
Prostitutes, mortality of, 21–24; number of, 24–28; number of inscribed, 40–46; supply of, 63–88.
Prostitution, cost of, 34–38; complexity of, 39–41, 105–106; definition of, 9–15, fluctuations in, 19–21; forms of, 28–31; involves two parties, 39, 107–109; legal attitude towards, 106, 111–117, 136–142, 288–292; medieval, 5, 6; modern, 6–8.
Prussia, venereal disease in, 368–371, 377–379.

Rescue work, 100.
Regulation, defined, 121–122; decay of, 266–267.
Regulation in various cities: see under names of cities.
Rendezvous houses, 96–98, 200–202.
Riehl process, 90, 185.
Rome, sanitary control in, 227.
Rotterdam, 328, 333.

Santoliquido, R., 352.
Scheven, K., 168, 173, 266.
Schjerning, O. v., 379.
Schmölder, R., 116, 138, 235.
Schneider, C. K., 22, 186.
Schreiber, Adele, 18, 63, 77, 80, 170, 177.

Seduction, 80.
Segregation, 175–179.
Servants and prostitution, 76–77.
Sex education, 52–58.
Souteneur, see Pimp.
Stockholm, regulation in, 134.
Stuttgart, regulation in, 130–136; street conditions in, 58–59.
Supply, sources of, 61–65.
Sweden, venereal disease in, 369.
Syphilis, 223, 250; amount discovered, 228–230; length of treatment, 238.

Venereal disease statistics, 366. (For various countries, see under countries, cities, armies.)
Vienna, regulation in, 132–136; street conditions in, 157–158; bordells in, 171, 188–189; text of regulations, 429–444.
Vigilance societies, 91.

Webb, Sidney and Beatrice, 365.
White, D., 364.
White Slave traffic, 92–94; dependent on bordells, 182–185.
Wolzendorff, K., 142.

Zurich, 324, 333; venereal disease in, 389–391.

L ERA

M

Lightning Source UK Ltd.
Milton Keynes UK
UKHW022242191218
334294UK00010B/965/P